Marrakech

timeout.com/marrakech

Published by Time Out Guides Ltd, a wholly owned subsidiary of Time Out Group Ltd.
Time Out and the Time Out logo are trademarks of Time Out Group Ltd.

© Time Out Group Ltd 2007
Previous editions 2003, 2005

10 9 8 7 6 5 4 3 2 1

This edition first published in Great Britain in 2007 by Ebury Publishing
Ebury Publishing is a division of The Random House Group Ltd,
20 Vauxhall Bridge Road, London SW1V 2SA

Random House Australia Pty Limited 20 Alfred Street, Milsons Point, Sydney, New South Wales 2061, Australia
Random House New Zealand Limited 18 Poland Road, Glenfield, Auckland 10, New Zealand
Random House South Africa (Pty) Limited Isle of Houghton, Corner Boundary
Road & Carse O'Gowrie, Houghton 2198, South Africa

Random House UK Limited Reg. No. 954009

Distributed in USA by Publishers Group West
1700 Fourth Street, Berkeley, California 94710

Distributed in Canada by Publishers Group Canada
250A Carlton Street, Toronto, Ontario M5A 2L1

For further distribution details, see www.timeout.com

ISBN 10: 1-84670-019-1
ISBN 13: 978184670 0194

A CIP catalogue record for this book is available from the British Library

Printed and bound by Firmengruppe APPL, aprinta druck, Wemding, Germany

The Random House Group Limited makes every effort to ensure that the papers used in our books are made from trees
that have been legally sourced from well-managed and credibly certified forests. Our paper procurement policy can
be found on www.randomhouse.co.uk.

Time Out Guides Limited
Universal House
251 Tottenham Court Road
London W1T 7AB
Tel + 44 (0)20 7813 3000
Fax + 44 (0)20 7813 6001
Email guides@timeout.com
www.timeout.com

Editorial

Editor Ros Sales
Copy Editors Jonathan Derbyshire, Hugh Graham, Charlotte Thomas, Elizabeth Winding
Consultant Lynn Perez
Listings Editor Lynn Perez
Proofreader Kieron Corless
Indexer Ismay Atkins

Managing Director Peter Fiennes
Financial Director Gareth Garner
Editorial Director Ruth Jarvis
Deputy Series Editor Dominic Earle
Editorial Manager Holly Pick
Assistant Management Accountant Ija Krasnikova

Design

Art Director Scott Moore
Art Editor Pinelope Kourmouzoglou
Senior Designer Josephine Spencer
Graphic Designer Henry Elphick
Junior Graphic Designer Kei Ishimaru
Digital Imaging Simon Foster
Ad Make-up Jodi Sher

Picture Desk

Picture Editor Jael Marschner
Deputy Picture Editor Tracey Kerrigan
Picture Researcher Helen McFarland

Advertising

Sales Director Mark Phillips
International Sales Manager Fred Durman
International Sales Consultant Ross Canadé
International Sales Executive Charlie Sokal
Advertising Sales (Marrakech) Aniko Boehler
Advertising Assistant Kate Staddon

Marketing

Group Marketing Director John Luck
Marketing Manager Yvonne Poon
Sales and Marketing Director North America Lisa Levinson

Production

Group Production Director Mark Lamond
Production Manager Brendan McKeown
Production Coordinator Caroline Bradford

Time Out Group

Chairman Tony Elliott
Financial Director Richard Waterlow
Time Out Magazine Ltd MD David Pepper
Group General Manager/Director Nichola Coulthard
Time Out Communications Ltd MD David Pepper
Time Out International MD Cathy Runciman
Group Art Director John Oakey
Group IT Director Simon Chappell

Contributors

History Dave Rimmer (*Glaoua power* Andrew Humphreys). **Marrakech Today** Richard Hamilton. **Architecture** Andrew Humphreys. **Rain Reigns** Dave Rimmer. **Where to Stay** Dave Rimmer, Richard Hamilton, Andrew Humphreys (*Fashion victim, The riad revolutionaries* Dave Rimmer). **Sightseeing** Richard Hamilton, Andrew Humphreys, Dave Rimmer (*On foot: A tour of the backstreets, Let me tell you a story, On foot: Souk safari, Mosques, muezzins, mourchidat, On foot: Museums, palaces and tombs* Richard Hamilton; *The exorcist, Exodus* Andrew Humphreys). **Restaurants** Dave Rimmer, Andrew Humphreys (*Putting on a show* Dave Rimmer; *Square meals, Moroccan menu* Andrew Humphreys). **Bars** Dave Rimmer. **Shopping & Services** Dave Rimmer, Andrew Humphreys (*Industrial revolution, Market forces* Dave Rimmer). **Children** Lynn Perez. **Film** Dave Rimmer. **Galleries** Dave Rimmer. **Music** Dave Rimmer, Andrew Humphreys (*The new sound of Marrakech* Dave Rimmer). **Nightlife** Dave Rimmer, Andrew Humphreys. **Sport** Richard Hamilton, Andrew Humphreys (*Surf Morocco* Cyrus Shahrad; *Lions of the Atlas* Peterjon Cresswell). **Essaouira** Dave Rimmer. **High Atlas & Sahara** Dave Rimmer. **Directory** Lynn Perez.

Maps john@jsgraphics.co.uk. The following maps are based on data supplied by New Holland Publishers: Essaouira, Marrkaech. Maps on pahes 69, 73 and 250-53 are based on data supplied by Jean Louis Dorveaux.

Photography by Olivia Rutherford, except: page 12 Bibliotheque Nationale, Paris, France/The Bridgeman Art Library; pages 14, 195, 197 Moroccan National Tourist Board; page 16 Mary Evans Picture Library; page 17 Getty Images; page 19 Time & Life Pictures/Getty Images; page 21 The Cecil Beaton Studio Archive at Sotheby's; pages 34, 186 Dave Rimmer; page 79 Tony Gibson; page 177 Pierre-Emmanuel Rastoin; page 198 Alan Keohane; page 221 Elan Fleisher.

The following images were supplied by the featured establishments/artists: pages 47, 48.

The editor and writers would like to thank Sofia Alami, Julia Bartel, Graham Carter, Mounat Charrat, Peterjon Cresswell, Jill Fechtmann, John Ross Fitzsimons, Adil El Fatimy, Viviana Gonzalez, Fouad Hmedi, Mike McHugo, Emma Wilson.

Contents

Introduction

Marrakech is a tourist phenomenon. Every day, a huge number of visitors fly into the small airport of this small provincial city. Many will then make the short journey to the narrow alleys of the medieval Medina, where they will stay in a riad. It is this very particular kind of boutique hotel that has done more than anything to revolutionise the Marrakech tourist industry: before its arrival visitors tended to fall into the backpacker or super-rich categories; now a far broader range can be accommodated in these beautiful converted Medina houses.

Aesthetics is a big part of the Marrakech visitor experience. This is not a city with a huge number of 'sights'. Instead, visitors are drawn by its looks and unique spirit: there is nowhere so close to Europe that feels as foreign or different. Artisanship and small-scale manufacturing still thrive in workshops across the Medina (even though much of what they produce is for visitors). Acrobats, musicians and storytellers work the Jemaa El Fna, the city's cultural and commercial hub – and they're not just here for the tourists.

West of Marrakech is the Atlantic coastal town of Essaouira, home to gnawa music and beloved of windsurfers. To the south, the High Atlas and Sahara, areas barely penetrated by westerners until the French Foreign Legion built roads and garrisons in the 1920s and '30s. Today, these rugged territories – home to tough Berber clans who have left their mark on the landscape with filmic kasbahs (fortified houses) and *ksour* (villages) – are far more accessible, but they still feel remote and exotic. Four and a half decades of French occupation and the subsequent influence of tourism has failed to erode the Moroccan 'difference'.

This may be set to change, though, as the government has adopted a pro-active stance in promoting tourism. Investments of two billion dollars have recently been approved for Marrakech alone, and a huge area to the south of the city has been pegged out as a new hotel zone. Elsewhere, new golf and ski resorts are set to change the country's landscape. If the 10 million tourists Morocco wants to attract annually by 2010 actually show up, it's hard to imagine quite what the place will look like.

Morocco is a poor country, and tourism is seen as a means of wealth creation and development. Whether promotion of this kind will succeed in the long run, or provide solutions for the country's problems, are tough questions – and we don't claim to have the answers. Our advice is to enjoy Marrakech and Morocco as it is today. We hope you find it as addictive, exhilarating and fascinating as we do.

ABOUT THE TIME OUT CITY GUIDES

This is the third edition of *Time Out Marrakech, Essaouira & the High Atlas*, one of an expanding series of Time Out guides produced by the people behind the successful listings magazines in London, New York and Chicago. Our guides are all written by resident experts who have striven to provide you with all the most up-to-date information you'll need to explore the city or read up on its background, whether you're a local or a first-time visitor.

THE LIE OF THE LAND

Marrakech is a small city that neatly divides into two: the Medina, or old city, which is contained within the city walls, and the new city, which is everything outside the city walls. For a map showing the different city areas and how they relate to each other, *see pp248-49*. We've divided the Medina into two main areas, which are north of the main square and south of the main square;

the square (Jemaa El Fna) and its surrounding neighbourhood also gets a chapter of its own. These area designations are a simplification of the city's geography and are not official names you'll see on signposts, we hope they'll help you to understand the city's layout and to find its most interesting sights. For consistency, the same areas are used in addresses throughout the guide. We've included map references in our addresses that point to our street maps at the back of the guide. For further orientation information, *see p64*.

ESSENTIAL INFORMATION

For all the practical information you might need for visiting the area – including visa and customs information, details of local transport, a listing of emergency numbers, information on local weather and a selection of further reference material – turn to the Directory at the back of this guide. It begins on page 224.

THE LOWDOWN ON THE LISTINGS

We have tried to make this book as easy to use as possible. Addresses, phone numbers, opening times and admission prices are all included in the listings. However, businesses can change their arrangements at any time. Before you go out of your way, we'd strongly advise you to phone ahead to check opening times and other particulars. While every effort and care has been made to ensure the accuracy of the information contained in this guide, the publishers cannot accept responsibility for any errors it may contain.

PRICES AND PAYMENT

We have noted where venues such as shops, hotels, restaurants and theatres accept the following credit cards: American Express (AmEx), Diners Club (DC), MasterCard (MC) and Visa (V). Many will also accept travellers' cheques. However, for important information regarding the use of credit cards, see p233.

The prices we've listed in this guide should be treated as guidelines, not gospel. If prices vary wildly from those we've quoted, ask whether there's a good reason. If not, go elsewhere. Then please let us know. We aim to give the best and most up-to-date advice, so we want to know if you've been badly treated or overcharged.

TELEPHONE NUMBERS

The country code for Morocco is 212; the area code for Marrakech is 024. You must dial area codes with all numbers, even when calling a number within the same area code – but drop the zero if calling from abroad. For more on telephones and codes, see p234.

LET US KNOW WHAT YOU THINK

We hope you enjoy the *Time Out Marrakech, Essaouira & the High Atlas Guide*, and we'd like to know what you think of it. We welcome tips for places that you consider we should include in future editions and take note of your criticism of our choices. You can email us your comments at guides@timeout.com.

There is an online version of this book, along with guides to over 100 international cities, at **www.timeout.com**.

L'ALBUM

A fascinating fusion of East and West

On sale exclusively at Le Comptoir de Marrakesh, at all Fnac , Virgin outlets and in other shops around the world.

Restaurant - Club - Boutique

In Context

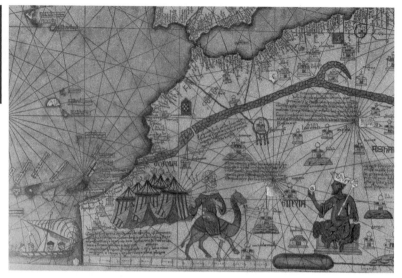

History

Tribalism, colonialism, nationalism – and bohemianism.

In the beginning, were the Berbers. Long before anyone thought of building a place called Marrakech, they were already here – before the Arabs came bearing Islam, before the rise and fall of Carthage and Rome, even before the Phoenicians. A Caucasian people, often light-skinned with fair hair and high cheekbones, their origins are lost in time. One theory is that they were descendants of the neolithic culture that stretched along Europe's Atlantic coast – a stone circle at Mzoura, near Asilah, is in similar style, and in a similar heathland location, to circles in Portugal, Brittany and southern England.

Over the centuries, the Berbers developed a complex clan system and dug into the Rif and Atlas mountains. There they remained unconquered, no matter what happened down on the plains. The Romans couldn't dislodge them. Neither could the Arabs, who ended up living alongside them. But though many Berbers had been unimpressed by Christianity, Islam took their fancy, and the eighth-century Muslim conquest of Iberia was achieved with an army of Berber converts.

Islam proved to be the cultural glue that would hold Morocco together. It condemned

petty interests and local loyalties, and enabled a central authority to draw legitimacy from respect for its teachings. From here on, the history of Morocco is one of dynastic rule, but also of tension between central government and tribal independence, between the relatively orderly plains and coast – known as the Bled El-Makzhen – and the ungovernable areas of mountain and desert – the Bled Es Siba. And, as tribe after tribe forayed out of the Atlas or Sahara to found dynasties in the north, Marrakech would watch history from the border between the two.

THE ALMORAVIDS (1062-1147)

The first such was the Almoravid dynasty. In the ninth and tenth centuries, trans-Saharan trade routes were established, mostly for gold – exchanged for salt in the Niger region. The main staging-post at this end was Sijilmassa, which stood near present-day Rissani in the Tafilelt oasis and thrived until the 14th century. There was ferocious competition for control of the caravan routes, but one tribe of nomadic Berbers came out on top. They ranged across the western Sahara from fortified religious settlements, known as *ribat*, and this gave them their name – El-Mourabitoun, or Almoravids.

One of their leaders went off to Mecca and returned preaching against palm wine and having more than four wives. Newly fired with missionary fervour, the Almoravids subdued the south, crossed the Atlas and paused for breath. Being nomads, they'd never done much in the way of founding cities, but as their dominions grew they saw the wisdom in having a central store of weapons and food, and as a pious people they wanted somewhere to build a great mosque. It was 1062. At a location offering control of the most important Atlas passes, they founded Marrakech.

'The Almoravids built what was by all accounts a spectacular city.'

It began as a military outpost – no more than an encampment circled by thornbush – but, well placed on the route between Sahara and Atlantic, it soon also became a trading post. The original name was Marra Kouch. No one knows what it meant but the name lives on in both 'Marrakech' and 'Morocco'.

From this new base, the Almoravids quickly went on to conquer the whole of Morocco. In 1086 they landed in Spain, defeated the Christians and absorbed much of the Iberian peninsula. By the early 12th century their empire stretched from Lisbon to West Africa and from the Atlantic to Algeria.

Back in Marrakech, the Almoravids built what was by all accounts a spectacular city. Sadly, nothing survives except one little piece of their great big mosque – the small but exquisite **Koubba El-Badiyin** (*see p77*). How grand must the Ali Ben Youssef Mosque have been if this was just its ablutions fountain?

The Almoravid legacy in Marrakech can still be felt in the city walls they erected and the palm groves they planted. They used their Saharan expertise to establish the water supply, building long underground pipes that conveyed Atlas meltwater to the fountains, pools and gardens of Marrakech.

THE ALMOHADS (1147-1269)

By the mid 12th century, the Almoravids had overstretched themselves. There were reverses in Spain and unrest at home. A rival confederation of Berber tribes, the Almohads, scented blood.

The Almohads had their own *ribat*, the mountain fastness of **Tin Mal** (*see p199)* in the High Atlas. Armed with interpretations of Islam even more strict than their predecessors,

the Almohads, whose name means 'unitarians', galloped out of the hills and placed Marrakech under siege. It took 11 unpleasant months, but in 1147 the city was theirs.

So they knocked it all down and rebuilt it – and, to be fair, did a beautiful job. The monumental architecture of this period still dominates Marrakech. The most stunning achievement was their own big mosque, the **Koutoubia** (*see p68*). Other significant period pieces include the **Kasbah Mosque** and **Bab Agnaou** (for both, *see p82* and the **Agdal** and **Menara gardens** (for both, *see p92*).

The greatest Almohad leader, Abdel Moumen, reconquered southern Spain and was victorious in Tunis, Tripoli and southern Algeria. During his reign, Marrakech became a bastion of Islamic civilisation and culture, a haven for scholars and philosophers.

THE MERENIDS (1248-1554)

Like the Almoravids before them, the Almohads had overreached, losing their religious drive and running into trouble in Spain. And of course yet another nomadic Berber tribe was waiting to charge in, this one the Beni-Merens – Merenids – from the empty lands between Tafilelt and Algeria. Fès fell to them in 1248; Marrakech in 1269.

The Merenids ruled from Fès and, compared to the glory of the Almohad period, Marrakech fell upon hard times, reduced to the status of provincial outpost. This is the era of the great Muslim geographers and explorers such as Ibn Khaldun and Ibn Batuta (the Muslim Marco Polo). But it was a golden age in which Marrakech played little part except as a bastion against attacks from the south.

Following the pattern established by previous dynasties, by the 15th century the Merenids too were in decline and Europe was on the attack. This was the epoch of the great discoveries. The Portuguese explored the African coast, grabbing Mogador (present-day Essaouira) and other ports. With maritime routes opening up to the 'gold coast', the overland trans-Saharan trade routes, and with them the whole south of Morocco, were declining in importance. And the Christian incursions, which the Merenids had proved unable to resist, spawned a new kind of Islamic movement, based around leaders called cherifs, who claimed descent from the Prophet. The Saadians were one such movement.

THE SAADIANS (1549-1668)

The Saadians arrived from Arabia in the 12th century and settled in the Drâa Valley. They lived peacefully among the palm groves and bothered no one for several hundred years. But

The ancient mosque at **Tin Mal**, built by the Almohads in 1153. *See p13.*

when the 16th century rolled around, with the Portuguese all over the coast, rebellious Berber tribes roaming the interior and the Merenids pretty much confined to Fès and Marrakech, the Saadians decided it was time to restore order and repel the Christians.

They needed time to establish themselves. In 1510 they took the Sous valley and used the Taroudant as their capital. In 1541 they defeated the Portuguese at nearby Agadir. And in 1549 they dethroned the Merenids at Fès.

The Saadians then returned the court to Marrakech and essentially refounded the city, which once more acquired the atmosphere of an imperial capital. Sultan Moulay Abdellah built a new Ali Ben Youssef Mosque and developed the similarly named *medersa* (*see p75*) into North Africa's biggest Qur'anic school. He gave the Jews their own quarter (*see p84*), the Christians their own trading centre at the heart of the Medina (roughly where Club Med is today), and sprinkled the city with fountains and hammams.

To celebrate victory over the Portuguese at Battle of the Three Kings (1578) – remembered as such because that's how many rulers lost their lives before it was over – the succeeding Sultan Ahmed El-Mansour ('the Victorious'; 1578-1603) oversaw the construction of the lavish **Badii Palace** (*see p83*), importing some 50 tons of marble from Italy. Another extravagance was the opulent mausoleums now known as the **Saadian Tombs** (*see p82*).

Much of this was paid for with gold from the Niger. In 1590 Ahmed led an army across the Sahara, reviving the trade routes, securing the salt mines, grabbing the gold and enslaving the locals. The whole area of the Western Sahara, Mauritania and Mali became a protectorate run by the Saadian pashas from Timbuktu.

ALAOUITE LONGEVITY

After Ahmed died in 1603, Morocco descended into civil war. Saadian rulers clung on to the Sous and Marrakech, while another tribe grabbed Fès and the strange pirate republic of the Bou Regreg briefly flourished in Rabat and Salé. It was clearly time for another dynasty to enter from the south.

The Alaouites were *cherifs* from Rissani in the Tafilelt, the same oasis that 600 years previously had nurtured the Almoravids. Like the Saadians before them, the Alaouites' route to power was a slow one; they took Taza and Fès before seizing Marrakech in 1668. Moulay Rachid was the first Alaouite Sultan, and though his reign was uneventful, his legacy lives on: the Alaouites still rule Morocco today.

As in any family, there are the members no one likes to talk about – in this case, Rachid's younger brother and successor Moulay Ismail (1672-1727). Ismail hated Marrakech and built a new imperial capital at Meknès. He stripped the Badii Palace and, such was the wealth there, this took a team of labourers 12 years to complete. Marrakchis must have been glad to see the back of him, particularly as he turned out to be one of the most cruel and depraved rulers in the whole of Moroccan history. He is said to have personally killed 30,000 people, chopping off heads and doing a bit of disembowelling when the fancy took him. He also sired 888 children, ensuring succession problems. But there was method as well as madness. He kept at bay both the Europeans and the Ottomans, by now camped next door in Algeria, and one way or another made Morocco strong again.

Until, after a 54-year reign, he died. Ismail's authority had been enforced by his Black Guard, an army of descendants of slaves taken by the Saadians on their Timbuktu expeditions. With Ismail gone this force owed loyalty to no one and spent 30 years on the rampage, rendering Morocco ungovernable.

> ### 'Moulay Hassan tried to stabilise the currency, play off the Europeans against each other and shore up national defences.'

Somehow the Alaouite ruler Sidi Mohammed Ben Abdellah (1757-90) managed to get the Black Guard under control. He also rebuilt the Atlantic port of Mogador and renamed it Essaouira – its rational, almost rectilinear medina dates from his reign – and then invited English, French and Jewish merchants to set up shop there. But chaos resumed as soon as he died, followed by a period of isolationism towards Europe.

ISOLATION AND DECLINE

By the early 19th century, Marrakech still hadn't progressed much beyond the Middle Ages. Dynasties had come and gone and it still made its living the same way it had done for 1,000 years, trading olive oil, corn, livestock, tanned leather, slaves and woven goods.

Meanwhile, the end of the Napoleonic Wars left European powers free to get on with colonial expansion. The French moved into Algeria in 1830, leaving Morocco under pressure and isolated from the rest of the Islamic world. France then defeated the Moroccan army at the Battle of Isly in 1844, the Spanish added Tetouan to their conquests on the Mediterranean coast and grabbed the area that is now Western Sahara, and the British forced Sultan Abdel Rahman (1822-59) to sign a preferential trade treaty in 1857. But quite amazingly, as the 19th century drew to a close, Morocco remained just about the only bit of Africa that wasn't under some form of colonial rule.

Sultan Moulay Hassan (1873-94), the last pre-colonial ruler with any real power, used Marrakech as his southern capital. By this time the city had long been in decline – the 1875 Encyclopaedia Britannica noted holes in the walls big enough for a horseman to ride through and a Medina 'defaced by mounds of rubbish and putrid refuse'.

But Moulay Hassan was a moderniser. He tried to stabilise the currency, play off the Europeans against each other and shore up national defences. For funds he had no recourse save the traditional *harka* – the Sultan would set off somewhere with an army and entourage, collecting tribute in the manner of a swarm of locusts. In 1893, he returned from such an expedition in the Tafilelt dying and with his forces in disarray. Crossing the Atlas towards Marrakech via the Tizi-n-Tichka pass, he was offered sanctuary at Telouet, the fortress of the Glaoua tribe.

Hassan's arsenal included an aged but still functional Krupp assault cannon. Such weapons had acquired a bizarre symbolic role as representative of the Sultan and his cherifian powers. People swore by them, prayed to them, kissed their barrels, brought them offerings of severed enemy heads, and believed them to possess healing powers.

Madani El-Glaoui somehow fed and sheltered the Sultan's entire army for several days. In gratitude, Hassan declared him his personal representative in the Atlas and Sahara and left behind most of his armoury, including the 77mm bronze Krupp cannon. The Glaoua tribe thus acquired both a weird legitimacy and a fearsome arsenal. They set about subjugating the south.

DEBT AND UNREST

Moulay Hassan died soon afterwards. He was succeeded by his young son, Abdel Aziz (1894-1908), but for the first few years Hassan's powerful vizier, Ba Ahmed Ben Moussa, carried on pulling the strings. He also spent the next six years building for himself the **Bahia Palace** (*see p87*). When Ba Ahmed died in 1900, Abdul Aziz was barely 20 years old.

Walter Harris, the *Times* correspondent whose *Morocco That Was* is a court insider's account of this period, paints a vivid picture of a country ripe for imperialist plucking. While his advisers feathered their nests, and the European powers contemplated a colonial carve-up of North Africa, the Sultan Abdel Aziz amused himself with games of cricket and bicycle polo, frittering away millions on toys and gadgets. These included a lift for a one-storey palace and a state coach for a country with no roads. Morocco was now heavily in debt to European banks.

The Marrakech slave market, 1908. Slaves were sold here until the early 20th century.

European powers met to discuss matters at the 1906 Conference of Algeciras. This established Tangier's status as an international free port and affirmed the independence of the Sultan, but it also paved the way for the Protectorate by giving Spain and France a mandate to restore order, if necessary.

> **'Emile Mauchamp was lynched outside his house by an angry crowd. The French used it as an excuse to move troops into the Moroccan town of Oujda.'**

In March 1907, Emile Mauchamp, a doctor sent by the French to set up a clinic in Marrakech, planted a pole on his roof. He did this as a kind of arrogant joke. Moroccan authorities were so worried about foreign powers establishing a wireless telegraph network, that a mass paranoia about radio antenna had been spreading across the country. Mauchamp's provocation worked too well – he was lynched outside his house by an angry crowd. The French used this as an excuse to move troops across the Algerian border and into the Moroccan town of Oujda.

Later, other Europeans were killed in Casablanca. The French stepped in and occupied that city too. Aziz was deposed by his brother, Moulay Hafid (1908-12), but faced with unrest, crippling debts and aggression from the Europeans, Hafid had little choice but to accept the imposition of French rule, formalised in the 1912 Treaty of Fès. He abdicated soon afterwards.

INTO THE 20TH CENTURY

The first French Résident Général (later Maréchal) of Morocco was Louis Lyautey, who had led the French troops in Oujda. Lyautey was to have an enormous effect on the country, building roads and railways, the ports of Casablanca and Kenitra, and adding new French-style towns to the old Medinas of Rabat, Fès, Meknès and Marrakech. The French basically dragged Morocco into the 20th century – except some of it didn't want to come along.

The old Bled El-Makzhen became what the French called *Maroc Utile* – the useful bits of Morocco whose resources they would set about exploiting. The rest of the country – the old Bled Es Siba of mountains and desert – remained recalcitrant and unruly. Hardly was the ink dry on the Treaty of Fès than a tribal warlord called El-Hiba appeared from the south and camped an army of 12,000 outside the walls of Marrakech. The French turned up to massacre them with machine-guns and mortars.

Machine-guns and mortars would soon also be firing in Europe, and the likelihood of war with Germany meant Lyautey would never have the forces needed to subdue the south. Instead, to keep a lid on the region, he struck a deal with the ruler of the powerful Glaoua tribe, Thami El-Glaoui, who, along with his brother Madani, had recently backed the coup that placed Moulay Hafid on the throne. Thami was installed as *bacha* (lord) of Marrakech, while Madani was given command of all lands and tribes of the south. They were allowed to rule as they saw fit and in return gave their full support to the occupying power. Madani died in 1918, but Thami was to carry on as bacha for the next 42 years. *See p17* **Glaoui power**.

Glaoui power

When the French first encountered Thami El-Glaoui in the early 20th century, he was little more than an uncouth tribal warlord with a mountain base in Telouet. Installing him as boss of Marrakech in 1912, the French seemed to take the view that he might be a ruthless despot, but at least he was their ruthless despot.

European society took a similar tack. Although at first he didn't speak a word of French, within 20 years 'the Glaoui' had become one of the most fashionable names to drop, imbued with all the mystique and exoticism of an Indian maharajah. While his political enemies rotted in dungeons below the opulent Dar El-Bacha, and his nephew-in-law Hammou ran Telouet as if medieval was going out of style, the Glaoui threw sumptuous banquets and lavished gifts on international guests – maybe a diamond ring, maybe a cute Berber boy or girl. While his subjects went hungry, the Glaoui diverted water from farmland to maintain an 18-hole golf course.

Europeans were less appalled by the Glaoui's excesses than they were suckered by his immaculate manners, generosity and *bons mots*. At one famous dinner party, the Glaoui overheard a young Parisian woman – who thought he understood no French – call him a pig, but admit to coveting his emerald ring. At the end of the meal, the Glaoui pulled her aside and said, in immaculate French, 'Madame, a stone like this emerald was never made for a pig like me. Permit me to offer it to you'. His comment on the French war minister, Daladier, was often quoted: 'He is like a dog without a tail – there is no way to tell what he is thinking.'

The Glaoui's refined exterior hid a voracious sexual appetite. His enormous harem – 96 women at his brother Madani's death in 1918, from whose harem he poached a further 54 – wasn't distraction enough and he put great effort into the pursuit of European women. A network of talent scouts scoured Morocco for likely conquests. White-skinned belles would be invited by aides to tour the palace. If they took his fancy, the Glaoui would make a 'surprise' appearance and invite them to dinner – and further seductions. Up in Telouet, Hammou's idea of a party was different. In 1931, three years before his death, he threw a huge banquet for Moroccan and French dignitaries. The guests were alarmed at the sound of gunfire outside. The kasbah had been surrounded by several thousand of Hammou's mounted warriors and, as the 'folkloric' demonstration began, he announced that he would like to see all Frenchmen in the country dead. Thami must have been mortified.

EXTRAVAGANT DESPOT

Ensconced in the lavish palace known as Dar El-Bacha ('House of the Lord'), Thami El-Glaoui took his place among the leading despots of Moroccan history, ruling Marrakech as would a Mafia boss. He hung the heads of his enemies from the gates, while his secret agents briefed him each evening on the goings-on in the Medina and brought in parades of suspects to be tried in his own personal *salon de justice*.

As the dungeons filled with prisoners and the coffers with cash, the Glaoui threw sumptuous banquets for European dignitaries while his henchmen combed the countryside for girls to stock the harem. The Glaoui funded his extravagant lifestyle by grabbing local monopolies in hemp, olives, almonds, saffron, dates, mint and oranges. Soon, he enjoyed greater power than the puppet Sultan and Marrakech rivalled in importance the new capital, Rabat.

But there was one snag. Madani had handed control of the lands beyond the Atlas to his son-in-law, Hemmou, who now sat in Telouet between Thami and the rest of the South. Wealthy, ruthless and equipped with an arsenal greatly expanded since the original Krupp cannon, he was also obstinately anti-French. For this reason the south was never 'pacified' – and the Protectorate not fully established – until after his death in 1934. It's also why the French Foreign Legion built the Tizi-n-Tichka road over a difficult route avoiding Telouet.

But despite all this, the Glaoui enjoyed the wholehearted support of the French administration. His despotic regime left them free to exploit Morocco's phosphates, iron, anthracite, manganese, lead and silver. Agriculture also flourished, as French companies turned traditional olive groves and orchards into industrialised enterprises.

COLONIALS AND LOCALS

Lyautey was on a civilising mission. 'I have always had two passions,' he said, 'policies regarding the natives and town planning'. Thus Marrakech acquired a *nouvelle ville* just outside the Medina, later to become known as Guéliz. Lyautey was explicit that this new quarter – like similar projects in other Moroccan cities – had to be separate from the Medina in order to 'protect the autonomy of each'. This can be read two ways: on the one hand, a respect for Moroccans and a commendable desire not to interfere with the traditional organisation of their cities; on the other, an enforced segregation with nice new quarters for the white folks and the natives confined to crowded and insanitary medinas.

For the new Marrakech a town planner named Henri Prost laid out a scheme of large *rondpoints* connected by broad, leafy avenues. Camp Guéliz, a military fort on a rocky outcrop just north of the new town, provided security. Almost as significantly, Prost was one of the architects behind the opulent new Mamounia hotel, built in 1922 by the Moroccan national rail company. Thus Guéliz received all the roads, railway connections, hospitals and schools; the Medina remained in squalor.

> **'The staggering inequality between the *colos* and the locals was a major factor in stoking support for a nationalist movement.'**

Lyautey's town-planning formalised the gulf between Moroccans and Europeans. By the 1930s there were 325,000 of the latter in the country. The staggering inequality between the *colos* and the locals was a major factor in stoking support for a nationalist movement. This found political voice in the Istiqlal (Independence) Party, formed in Rabat and Fès. World War II provided further momentum. The French army had included 300,000 Moroccan soldiers. These acquitted themselves so ably that Franklin D Roosevelt, who had travelled to Casablanca to meet Winston Churchill for a conference, hinted to the new Sultan, Mohammed V, that, after the war, the country would become independent.

WORKING FOR THE CLAMPDOWN

Mohammed V had succeeded his father in 1927. He was young but in no way content to be a puppet. After the war, he began to press for independence. With membership of the Istiqlal Party mushrooming, the French began to get nervous. In 1953, with the help of the Glaoui (who imprisoned his own son for nationalist sympathies), they sent Mohammed V into exile. This proved a mistake, confirming him as a nationalist figurehead. His expulsion sent the country into turmoil, triggering riots in Marrakech and Casablanca. There was a clampdown on both cities, with curfews, arrests and interrogation under torture. A week after the Sultan's expulsion, 13,000 Moroccans had been arrested for treason.

By the summer of 1955 a campaign for the Sultan's return had escalated into armed rebellion. Terrorists tossed a bomb into a Casablanca café, killing seven Europeans. In Marrakech, a bomb was lobbed into the Berima Mosque where Ben Arafa, France's new puppet Sultan, was praying.

High rollers: the good life in the *nouvelle ville*, 1952.

The Glaoui advised the French to 'do as the British did with the Mau Mau' – a reference to the particularly brutal campaign in Kenya, where nationalists had been slaughtered in their thousands. Given such an attitude towards his fellow Moroccans, it's perhaps not surprising that, when being driven around in his Bentley, the Glaoui only felt safe on the floor with a submachine gun clutched to his chest.

Hands already full with a bloody nationalist revolt in Algeria, the French decided to cut their losses in Morocco. In November 1955 Mohammed V was permitted to return. The Glaoui was furious, but kissed the Sultan's feet and begged for mercy. Punitive measures were unnecessary as the Glaoui was dying of cancer. He succumbed on 30 January 1956.

What should have been a joyous occasion for Marrakech quickly turned ugly – as if even in death the Glaoui could bring terror to the streets. A rampaging mob chanted 'Death to the traitors!'. Old allies of the Glaoui were hunted down, stripped, stoned and dragged outside the city walls to be doused in petrol and set alight. Children gathered around, laughing and cheering as victim upon victim was thrown on to the bonfires.

The new governors of Marrakech did nothing to halt the rioting but placed guards round the smouldering bodies so that women could not take pieces of them for black magic. The c orpse of the Glaoui himself was spared any indignities and interred, with full French

military honours, at the Shrine of Sidi Ben Slimane. Three months later, with France fully engaged in a bloody war against the nationalists in Algeria, Morocco was granted its independence.

MOHAMMED V AND INDEPENDENCE
The date was 2 March 1956. The first act of the Sultan was to restyle himself as King Mohammed V, a modern constitutional monarch. But not too modern: the monarchy was still at the centre of political life, and the King kept the military on a short leash. He was rightly worried that the jubilation following independence would be short-lived; the nationalist movement quickly disintegrated into rival factions. The left-wing of the Istiqlal Party broke away to set up the socialist UFSP, with the King lending his support to the more moderate Mouvement Populaire.

Mohammed V never lived to see the first democratic election. Presided over by his son, King Hassan II, in 1963, it was won by a coalition of royalists and the Mouvement Populaire. The socialists claimed the polls had been rigged. Their leader, Ben Barka, denounced the monarchy and was exiled to Paris, where he was assassinated by secret agents. So much for the new Morocco. Much of the period's civil unrest was the result of poverty compounded by a series of natural disasters. In 1961 locusts devastated crops around Marrakech. Severe drought added to the country's woes, as did the catastrophic 1961 earthquake in Agadir, which killed 15,000. Hassan II nationalised much of the economy, expropriating land from French companies. But most of this land was reserved for export crops and did nothing to feed the domestic population. By the mid 1960s Morocco – once called 'the bread basket of the Roman Empire' – had become a net importer of cereals.

As poverty increased, mass migration to the cities followed. Sprawling, overcrowded shanty towns – known as *bidonvilles* – sprang up on the edge of Marrakech and other major cities. A whole uncontrolled economy developed. Marrakech was soon packed with illegal taxi drivers, street peddlers and hustlers. The rise of hashish farming also fuelled the black economy and helped spawn a new kind of tourism.

Marrakesh Express

'*Wouldn't you know we're riding on the Marrakesh Express?*' Jimi Hendrix might have been Morocco's most celebrated visitor from the Woodstock generation, but it was Crosby, Stills and Nash who released the hippie holiday anthem. Graham Nash wrote 'Marrakesh Express' after a 1966 train journey from Casablanca, recording postcard impressions of clear skies, snake-charmers, and jellebas 'we can wear back home', all the while 'blowing smoke rings' from the corners of his mouth.

In the decade between 1965 and 1975, tourism revenue doubled in Morocco. And the main reason was its sudden popularity with the hippie generation. Even before *Casablanca*, made in 1942, Morocco had been Hollywood shorthand for 'exotic', but it was the Beats who put it on the countercultural map. William Burroughs' association with Tangier, and much-mythologised visits by Allen Ginsberg, Jack Kerouac and Timothy Leary, drew the first curious bohemians. By 1965 there were so many longhairs in the Socco Chico that it helped drive Burroughs away from Morocco for good.

What became known as the Hippie Trail led from London or Paris to Istanbul, and then on to India and Nepal. Morocco was more of a side trip, a quicker and more convenient blast of Third Worldliness and alien spirituality, offering strange, colourful clothes and a plentiful supply of cheap marijuana. Its culture mostly impenetrable to the casual visitor, it was a blank wall on which the hippies could daub their own psychedelic mural.

Tangier and Marrakech were the principal hippie destinations, but there were also plenty to be found in Asilah, Chefchaouen, Ketama and other towns of the Rif. A commune established itself in Diabat, just south of Essaouira, and, to this day,

further down the coast towards Agadir, the occasional longhair can still be found nodding to Bob Marley tunes in the village of Taghazoute.

It's impossible to say just how many made the trip, but Ed Buryn's guidebook for the love generation, *Vagabonding in Europe and North Africa*, had 50,000 copies in print by 1973. By that time the Moroccan authorities were getting sick of the hippies, refusing to let in some longhairs and obliging many others to make a quick trip to the barber at Casablanca airport. Though that establishment can have had few complaints, hippies were widely perceived as contributing little to the local economy. Anti-drug laws that were usually ignored or enforced only loosely were used to harrass the hippies by authorities increasingly worried about their potential effect on local youth.

But potential was all it ever was. It's a sad paradox that the very decade during which western youth was acting out a Maghrebi fantasy of freedom was also the most heavy-handed and repressive period in Morocco's post-Independence history. Moroccans call it *Les Années de Plomb* – the 'Years of Lead'. Student actions were ruthlessly repressed, with the army killing over 1,000 people after the 1965 student riots in Casablanca, and closing down Mohammed V University in Rabat after strikes in 1971 and 1972. The period included two failed coups and came to end only with the 1975 Green March into Western Sahara, when the monarchy managed to channel dissent into a resurgent nationalism.

The hippies never connected with any of this at all, smoking kif and staring out of the train windows. Graham Nash sang of seeing 'ducks and pigs and chickens'. Well, there are hardly any ducks in Morocco and you could live your whole life there without ever seeing a pig. The hippies' detachment was absolute and, eventually, they went home.

The Rolling Stones in Marrakech, photographed by Cecil Beaton in 1967.

JOHN, PAUL, MICK AND KEITH

North Africa had long held romantic resonance for European intellectuals: a haven for 19th-century bohemians, it had been a source of inspiration for writers and painters from Gustave Flaubert and Eugène Delacroix to André Gide and Henri Matisse.

The bohemian tradition continued into the 20th century when the licentious enclave of Tangier – designated an International Zone under the joint rule of France, Spain, Britain, Portugal, Sweden, Holland, Belgium, Italy and the USA – attracted the likes of Paul Bowles and William Burroughs. In 1956 the International Zone was absorbed into independent Morocco and the expats began drifting south to Marrakech, lured by its balmy climate and colourful exoticism.

In accordance with Beat philosophy, the spiritual went hand in hand with the sexual. The Marrakech brothels were infamous, particularly among gays (sun and sex in Marrakech remains a favourite with ageing American and European queens to this day). And, of course, there was the *kif*, or cannabis, which was smoked openly.

Brian Jones of the Rolling Stones made his first trip in 1966 with his girlfriend Anita Pallenberg. He brought the rest of the band with him on the next visit; they drove from Tangier to Marrakech and checked into the Hotel Es Saadi. There they tripped on LSD and ran into Cecil Beaton, who photographed Mick and Keith by the pool. At the centre of the scene were the American oil heir John Paul Getty Jr and his wife Talitha. The Gettys owned a place in the Medina, where they were famously photographed in kaftans up on the roof terrace against a backdrop of Koutoubia and the Atlas Mountains. Here they hosted parties that went on for days at a time. An entry in John Hopkins's *The Tangier Diaries* for 1 January 1968 reads: 'Last night Paul and Talitha Getty threw a New Year's Eve party at their palace in the Medina. Paul McCartney and John Lennon were there, flat on their backs.'

Portrait of a leader

Portraits of leaders are a feature of authoritarian societies, where the nation is supposedly embodied in the person of a charismatic leader. Hanging one up on the wall is a sign of loyalty. Or conformism. Or simply because to do otherwise would be to invite unwelcome attention from the secret police. You might not particularly want to put up a picture of the King, but if you don't then people might talk.

The days are probably gone when ordinary Moroccans need worry about being dragged off to some dungeon. The heavy-handed Hassan II inspired considerable fear, but Mohammed VI is clearly a more liberal-minded ruler. Still, you'll see his likeness everywhere, on roadside banners and billboards, in both government offices and private businesses. On some hillsides in the south, white stones are laid to spell out in giant letters: 'God, Country, King'. Moroccans, like Britons, are subjects, not citizens. And here the King still rules OK.

But there aren't really official portraits in the way there were in, say, Communist-era Russia or China. A Mao or Stalin was represented by a unitary, approved image that – as Andy Warhol twigged – was more of a graphic icon than a human likeness. Portraits of Mohammed VI are as varied

as can be, and seem to show a human being rather than an idealised symbol of authority.

The game in shops and businesses, given that they more or less have to have one, is finding a picture appropriate to their enterprise. A café might show Mohammed VI drinking a coffee. In a kaftan shop, he'll be wearing traditional garb. At the fake Ray-Ban stall, he'll be sporting designer shades. Even the humble shoeshine guy might pin on his wooden box of brushes a picture of the King shod in something highly polished. In a *téléboutique*, he is pictured talking on the phone.

Portraits of Hassan II are still common and, comparing pictures of father and son, you can see a distinct shift in style. When Hassan II was shown riding a stallion or teeing up at the 18th hole, it was to present him as master of everything, first Moroccan in all things. The more informal pictures of Mohammed VI, holding his baby or laughing at something off-camera, are saying that he shares these ordinary human things with everyone, that he is close to the people.

If you feel like hanging one at home or in your workplace, pictures of Mohammed VI can be found at stationery or photographic shops, and on book and newspaper stalls around the Jemaa El Fna.

They couldn't get off the floor let alone talk. I've never seen so many people out of control.'

COUPS AND MARCHES

While the foreigners carried on, members of the royal court were plotting to get rid of their ruler. In 1971 the King's 42nd birthday party was gatecrashed by 1,400 army cadets who loosed machine-gun fire at the 800 or so diplomatic guests lounging around the pool. The coup leader was accidentally killed in the crossfire and the cadets panicked, at which point the King, who had hidden in a bathroom, emerged and coolly stared down his would-be assassins, who dropped their weapons and rushed to kiss his hands and feet. The failed coup had left 98 guests dead.

> 'Islamic extremists attacked a hotel in Marrakech, spraying the lobby with machine-gun fire and killing two Spanish tourists.'

Thirteen months later the King's Boeing 727 was attacked in the air by six F5 fighters from his own airforce. One of the jet's engines was destroyed but the pilot managed to land at Rabat. As the King and his party ran for cover three more rebel aircraft continued to strafe the runway and the officials who had been waiting to greet the plane. Eight people on the ground were killed and close to 50 wounded. The minister of defence committed suicide, there were summary executions, the pilot was promoted – and the King got back to ruling the country.

In 1975 he seized the Spanish colony of Rio del Oro in the Western Sahara. He did so by organising the 'Green March', in which 350,000 citizens marched into the territory from Marrakech. General Franco had just died and Spain relinquished the colony without much fuss. But the colony's residents had other ideas. Polisario, a nationalist group comprised of the indigenous Sahrawi tribe, proclaimed a republic. Backed by the Algerians, they waged a guerrilla war of independence against Morocco until a ceasefire in 1991. The situation remains unresolved today.

The same year as the Polisario ceasefire, the King dispatched 1,200 troops to Saudi Arabia as a gesture of support to the US-led Gulf War operation. It was not a popular move – Arab versus Arab – and resulted in rioting and worse: in 1994 Islamic extremists attacked a hotel in Marrakech, spraying the lobby with machine-gun fire and killing two Spanish tourists. Hassan II reacted with the ruthless suppression characteristic of his reign, involving arbitrary arrests, 'disappearances' and widespread abuses of human rights and judicial norms. It's a darker side to the King's rule that has only recently been aired in public, most notably in the furore surrounding 2004's publication of a novel by Moroccan writer Tahar Ben Jelloun (*see p240* that focused on the fate of detainees in Hassan II's desert concentration camps.

MOHAMMED VI AND HUMAN RIGHTS

Hassan II died of a heart attack in July 1999 and was succeeded by his 36-year-old eldest son, who became King Mohammed VI. Popular approval greeted his pledge to a multi-party political system, respect for human rights and improved rights for women. Some progress has been made towards these goals. The King dismissed his father's much-feared interior minister, political exiles were allowed to return and political detainees were released.

In 2004 a Justice and Reconciliation Authority was set up to investigate the human rights abuses of the past. The same year, the rights of women were improved by a rewriting of the *moudawana* (the laws governing personal rights) to restrict polygamy and give women equal rights to men in marriage, divorce and the care of children. Meanwhile, the May 2003 Islamist suicide-bomb attacks on various targets in Casablanca helped gather support for a crackdown on this new breed of dissident. In April 2007, there were several more explosions in Casablanca, as terrorists blew themselves up rather than be taken prisoner in a massive police operation.

Marrakech has remained free of such problems and has definitely prospered under the influence of the new King. Although his official residence is in Rabat, Mohammed VI spends as much time as he can in the Pink City – and built himself a new, more modest palace rather than occupy the gigantic old one that sprawls across half of the kasbah district. Mohammed VI removed the red tape obstructing foreign investment, triggering the current property boom in the Medina, and cracked down on the touts and hustlers.

The young King remains popular, despite press revelations that he costs Moroccan taxpayers £144.6 million a year – 18 times more than Queen Elizabeth II. But it's hard not warm to someone who speaks with such frankness: *Time* magazine asked him what advice his father gave him; the King answered: 'He told me that the most important thing was 'to last'. I do not know what he meant.'

Marrakech Today

When it comes to tourism, how much is too much?

So near and yet so exotic: one of Marrakech's attractions has always been that it's the *Arabian Nights* within easy travelling distance of Europe. Some would say it has become too easy. Budget airlines have noted Marrakech's popularity and now whisk holidaymakers to the Red City for peanuts. In 2006, more than one and a half million tourists descended on a city of fewer than one million residents. And those numbers are set to grow, with the Moroccan government aiming for a 50 per cent increase in capacity in the city's hotels and guesthouses by 2010.

THE QUESTION

The big question is whether Marrakech can absorb these kinds of tourist numbers without compromising the unique qualities that attract visitors in the first place. Back in the 1960s, Gavin Maxwell wrote that 'Marrakesh has become perhaps the greatest tourist attraction of all North Africa, but the tourists, however great an impression Marrakesh makes upon them, make little impression on Marrakesh.' It's not clear that you could say the same today. While it is true that sensitive restoration means the Medina looks pretty much as it did when Maxwell was there, it is now home to what is officially estimated as around 500 riad hotels (and other estimates are much higher).

In 2006 the Moroccan government approved investment projects around the city worth two billion dollars, mainly consisting of new five-star hotels and golf estates that will stretch water supplies to the limit. The area around the Palmeraie seems to be a permanent building site, and 100 hectares or so of land on the southern outskirts of town have been set aside as an 'international hotel zone', reserved for a number of five-star chain properties . The long-term effects of this on the city remain to be seen, but there is no doubt that full occupancy of the new facilities would skew the local-tourist balance still further.

THE CITY GOES HASSLE-FREE

One change surely welcomed by all visitors is the drastic reduction of hassle and hustle. Mindful that tourists were being put off by the over-attention that was an unavoidable part of any visit to Marrakech until a few years ago, the government formed the *brigade touristique*, a tourist police force whose officers patrol the Medina watching over foreigners. They'll step in if they spot hassle and haul away persistent nuisances. The result is a much calmer experience.

However, this is not to say that Marrakech has become a little Switzerland: it's still hard to walk from one corner of Jemaa El Fna to another without someone trying to persuade you that a photograph of you with a barbary ape on your shoulder is just what you've always wanted.

LOCAL ATTITUDES

Local attitudes to the tourist influx vary. European riad- and home-owners have often found locals keen to sell Medina property at inflated prices, and there is no doubt that foreign money has restored many old buildings that were on the verge of disintegration. In addition, the riad industry has done much to provide work for Marrakech's artisans, and has stimulated a revival of traditional crafts and skills. But not everyone is happy. The more traditionally minded, and particularly the Islamists, find the presence of the visitors alarming. 'Tourism brings only illnesses and social deviance,' said one young man in a recent survey.

Moroccan newspapers have written of street children being lured with gifts to houses where they were abused and filmed by foreigners. According to the association Ne Touche Pas à Mon Enfant, of 80 cases of child sexual abuse documented in Marrakech between 2004 and

Strands of Islamism

Morocco has always prided itself on its moderate form of Islam. The country follows the Maliki school of religious law, which interprets the Qur'an in a flexible way. In addition, many Moroccans are devoted to saints, shrines and other unorthodox elements of folk religion. However, they woke up to a devastating new reality on 16 May 2003, when 45 people were killed in a series of suicide bomb attacks in Casablanca. What these attacks revealed to Moroccans was a home-grown strain of Islamic fundamentalism – disaffected youth from the city's shanty towns who had become attracted to radical teachings.

After the Casablanca bombings the authorities conducted a crackdown and arrested thousands of suspected Islamists, the vast majority of whom had nothing to do with the attacks. Needless to stay, this further radicalised the young detainees and other Moroccans, and the prisons became a breeding ground for extremists. Since then, the security forces periodically announce that they have broken up other terrorist cells elsewhere in the country.

After the attacks of 16 May, King Mohammed VI introduced a reform programme to try to boost liberal Islam. Measures included reform of the family law (covering issues like divorce and

child custody) and even the introduction of women religious guides, or *mourchidat*.

It is not just violent *jihadi* elements that worry the state; it also regards certain non-violent Islamist groups as a threat. While the moderate Party for Justice and Development (PJD) has done well in elections and is expected to increase its support, the government has banned another group, Justice and Charity, on the grounds that it advocates the abolition of the monarchy and disputes the king's claim to be a descendent of the Prophet Mohamed. Much of the monarchy's legitimacy rests on this claimed succession. For many Islamists, on the other hand, there can be no concept of monarchy in Islam. However, continuing concerns about poverty and inequality probably have as much to do with support for Islam as a political solution as anything else. General unease over westernisation is exacerbated by the state's close relationship with the United States (it is an ally in the so-called 'war on terror').

It's worth remembering that around a million people came out on to the streets of Casablanca to protest against terrorism after the 2003 bombings: those who advocate violence are a tiny minority. But Islamism will continue to have political appeal in a nation polarised by economic divisions.

2007, eight involved foreigners. While this isn't a large percentage, there is a feeling that this it is the tip of the iceberg. Whatever the truth of the matter, the fact remains that there is a concern about the impact of outsiders.

NOTHING NEW UNDER MARRAKECH'S SUN

For all the recent upheaval that increased visitor numbers have brought, it is important to remember that tourism is nothing new in Marrakech. Unlike the more conservative cities of Rabat and Fes, Marrakech has a tradition of welcoming strangers. In the days of camel caravans, the city was a gateway to the south. In the main square, Jemaa El Fna, peasants from the Atlas, Souss and Draa would mix with Senegalese traders and Tuaregs. And before the likes of Jude Law, Sienna Miller, or Hugh Grant set foot on Moroccan soil, far more illustrious visitors were drawn to the city, among them Flaubert, Matisse, Orwell and Churchill. In the 1960s Marrakech was a major stop-off on the hippy trail – as exemplified in Crosby, Stills and Nash's 'Marrakesh Express'. The writer Wilfred Thesiger was a frequent visitor – he would arrive with his aged mother in the back of a beaten-up Peugeot 404. Paul McCartney and John Lennon were seen on John Paul Getty Jr's rooftop and Cecil Beaton took snaps of Mick and Keith lounging by the pool at the Hotel Es Saadi. Cat Stevens is supposed to have discovered Islam here. Jimi Hendrix

visited, as did Beat author William Burroughs. Paul Bowles was a frequent visitor, on one occasion turning up with Alan Ginsberg in tow. And the period saw its own property gold rush. According to one story – probably apocryphal – an estate agent was so overwhelmed that he closed his office to evade the clutches of yet another group of inquiring Europeans. 'Dad', his daughter is said to have asked him, 'why have the Rolling Stones followed you home?'

THE FUTURE

There are signs that the property frenzy is calming down, however. Prices in the Medina, which have gone up by five times in the last decade, look to be reaching their ceiling and there are few bargains to be had. But the inescapable fact is that Marrakech's economy is heavily reliant on tourism and will become more so. Today, the city is a centre for diverse holiday activities, whether it's wandering and general hanging out, shopping, dancing or drinking, gambling, spa treatments, eating in first-class restaurants, or golfing. In addition the town is a base for trekking, skiing and more. You can even get married in Marrakech (just have a word with Maggie Perry of Riad Magi). Marrakech has always drawn outsiders. Perhaps those increased tourist numbers will merely add to the mix. We certainly hope that Marrakech doesn't become a holiday theme park, robbed of the real local life that makes it such a chaotic and charismatic city.

A quintessential Marrakech scene: with monkeys in Jemaa El Fna.

Ben Youssef Medersa. *See p29.*

Architecture

Unique use of colour, natural materials, distinctive design: it can only be Marrakech.

When the Arab commander Oqba Ben Nafi spurred his horse into the surf of the Atlantic in AD 682 and swore, 'O God, I take you to witness that there is no ford here. If there was I would cross it', it marked the completion of the Islamic conquest of North Africa, confirmed when Idris II established the wholly Islamic city of Fès. In 818 a failed rebellion in Córdoba sent a flood of Arab refugees to Fès, and a decade later a similar rebellion in Tunisia brought more. In just a few decades Morocco had gained its defining architectural influences and the communities of craftsmen that would give it shape and form.

ANDALUCIAN INFLUENCE

Morocco became the inheritor of the architectural and craft traditions of Muslim Spain and the Córdoban empire (whose glory was enshrined in the glorious Mezquita, Córdoba's Great Mosque). The Almoravids (1062-1147), who were the next dynasty to reunite Morocco after the country dissolved into principalities on the death of Idris II,

further opened the doors to the influx of Spanish Muslim culture. They founded Marrakech (1062) as their capital and, under the influence of the Spanish, built some monumental structures, importing into Morocco the horseshoe arch and cusp arch (the one that looks like a broccoli section). Under the Almoravids the fine carving of stucco also first appears. Incredibly, some of those earliest designs (stylised, paisley-like flowers), which appear in the *mihrab* (prayer niche) of the Karawiyin Mosque in Fès and are reproduced in the erudite *A Practical Guide to Islamic Monuments in Morocco* by Richard Parker, are still being reproduced in Marrakech in 2003 by craftsmen furiously chiselling swirls and flourishes into bands of damp plaster.

In terms of surviving monuments, the only complete Almoravid building in the whole of Morocco is Marrakech's **Koubba El Badiyin** (*see p77*), which displayed for the first time many of the elements and motifs that have since come to characterise Moorish building.

During the reign of the successors to the Almoravids, the Almohads (1147-1269), the Spanish-Moorish synthesis reached its peak. Moroccan architectural styles were developed dramatically. Building materials of choice remained mud brick and *pisé* (reinforced mud), but stone was employed for certain structures, notably the **Bab Agnaou** (*see p82*), the splendid Marrakech gate. Decoration was simplified and made more masculine: whereas the Almoravids went in for flowers, their successors favoured geometric patterns. But these austere rulers eventually softened: witness the lovely trellis-like brickwork and faience tiling lavished on the minarets of the **Koutoubia Mosque** (*see p68*; **photo** *p30*) and the **Kasbah Mosque** (*see p82*).

Under the Merenids (1276-1554), Marrakech may have languished as attention switched to the northern imperial cities of Fès, Meknes and Salé, but artistic interchange continued with Spain. Some of the Merenids' finest monuments – including the Karaouiyine Mosque and Bou Inania Medersa, both in Fés – share similarities with the other great Moorish architecture of the time, the extraordinary Alhambra palace complex, across the Strait in Granada.

ARABESQUE INTERIOR DESIGN

It was the Merenids who introduced most of the familiar interior design repertoire into Morocco, including carved stucco and carved wood, as well as *zelije*, the creation of intricate mosaic design using hand-cut tiles.

Islamic tradition forbids any representation of living things, a policy defined in the formative years of the religion when the Prophet Mohammed first started preaching against the idol worshippers of Mecca. Hence, creativity flourished in more abstract forms. The tradition of tiling was carried west by the Arabs, who had been inspired by the bright turquoise domes and mausoleums of ancient Persia and Samarkand. The Central Asians, in their turn, had picked up the idea from Chinese porcelain, hence the devotion to blue. The Moors of Morocco and Andalucia widened the colour palette courtesy of the Berber influence. Tribal inhabitants of the Atlas Mountains, the Berbers added pink, purple, orange, red and yellow to the existing blue, green and white palette of Islamic culture.

Zelije takes the form of complex geometrical patterns executed in small glazed tiles like a massive jigsaw puzzle. The tiles are formed in large sizes and then cut to shape. This remains the case even today. Visit a building under construction and there will be a group of craftsmen employed to do nothing but cut tiles, which are then stockpiled awaiting the attention of the *zelayiya*, the zelije master craftsman, who will assemble them according to designs passed from father to son and retained in memory only.

There are, it is claimed, 360 different shapes of cut-clay pieces, called *fourma*, and the permutations of colour and pattern are endless. The craft has always been a speciality of the artisans of Fès, but Marrakech has no shortage of kaleidoscopic tiling either, exhibited in its various palaces and religious monuments.

'Berber architecture is quite literally of the earth.'

The other great Merenid addition to architecture is woodworking. Wood has rarely been used as a primary structure (walls and floors are made of stone and mudbrick) but it was frequently employed for ceilings, lintels, capitals and, of course, doors – frequently massive and imposing pieces of work, and decorated with carving, incising and inlays.

Unfortunately, much of the best wood-working has traditionally been reserved for holy institutions such as mosques, shrines and *medersas* (Koranic schools; a building type also introduced by the Merenids), most of which are off-limits to non Muslims. However, some impressive examples of historic craftsmanship can be seen in Marrakech at the engrossing **Dar Si Said Museum** (*see p88*).

PALACES AND HOUSES

Post Merenid, Moroccan architecture went into a period of stagnation. The Moors had retreated from southern Spain in the late 15th century and the Moroccan empire had collapsed inwards. Under the Saadians (1549-1668), Marrakech became the capital again and was embellished with grand new monuments, including the delightful **Ben Youssef Medersa** (*see p74*; **photo** *p27*) and the dazzling **Saadian Tombs** (*see p82*). The former is notable for its acres of carved stucco and wood, the latter for floor-to-ceiling zelije. Architectural historians dismiss these buildings as inferior repetitions of earlier techniques and motifs. That may be so, but at least through them visitors gain an idea of the glorious old buildings that have disappeared.

What the Saadians excelled at were palaces. Sultan Ahmed El Mansour (1578-1607) took 25 years to build the **Badii Palace** (*see p83*). Unfortunately, Moroccan dynasties have not only had a habit of shifting the centre of power around, they've also been inclined to destroy whatever had been created by their predecessors. Right at the start, the Almohads pulled down the original founding fortress of Marrakech to replace it with the Koutoubia Mosque, and, later, Moulay Ismail, who succeeded the Saadians, dismantled the Badii Palace – all that remains are impressive ruins.

Essentially the palaces echoed the design of a traditional house or *dar*. Both followed the principle of an anonymous exterior of blank walls with an entrance leading via a passage – kinked so that anyone at the door or gate couldn't see directly inside – to a central open court. The whole palace or house looks inward rather than outward, with windows and terraces addressing the courtyard, which serves to introduce both light and air into the rooms set around it. On the ground floor these are public reception rooms and salons; the private quarters are on the floor above.

The central open spaces are also rooms in themselves, used for eating and entertaining. In larger houses the courts often have *bahou*, small recessed seating areas. A *douiriya*, or annex, contains the kitchens and servants' rooms. At roof level, flat terraces provide additional space for storage, drying washing or keeping goats and chickens.

The iconic **Koutoubia Mosque**. *See p29.*

BERBER HERITAGE

All that has been described so far is essentially Arab architecture, imported into Morocco since the arrival of Islam. But Marrakech is different to the imperial cities of the north because of the influence of the indigenous Berbers.

These desert and mountain tribal people were the original inhabitants of Morocco long before the Arabs and their city of Fès, long even before the Romans established their outpost at Volublis. Their architecture is quite literally of the earth. The typical fortified Berber village, known as a *ksar*, has traditionally been built of soil reinforced with lime, straw and gravel, mixed into a thick mud paste and applied by hand to a wooden frame. It dries so hard that it takes a hammer and chisel to mark it. At the same time, it has a beautifully organic quality; if another house or extension is needed it's simply welded on and the village grows like a bees' nest.

Similar to the ksour is the *kasbah*, which can be described variously as a castle, a fortress, a palace or a garrison – but essentially it is the residence of a tribal ruler. These ancient structures predominate in southern Morocco, built as much to protect the Berbers from one another as from invaders. They are often sited on a hill, with towers at each corner serving as lookout posts. The interiors are simple, often claustrophobic, with narrow windows (terraces and courtyards bring in light). They might rise to five storeys, with the living quarters and grander reception rooms on the upper floors. Decoration comprises bold geometric motifs – the Berbers were early converts to Islam so share the Arab aversion to figurative representation. At the same time, they held on to many pre-Islamic superstitions and adorned walls with simple carved motifs, designed to ward off evil.

A guaranteed way to breach the defences of a kasbah was to reroute a river and let the water wash away the foundations.

Sadly, many kasbahs and *ksours* have been abandoned over the decades as tribal power has waned. The south of Morocco, especially the High Atlas region, is studded with grandly decaying hilltop ruins, most spectacularly at **Telouet**, the former stronghold of the Glaoui tribe. On a brighter note, there are also impressive partially and wholly restored kasbahs at **Aït Benhaddou**, **Taouirt**, **Tiffoultoute** (for all of the above, *see pp203-207*) and **Skoura** (*see p208*).

MAURESQUE MODERNISM

Following the Saadian dynasty, Marrakech and Morocco on the whole endured a succession of weak, ineffectual imperial figureheads who

In Context

Colour codes

A bit of enlightened ordinance set down during the time of French rule specifies that all buildings in Marrakech must be painted **pink**. Except it's not really pink. The colour is more **ochre**, natural hue of the earth on which the city is founded. Earth has always been the prime building material, mixed with crushed limestone and straw to make *pisé*. No painting required. It's already the right colour. It was only when the French began building the nouvelle ville now known as Guéliz in the early 20th century and introduced new building materials such as concrete that colour became an issue. Even so, even most newer buildings stay somewhere in the pink palette. There's no prescribed paint number or swatches to match, and as a result the tones vary from **pale flesh** to **fiery vermilion**. It's all highly practical, as the colour takes much of the glare out of the sunlight (by contrast Casablanca, which frequently labours under overcast skies, is, as its name suggests, uniformly white). Doors, woodwork and trim are usually done in a complementary shade of **pale green** – the minor term in the city's equation of colour. Some recent buildings in the new town, however, have begun contrasting Marrakech pink with **Majorelle blue** – the intense, luminous blue developed by French artist Jacques Majorelle.

were largely unable to halt the country's descent into intermittent civil war. Architecture rarely flourished. Marrakech briefly grew wealthy during the reign of free-trade fan Sultan Abdel Rahman (1822-59), with the wealth accrued resulting in the building of the **Bahia Palace** (*see p85*). Half a century later the Glaoui's rapacious taxes financed the **Dar El Bacha** (*see p79*). However, if the Saadian monuments were just imitations of greater glories past then these later buildings are third-hand pastiche, only sporadically enlightened by the skills of local artisans.

The arrival of the French in 1912 drew a line under all that had gone before. With foreign rule came a new style of architecture, a mix of European modernistic and Moorish, dubbed 'Mauresque'. Marrakech gained a new town but few buildings of distinction.

In Marrakech, the Protectorate was a mixed blessing. The city was introduced to new architectural ideas, but traditional forms and crafts were largely sidelined in the process. It's only recently, almost 50 years after the departure of the French, that architecture in the city has begun to move on. Gratifyingly,

the inspiration for much of what is happening is Berber simplicity, with current high-profile architects such as Charles Boccara and Elie Mouyal looking to the logic, economy and organic-stylings of mud building.

According to Boccara, when he first began working in Marrakech in the 1980s there was 'no competition'; now he estimates there are maybe more than 50 small architectural practices. He singles out for attention Mohammed Amine Kabbaj, originally from Casablanca, trained in Strasbourg with a diploma from Paris and resident in Marrakech since 1980. Along with two partners, Kabbaj operates out of a hi-tech basement office in the New City, balancing big-bucks projects like a new factory for Coca-Cola with riad rebuilds in the Medina and a personal project to revitalise the small Berber town of Tamesloht and conserve its kasbah.

At the same time, thanks to the patronage of a new wave of designers and decorators, the traditional skills of the city's artisans (zelije workers, the wood and stucco carvers) are back in vogue. After what has been the best part of four centuries of lassitude, a new Marrakech style looks set to shake things up.

Marrakech palmeraie. *See p33.*

Rain Reigns

Where water is scarce, water is everything.

Marrakech is horrible when it rains. It doesn't do it very often, but any time between November and March it can suddenly start coming down in buckets. The alleys of the medina turn into miniature flash floods, leaving behind mud and ankle-deep puddles. Courtyards become gloomy and inhospitable, riad rooms turn chilly and damp. Overworked drainage pipes splash water down the back of your neck as you try to hop between dry patches, suddenly curious about just where Marrakchis buy those waterproof djellabas and wishing you'd booked a place with an open fire.

But while holidaymakers curse, the locals perk up. Rain is welcome, a positive relief. If it doesn't come when it's supposed to, they get nervous and talk about little else. In recent decades too many winters have remained frustratingly dry. Drought affects every Moroccan, from subsistence farmers in the Saharan oases to traders on the Casablanca Stock Exchange. The entire economy suffers from a dry winter, while a few weeks of

decent rainfall can boost GDP by as much as ten or 12 per cent. The French Resident-General, Marshal Lyautey, wasn't kidding when he came out with his much-quoted maxim: 'Au Maroc, gouverner c'est pleuvoir' – in Morocco, rain reigns.

MARRAKECH AND OTHER OASES

It's not immediately obvious, but Marrakech is an oasis – a very big one. While the city's immediate hinterland includes large areas of irrigated agricultural land, you don't have to drive too far out of town to discover that the plain it stands on is fundamentally arid. When the Almoravids came out of the Sahara and founded Marrakech in the 11th century, part of the job was to construct a system of subterranean irrigation channels – *khettaras* – that brought water in from the Atlas. Except for a few bits and pieces, the rest of the city they founded vanished long ago. But their water supply system carried on nurturing Marrakech's parks and gardens for centuries, eventually to be replaced by a system of reservoirs and artesian wells.

The clearest sense of Marrakech as oasis is garnered by a quick trip to the Palmeraie, where a forest of tens of thousands of trees has stood since the area was first planted back in those Almoravid days. Today the palms, many of them sadly stunted and diseased, stand on dry and dusty land, framing what is essentially an affluent suburb of palaces, hotels and golf courses.

It's not, then, either the most beautiful nor the most typical of oases. But the basic features are common to all. Oases depend on there being water present or accessible, but they are not natural features. They're the work of men who dig wells, build reservoirs, channel water from rivers, construct underground water galleries, and continue to maintain and extend the irrigation systems which make them possible. They are also basically palm forests. Occasionally the habitations are among the trees, but more usually are built alongside them, so that no bit of fertile land will be lost to cultivation.

'The kasbahs remind us of the valley's historic wealth and importance.'

The desert proper doesn't begin until the other side of the Atlas mountains. To see an oasis both more characteristic and more appealing, take a drive over the Tizi-n-Tichka to Skoura (*see p208*) – first of the string of oases that run along the Dades Valley and eventually down to the Tafilelt. After the barren landscape along the road, its riot of lush greens is all the more surprising and sensual. Birdsong fills the air as you pass along its narrow alleys, and palm trees tower above the tidy mud walls. Smaller trees – almond and fig, olive and orange – grow between them. Every scrap of land below, carved into squares by narrow channels of water, is planted with wheat and vegetables. Around 20 ancient kasbahs, big fortified mansions, their mud-and-straw façades smoothed and decorated with indentations, tapering towers at their four corners, add to its distinction. And if all that wasn't beautiful enough, the Atlas mountains, snow-covered in winter, stand as a breathtaking backdrop.

The kasbahs, some of which are now converted into hotels, remind us of the valley's historic wealth and importance. Pre-Saharan oases like Skoura were stages on the caravan routes connecting sub-Saharan Africa with the cities of the north, centres of trade as well as pockets of agriculture, and a source of supplies for outlying areas.

The bigger ones are still market towns, but the wealth slowly vanished with the opening of sea routes to the south. Still, as recently as 1934, Paul Bowles found that he could still catch a caravan from Erfoud to Timbuktu. The journey would take, he was told, around 16 to 20 weeks. And how would he get back? Oh, no problem, the caravan would be returning same time next year. 'They were surprised to see that this information lessened my interest. How could you expect to do it more quickly?'

RAIN, GLORIOUS RAIN

In February 2007 it rained in these valleys for the first time in a dozen years. Yellow and purple flowers appeared by the roadside, normally barren hillsides were dusted with green as long-dormant seeds finally got a little of what they'd been waiting for. At an area of ancient wells outside Jorf, marking the line of ancient *khettaras* (**photo p34**), a guy selling trinkets by the roadside told us that he'd lived here all his life and never seen the area so green as it was that day. He was 36 years old. The last well had dried up around the time he was born.

Everyone was relieved that rain had fallen. The water tables had been replenished, the harvest was secured. But sudden rain also has some quite disastrous consequences. The dry river beds fill with rushing torrents that sweep all before them. Desert architecture of mud and straw is fragile, with shallow foundations. A May 2006 flash flood in Merzouga severely damaged a number of the hotels beside the dunes, and completely destroyed the Riad Maria, our pick of the bunch in the last edition of *Time Out Marrakech*. Locals, however, were celebrating. News crews interviewed people who'd lost everything, sheltering in bivouacs because their houses had been washed away. But they were beaming from ear to ear: the date harvest would be bountiful! That far south, on the very edge of the vast Saharan wasteland, there's not much to the economy but tourists and dates.

A CHANGE IN THE WEATHER

The oases are in trouble these days. A combination of demographic pressure and new-fangled agricultural methods has disrupted the delicate balance between man and nature that the oases had long maintained. Add in steadily shrinking rainfall and it's a recipe for a slowly simmering disaster – increasing poverty, creeping desertification. Morocco is one of the countries most threatened by climate change. And it's not just a problem in the south.

In 1993, King Hassan II told a French journalist: 'Faced with a choice between an intelligence report and the weather bulletin, I will put the intelligence report on one side.'

He has a point. Since the late 1970s there have been more and more dry winters. The average annual growing period in Morocco contracted from 180 days in the late 1960s to 110-130 days in the late 1990s. Meanwhile, nearly half of the population still lives off the land. When the rains fail, the economy shrinks, and when the economy shrinks, poverty and unrest increase.

A BRAVE NEW IRRIGATED WORLD

Hassan II tried to tackle the problem with a programme for large-scale irrigation, building dozens of dams in the 1970s and '80s. This was meant to raise rural standards of living, earn foreign currency and provide for national food needs. It failed on all counts. Decreasing rainfall means the reservoirs behind those dams are rarely full. And the huge investment has mostly been to the benefit of a post-colonial landowning elite growing export crops on the coastal plains, further widening the gap between rich and poor. It has been calculated that 17 per cent of cultivated land benefits from irrigation schemes, and this 17 per cent brings in 45 per cent of agricultural earnings. The majority of rural Moroccans live in unirrigated mountain regions, growing grains and raising sheep, completely vulnerable to fluctuating rains. Neighbouring villages occasionally erupt into disputes over water rights, relaying pipes and diverting streams in the dead of night, or going at each other with picks and scythes. While the number of people living below the

official poverty line of just $1 a day continues to increase, the country is now worryingly dependent on food imports, including wheat and corn, vegetables and dairy products, half of its sugar, and 90 per cent of its cooking oil.

Rural poverty also means that more and more people are leaving the land and flooding into the bidonvilles that surround Moroccan cities. Here families pile in ten to a room, and people scrape a living from the informal economy. Today they're the main recruiting grounds of militant political Islam. It's no great stretch to say that the Casablanca terrorist attacks of May 2003 were at least in part a result of the disastrous drought of 1998-2000. Truly, as the man said, rain reigns.

As long as stability and growth depend on the weather, the economy remains hard to manage. Tourism is these days the biggest earner of foreign exchange. In 2000, around three million visitors brought in an estimated $2 billion. The following summer, Mohammed VI announced he was giving the industry top priority, with the aim of attracting ten million visitors by 2010. In the Atlas mountains, along the Atlantic coast, gargantuan golf and skiing resorts are in development. A huge area south of Marrakech, at the far end of avenue Mohammed VI, has been pegged out as a new hotel zone. Of course, all these things put a further strain on limited water resources. But at least tourists won't mind if there's no rain to disturb their sunbathing, or turn the Medina into a warren of mud.

Landscape near Jorf, after rain. Wells mark the site of an ancient *khettara*. See p33.

Where to Stay

Riyad Edward. *See p53*.

Where to Stay

The riad revolution has given birth to a new kind of hotel.

The piecemeal conversion of the Medina into a vast complex of boutique hotels continues apace. Marrakech probably boasts more boutique hotels per square mile than any other city in the world. Current estimates of the number of riads, as they're now generically known, start at 500 and climb to over 1,000. In some districts, such as the R'mila area in the north-western Medina – more developed than most because of good vehicle access – there already seem to be more guesthouses than houses. And though rocketing property prices mean there are few real bargains left on the market, all the signs are that this trend will continue, if a little more slowly than in the last few booming years. And it all makes a certain sense. If your city is low on conventional sights, then make the accommodation the destination. It's just that Marrakech has taken this further than most places.

'Riad' means garden house, though for 'garden' you can usually read 'courtyard'. The city's riad guesthouses are organised around one or more of these courtyards, reflecting the traditions of Moroccan domestic architecture, which are inward-looking with thick blank walls to protect the inhabitants from heat, cold and the attentions of the outside world. Grander riads involve two or more houses knocked together, but many consist of just half a dozen or so rooms around a single courtyard. Most are privately operated affairs, which generally means excellent personal service and a high degree of individuality.

In all but the cheapest riads, rooms have en suite bathrooms, but air-conditioning, TVs, telephones, hairdryers and other mod cons are often dispensed with in the name of authenticity and getting away from it all. Marrakech can be decidedly chilly during the winter; we have listed riads with central heating, but anyone who is travelling in winter and feels the cold should check before booking. Breakfast is commonly taken on a roof terrace shielded from the sun under tent-like awnings, while lunch and dinner are provided on request. Many riads have excellent cooks, producing food as good as, if not superior to, anything dished up in the city's restaurants.

In deference to local aesthetics, most riads forgo any kind of tell-tale frontage, signboard or even nameplate. Given that they often lie deep within the obscure twists of narrow alleys, this makes them a swine to locate. Guests are generally met at the airport (for which there may or may not be an additional charge in the region of 80dh-150dh), but after that it's just you and your sense of direction. With that in mind, it's always wise to carry your riad's business card to show locals in case you get lost.

Gaining in favour of late is the out-of-town retreat. There are a growing number of villas and new-build compounds on the outskirts of the city – scattered throughout the Palmeraie

The best Hotels

For gorgeous gardens
Dar Zemora (*see p60*). **Les Jardins de la Medina** (*see p41*).

For foodies
Ksar Char-Bagh (*see p60*). **Riyad Al Moussika** (*see p47*).

For getting cool in the pool
Caravanserai (*see p62*). **Les Jardins de la Koutoubia** (*see p41*). **Sultana** (*see p47*). **Tichka Salam** (*see p58*).

For budget travellers
Dar Fakir (*see p49*). **Jnane Mogador** (*see p57*). **Nejma Lounge** (*see p57*). **Riad Magi** (*see p57*).

For soothing minimalism
Riad Mabrouka (*see p51*). **Riad W** (*see p53*).

For brilliant bathrooms
Les Deux Tours (*see p60*). **Riad Enija** (*see p45*). **Riad Farnatchi** (*see p39*).

For organic eats
Jnane Tamsna (*see p60*). **Riad El Fenn** (*see p43*).

For rurally retreating
Tigmi (*see 62*). **Villa Vanille** (*see p61*).

> ❶ Green numbers given in this chapter correspond to the location of each hotel on the street maps. *See pp250-254.*

Riad Enija. *See p45.*

NIKKI BEACH
MARRAKECH

TELL ONLY YOUR BEST FRIENDS

Circuit de la Palmeraie - Marrakech - Tél : +212 (0) 63 51 99 92 / +212 (0) 24 36 87 27

and further afield – that serve as semi-private retreats dedicated to indolence and pampering, with teams of cooks, masseurs, manicurists, maids and assorted flunkies to obviate the need for any exertion on the part of the guest. Marrakech is on hand simply to provide blasts of colour and exoticism between early afternoon waxings and evening cocktails. One way to holiday is to spend a couple of days at a riad in the Medina followed by a couple of days in self-indulgent retreat. Independent tour operators are now pushing this sort of package.

Whichever way you choose to go, we highly recommend pushing the budget. Marrakech is not a place to scrimp on the accommodation – not when your hotel could turn out to be the highlight of the trip.

The chain gang

The heavy hitters of the hotel world are staking their claims on Marrakech. At the time of writing, Four Seasons, Mandarin Oriental and Banyan Tree among others have hotels at various stages of planning and construction in and around the city. For the moment, though, those in search of the comfortable familiarity of the chain experience can choose from the following:

● **Le Meridien N'Fis** (avenue Mohammed VI, Hivernage, 024 44 87 72, www.le meridien.com) offers 278 rooms including 12 suites, two restaurants, a bar, a tearoom, a pool and all the other usual amenities. The hotel is a five-minute taxi ride from the Medina.

● The **Royal Mirage Marrakech** (avenue de la Menara, Hivernage, 024 44 89 98, www.royalmiragehotels.com) was formerly the Sheraton. It has 219 rooms, ten suites and a royal villa, plus five restaurants, a bar, a pool, a putting green and tennis courts. It's also a taxi ride from the Medina.

● We rate the **Sofitel Marrakech** (rue Harroun Errachid, 024 42 56 00, www.sofitel.com) as the city's best chain hotel. It has a lovely garden with a big pool. It's also the closest to the Medina walls and within walking distance of Jemaa El Fna. There are 260 rooms and suites, each with private balcony or terrace (ask for south-facing, overlooking the garden with the mountains in the distance), as well as all the usual facilities.

THE MAMOUNIA
Out of action and in the process of a revamp at the time of writing is the grand old Mamounia, the most famous hotel in Marrakech, if not all of Morocco. For more on its history and future, *see p43* **Fashion victim**.

RATES AND BOOKING
There are significant seasonal variations in room rates, with prices at some hotels rising by up to 25 per cent at peak periods. What constitutes peak period varies by establishment, but generally speaking you'll pay considerably more for a room any time over Christmas/New Year and Easter, plus from late September through to October, when the fierceness of the summer heat has abated and temperatures are near perfect. Rooms are scarce at peak times and booking well in advance is a must.

When it comes to making a reservation, even though most hotels boast websites, bear in mind that Moroccan servers are prone to meltdown. Book through the website by all means, but be sure to follow up with a phone call.

A new internet booking service, www.so-maroc.com, is a particularly useful resource to check on last-minute room availability, and to make online bookings.

We've divided this chapter by area, then price: deluxe from 3,200dh (currently around £200/$400); expensive 1,950dh-3,200dh (£120-£200/$240-$400); moderate 970dh-1,950dh (£60-£120/$120-$240); and budget up to 970dh (£60/$120). Breakfast is usually included. Payment is typically cash only, and made in local currency. Even places that purport to take credit cards usually prefer cash – you might too, given that a five per cent surcharge may be added on top to cover the transaction costs.

Medina

Aka the Old City. A room here puts you right in among the souks and sights, and the nearer to Jemaa El Fna the better. Remember that much of the Medina is inaccessible by car, so accommodation close to a taxi-friendly main street is always preferable.

Deluxe

Riad Farnatchi
2 Derb Farnatchi, Kat Benahid (024 38 49 10/fax 024 38 49 13/www.riadfarnatchi.com). **Rates** *Jan, June-July* 3,100dh-4,100dh suite. *Feb-May, Sept-Dec* (excl Christmas) 3,400dh-4,750dh suite. **Credit** AmEx, MC, V. **Map** p251 D4 ❶
Farnatchi is the creation of Jonathan Wix (42 The Calls in Leeds, the Scotsman in Edinburgh and Hotel de la Tremoille in Paris). Originally intended as his

private residence, it's now an intimate, top-class hotel. Five suites are arrayed off two small court-yards, one of which has a modestly sized heated pool. The suites are vast and supremely luxurious, with large sunken baths, shower rooms, under-floor heating, desks and armchairs and private balconies. The design throughout is a striking update of the local aesthetic, with stark black and white as a neutral backdrop to intricate woodworked screens and finely carved stucco. All the furniture has been specially designed and manufactured in Marrakech, except for bathroom fittings by Philippe Starck. The hotel is superbly run (Canadian manager Lynn Perez is a walking directory of Marrakech) and right in the middle of the Medina, just north of the Ben Youssef Medersa; taxis can get to within 200m. Rates include complimentary hotel transfers. The hotel is closed annually during August. **Photo** *p44*.
Air-conditioning. Cook. Hammam. Heating. Internet (Wi-Fi). Plunge pool (outdoor). TV: DVD, satellite.

Villa des Orangers

6 rue Sidi Mimoun, place Ben Tachfine (024 38 46 38/fax 024 38 51 23/www.villadesorangers.com). **Rates** 2,900dh-3,800dh double; 4,000dh-6,800dh suite. **Credit** AmEx, MC, V. **Map** p252 B7 ❷
Built in the 1930s as the residence of a judge, the Villa des Orangers was acquired by a French husband-and-wife team with a successful hotel business in Paris. After gaining an additional storey, it opened to paying guests in December 1999. The style is Moorish palatial, and it has 19 rooms and suites arranged around three beautiful courtyards – one filled with the eponymous orange trees, the others lavishly decorated with lacy carved plasterwork. Six suites have private upstairs sun terraces, although all rooms have access to the roof with matchless views of the nearby Koutoubia minaret – doubly enchanting when the storks come wheeling round at dusk. The service is outstanding, and airport transfers are included in the price.
Air-conditioning. Bar. Hammam. Heating. Internet (Wi-Fi). Pool (2 outdoor). Restaurant. TV: satellite.

Expensive

Dar Karma

51 Derb el Mennabha, Kasbah (024 38 58 78/fax 024 37 58 78/www.dar-karma.com). **Rates** 1,700dh-2,240dh double; 2,520dh-3,130dh suite. **Credit** MC, V. **Map** p252 C9 ❸
For much of its century-long existence, this big old house near the Royal Palace was the home of Mohammed V's French translator. An elegant *maison d'hôte* since 2003, it still retains something of a homely air, despite now being kitted out with such mod cons as a small swimming pool and a water-mist cooling system to alleviate searing summer temperatures on the roof terrace. The five bedrooms are smart but unfussy, with fine bedlinen from Via Notti (*see p135*) and spacious bathrooms finished with marble and *tadelakt*. Communal salons are

comfortable, the hammam is very grand indeed, and the card supplied to guests bearing a map with the hotel's location and instructions for what to tell taxi drivers is an innovation other establishments would do well to imitate.
Air-conditioning. Cook. Hammam. Heating. Internet (Wi-Fi). Pool. TV.

Jardins de la Koutoubia

16 rue de la Koutoubia (024 38 88 00/fax 024 44 22 22/hoteljardinkoutoubia@menara.ma). **Rates** 1,950dh-2,600dh single; 2200dh-2,800dh double; 3,500dh mini-suite; 4,500dh-5,000dh junior suite. **Credit** AmEx, MC, V. **Map** p250/252 B5 ❹
If you want to be in the Medina but prefer the relative impersonality of a hotel over the intimacy of a *maison d'hôte*, then this comfortable, well-run establishment is the place. It's brilliantly located, two minutes from the Jemaa El Fna in one direction, two minutes from the Koutoubia mosque and a steady stream of taxis in the other. The courtyard pool is heated, they can shake a proper cocktail in the Piano Bar (*see p117*), the patio restaurant (*see p103*) is a fine spot for lunch, and everything is nicely spacious. The faux traditional design may be nothing for the style supplements, but it isn't too shabby and both beds and bathrooms are big and welcoming. A huge new extension has brought the total number of rooms up to around 100 and added another garden, a couple more swimming pools and a subterranean fitness centre.
Air-conditioning. Bar. Hammam. Heating. Restaurants (3). Pool (outdoor). TV: satellite.

Les Jardins de la Medina

21 Derb Chtouka, Kasbah (024 38 18 51/fax 024 38 53 85/www.lesjardinsdelamedina.com). **Rates** 1,700dh-3,300dh double. **Credit** AmEx, MC, V. **Map** p252 C9 ❺
At the southern end of the kasbah, this former royal residence has been a luxurious 36-room hotel since 2001. You enter a beautiful reception area eccentrically decorated with a tree and wooden birds hanging upside down from a painted dome. From there, you emerge into a seriously big garden with rows of orange trees and a heated swimming pool actually large enough to swim in – which makes it a great place for families. Comfortable rooms, decorated in a sort of Moroccan-international style, come in three categories but most are in the middle 'superior' class – big enough to have sofas as well as beds, and all of them with DVD players and iPod docks. A big international restaurant, a splendid hammam, a decently equipped gym and a beauty salon round off the range of services. They also run a cookery school.
Air-conditioning. Gym. Hammam. Heating. Internet. Pool (outdoor). Parking. Restaurant.

Maison Arabe

1 Derb Assehbe, Bab Doukkala (024 38 70 10/fax 024 38 72 21/www.lamaisonarabe.com). **Rates** *July & Aug* 1,500dh-2,000dh double; 2,500dh-4,800dh suite. *Sept-June* 1,900dh-2,500dh double; 3,000dh-6,000dh suite. **Credit** MC, V. **Map** p250 A4 ❻

*Marrakech : the Villa Dar Zina,
one of the most beautiful villas riad of Morocco
opens the doors of paradise for you ...*

Marrakech – The Villa Dar Zina, one of the most beautiful Villa-Riad of Morocco opens the doors of paradise for you.

Two formulas are available :

1) **Renting of the Villa in a "hotel formula"** (4 suites + 4 bedrooms + 8 bathrooms)

2) **Renting of the entire Villa in exclusivity** (the 4 suites and 4 bedrooms).

In the two formulas the Villa offers twenty competent and discreet employees : butler, masseuse, masseur, driver, chief cook (morrocan and international gastronomy). The **Villa Dar Zina of Marrakech** is an unique place for unique guests. Unique position offering luxurious amenities, refined decoration. Exceptional place.

Villa Dar Zina
Marrakech

Tel. + 212 24 34 66 45   Fax + 212 24 49 56 55
Mob + 212 64 16 69 10   Email info@villadarzina.com
Visits on internet : www.villadarzina.com

Maison Arabe began life in the 1940s as a restaurant run by two raffish French ladies. It rapidly gained fame through its popularity with illustrious patrons such as Winston Churchill. The last tagines were served in 1983, and the place lay dormant for over a decade before reopening under Italian ownership in January 1998 as the city's first *maison d'hôte*. Today, there are nine rooms and eight suites set around two leafy, flower-filled courtyards.

Inside, the prevailing style is Moroccan classic with French colonial overtones – lots of Orientalist paintings and antiques, high-backed armchairs and an elegant cedarwood library. The rooms and suites are supremely comfortable, most with their own private terraces and a couple with fireplaces. Our favourite is Sabah (the rooms have names), which is ingeniously fitted around the curve of a dome. The hotel pool may be a 20-minute drive away on the outskirts of town (serviced by hourly shuttles), but it's set in a lovely garden planted with olive and fig trees; in their shade, lunch is served at Le Figuier snack bar. Back at the hotel, the smart restaurant (*see p98*) is excellent, there's a fine bar, Le Club (*see p117*), and guests can also sign up for Moroccan cookery workshops.
Air-conditioning. Bar. Hammam. Heating. Internet. Pool (outdoor). Restaurant. TV: satellite.

Palais Calipau

14 Derb Ben Zina, Kasbah (024 37 55 83/ www.palais-calipau.com). **Rates** 2,460dh-6,160dh suite. **Credit** MC, V. **Map** p252 C8 ❼

A bright and stylish conversion of three houses, Palais Calipau opened in March 2006. It's French-owned, although the majority of guests are from the UK and USA. There are 12 suites – four on the ground floor and eight upstairs – though some are more suite-like than others. We liked the cedar ceiling and cosy fireplace area of 'Zagora', the stained-glass in 'Tanger' and the green-tiled bathroom in 'Marrakech', but all of the rooms are colourful, comfortable and well-furnished, with high-definition TVs complementing traditional touches. There are also two heated pools, a hammam in elegant grey *tadelakt*, a bar and restaurant, and a huge roof terrace for eating or sun-lounging. A great set of services, but somehow it could use a little personality.
Air-conditioning. Bar. Hammam. Heating. Internet (Wi-Fi). Pool. Restaurant. TV: satellite.

Riad El Fenn

2 Derb Moulay Abdallah Ben Hezzian, Bab El Ksour, Medina (024 44 12 10/www.riadelfenn.com). **Rates** 3,580dh-4,360dh double; 5,500dh douiria. **Credit** AmEx, MC, V. **Map** p250/252 B5 ❽

Fashion victim

The grande dame of Marrakech hotels has closed her doors for a makeover. So when will she be ready for her close-up?

One side-effect of the riad explosion has been to make the **Mamounia** (avenue Bab Jedid, www.mamounia.com), Morocco's most famous hotel, look distinctly old-fashioned. The textbook 'destination hotel' was opened in 1923 to coincide with the arrival of the French-built North African railway network. In the inter-war years, it became more or less synonymous with a trip to Marrakech, and an exclusive clientele of writers, artists, colonial rulers and well-to-do adventurers would sip scotch in the piano bar or stroll around its well-watered gardens. Winston Churchill was a regular, executing a number of watercolours on the balcony of his favourite suite. In room 414, Doris Day sang 'Que Sera, Sera' in Hitchcock's *The Man Who Knew Too Much*. For the rich and famous, it carried on being simply the only place to stay well into the late 20th century – until all the new boutique hotels started making it feel its age.

A kitsch 1986 makeover didn't help, adding a conference centre but eradicating the cool elegance of the past. Nor did a 2001 overhaul of the rooms, with a clutch of tawdry themes (Orient Express, 1930s, Nuptial), usher it back into fashion. And so in July 2006, it closed again for major renovations.

In spring 2007 it was still shut, the main building a gutted shell. No one at the Leading Hotels of the World group would admit to knowing anything about how it will look on reopening, but a major makeover is clearly under way. The choice of Parisian designer Jacques Garcia, the man with the motto 'luxury is knowledge', whose most recent project was the Hotel Fouquet's Barrière on the Champs Elysées, suggests the result will be an opulently classicist reassertion of the Mamounia as grand, historic hotel. Whether they keep the Piano Bar and Churchill Suite remains to be seen, but we hope the Trois Palmiers poolside lunchtime buffet manages to survive.

An original completion date of 'summer 2007' has been put back to an even vaguer 'sometime in winter 2007-08'. We suspect it could be even later than that.

Moorish, modish **Riad Farnatchi**. *See p39*.

This riad has received plenty of media attention, partly because it's co-owned by Vanessa Branson (sister of Richard) and partly because it is such a fine place. Two historic houses have been joined to create nine spacious, sorbet-coloured bedrooms. Clutter-free, each room is dominated by an Egyptian cotton-swathed imperial-sized bed. There's also a split-level suite (the Douiria) that is arguably the most striking room for rent in the whole of Marrakech. At press time the owners were just completing the conversion of a third house, adding six new rooms – including a huge garden suite with a sunken bath in the bedroom and a steam room in the bathroom. Another new suite has a private pool on the terrace above, accessed by a spiral staircase. Despite the grandeur of the architecture and some serious modern art on the walls, the mood is relaxed, with plenty of private spaces and two obligatory rooftop terraces. A garden in the foothills of the Atlas provides organic produce for the kitchen. Top-rank facilities include two pools, a DVD screening-room, an excellent library and – not finished at the time of writing – a 120-seater restaurant that can double as a theatre. But arguably the greatest assets are managers Frederic and Viviana, who ably live up to the riad's name: 'fenn' being local slang for 'cool'.
Air-conditioning. Cook. Hammam. Heating. Pool (2 outdoor).

Riad Enija

9 Derb Mesfioui, off rue Rahba Lakdima (024 44 09 26/fax 024 44 27 00/www.riadenija.com). **Rates** 2,300dh-3,500dh double. **No credit cards.** **Map** p251/253 D5 ❾
Anyone lacking the pose and hauteur of a Karl Lagerfeld model risks being made to look shabby by comparison with the drop-dead gorgeousness of their surrounds at Riad Enija. Its 12 rooms and suites variously boast glorious old wooden ceilings, beds as works of art (wrought-iron gothic in one, a green muslin-wrapped four-poster in another), some striking furniture (much of it designed by artist friends of Swedish/Swiss owners Björn Conerding and Ursula Haldimann) and grand bathrooms resembling subterranean throne chambers. Central to the three adjoined houses (which originally belonged to a silk trader from Fes and 64 members of his family) is a Moorish courtyard garden gone wild, where maroon-uniformed staff flicker through the greenery. Distractions such as televisions and telephones are dispensed with (although there is a sweet little 'internet salon'), but alternative services include anything from a visiting aromatherapist and masseurs to cookery classes and heli-skiing excursions (in season). The service and food are both excellent, and the riad is just a few minutes' walk from Jemaa El Fna. The only downsides to this place are the lack of a swimming pool and the fact that taxis can't get you anywhere very near. Then there's the nuisance of having the latest fashion shoot going on outside your window – we warned you this place was a looker. **Photo** *p37.*
Cook. Internet. Plunge pool (outdoor).

Riad Kniza

34 Derb l'Hôtel, Bab Doukkala (024 37 69 42/ www.riadkniza.com). **Rates** 2,230dh-3,920dh. **Credit** AmEx, MC, V. **Map** p250 A3 ❿
This grand and well-located 18th-century house has belonged to the family of current owner Mohammed Bouskri for two centuries, but only opened as a *maison d'hôte* in 2004. It's the most Moroccan of upmarket riads, decorated entirely in a conservative and traditional style. There are four suites and three rooms, and even the smallest is pretty spacious. The suites all have separate sitting rooms and there are working fireplaces throughout. The Bouskri family are antique dealers, which means a lot of old pieces in alcoves and cabinets. Mohammed Bouskri has also been a professional guide for over 30 years, so it's a useful place for anyone who wants to 'do' Marrakech in an old-school kind of way. They offer a free half-day tour for anyone staying for three nights. It deserves its reputation as a well-run establishment – the only downside is a slightly staid atmosphere. An extension containing a hammam, a pool and four more suites should be completed by autumn 2007. No children under 12. **Photo** *p47.*
Air-conditioning. Heating. Internet (Wi-Fi). TV: satellite.

Riad Lotus Ambre

22 Fhal Zefriti, Bab Laksour (024 44 14 05/fax 024 44 14 07/www.riadslotus.com). **Rates** *Jan, June-Aug* 1,550dh-2,200dh double; 2,700dh suite. *Feb-May, Sept-Dec* 1,850dh-2,550dh double; 3,000dh suite. **Credit** MC, V. **Map** p250/252 B5 ⑪
In contrast to most riads, where the gone-native aesthetic means you're lucky to get a table lamp in your bedroom, let alone a TV, the Lotus lays on the extras big time. The four doubles and one suite all come with logo'd bed linen, towels and toiletries, high-speed internet access and a Bang & Olufsen plasma screen, sound system and DVD player. Not to mention the huge Warhol-copy Pop Art pieces (Jackie O, Marilyn, Goëthe and Mao) that dominate each room. All the lighting is touch-sensitive B&O, the crystalware comes from Italy and there's a jacuzzi on the roof. If bling's your thing, then here's your Marrakech home from home. Rooms, however, vary greatly in size (Marilyn, in particular, is a bit mean). Owner Reda Ben Jelloun, Marrakech-born but previously a travel agent working in Florence, says his aim is to offer five-star service in intimate, stylish surroundings. In 2005 he opened the Lotus Perle, on similar lines (neo-classical columns, black and white marble floors, gadgetry and a retro American theme reflected in room names like Kennedy, Gatsby and Coco Chanel). He's now also opened the even more upmarket Lotus Privilege near the Dar El-Bacha, with a similar array of gadgets, five suites around an enormous courtyard where mirrored obelisks flank a huge plunge pool, and rather too much black marble throughout. See the website for details of the Perle and Privilege.
Air-conditioning. Cook. Hammam. Heating. Internet portal. TV: DVD, satellite.

Le Tanjia

Restaurant Bar
Marrakech

The unique Chill out spot
beetwen two of the most
beautiful monuments Bahia
and Badii Palaces.
Belly Dancers Show.

Moroccan and Internationale cuisine

Restaurant Bar from 11:00 am to 1:30 am www.le-tanjia.com

14, Derb J'did (Mellah) Médina Marrakech Tel : +212 63 51 99 92 +212 24 38 38 36 letanjia@yahoo.fr

Riad Kniza. *See p45.*

Riyad Al Moussika

*62 Derb Boutouil, Kennaria (024 38 90 67/
fax 024 37 76 53/www.riyad-al-moussika.ma).*
Rates 2,200dh-2,860dh double; 3,850dh suite.
Credit AmEx, MC, V. **Map** p253 D6
One reason laid-back Turinese owner Giovanni
Robazza opened this former pasha's palace as a
guesthouse was to showcase the Cordon Bleu cooking of his son Khalid. This is a riad for gourmands,
dedicated, as their publicity puts it, 'to the art of good
living', with a touch of pretension but a comfortable,
worn-in feel. Both a big breakfast and two-course
lunch are included in the rates, and it's not a place
to lose weight. The palace has been restored in a relatively traditional style: fountains splash and birds
sing in trees, while six bedrooms are complemented
by a hammam, a formal dining-room, a music room
with piano and a small library with some interesting volumes. There are three courtyards, one with a
long, thin, 'Andalucian' pool for swimming, along
with two flower-filled roof terraces for sunbathing,
breakfasting or dining. Minimum stay of three nights.
*Air-conditioning. Hammam. Heating. Pool
(outdoor) Restaurant.*

Riad Noir d'Ivoire

*31 Derb Jdid, Bab Doukkala (024 38 09 75/fax 024
38 16 53/www.noir-d-ivoire.com).* **Rates** 1,980dh-
3,520dh. **Credit** MC, V. **Map** p250 A3
Opened in December 2006, Riad Noir d'Ivoire has that
gratifying combination of looking spectacular while
feeling exceedingly comfortable. Interior designer

and co-owner Jill Fechtmann has mixed specially
commissioned Moroccan elements with assorted
curiosities from sub-Saharan Africa (inspired by
years in Swaziland), Europe (years more in Paris and
the Dordogne) and India. Some of the more idiosyncratic details are the work of her husband, Jean-
Michel Jobit. Three suites and one double room have
huge beds imported from the USA, sheets of
Egyptian cotton, big bathrooms and pleasingly
eccentric furnishings that vaguely reflect an animal
theme. Our favourite is the 'Chameau' suite, with its
open fire, golden masks in alcoves, treacherously
comfortable armchairs and sculpted wooden camel,
as big as a mule. Off the chandeliered courtyard with
plunge pool and baby grand there's a hammam in
Tiznit marble, plus a lounge/library, small boutique,
dining area and cosy bar. The vibe is essentially
sociable – Jill is an able and amiable hostess who
gets everyone talking – but that may make it the
wrong place if you vant to be a-lone. There's also
nowhere save the roof terrace to escape the Sting
tunes and jazz standards played by the tempera-
mental Georgian pianist some evenings. But these
are quibbles. This is a great place. **Photo** *p48.*
*Air-conditioning. Cook. Hammam. Heating.
Plunge pool (outdoor).*

Sultana

*Rue de la Kasbah, Kasbah (024 38 80 08/
fax 024 38 77 77/lasultanamarrakech.com).*
Rates 2,560dh-3, 815dh double; 4,630dh-7,085dh
suite. **Credit** MC, V. **Map** p252 B8

Opened in 2004, the Sultana is astonishing in that it's a completely new-build hotel of considerable size and scale slapped down in the middle of the Medina. And you'd never know it was there. It has no frontage to speak of, but beyond the arched street door are 11 guestrooms and ten suites, connected by seemingly acres of arcaded corridors, courtyards, landings and galleries and serviced by 62 staff. There's a good-sized swimming pool, a full spa complex (*see p165*), a row of boutiques and a vast roof terrace that overlooks the gardens of the Saadian Tombs. The hotel boasts all the facilities and amenities of a five-star but is packaged to look like a *maison d'hôte*. The architecture (Moorish-gothic) and decoration is sumptuous going on camp (check out the life-size bronze camel beside the pool), piling Indian, African and Oriental on the Moroccan. Serving French and Moroccan cuisine, the restaurant is open to non-guests who reserve in advance, but the basement bar is residents only. Kitted out to resemble a ship's cabin, the bar even has a window into the deep end of the swimming pool.

Air-conditioning. Bar. Fitness room. Hammam. Heating. Internet portals. Pool (outdoor). Restaurant. Spa. TV: satellite, DVD.

Talaa 12

12 Talaa Ben Youssef, El Moqf (024 42 90 45/ fax 024 44 26 07/www.talaa12.com). **Rates** 1,500dh-3,000dh double. **Credit** AmEx, MC, V. **Map** p251 D4 ⓮

A serene, minimalist-style riad in the north-east of the Medina, Talaa 12 is owned by Belgian interior designer Marianne Lacroix. Three years of painstaking renovation have paid off well. Walls are white and shutters are grey, with judicious bolts of colour provided by rugs, furnishings and hangings. The courtyard is planted with lemon trees, and Arabic chill-out and gnawa-style music plays on the CD player. There are eight comfortable bedrooms, with limestone *tadelakt* bathrooms. Location is another plus factor: Talaa 12 is in the El-Moqf section of the Medina, close to Foundouk restaurant (*see p103*) and the Musée de Marrakech, and just a ten-minute walk from Jemaa El Fna. The roof terrace has a 360-degree view of the rooftops of Marrakech and the peaks of the Atlas mountains.

Air-conditioning. Cook. Hammam. Internet (Wi-Fi).

Moderate

Casa Lalla

16 Derb Jamaa, off Riad Zitoun El Kedim (024 42 97 57/fax 024 42 97 59/www.casa lalla.com). **Rates** 972dh-1,240dh double. **Credit** MC, V. **Map** p252 C6 ⓰

Lalla is a beautiful little guesthouse, with eight rooms ranged on two floors around a grand central courtyard. It's elegant yet homely, with lots of attractive *tadelakt* surfaces in prevailing tones of off-white, mushroom and chocolate. Two of the rooms have

The opulent, eclectic **Riad Noir d'Ivoire**. *See p47.*

fireplaces, some of the bathrooms are wonderful and a couple of the suites have their own mezzanine areas. A lounge area off the courtyard has a fireplace, a small library and a couple of tables set up for chess; for more rest and relaxation, there's a plunge pool which you can set fizzing with bubbles and a nice green-tiled hammam. If you've heard of this place before, however, its probably because of its former connection with Michelin-starred British chef Richard Neat. He's now departed for Costa Rica, but word has it that French owner Pierre Olivier is no slouch in the kitchen either.

Air-conditioning. Hammam. Heating (fireplaces). Plunge pool (outdoor). Restaurant.

Dar Atta

28 rue Jebel Lakhdar, Bab Laksour (024 38 62 32/ fax 024 38 62 41/www.daratta.com). **Rates** 650dh-750dh double; 1,250dh suite. **No credit cards.** **Map** p250 B4 ⑰

At first sight it seems an unpromising location – a not very picturesque part of the Medina, opposite the gaudy Alanbar. But you can get a taxi right to the door, or walk to the Jemaa El Fna or Koutoubia in ten minutes, and once you're inside, this Italian-owned *maison d'hôte* reveals itself to be a very pleasant place indeed. Seven stylish double rooms and three spacious suites are ranged around a sunken patio and two terraces. We liked the big and faintly ramshackle-looking wooden partitions that separate the comfortable double beds from the wardrobe areas, and the generally unobtrusive design – it's cool, without being in your face. Staff are equally discreet, drifting around in black uniforms. There's also a charming small hammam and massage area and a restaurant that serves Moroccan and Italian dishes. When it's time to leave, you're on the right side of town for a quick dash to the airport.

Air-conditioning. Hammam. Heating (fireplaces). Restaurant.

Dar Attajmil

23 rue Laksour, off rue Sidi El Yamami (024 42 69 66/www.darattajmil.com). **Rates** 800dh-1,200dh double. **Credit** MC, V. **Map** p250/252 B5 ⑱

With just four bedrooms, Dar Attajmil is nothing if not cosy. It's run by the lovely (English-speaking) Italian Lucrezia Mutti and her small body of staff, which includes two slothful black cats. There's a tiny courtyard filled to bursting with banana trees and coconut palms that throw welcome shade on to a small recessed lounge and a library. Bedrooms overlook the courtyard from the first floor, and are beautifully decorated in warm, rusty tones with dark-wood ceilings and lovely *tadelakt* bathrooms. Best of all, though, is the astonishingly peaceful roof terrace, scattered with cushions, wicker chairs and sofas – guaranteed to get you in the holiday spirit. Dinner (trad Moroccan with Italian leanings) is available on request for 150dh per person. It's an easy six-minute walk from the house to the Jemaa El Fna, Mouassine and the main souks.

Cook. Hammam.

Dar Doukkala

83 Arset Aouzal, off rue Bab Doukkala (024 38 34 44/fax 024 38 34 45/www.dardoukkala.com). **Rates** 1,600dh-1,800dh double; 2,100dh-2,400dh suite. **Credit** MC, V. **Map** p250 B4 ⑲

A bizarre mix of English country mansion and Moroccan townhouse, Dar Doukkala is like the home of some demented Victorian explorer-inventor with an obsession for the Orient. Its four bedrooms and two suites are filled with gorgeous period details and furnishings, including claw-foot tubs and pedestal basins in the bathrooms. Other wonderfully eccentric touches include Guimard-like glass canopies projecting into the central garden courtyard, and an artful array of lanterns patterning the wall behind the terrace-level pool. It's one of the most fun and delightful *maisons d'hôtes* in town. Both suites have two extra beds each for kids, while one of the doubles also comes with an extra bed. The location is good too, opposite the wonderland warehouse of Mustapha Blaoui (*see p130*) and close to the taxis ranked outside the Dar Marjana restaurant.

Air-conditioning. Cook. Hammam. Heating. Pool (outdoor). TV: satellite.

Dar Fakir

16 Derb Abou El Fadal, off Riad Zitoun El Jedid (024 44 11 00/fax 024 44 90 42/darfakir@ yahoo.fr). **Rates** 1,000dh-1,300dh double. **Credit** MC, V. **Map** p252 C6 ⑲ⓐ

The riad for the clubbing generation. Dar Fakir's central courtyard and surrounding salons are layered with casually strewn rugs and scattered with glittery throw cushions. The heady scent of incense hangs heavy in the air and tea candles serve for illumination. There's a bar counter, and every corner and recess is filled with exotic plunderings from South-east Asia and the Levant. A chilled soundtrack adds to the Buddha Bar vibe. Of the eight guestrooms, two are on the ground floor and six are upstairs; they're very simply done but attractive, including *tadelakt* bathrooms. Owner Noureddine Fakir, an ambitious young Casablancan, also runs the Le Tanjia (*see p100*) and Marrakchi (*see p99*) restaurants. The latter is nearby and residents can order from its menu and have the food delivered within around 20 minutes.

Bar.

Riad Alma

77 Derb Kbala, Kasbah (024 37 71 62/www.riad alma.com). **Rates** 1,100dh-2,200dh double. **Credit** AmEx, MC, V (4% surcharge). **Map** p252 B9 ⑳

Created out of two adjoining houses in the Kasbah, Riad Alma has adopted a design ethos mixing Moroccan features – judicious use of *tadelakt*, rugs, artefacts and so on – with pieces from India and the East. The style is restrained, though: comfortable but considered, with no random mixing. Colour is used to dramatic effect against an overall white paint job. One of the seven rooms has a pink theme, with fuchsia Indian fabrics; in another, dark grey *tadelakt* makes for a dramatic bathroom; in a third

Jnane Tamsna

Country Guesthouse

24 bedrooms spread over 5 villas
on 9 acres in the Palmgrove
Tel: 212 24 329423   Fax: 212 24 329884
Email: meryanne@jnanetamsna.com
www.jnanetamsna.com
www.diversity-excursions.co.uk

the *tadelakt* is chocolate brown. A comfortable suite features a fireplace and a bath, and some rooms have CD players. In the second courtyard is a plunge pool, and there's a hammam on the premises. The roof terrace is extensive, with great views.
Air-conditioning. Cook. Hammam. Heating.

Riad Azzar

94 Derb Moulay Abdelkader, off Derb Debbachi (061 15 81 73/fax 024 38 90 91/www.riad azzar.com). **Rates** 1,200dh-1,600dh double; 2,500dh suite. **No credit cards. Map** p251/p253 D5 ㉑
Owned by a friendly, English-speaking Dutch couple, Azzar is a neat little six-room riad with the feel of a B&B. It's distinguished by a small, emerald green, heated plunge pool in the middle of the courtyard – nice enough, but if the riad is full it could be a bit like bathing in the main lobby. Walls are whitewashed and the decor is understated: it's a very tasteful place. Three of the rooms are suites and come with fireplaces and air-conditioning (as does one of the doubles); of these, the Taznarth suite also boasts a beautiful *mashrabiya* (wooden lattice) window overlooking the courtyard and a particularly lovely grey *tadelakt* bathroom. The owners admit with admirable honesty that the hammam is of a size suitable only for petite French ladies. Also admirable is Riad Azzar's support of a local orphanage; guests are encouraged to contribute by bringing children's toys and clothing or school materials for donation.
Air-conditioning (4 rooms). Cook. Hammam. Heating (4 rooms). Plunge pool (outdoor).

Riad Hayati

27 Derb Bouderba, off Derb El Bahia, Riad Zitoun El-Jedid (UK 07770 431 194/www.riad hayati.com). **Rates** 2,000dh double. **Credit** V. **Map** p253 D7 ㉒
Could this be the most tasteful riad in town? It's a little piece of visual perfection, with three all-white bedrooms set around the galleried first floor of a white courtyard; intricately carved dark wooden doors complement the snowy expanses. If needed, the ground-floor study can serve as a fourth bedroom, with its own en suite bathroom. Complementing the classic Moorish architecture are subtle references to Ottoman Turkey, Persia and Arabia (a mirror modelled on one seen in Istanbul's Dolmabahçe Palace, a fountain from Damascus), mementos of the British owner's many years in news broadcasting from the Middle East (*hayati* means 'my life'). The location is extremely peaceful but only six or seven minutes' walk from the Jemaa El Fna. Evening aperitifs are included, ideally taken on the roof terrace with its lovely Atlas views. A separate garden suite was due to open as we went to press, with its own terrace, courtyard garden, fountain and plunge pool.
Cook. Heating (fireplace).

Riad Ifoulki

11 Derb Moqqadem, Arset Loghzail (tel/fax 024 38 56 56/www.riadifoulki.com). **Rates** 1,000dh single; 1,500dh double; 3,000dh suite. **Credit** MC, V. **Map** p253 D6 ㉓

This may well be the only riad in Marrakech at which Latin is spoken; Latin and nine other languages, in fact – including Danish, which is the nationality of owner Peter Berg. The property is a former palace (or at least, four-fifths of one), with a total of 14 rooms arranged on several levels around numerous whitewashed courtyards, large and small. For all its imperial origins and size, this is one of the least showy and 'designed' of riads; the rooms are simple and unpretentious, with big beds swathed in translucent shimmery fabrics. Parts of the residence are self-contained with their own doors, making them ideal for families, and have gates at the top of stairs for child safety. There's a small library with volumes on Morocco in various languages, some of which are signed by their authors with gratitude to the erudite Berg. More energetic guests can take lessons in the arts of *tadelakt* (plastering), *zelije* (tiling) and calligraphy, and are welcome to accompany the kitchen staff on shopping expeditions and help with cooking. Airport transfers are free.
Cook. Fitness room. Hammam. Plunge pool (outdoor). TV.

Riad Kaiss

65 Derb Jedid, off Riad Zitoun El Kedim (tel/fax 024 44 01 41/www.riadkaiss.com). **Rates** 1,770dh-2,425dh double. **Credit** MC, V. **Map** p252 C7 ㉔
Renovated, owned and managed by architect Christian Ferré, who lives on the premises, the eight-room Kaiss is small but exquisite. Its Rubik's Cube layout has rooms linked by galleries, multi-level terraces and tightly twisting stairs, all around a central court filled with orange, lemon and pomegranate trees. The decor is traditional Moroccan: earthy ochre walls with chalky Majorelle-blue trim, stencilled paintwork (including some gorgeous ceilings), jade *zelije* tiling and frilly furniture (including four-poster beds). Guests are greeted by red rose petals sprinkled on their white linen pillows. It's the Merchant Ivory of riads. Modern tastes dictate a cool plunge pool on the roof and a well-equipped fitness room – it's worth a workout for the ache-relieving pleasures of the visit to the in-house hammam that comes afterwards.
Cook. Fitness room. Hammam. Plunge pool (outdoor).

Riad Mabrouka

56 Derb El Bahia, off Riad Zitoun El Jedid (tel/fax 024 37 75 79/www.riad-mabrouka.com). **Rates** 1,540dh double; 1,980dh suite. **Credit** MC, V. **Map** p253 D6 ㉕
The Mabrouka is a vision of cool, understated elegance. Architect Christophe Siméon has gone for a Moroccan minimalist look, with whitewashed walls, billowing canvas in place of doors and some fabulous painted ceilings and shutters; kilims add selective splashes of colour. The result is stylish, but also very comfortable. Bathrooms are seductively sensuous; all soft corners and rounded edges, they look as if they've been moulded out of coloured clay. With just two suites, three doubles and a lone single room, it has a very intimate feel. There's a

pleasant cactus-potted roof terrace with a canvas-shaded breakfast area, and a good kitchen turning out Moroccan, Mediterranean, French and Italian cuisine. *Beauty treatments. Boutique. Cook. Pool (outdoor).*

Riad Noga

78 Derb Jedid, Douar Graoua (024 38 52 46/ fax 024 38 90 46/www.riadnoga.com). **Rates** 1,451dh-2,121dh double. **Credit** MC, V. **Map** p253 D5 ㉖
One of the most homely of Marrakech's riads. Behind salmon-pink walls lies a bougainvillaea and orange tree-filled courtyard (complete with chatty grey parrot), serving as an antechamber to an inner, more private court centred on a shimmering, green-tiled, solar-heated swimming pool. Noga is very spacious (it's made up of three old houses knocked into one), and shared by just seven bedchambers. All of the rooms are bright, bold and cheery, displaying the hospitable touch (small libraries of holiday-lite literature, for instance) of the garrulous German owner, Gaby Noack-Späth. Expansive roof terraces filled with terracotta pots and lemon trees offer terrific views over the Medina and make for the perfect spot to enjoy aperitifs or fine cooking from the excellent in-house Moroccan chefs. The riad is closed during August.
Air-conditioning. Cook. Heating. Internet. Pool (outdoor). TV: satellite.

Riad 72

72 Derb Arset Aouzal, off rue Bab Doukkala (024 38 76 29/fax 024 38 47 18/www.riad72.com). **Rates** *June-Aug* 1,100dh-1,550dh double; 2,200dh suite. *Sept-28 Feb (excl Christmas & New Year)* 1,250dh-1,750dh double; 2,750dh suite. *21 dec-6 Jan, Mar-May* 1,440dh-1,920dh double; 3,000dh suite. **Credit** AmEx, MC, V. **Map** p250 B4 ㉗
Italian owned, this is one sleek and good-looking place – Marrakech has it away with Milan. The result is a trad townhouse given a black, white and grey *tadelakt* makeover. The structure, space and detailing are Moroccan, the furniture and fittings imported. There are just four guest bedrooms, all up on the first floor and arrayed around the central courtyard. Rooms include a master suite that's laugh-out-loud large; five metres or more in height and crowned by an ornate octagonal fanlight.
  The roof terrace boasts one of the best views in town, with the green-tiled roofs of the Dar El-Bacha in the foreground and a cinemascopic jagged mountain horizon beyond. Being that much higher than the neighbours means sunbathing is no problem (many riads are overlooked and modesty can be an issue). The Milanese owner and designer, Giovanna Cinel, has now also opened two other riads in the area, each with four more rooms and a similar aesthetic. The cosy Riad 12, off nearby rue Dar El-Bacha, includes a single room – a real rarity in Marrakech. Riad 2, just beyond the souks' northern tip, is more grand and spacious, with an enormous suite sporting a big copper bathtub in the huge main room. Both also have higher-than-usual roof terraces

(Riad 12's is the better one) and all three houses have the same menu and portfolio of services. Riad 72, with its superior vehicle access, remains this small chain's main rendezvous point.
Air-conditioning. Cook. Hammam. Heating. Plunge pool (outdoor).

Riad Tizwa

26 Derb Gueraba, Dar El-Bacha (068 19 08 72/ UK +44 7973 238 444/www.riadtizwa.com). **Rates** 745dh-1,980dh double. **Credit** AmEx, MC, V. Map p250 B4 ㉘
Small (five rooms), relaxed and comfortable, Riad Tizwa has a slightly rough-around-the-edges charm that is all its own. Laid out in the usual fashion on three open-fronted floors around a central tiled courtyard, this place is a great antidote to design excess. Rooms are white with splashes of colour, some with wood-beamed ceilings; bathroom *tadelakt* is in a limestone shade. Design solutions are simple but striking, like the thick, high azure *tadelakt* headboard that conceals clothing rails behind it in one of the rooms. There is a hammam, and each room is equipped with an iPod docking station. The roof terrace has a shaded area for al fresco dining (there's also an indoor dining area downstairs) and offers privacy for sunbathing. The friendly owners encourage exclusive rentals of the whole riad as well as individual guests. One big advantage of this place is that it's accessible to taxis, just a few yards down a narrow alley off rue Dar El-Bacha. *Photo p57. Cook. Hammam. Internet (Wi-Fi).*

Riad W

41 Derb Boutouil, Kennaria (065 36 79 36/ www.riadw.com). Rates 990dh-1,650dh double. **No credit cards. Map** p253 D6 ㉙
Working on the premise that guests would get quite enough sensory input from their forays into the Medina, Spanish owner Elsa Bauza designed her four-room riad with a philosophy of simplicity and 'quiet in the head'. The bedrooms – one huge, one big, one small – have white walls, unadorned save for a few framed textiles. Downstairs, zen-like lines are matched by some quietly retro furnishings. It makes a refreshing change in a town where there's often too much colour and clutter. Up top are two roof terraces, each shared by two rooms. Below is a spacious courtyard, a plunge pool, two sitting-rooms (one with a piano), and Bauza and her daughter's appartment. Breakfast is included, and dinner can be arranged on request.
Air-conditioning. Cook. Heating. Plunge pool. TV.

Riyad El Cadi

87 Derb Moulay Abdelkader, off Derb Debbachi (024 37 86 55/fax 024 37 84 78/www.riyadel cadi.com). **Rates** 1,230dh single; 1,476dh-1,845dh double; 2,460dh-2,950dh suite. **Credit** MC, V. **Map** p251/p253 D5 ㉚
Comprising eight interconnected houses, El Cadi is a rambling maze of a residence in which getting lost is a pleasure – luckily, for it'll happen quite a lot in your first few days. The 12 well-appointed suites

The riad revolutionaries

Tadelakt walls, carved stucco, colourful *zelije* tiling, rugs on the walls – it sometimes seems like every riad has been designed from the same Marrakech Style handbook. The basic forms and materials are native, of course, as is the palette – the pinks and ochres of local earth, lemon yellow, the blue of cobalt skies. But for traditional Moroccan and Berber crafts and methods to result in an internationally known style required outside intervention. Enter Bill Willis, the man who ignited the Marrakech interiors explosion.

A native of Memphis, Tennessee, Willis moved to Marrakech in the 1960s and began working for clients such as Paul Getty Jr and Yves St Laurent. He developed a style based on traditional Moroccan references (arches, painted woodwork, geometric patterns in tiling), but imbued with his own slightly camp sense of humour. Look at his candy-striped, onion-domed fireplaces at Dar Yacout (*see p98*), or the palm tree columns at the **Tichka Salam** hotel (*see p58*).

While his particular twists are wholly modern, the techniques are age-old – intricate mosaic work, wood carving, stone masonry. And because his interiors demanded local craftsmen to adapt and stretch, Willis also helped to revive the city's artisan traditions.

He worked on the Tichka with architect Charles Boccara, who also used traditional elements to convey a strong sense of place while striking an unmistakably modern pose. His interiors make stunning use of *tadelakt*, the polished wall finish traditionally employed in hammams, where heat and moisture are a problem. Surfaces are trowelled in a plaster of powdered limestone mixed with coloured dust to provide the requisite hue. The plaster is then polished hard with flat stones, sealed with a glaze of egg white, and polished again with Moroccan black soap. Boccara brought *tadelakt* out of the steam room and into style. Since the example set by his signature **Les Deux Tours** (*see p60*), completed in the early 1990s, Marrakech has gone *tadelakt* mad.

French-Senegalese architect Meryanne Loum-Martin also schooled herself in traditional crafts and methods, then applied the knowledge to a half-built concrete shell in the Palmeraie. The result was Dar Tamsna, the protoype boho-chic villa and the place that really introduced Marrakech to the international lifestyle press (eight pages

in *Condé Nast Traveller*!). Like Willis, she reinterpreted local ingredients, but with a beautifully restrained simplicity – an approach refined with her **Jnane Tamsna** (*see p60*), completed in 2002.

Meanwhile, the riad scene began to boom in the Medina. Low property prices and the abundance of local artisans encouraged designers to buy houses and go to town on them. Each started with the same traditional references, but the beauty of the whole modern Marrakech thing is how readily traditional methods lend themselves to experimentation and innovation.

Thus Björn Conerding and Ursula Haldimann took trad Moroccan into the realm of gothic fantasy with their **Riad Enija** (pictured, *see p45*). Christian Ferré played heavily on colour and patterning in his **Riad Kaiss** (*see p51*). Christophe Siméon develped a Moroccan minimalism with his **Riad Mabrouka** (*see p51*). Giovanna Cinel married Marrakech to Milan at her **Riad 72** (*see p53*). And Jill Fechtmann and Jean-Michel Jobit have mixed local elements with an idiosyncratic eclecticism in their **Riad Noir d'Ivoire** (*see p47*). It's astonishing how many riads are now owned by designers turned hoteliers: Marrakech has become their playground.

and bedrooms, as well as the various salons, corridors, staircases and landings, also double as gallery spaces for an outstanding collection of art and artefacts gathered by late former owner Herwig Bartels. The reception area alone boasts an ancient Berber textile with a Bauhaus chair and a Rothko-like abstract. Despite the rich details, the overall feel is uncluttered, cool and contemporary. Bartels's daughter Julia now runs the riad, with the assistance of the dapper and charming general manager Ahmed El-Amrani, and standards remain high. Extensive roof terraces with tented lounging areas further add to the appeal of what, for the money, is some of the classiest accommodation in town. The only drawback is its distance off from taxi dropping-off points, though cars can get quite near at the top end of the Jemaa El Fna up to 1pm. *Photo p59.*
Air-conditioning. Boutique. Cook. Hammam. Heating. Plunge pool (outdoor). TV.

Riyad Edward

10 Derb Marestane, Zaouia El-Abbasia (024 38 97 97/024 38 48 55/www.riyadedward.com). **Rates** 1,320dh-1,980dh. **No credit cards. Map** p250 C2 ③
Up in the north of the Medina, near the Shrine of Sidi Bel Abbas, Riyad Edward is a rambling conversion of two houses, both around 500 years old. An ancient cypress tree towers from the main courtyard, affording a little shade over the swimming pool and marking the location from a distance. Amiable English owner Stephen Skinner formerly rented it all out as a house, and it was only converted into a *maison d'hôte* in 2006, when the charming Beatriz Maximo, who used to run Caravanserai (*see p62*) got involved. The style is unpretentious Moroccan, with some surviving original detailing and an odd scattering of pictures and objects from Skinner's collection, and there's a kind of weathered feel about the place. Maximo, meanwhile, ensures the place is run with a feminine touch. Of the ten rooms, we favour those on the rooftops and the big square suite. There's also an annex with its own entrance that can be rented as a separate house. Skinner is now building a new place on a hilltop at the mouth of the Ourika Valley, which he hopes will be open by early 2008.
Cook. Hammam. Pool.

Tchaikana

25 Derb El Ferrane, Kaat Benahid (tel/fax 024 38 51 50/www.tchaikana.com). **Rates** *July, Aug* 800dh double; 1,300dh suite. *Sept-June* 900dh double; 1,500dh suite. **No credit cards. Map** p251 D4 ③
Run by a young and charming (English-speaking) Belgian couple, Jean-François and Delphine, Tchaikana has just four rooms. However, most of these rooms are enormous, particularly the two suites, each of which measures 11 metres by five metres (36ft by 16ft). The decor is beautiful, with a sort of *Vogue* goes Savannah look, and the central courtyard, laid out for dining, is gorgeously lit at night. Rates are per room, and given that all have banquettes in addition to double beds, each could sleep four or more impecunious souls – Jean-François has no objections (although no more than four breakfasts per room). Soft drinks and orange juice are free, and there's a library of comic books. Delphine is a buyer for several major UK high-street stores, and is the ideal person for advice on shopping the souk. In case you're wondering, a 'tchaikana' is a Central Asian teahouse.
Air-conditioning. Cook. Heating. Internet (Wi-Fi).

Budget

Let's just reiterate this: Marrakech is not the place to scrimp on accommodation. But for those who just don't have the cash, there are plenty of budget hotels between rue Bab Agnaou and Riad Zitoun El-Kedim, south of Jemaa El Fna. The very best of the budget options are listed below.

Grand Tazi

Corner of avenue El-Mouahidine & rue Bab Agnaou (024 44 27 87/fax 024 44 21 52). **Rates** 320dh single; 500dh double. **Credit** MC, V. **Map** p252 C6 ③
More accurately, the 'No Longer So Grand Tazi' – although we doubt it was ever particularly salubrious. It's a well-known two-storey, two-star establishment that retains its popularity because of its plum location just a minute's walk from Jemaa El Fna, combined with cheap room rates and the added benefits of a swimming pool and bar. Rooms vary wildly in quality: ask to view a few before settling. Up on the first floor, what must be the longest corridor in Marrakech leads to the good-sized outdoor swimming pool, bordered by sunloungers. In the evening the area beside reception takes on a life of its own as a lounge bar (*see p117*), the only place in the central Medina for a cheap beer. We have heard less-than-favourable reports about the food in the in-house restaurant.
Air-conditioning. Bar. Pool (outdoor). Restaurant. TV.

Hotel Gallia

30 rue de la Recette, off rue Bab Agnaou (024 44 59 13/fax 024 44 48 53/www.ilove-marrakech. com/hotelgallia). **Rates** 320dh single; 500dh double. **Credit** MC, V. **Map** p252 C6 ③
The lanes off rue Bab Agnaou – seconds from the Jemaa El Fna – are thick with budget options, but Gallia comes top of the class. This small, French-owned operation gets ticks in all the right boxes: it's smack-bang central, impeccably clean and aesthetically pleasing. Nineteen en suite double rooms open on to two picture-pretty, flower-filled courtyards, where an excellent breakfast is served. Bathrooms are big, modern pink affairs with limitless hot water. The well-kept flowery roof terrace is an ideal spot for lounging. Unsurprisingly, Gallia is popular. Bookings should be made by fax and it is advisable to book at least one month in advance.
Air-conditioning. Heating. TV: satellite.

CASA LALLA

A refined dinner and an unforgettable stay wait for you behind the doors at Casa Lalla.

The table d'hôte

Annabel and Pierre-Olivier welcome you to dine under the stars and experience the wonderful gastronomical kitchen. A refined, exquisite and varied cuisine that will satisfy your papillas!

Every evening, the chef invites you to discover a personally created and inventive gourmet menu. Every dish is visually tantalising, with a blend of enticing flavours, appealing to the discerning palate. Emotion and sensuality go hand-in-hand with the legendary hospitality of this convivial country. We provide a warm and special environment for all our guests!

The house guest

By staying in Casa Lalla, you will be warmly greeted by its guest house, entering a world of serenity, comfort and refinement. It's a delicate alliance between a traditional riad and sober décor with a contemporary feel and subtle oriental touches. Our suites include fireplaces and finely decorated bedrooms with tadelakt and cedar woodworks.

For accommodation that provides a calm and tranquil environment, we offer top-of-the-range prestations at reasonable prices.

Meditate in the living-room library with the fire burning, enjoy the jaccuzi, day-dream on the panoramic and hazed terrace, allow yourself to be seduced by a massage after a traditional hammam.

CASA LALLA

Riad Zitoun Lakdime 16 Derb Jamaa, Marrakech Medina
Tel: 00 212 (0) 24 42 97 57   Fax: 00 212 (0) 42 42 97 59
www.casalalla.com   contact@casalalla.com

Jnane Mogador

116 Riad Zitoun El Kedim (024 42 63 24/fax 024 42 63 23/www.jnanemogador.com). **Rates** 290dh single; 380dh double; 460dh triple; 520dh quadruple. **Credit** MC, V. **Map** p252 C6 ㊱

Arguably offering the best value accommodation in town, the Mogador is a small riad with considerable charm and warmth. And it's clean. All this for an unbelievable 380dh per double with en suite bathroom – just don't expect a power shower. The 17 rooms are simple and predominantly pink with light pine and wrought-iron furniture and *tadelakt* bathrooms. Public areas are much more ornate, with fountain courtyards, stucco arches and a large roof terrace used for breakfast. Be prepared, however, to dress warmly in winter as there is no heating. Advance reservations are essential as the place is permanently full; prices are due to go up in autumn 2007 (rates still to be established at time of writing). English may or may not be spoken, but if the riad's website is anything to go by ('This supernatural riad opens to those that conjugate their dreams in the present'), you're unlikely to understand anything even if it is. **Photo** *p61.*

Nejma Lounge

45 Derb Sidi M'hamed El Haj, Bab Doukkala (024 38 23 41/www.riad-nejmalounge.com). **Rates** 460dh-740dh double. **No credit cards. Map** p250 A3 ㊲

This notable new budget option, conveniently close to Bab Doukkala, shuns the traditional in favour of black and white floor tiles, playful accents in pinks and purples, and furniture by Laurence Corsin, who owns African Lodge (*see p129*). It's the riad as pop art. The six rooms are named to reflect the colours that predominate – 'Rose' is pink, 'Rouge' is red and 'Chocolate' is, well, chocolate. They're not the biggest bedrooms in town but they're nice for the price. Young, anglophile French owners maintain a cool but animated atmosphere. There's a small bar off the courtyard, snacks and drinks are served all day long, and you can even imbibe from floating trays in the modest plunge pool. Naturally, there's also a roof terrace, but no TV anywhere on the premises. Closed for most of August.

Air-conditioning. Cook. Heating. Internet.

Riad Magi

79 Derb Moulay Abdelkader, off Derb Dabbachi (tel/fax 024 42 66 88). **Rates** 800dh single; 1,040dh double. **No credit cards. Map** p251/p253 D5 ㊳

Petite, unpretentious and homely, Riad Magi has six carefully colour-coordinated rooms on two floors around its central orange-tree shaded courtyard. The first-floor blue room is particularly lovely, with its step-down bathroom. Breakfast can be taken on the roof terrace or in the courtyard (which may or may not sport tree-clinging chameleons); other meals are available by arrangement. When in town, English owner Maggie Perry holds court from her corner table, organising guests' affairs and spinning stories of local absurdity – at such times Riad Magi becomes possibly the most entertaining hangout in Marrakech. Maggie and husband Clay also own a farm, complete with donkey and horse, down in the Ourika Valley. It's a 30-minute drive south of the city, and riad guests are invited to visit or even stay overnight on the property.

Cook.

Riad Omar

22 rue Bab Agnaou (024 44 56 60/fax 024 38 75 22/www.riadomar.com). **Rates** 500dh rooms; 700dh suites. **No credit cards. Map** p252 B7 ㊴

A brusque atmosphere and cramped rooms with no frills are the trade-off for budget prices and an excellent location on the pedestrianised rue Bab Agnaou, a short stroll south of the square. This is a hotel rather than a *maison d'hôte*, with 17 rooms and four

Riad Tizwa. *See p53.*

suites set around a central courtyard with a small fountain. They're all air-conditioned and en-suite, though only eight of them have bathtubs. The four suites have small sitting-rooms with fireplaces, but in the normal doubles you can either sit on the beds or lie on them, and that's pretty much it. The hammam is rather plain, but at least they have one. On the roof there's a tented restaurant that looks over-priced (menus at 150dh and 200dh) and bears no relation to the Snack Omar on the street downstairs. *Air-conditioning. Hammam. Heating.*

Riad de l'Orientale

8 Derb Ahmar, Laksour (024 42 66 42/www. riadorientale.com). **Rates** 620dh single; 720dh double; 980dh suite; 100dh extra bed. **Credit** MC, V. **Map** p250/p252 C5 ⑳

In the quarter behind Bab Fteuh, just a few minutes' walk from the Jemaa El Fna, this 250-year-old house has been a seven-room guesthouse since 2000. The owners are English but the style is traditional Moroccan – no radical design concepts here, just small but comfortable rooms ranged around the usual courtyard with fountain. The best deal, though, is the rooftop suite, which has two rooms, a bathroom, an open fire and a private terrace with its own fountain. It sleeps up to four. *Cook. Internet (Wi-Fi).*

Sherazade

3 Derb Djama, off Riad Zitoun El-Kedim (tel/fax 024 42 93 05/www.hotelsherazade.com). **Rates** *En suite bathroom* 210dh-510dh single; 260dh-650dh double. *Shared bathroom* 160dh single; 210dh double. **Credit** MC, V. **Map** p252 C6 ㉑

Probably the most popular budget accommodation in the Medina. Why so? Perhaps because it's so much better run than most of its competitors. The desk staff speak a variety of languages, English included, rooms come with meal menus, services and trips out of town, the place is cleaned regularly, and there's a general air of competency, which isn't always a given down at this end of the market. Some rooms are better than others; those on the roof share toilets and soon become overly hot in summer, while only a handful of the most expensive have air-conditioning. Breakfast is charged extra at 50dh per person. During high season an extra 50dh is added to room charges.

Villa El Arsa

18 Derb El-Arsa, off Riad Zitoun El-Jedid (tel/fax 024 42 63 26/www.villaelarsa.com). **Rates** 850dh-1,200dh. **No credit cards. Map** p253 D6 ㊷

Owned by a British couple, David and Susie Scott, this is a modest little house, but utterly charming with it. There's a rustic, vaguely Spanish air about the place, suggested by whitewashed walls, potted plants, and bare, weathered wooden doors and furniture. There are two attractive cushion-filled lounging salons off a central courtyard that comes with a tub-sized underlit plunge pool. The four bedrooms are ranged off the irregularly shaped upper gallery.

Two of the rooms are on the small side, but the other pair are generous; all are rendered in calm neutral tones with splendid en suite bathrooms. One of the larger rooms contains an additional single bed and is air-conditioned. Plus there's the ubiquitous roof terrace, in this case with an open fireplace for chill winter evenings. The Scotts have good connections with a pair of mountain guides, and can arrange one-day or overnight trekking in the Atlas. *Cook. Plunge pool (outdoors).*

Guéliz & Semlalia

Guéliz offers a continental-style café scene, boutique shopping, good eating and what passes locally for nightlife. It's a good antidote to the foreignness of the Medina, which is still only five minutes from central Guéliz by taxi. Semlalia is just a few minutes' north of Guéliz on the route de Casablanca.

Moderate

Tichka Salam

Route de Casablanca, Semlalia (024 44 87 10/fax 024 44 86 91). **Rates** *6-31 Jan, June-Aug, Nov-21 Dec* 950dh single; 1,200dh double; 1,700dh-2,700dh suite. *Feb-15 Mar, May, Sept-Oct* 1,000dh single; 1,300dh double; 1,800dh-3,000dh suite. *16 Mar-Apr, 22 Dec-5 Jan* 1,100dh single; 1,300dh double; 2,000dh-3,300dh suite. **Credit** AmEx, MC, V. **Map** p248 B1.

Jaws dropped when the Tichka first opened in the 1970s. It's said that Jagger checked out of the Mamounia and shimmied straight over here, swiftly followed by the great and good of the society pages. The big wow was the design, courtesy of louche Texan Bill Willis (*see p54* **The riad revolutionaries**). Since then, Marrakech has been hip-hotelled to excess and some of the sheen has come off the Tichka, but the public spaces are nevertheless still tremendous fun. The bar and restaurants, in particular, are a riot of rich colouring and tongue-in-cheek detail – check out the palm-leaf column capitals. The back garden's pool, complete with giant birdcage on stilts, remains arguably the best in town. Rooms (130, plus eight suites), though blessed with Willis furniture, are badly in need of a little TLC, especially the drab bathrooms. *Air-conditioning. Bar. Hammam. Heating. Pool (outdoor). Restaurants (2). Shops. TV: satellite.*

Budget

Hotel du Pacha

33 rue de la Liberté, Guéliz (024 43 13 27/fax 024 43 13 26). **Rates** 312dh single; 424dh double. **No credit cards. Map** p254 B2 ㊸

A standard two-star joint, nondescript and of a kind common to cities the world over. The only indication that this is Morocco is a handful of aged tourist office posters. The better rooms have small

balconies overlooking a central courtyard. All are in need of a little investment, with worn furniture and broken fittings, but the beds are comfortable and the en suite bathrooms are kept clean. For the price it's a reasonable deal – and one that has considerable appeal for independent tour groups, judging by the logo'd stickers on the door. The hotel business card announces that it has a 'restaurant gastronomique' but that's hardly the case – this is not a problem, though, as there are plenty of good dining options in the neighbourhood. Note that breakfast is charged extra (30dh).
Air-conditioning. Bar. Heating. Restaurant. TV lounge.

Moroccan House Hotel

3 Rue Loubnane, Guéliz (024 42 03 05/ fax 024 42 02 97/moroccanhousehotels@ menara.ma). **Rates** 490dh-770dh double. **Credit** AmEx, MC, V. **Map** p254 A2 ㉔
There are 52 rooms in this Moroccan-run hotel, open since 2004. Having struggled a little too hard to simulate a traditional atmosphere in a modern building, it's all a bit lurid and frilly. But there's a

Riyad El Cadi. *See p53.*

swimming pool and hammam, the location is central for Guéliz, the atmosphere is friendly and it's not a bad option for the price. Table football by the pool is a pleasingly inauthentic touch, and there's a lift for people daunted by too many Medina staircases. A few doors away at No.12, Le Caspien (024 42 22 82/fax 024 42 00 79/www.lecaspien-hotel.com) offers similar services at a similar price in slightly less 'Moroccan' surrounds.
Air-conditioning. Hammam. Heating. Pool (outdoor).

Hivernage

Aka the international enclave. Hivernage is between the airport and the walls of the Medina (five minutes from each), so the location is good, but the architectural neighbours are puffed-up villas and civic buildings and it's a taxi journey to get anywhere of interest.

Moderate

Hotel Es Saadi

Avenue El Qadissia (024 44 88 11/fax 024 44 76 44/www.essaadi.com). **Rates** *4-31 Jan, 7 June-20 Dec* 1,650dh-1,950dh double; 3,150dh-3,750dh suite. *Feb-6 June, 21 Dec-3 Jan* 1,950dh-2,550dh double; 3,450dh-4,050dh suite. **Credit** AmEx, MC, V. **Map** p254 C5 ㊹
The Saadi has been around forever. Cecil Beaton snapped the Rolling Stones beside its pool back in the late 1960s. Undoubtedly, then it looked like the chicest thing on the planet; now it looks more like a municipal hospital. Guests tend to be of the same era as the hotel (that is, a good few decades past their prime), but a lot of them are repeat customers, so folk are obviously well looked after here. Rooms (150 of them) are dated but comfortable, but be sure to get one facing south, overlooking the verdant gardens. We like the way the glass rear wall of the lobby slides up during the day so that the hotel blends seamlessly with the poolside terrace – and the irregularly shaped pool remains one of the biggest and best in town. Even if you aren't staying here, the terrace is a good lunch option and house club Théatro (*see p156*) is currently one of the hippest nightspots in town.
Air-conditioning. Bar. Casino. Golf driving range. Hairdressing salon. Hammam. Pool (outdoor). Restaurants (2). Sauna. TV: satellite. Tennis courts.

Ryad Mogador Menara

Avenue Mohammed VI, Hivernage (024 33 93 30/ fax 024 33 93 33/www.ryadmogador.com). **Rates** 1,600 single; 1,800dh double. **Credit** AmEx, MC, V. **Map** p254 A4 ㊻
Opened in 2005, the Mogador Menara in Hivernage (directly opposite the Palais des Congrès) has all the comfort and facilities one would expect from a smart international hotel – the outdoor swimming pool and poolside area with snack bar are particularly impressive – as well as the common drawback

of a slight lack of personality. On the plus side, with 244 rooms it's a good bet you'll find a bed for the night here, even during busy periods.

Air-conditioning. Business centre. Fitness centre. Hammam. Heating. Parking. Pools (indoor and outdoor). Spa.

Location of choice for the moneyed and famous, accommodation among the palms is mostly select and top end. Personally, we find the 20-minute drive into town a drag (not to mention expensive if you have to take taxis), but if luxury isolation is your thing, look no further.

Deluxe

Dar Zemora

72 rue El Aandalib, Ennakhil (024 32 82 00/ fax 024 32 82 01/www.darzemora.com). **Rates** 2,240dh-4,480dh. **Credit** MC, V.
Set in a hectare of lush gardens filled with roses and hibiscus, fragrant bougainvillea and palm trees, Dar Zemora is Marrakech's answer to the English country-house hotel – perhaps because it's owned by an English couple, who remodelled this former private abode beyond all recognition and opened it in December 2003. Apart from two large sitting rooms, a dining room and a library with leather-upholstered armchairs, the main house contains just three rooms and two big suites. The 'Perla' suite has a simply colossal private terrace with plant life spilling from pastel-coloured urns and a view over the garden's big heated pool. 'Zahara' has a smaller terrace but a better sitting room and a huge bath. Both have fireplaces, king-size four-posters and dressing rooms. The other rooms are less impressive but just as gorgeous. In the garden there's also a two-bedroom pavillion with a kitchen and big living room. All in all, there's so much space you might get agoraphobic, but you could probably wander among the vegetation all day long without bumping into another guest. **Photo** *p62.*

Air-conditioning. Heating. Restaurant. Pool (outdoor).

Jnane Tamsna

Douar Abiad (024 32 94 23/fax 024 32 98 84/ www. jnanetamsna.com). **Rates** 3,000dh-4,500dh double. **Credit** MC, V.
The creation of designer Meryanne Loum-Martin and her ethnobotanist husband Dr Gary Martin, Jnane Tamsna is a 'Moorish hacienda' with seven opulent suites and 17 gorgeous rooms, set in five buildings scattered around some beautiful gardens, each with its own pool. The architecture is vernacular chic, coloured in the palest tones of primrose, peppermint and clay and enhanced by Loum-Martin's own inspired furniture. Surrounding fruit orchards, herb and vegetable gardens provide organic produce for the kitchen. A second kitchen is used for 'culinary adventure' programmes. The

combination of rural tranquillity, Zen-like aesthetics and ecological initiative makes for an almost utopian (no locks on the doors!) scenario. There's also an art gallery and boutique, open by appointment (061 24 27 17), and non-guests are able to take advantage of 'pool, lunch and tennis' packages or visit for dinner, prepared by a former executive chef of the Quinta do Lago Four Seasons: call for details. *See also p54* **The riad revolutionaries**.

Air-conditioning. Art gallery. Boutique. Cook. Garden. Heating. Pool (5, outdoor). Restaurant. Tennis courts. TV: satellite.

Ksar Char-Bagh

Palmeraie (024 32 92 44/fax 024 32 92 14/www. ksarcharbagh.com). **Rates** 5,940dh-7,020dh suite; 9,180dh pool apartment. **Credit** MC, V.
Char-Bagh takes the whole Moroccan fantasy trip to its absolute extremes. A charming French couple (she works in advertising, he's in publishing) have re-created an Alhambran palace court that defies belief; it's been built from scratch on a kasbah-sized scale. A moated gatehouse with six metre-high beaten metal doors fronts an arcaded central court with a central pool. Extensive grounds contain herb and flower gardens, an orchard, an open-air spa and the deepest of pools. OTT indoor amenities include a cigar salon and wine cellar selected by the house sommelier. Lunch or dinner can be served out on the terrace or by the pool, and the chef trained under Alain Ducasse and Joël Robuchon. All this is shared by just a handful of sumptuous, not to mention spacious, suites, each with its own private garden or terrace, and one with its own exclusive swimming pool. Guests are collected from the airport in a reconditioned London taxi, one of a pair shipped here via Casablanca.

Air-conditioning. Gym. Hammam. Heating. Pool (outdoor). Restaurants. Tennis courts. TV: DVD, satellite.

Expensive

Les Deux Tours

Douar Abiad (024 32 95 27/fax 024 32 95 23/ www.les-deuxtours.com). **Rates** 5-31 Jan, 16 June-30 Sept, 1-19 Dec 1,750dh double; 2,500dh deluxe; 4,000dh suite. Feb-15 June, Oct, Nov, 20 Dec-4 Jan 2,000dh double; 3,000dh deluxe; 4,000dh suite. **Credit** MC, V.
One of the longer established guesthouses in the Palmeraie, Les Deux Tours (named for its distinctive twin-towered gateway) is the sublime work of premier Marrakchi architect Charles Boccara. Approached via a cactus-lined driveway, it's a walled enclave of earthen-red villas that together offer 24 chic rooms and suites in a lush blossom and palm-filled garden setting. No two rooms are the same, but all feature glowing *tadelakt* walls and *zelije* tiling with stunning sculpturally soft bathrooms, several seductively lit via glassy punch-holes in pink mud-brick domes. Guests share the most attractive of outdoor pools, keyhole shaped and

fringed by perfectly maintained grassy lawns, as well as a stunning subterranean hammam. Breakfast is charged extra (100dh).

Air-conditioning. Cook. Hammam. Pool (outdoor).

Villa Vanille

Palmeraie (024 31 01 23/www.villavanille.com). **Rates** 1,540dh-2,370dh ddouble. **Credit** MC, V.

French-Swedish couple Pierre Blanc and Pia Westh set up their private family home in these generous grounds, and then built a bungalow in the garden where friends could stay. Soon they were renting it out, then building another small bungalow, and another. Almost by accident they ended up with a unique hotel. 'Suite Atlas' is the oldest, with a bedroom and sitting room, the latter with an open fire. Along with 'Room Gibilette', it has a TV, minibar and private terrace. 'Suite Soleil' has two rooms separated by a bathroom, and would suit a family. The earth-toned 'Room Nature' is relatively austere, but cheaper and handy for the heated 20-metre swimming pool. Scattered around the big garden under shady mimosa trees are tables and chairs, tents and hammocks, and lunch or dinner can be served wherever you want it. It's a great place for children, with lots of space to run around and a small playground with a swing, slide and sandpit. For grown-ups there's a gym and massage room. Pia is a trained masseur (*see p165*), and has a wall of diplomas to prove it.

Air-conditioning. Cook. Gym. Heating. Pool (outdoor).

Further afield

All of the places below are a 15- to 30-minute drive from the Medina – far enough away to be rural, but close enough to pop to town for dinner.

Deluxe

Amanjena

Route de Ouarzazate, km12 (024 40 33 53/fax 024 40 34 77/www.amanresorts.com). **Rates** 8,100dh-14,400dh pavilion; 21,150dh-24,750dh maison. **Credit** AmEx, MC, V.

Yep, those prices are right. The Amanjena is part of the Amanresorts group, the world's most luxurious international hotel chain. It caters to a very specific and highly pampered clientele: Amanjunkies are not the kind to worry about a few hundred dollars here and there. What they get for their money is an exclusive gated complex a few miles south of town, well away from the masses (and secure from paparazzi). The architecture is low-rise palatial, rose pink and frilly, trimmed with green-tiled roofs. At the heart of the resort is the *bassin*, a massive fish-filled reservoir of water that feeds two shallow canals running between the 34 'pavilions' and six 'maisons'. These are vast and lavish private residences, some with their own walled gardens, all filled with every conceivable luxury. Services range from spas and facials to hot-air ballooning

Jnane Mogador. *See p57.*

Understated luxury at **Dar Zemora**. See p60.

There's a TV room, a beautiful outdoor pool, food (and wine) when you want it and a small Berber village for company, but no phones and otherwise little to do but kick back and relax. A rental car would extend your options but, then again, as David Byrne once sang, 'Heaven is a place where nothing ever happens'.

Cook. Hammam. Pool (outdoor). TV: cable, DVD.

Moderate

Caravanserai

264 Ouled Ben Rahmoun (024 30 03 02/ fax 024 30 02 62/www.caravanserai.com). **Rates** 700dh-1,250dh single; 1,250dh-2,500dh double; 1,750dh-3,250dh suite; 3,250dh-3,500dh Majorelle suite; 3,750dh-4,000dh pool suite. **Credit** MC, V.

Outwardly it's indistinguishable among the compressed mudbrick walls that make up the impoverished hamlet of Ouled Ben Rahmoun, but behind its wooden door Caravanserai offers a super-sophisticated take on rural life – right down to a water-mist cooling system. It's a seductive, unmistakably luxurious ensemble of pale pink walls, rough-hewn eucalyptus ceilings, earthenware fittings and plenty of white canvas-draped banquettes for indolent hours spent lounging. Best of all is the magnificent central swimming pool, framed by a massive gate-like structure. There are five rooms and 12 suites, including a couple that feature their own courtyards and pools. In the evenings, sip a drink at the bar and listen to live performances by traditional musicians. For guests who can tear themselves away, a minibus shuttles into central Marrakech three times a day (15 mins) and there's a 24-hour taxi service.

Air-conditioning. Bar. Beauty treatments. Boutique. Hammam. Heating. Parking. Pool (outdoor). Restaurant.

La Pause

Douar Lmih Laroussiène, Commune Agafay Marrakech (061 30 64 94/www.lapause-marrakech.com). **Rates** 1,650dh per person half-board. **No credit cards.**

La Pause is the closest thing you'll get to a desert experience within the vicinity of Marrakech. At this country retreat it's all about big skies, magnificent sunsets, rolling hills and nothing much else for miles and miles around. By reservation only, La Pause will serve lunch or romantic, lantern-lit dinner in traditional tents, with entertainment from gnawa musicians. Overnight guests are accommodated in beautifully simple country-style rooms. Owner Fréderic Alaime fell in love with the spot while horseback riding, and outdoor activities are a big part of the La Pause experience. There's horseriding (riders of all standards are catered for), mountain biking and camel trekking – not to mention an intriguing form of cross-country golf. There really isn't anything else quite like it in Marrakech.

Air-conditioning. Cook. Heating.

and the loan of clubs for use on the Amelkis golf course next door. Yes, that might be Sting by the pool, but if you can afford to stay here you're probably as rich and famous as he is.

Air-conditioning. Bar. Beauty centre. Gym. Hammam. Heating. Pool (outdoor). Restaurants. Room service. Shops. TV: cable, DVD, video. Tennis courts.

Expensive

Tigmi

Douar Tagadert El Cadi, km24 route d'Amizmiz (+44 (0)845 026 4588/www.tigmi.com). **Rates** June-Aug 1,795dh suite; 5 Jan-19 Mar, 5 Apr-May, Sept-19 Dec 2,038dh suite. 20 Mar-4 Apr, 20 Dec-4 Jan 2, 610dh suite. **Credit** MC, V.

The ultimate rural retreat, Tigmi is a mud-walled eight-suite haven of solitude lying in the middle of nowhere, halfway to the foothills of the Atlas, some 15 miles (24km) south of Marrakech. The hotel's architecture and interiors are rustically simple but fashion-shoot stylish – lots of white-washed arches, arcades and alcoves, covered walkways and terraces with beguiling views over raw, dusty pinkish landscapes; think Sergio Leone with citrus fruits. Most suites have courtyards (one has its own little pool), terraced chill-out areas and sweet, cosy bedrooms with fireplaces that are lit in winter.

Sightseeing

Features

Maps

Introduction

The best way to explore Marrakech? Just get lost.

If you want to, you can take a London-style open-top bus for a whirlwind tour of Marrakech's sights. But you'll be missing the point: 'sights' per se are not what this city is all about. For a start, conventional sights are limited and some are frankly disappointing. But more than that, it's just the wrong way to approach the Red City. Rather than listening to the patter of a tour guide you might do better to just get lost, because losing yourself is the best thing you can do here. Wander aimlessly. Explore. The longer you stay in Marrakech the more it grows on you, but you can't rush it: if you take your time it will open up gradually like a flower. To sample the atmosphere of Marrakech, amble slowly down its alleyways, immerse yourself in its colours and sounds, step on some donkey droppings and smell everything from ginger and cinnamon to open drains.

THE MEDINA

The area in which to idle is the Medina (Arabic for the 'city') the district enclosed by the old walls. This is where you will spend most of your walking hours. The city's few monuments are here, typically hidden in warrenous quarters and down dead-end, nameless alleys. There's little logic in the layout but navigation is aided by two landmarks: the minaret of the **Koutoubia Mosque**, helpfully flagging the location of the adjacent central square, the **Jemaa El Fna**. Also known simply as 'la place', it is the place you always seem to end up – the sink-hole around which Marrakech swirls.

The open space of the main square also neatly divides the Medina into two zones: north of Jemaa El Fna is commercial, with a fibrous network of souks (bazaars), and beyond them a grouping of three of the city's moderately interesting monuments: the **Musée de Marrakech** (*see p73*), **Koubba El-Badiyin** (*see p77*) and **Ben Youssef Medersa** (*see p75*). South of Jemaa El Fna is imperial, the quarter of the palaces and location of the melancholic **Saadian Tombs** (*see p82*).

Away from tourist paths, alleys become even more shambolic. Stray into the far northern or eastern parts of the Medina to see a backstage world of Marrakech *au naturel*. About street etiquette: pedestrians stick to the right to make room for scooters, pushbikes and donkeys.

THE CITY WALLS

Around 1126, in the face of threat from the aggressive Almohads, Almoravid Sultan Ali Ben Youssef encircled Marrakech with walls. He erected a circuit of ten kilometres (six miles) of ten-metre (30-foot) walls defended by 200 towers and punctuated by 20 gates. Despite extensions and repairs, the current walls follow roughly the same lines as the originals.

The walls are built of reddish *pisé* (dried mud mixed with lime). Although beautiful at times – especially when glowing pink under a setting sun – they are fairly featureless. A walk around the whole circuit is a slog, but a whirl in a horse-drawn *calèche* is fun. Carriages wait on the north side of place de Foucauld. A complete circuit, heading north up avenue Mohammed V and right out of Bab Nkob, takes about an hour; state-fixed prices are posted on the carriages.

BEYOND THE MEDINA

North-west of the old walls is the 'new city', a French colonial creation of the 1930s, which goes by the name of **Guéliz** (see p89). Old city and new are connected by the broad, tree-lined avenue Mohammed V (pronounced 'M'hammed Sanc'). Named for the king who presided over Morocco's independence, it's the main street of Guéliz. Few visitors bother with this part of town but middle-class Marrakchis and expats favour it for car-friendly streets, modern apartment blocks and decent restaurants and shops, plus most of what passes for nightlife.

South of Guéliz and immediately west of the city walls, is **Hivernage** (see p90), a small, low-density neighbourhood of villas and international five-star hotels. Also out this way, where Hivernage shades into Guéliz, are civic trappings such as the railway station, new Royal Opera House, Palais des Congrès and, beyond them all, the airport.

On the opposite (north-east) side of the Medina is a vast oasis of palm trees known as the **Palmeraie** (see p94). While not particularly pretty, its distance from the hoi polloi, low population density and lavish new houses have made it a favourite home of the rich – both Moroccans and foreigners.

GETTING AROUND

The only way to tackle the Medina is on foot. It looks daunting on the map but the area within the walls isn't huge. However, the miles do add up with all the wrong turns you'll make, and many streets are too narrow for cars (watch out for motorcycles, scooters and pushbikes). A taxi is sometimes handy for navigation – some hotels and eateries are so well hidden that only natives can find them.

Taxis are necessary for shuttling between the Medina and Guéliz, which is only a five-minute ride (roughly 20dh by day, 30dh by night; should be less but taxi drivers often don't use their meters) but a half-hour walk. The green horse-drawn carriages (known as *calèches*) are a fun way to meander, particularly for a trip round the city walls (see p64), and aren't too expensive. Rental of a two-wheeler is good for exploring beyond the walls and in the Palmeraie.

For more information on getting around the city, see pp224-226.

GUIDES

Hotels tend to push them on to clients, warning of the dangers of unaccompanied exploration, but do you really need a guide? The answer is an unequivocal 'no'. Yes, you'll probably get lost but you'll never stay that way for long – any local will graciously set you back on track.

In any case, in a city of so many hidden surprises, there's no such thing as a wrong turn, only alternative routes.

However, if you have special interests or wish to hire someone whose knowledge goes beyond the confines of this book, then we can recommend Ahmed Tija, who's been guiding visitors for more than 20 years. He's fluent in English and a mine of information, anecdotes and legends of the city. We used him as an interpreter to listen to the storytellers in Jemaa El Fna (see p70 **Let me tell you a story**). He and his father were great friends of the author Gavin Maxwell, whose *Lords of the Atlas* is the definitive local history book (Ahmed did the illustrations in the paperback edition). We've also heard good things about the other guides listed below, all of whom speak English. Expect to pay around 300dh per half day. Beware picking up *faux guides*/unofficial guides (official guides carry accreditation) – they are usually an expensive waste of time.

Ahmed Tija
024 30 20 50/mobile 061 08 45 57.

Moulay Youssef
Mobile 061 16 35 64.

Mustapha Chouquir
Mobile 062 10 40 99.

Mustapha Karroum
Mobile 061 34 07 78.

Don't miss Sights

Quintessential Marrakech
Snake charmers, storytellers, henna artists: all life is at **Jemaa El Fna**. See p69.

A sense of proportion
Tiling and stucco, a courtyard with central pool, and beautiful proportions throughout, turn the **Ben Youssef Merdersa** into a haven of serenity. See p75.

Pre-industrial manufacturing
Many of the Medina's ancient *fundouks* now function as workshops. See p66.

Souk couture
Slippers or scorpions? Find them both, and more, in Marrakech's shopping city. See p72.

Blue
See Jacques Majorelle's intense cobalt shade, paired with ochre or dusky yellow, at the **Majorelle Gardens**. See p92.

On foot A tour of the backstreets

Allow two and half to three hours.
This walk was recommended by the tour guide Ahmed Tija (*see p65*). The route takes you off the beaten tourist track.

Start in **Jemaa El Fna**. Standing with your back to the Café de France (*see p115*) take a right and head down the busy **Derb Dabachi** for about 700 metres or five minutes. You are heading right or east of the square in the rough direction of the tanneries. Take a left turn (at a *teleboutique*) towards the Sidi Ben Salah shrine and mosque. This road has a traditional dentist on the right (the kind who pulls out teeth with pliers). Walk on, noticing the Moroccan wedding shop on your right: everything for the traditional wedding party can be hired here, from elaborately decorated kaftans to singers.

Immediately opposite the wedding shop on the left hand side is a *tahana*, a small-scale business for grinding corn, barley and wheat to make flour. The grinding machines are around 70 years old.

Opposite the *tahana*, on your left, is the first of several **fundouks** or *caravanserai* (merchants hostels). This one is 200 years old. It looks tatty but from the inside you have an excellent view of the **Sidi Ben Salah Mosque**, and if you walk up the stone steps on your right you can peer into some fascinating old workshops, including one belonging to two traditional *jellaba* makers. The mosque is on the east side of the picturesque **Ben Salah Square**. In another corner is one of the weirdest houses in Marrakech – a sort of tiled penthouse piled on top of other flats, like something from a Terry Gilliam film.

From the square take a right and an immediate left and follow the street as it bends in a slight zig-zag past another *teleboutique.* The road then veers left and heads northwards. By this time you have come into the quarter known as El-Moqf. The street turns into a covered market area. On the right is a door that opens into one of the oldest *fundouks* in Marrakech, dating back to the 16th century. These days it's home to chicken and sheep. Opposite the *fundouk* on the left-hand side of the street is another little gem: a shop selling magic requisites – lizards, amulets, gourds and dried animal skins.

When you come out of this covered section take the first left and head towards the Medersa Ben Youssef and the Foundouk restaurant. As you pass the restaurant you can see yet another old 18th-century *fundouk* that is being restored. At this point walk towards a mini fork in the road and keep to the right, walking past another dilapidated *fundouk* where you can see craftsmen making leather shoes.

As you follow the street around you will see in front of you a series of keyhole arches leading towards the Medersa Ben Youssef. Don't go this way. Instead turn right and follow the alleyway, which bends left. On your right there's a hammam dating back to the Saadian era. Next door, peep into the huge furnace where the water is heated for the hammam. The man who runs the furnace is a gnawa musician; he may be prepared to give a recital for few dirhams.

As you walk on from here you enter another covered section. As you emerge, go straight across the crossroads and head towards the **Shrine of Sidi Abdel-Aziz**. An 18th-century doctor famed for his ability to help the mentally ill, Abdel-Aziz promises help for modern suffering too. People with mental illnesses come to his shrine hoping for a cure. They chain padlocks to the window bars of his mausoleum; if they recover they remove the padlock.

After you've seen the mausoleum, retrace your steps for a little way and turn right down **Riad El-Arous**. On the right-hand side is an old bakery. Continue for several minutes and you should be able to see the **Mosque and Shrine of Sidi Ben Slimane** (one of Marrakech's seven holy men) ahead of you. Take the next left turn and then left again into rue Bab Taghzout which opens up into **Bab Taghzout square**, which provides a useful landmark for taking your bearings and has a taxi rank – useful if you're getting tired.

Now walk left towards the mosque and mausoleum of **Sidi Bel Abbes** (the greatest of the city's holy men), past the quaint little 60-year-old Marhaba cinema. Walk under an archway and turn immediately right where you will be able to enter the courtyard of the mausoleum. Here blind people gather to ask for alms. Walk through more courtyards and you can take an alleyway that goes round the whole building and takes you back to rue Bab

Sightseeing

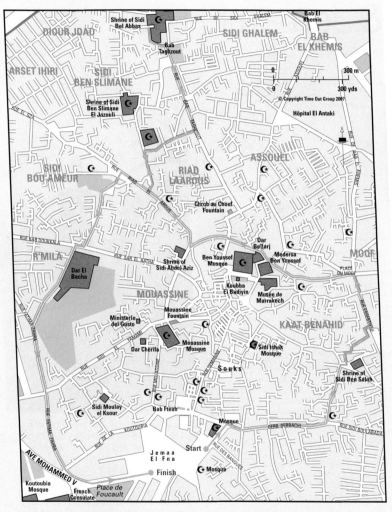

Taghzout. From here you will have to retrace your steps back towards Ben Slimane. From the small square of Riad El-Arous take another right turn and then a left and walk towards **Dar El-Bacha** (House of the Pasha – it belonged to the notorious despot, Thami El-Glaoui). A new museum is under construction

here. Bear left keeping the high walls of the palace on your left and head down the long stretch of rue Fatima Zahra. On your right is Marrakech's most famous hammam – **Hammam El Bacha**. Rue Fatima Zahra eventually leads you back towards the Koutoubia mosque and the Jemaa El Fna.

Koutoubia Mosque & Jemaa El Fna

The beating heart of the city.

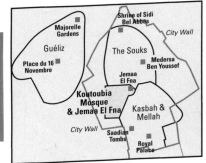

The square, towering minaret of the Koutoubia Mosque is the city's pre-eminent landmark and most recognisable icon. It's also one of the city's oldest structures. The mosque and its minaret are unquestionably the heart of Marrakech; the soul lies 200 metres to the west in the amorphous form of Jemaa El Fna, market place and forum to the city almost since its foundation.

Koutoubia Mosque

The minaret of the Koutoubia Mosque – Marrakech's most famous symbol – is visible from near and far. It is not actually very high (77 metres, 252 feet), but thanks to local topography and a local ordinance that forbids any other building in the Medina to rise above the height of a palm tree, it towers majestically over its surroundings. The original mosque, built in 1147, was demolished because it was not correctly aligned with Mecca (don't you just hate it when that happens?). It was rebuilt, and its new minaret was constucted more than half a century later under the patronage of the Almohad Caliph Yacoub El-Mansour.

The name Koutoubia is derived from *el-koutoubiyyin* – Arabic for booksellers – since a booksellers' market once filled the surrounding streets. The mosque's exterior is of red stone, but it's thought to have originally been covered with plaster. The tower is 13 metres (43 feet) wide. Six rooms, one above the other, constitute

Koutoubia Mosque.

the interior; leading around them is a ramp by way of which the muezzin could reach the balcony – it was supposed to be wide enough for him to ride a horse to the top.

The Koutoubia is built in a traditional Almohad style and the minaret is topped with four copper globes; according to legend, these were originally made of pure gold. There were also supposed to have been only three of them: it is said that the fourth was donated by the wife of Yacoub El-Mansour as compensation for failing to keep the fast by eating four grapes during Ramadan. As penance, she had her gold jewellery melted down to fashion the fourth globe. Hardly more credible is the claim that in times past only blind muezzins were employed because a sighted person would have been able to gaze into the royal harem from the minaret. Modern life does seem to be imitating legend, though: the Moroccan authorities have blocked the internet application Google Earth to avoid Moroccans being able to see into the grounds of the king's many palaces.

Glassed-over, sunken areas on the plaza outside the mosque are the remains of reservoirs that belonged to the **Dar El-Hajar** (House of Stone), a fortress built by city founder Youssef Ben Tachfine towards the end of the 11th century, and the first permanent structure in the encampment that became Marrakech. The fortress was short-lived, destroyed by the conquering Almohads who replaced it with the site's first mosque.

The small white-domed structure on the plaza is the **Koubba of Lalla Zohra**, a shrine that used to be open to the public until the inebriated son of a former city mayor ploughed his car into the structure and, as part of the repairs, the door was sealed up.

It's possible to walk around either side of the Koutoubia, clockwise between the main entrance and the wall that encloses the grounds of the French Consulate, or anti-clockwise along the top of the Almohad ruins. Either route leads into the rose-filled Koutoubia Gardens, which spread south and west of the mosque. Across avenue Houman El-Fetouaki, south of the gardens, a high wall cuts from sight a modest crenellated building; this is the humble **Tomb**

of **Youssef Ben Tachfine**, founder of Marrakech. A padlocked gate ensures that the great desert warrior rests in peace, his mausoleum off limits to the public.

Jemaa El Fna

It's the main open space in Marrakech but to call Jemaa El Fna a public square is misleading. Uncontained, disorderly, untainted by grandeur or pomp, untamable by council or committee, Jemaa El Fna is nothing less than bedlam. It's an urban clearing, as irregular in shape as an accident of nature, and thronged day and night with a carnival of local life – totally at odds with its name, which roughly translates as 'Assembly of the Dead'.

The square is as old as Marrakech itself. It was laid out as a parade ground by the Almoravids in front of their royal fortress (the **Dar El-Hajar**). When the succeeding Almohads built a new palace to the south, the open ground passed to the public and became what it remains today – a place for gathering, trading, entertainment and even the occasional riot. The name (pronounced with its consonants tumbling into each other to come out something like 'jemaf'na') refers to its former role as a venue for executions, with the decapitated heads put up on spikes for public display. The French put a stop to that.

In more recent times, during the 1970s, the municipality attempted to impose order with

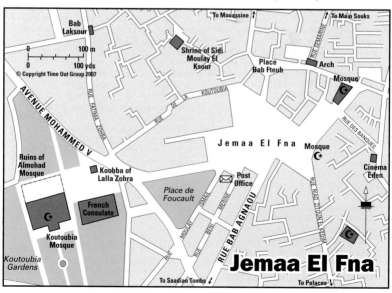

Let me tell you a story

They may not be the most obvious people to spot in the Jemaa El Fna and they are certainly not the loudest, but if you can find a storyteller, you are in for a treat. The storytellers, or *halakis*, claim to know by heart all the stories from *A Thousand and One Nights* as well as assorted tales from the Old Testament. They get started at around five in the afternoon as the sun gets cooler in the square; one storyteller usually sits outside the Café de France. If you can find an interpreter, it's worth sitting down for an hour with the locals and listening to one of these old men spin their yarns. Even if you don't understand a word of Arabic it's still an experience, as Elias Canetti describes in *Voices of Marrakesh*. 'Their words come from farther off and hang longer in the air than those of ordinary people. I understand nothing and yet whenever I came within hearing I was rooted to the spot by the same fascination. They were words that held no meaning for me, hammered out with fire and impact: to the man who spoke them they were precious and he was proud of them.'

In a culture where few could read and write, the oral tradition provided more than just entertainment; it was a vital means of passing down ideas, values and philosophy. Even today, around 40 per cent of Moroccans are illiterate. But there is no doubt that after a thousand years, the art and practice of storytelling in Jemaa El Fna is dying out. Young Marrakchis prefer modern forms of entertainment: they would rather watch Egyptian soap operas or play computer games than listen to a storyteller – let alone become one. There used to be 20 or so *halakis* in the square; now there are only half a dozen, and they are all elderly men.

But help is at hand. Writer and Marrakech resident Juan Goytisolo is at the forefront of efforts to preserve the storytellers' tradition and UNESCO has also intervened. It named the 'cultural space' of Jemaa El Fna as one of 19 'proclaimed masterpieces of the oral and intangible heritage of humanity' in 2001. As part of its efforts, the UN organisation is recording some of the *halakis*' stories and putting them on the internet. Ironically, modern technology – largely responsible for the demise of the art of public storytelling – may be responsible for preserving this part of the world's oral heritage.

a scheme to tarmac the square and turn it into a car park. This was opposed and defeated. Since then, thanks in part to the lobbying efforts of Spanish writer Juan Goytisolo (who has lived just off the square since the late 1970s), Jemaa El Fna has been recognised by UNESCO as part of the mankind's cultural heritage and its preservation is secured (*see also p70* **Let me tell you a story**). There's still some tidying-up impulse at work, however. The design of the orange-juice carts has recently been regularised in a faux traditional style and the whole square has been gradually paved over.

A DAY IN THE LIFE

During the early part of the day the square is relatively quiet. The orange-laden carts of the juice-sellers line the perimeter, wagon-train fashion, but otherwise there's only a scattering of figures, seated on boxes or rugs, shaded under large shabby umbrellas. The snake-charmers are early starters with their black, rubbery reptiles laid out in front or sheltered under large drums (be careful what you kick). For a few dirhams visitors can have a photograph taken with a large snake draped over their shoulders; for a few more dirhams they can have it removed. Gaudily clad water-sellers wander around offering to pose for dirhams. Other figures may be dentists (teeth pulled on the spot), scribes (letters written to order), herbalists (good for whatever ails you) or beggars (to whom Moroccans give generously). Overlooking all, the prime morning spot for unhurried businessmen and traders is the patio of the landmark Café de France (*see p115*), on the square for the last 50 years.

The action tends to wilt beneath the heat of the afternoon sun, when snake-charmers, dancers and acrobats can barely manage to stir themselves for camera-carrying tourists. It's not until dusk that things really kick off. As the light fades, ranks of makeshift kitchens set up with tables, benches and hissing flames, constituting one great open-air restaurant where adventurous eaters can snack on anything from snails to sheep's heads (*see p113* **Square meals**).

Beside the avenues of food stalls, the rest of the square takes on the air of a circus. Visiting Berber farmers from the surrounding plains and villages join Medina locals in crowding around the assorted performers. These typically include troupes of cartoon-costumed acrobats, musicians and their prowling transvestite dancers, storytellers and magicians, and boxing bouts between underage boys who can hardly lift their hands in the heavy leather gloves. The tourists and

visitors who provided the raison d'être for the afternoon entertainers are now negligible in this far more surreal evening scene.

Approaching midnight the food stalls begin to pack up, the performers wind down, and the crowds thin. Only the musicians remain, purveyors of seedy mysticisms, attended by wild-eyed devotees giddy on repetitive rhythms, helped along by hash. At the same time, the place becomes one great gay cruising ground, busy with tight-shirted, tight-trousered teens, sharp and cynical beyond their years.

SPECTATING THE SQUARE

The best place to be at any time of the day is in among it all (watch your wallet and bags), but several of the peripheral cafés and restaurants have upper terraces with fine ringside seating, among them the Café de France, Argana (*see p115*), Terrasses de l'Alhambra (*see p105*) and – with the best view of the lot – the Café Glacier, above the Hotel CTM. Here, the purchase of one soft drink (*'obligatoire'*) for 10dh allows you access to the café's grand balcon with its sweeping panorama.

Day or night, whether you choose stealthy observation from the terraces or a headlong plunge into the mêlée, Jemaa El Fna always remains somewhat elusive. 'All the guidebooks lie', writes Juan Goytisolo, 'there's no way of getting a firm grasp on it.'

Jemaa El Fna.

The Souks

Trading places.

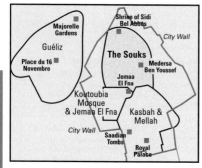

North of the Jemaa El Fna are the souks (markets), with alleyway upon alleyway of tiny retail cubicles. In the most heavily touristed areas, the overwhelming number of shops is offset by the fact that most seem compelled to offer exactly the same non-essential goods: slippers (*babouches*), embroidered robes, and brass platters. It is hard to believe that so many people sell so many of the same thing to such ambivalent customers. These areas are where you are most likely to hear entreaties such as: 'Look for free, no charge just to look' (as if any shop charges you to look). It's all a lot quieter than it used to be, though. The Moroccan authorities twigged that foreigners dislike full-on hassle and souk shopkeepers are models of good behaviour compared to some years ago.

The further into the souks you venture the more interesting they become. Our Shops & Services chapter (*see pp121-139*) picks out some of the highlights. The two main routes into their heart are rue Semarine and rue Mouassine; the former offers the more full-on blast of bazaar, the latter is a more sedate path leading to choice boutiques.

Semarine & the Great Souk

Entrance to the rue Semarine (aka Souk Semarine) is via an elaborate arch one block north of Jemaa El Fna – reached via either the spice market or the egg market, both pungent experiences, one pleasant, the other not. Semarine is a relatively orderly street, broad and straight with overhead trellising dappling the paving with light and shadow.

Every section of the souk has its own speciality and here it has traditionally been textiles, although these days cloth merchants have been largely supplanted by souvenir shops.

About 150 metres along, the first alley off to the east leads to a wedge-shaped open area known as the **Rahba Kedima**, or the 'old place'. The way between Semarine and the Rahba Kedima is a perpetual crush because it also leads to a small court, the **Souk Laghzel**, formerly the wool market but now a car-boot-sale of a souk where women – and only women – come to sell meagre possessions such as a single knitted shawl or a bag of vegetables. The Rahba Kedima used to be the city's open-air corn market but it's now given over to an intriguing mix of raffia bags and baskets, woollen hats and sellers of cooked snails. Around the edges are spice and 'magic' stalls (*see also p79* **The exorcist**).

The upper storeys of the shops on the northern side of the Rahba Kedima are usually hung with carpets and textiles, an invitation to search for the partially obscured passageway that leads through to the **Criée Berbère** (Berber Auction). These days this partially roofed, slightly gloomy section of the souk is the lair of the rug merchants, but until well into the 20th century it was used for the sale of slaves, auctioned here three times weekly. According to North African historian Barnaby Rogerson, the going rate was two slaves for a camel, ten for a horse and 40 for a civet cat.

Back on rue Semarine, just north of the turning for the Rahba Kedima, the street forks: branching to the left is the **Souk El-Attarin**, straight on is the **Souk El-Kebir** (Great Souk). Between the two is a ladder of narrow, arrow-straight passages, little more than shoulder-width across and collectively known as the **Kissaria**. This is the beating heart of the souk. Stallholders here specialise in cotton, clothing, kaftans and blankets.

Further along the Souk El-Kebir are the courtyards of carpenters and wood turners, before a T-junction forces a choice: left or right. Go left and then immediately right at the Meditel shop to emerge once again into streets that are wide enough for the passage of cars.

Just north is the dusty open plaza of the place Ben Youssef, dominated by the **Ben Youssef Mosque**, which is easily identifiable by its

The Souks

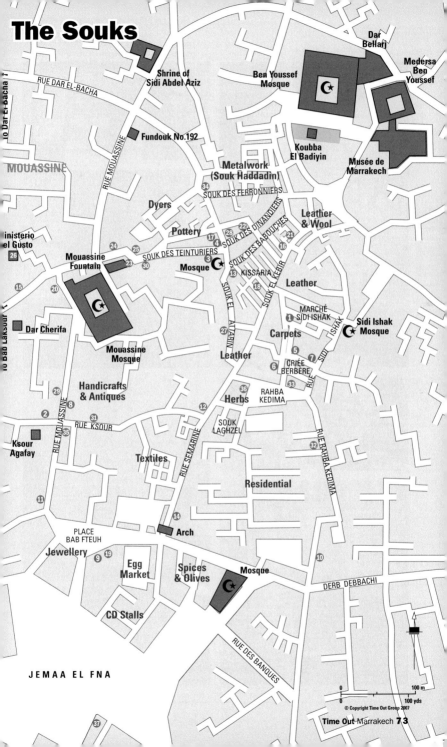

TO DAR EL-BACHA
RUE DAR EL-BACHA

Dar Bellaj

Shrine of Sidi Abdel Aziz

Ben Youssef Mosque

Medersa Ben Youssef

RUE MOUASSINE

Fundouk No.192

Koubba El Badiyin

MOUASSINE

Metalwork (Souk Haddadin)

Musée de Marrakech

SOUK DES FERRONNIERS

Dyers

SOUK DES DINANDIERS

Leather & Wool

Pottery

inisterio el Gusto

26

24

25

SOUK DES TEINTURIERS

17 28 22

4

SOUK DES BABOUCHES

21

16

Mouassine Fountain

23   30

3

Mosque

13 KISSARIA

SOUK EL KEBIR

Leather

15

20

Dar Cherifa

18

MARCHÉ SIDI ISHAK

1

Carpets

Sidi Ishak Mosque

SOUK EL ATTARIN

27

Leather

5

7

SOUK SIDI ISHAK

Mouassine Mosque

6 CRIÉE BERBÈRE

Handicrafts & Antiques

29

8

36

Herbs

RAHBA KEDIMA

33

2

35

31

RUE KSOUR

12

SOUK LAGHZEL

Ksour Agafay

RUE MOUASSINE

Textiles

RUE SEMARINE

RUE RAHBA KEDIMA

32

11

Residential

14 Arch

PLACE BAB FTEUH

Jewellery

9 19

Egg Market

Spices & Olives

Mosque

10

DERB DEBBACHI

CD Stalls

RUE DES BANQUES

37

JEMAA EL FNA

0   100 m
0   100 yds

© Copyright Time Out Group 2007

Whatever you want: a small selection of what's for sale in the souks.

bright-green pyramidal roofs. The original mosque went up in the 12th century and was the grandest of the age, but what stands now is a third and lesser incarnation, dating from the early 19th century. Non-Muslims may not enter. However, in the immediate vicinity of the mosque is a cluster of tourist-friendly sights, including the decidedly average **Musée de Marrakech** (*see p77*), the enchanting **Ben Youssef Medersa** (*see below*) and the venerable **Koubba El Badiyin** (*see p77*).

DYERS' QUARTER

Back at the fork on rue Semarine, bearing left brings you on to **Souk El Attarin**, or the Spice Souk. Contrary to the name, this part of the souk no longer deals in spices. Instead its traders largely traffic in tourist tat, from painted wooden thingamies to leather whatjamacallits. Almost opposite the subdued entrance to a workaday mosque is the **Souk des Babouches**, a whole alley devoted to soft-leather slippers – and their almost identical synthetic counterparts.

Further along Attarin, ringing hammer blows announce the **Souk Haddadin**, the quarter of the ironworkers. One of the most medieval parts of the souk, it's full of dark, cavern-like workshops in which firework bursts of orange sparks briefly illuminate tableaux of grime-streaked craftsmen, like some scene by Doré.

West of Attarin three alleys run downhill into the **Souk des Teinturiers**, which is the area of the dyers' workshops. Labourers rub dyes into cured hides (to be cut and fashioned into *babouches*) and dunk wool into vats of dark-hued liquids. This results in brightly coloured sheafs of wool which are then hung over the alleyways in a manner irresistible to passing photographers. It also results in the labourers having arms coloured to their elbows. You know you're nearing this part of the souk when you start seeing people with blue or purple arms.

The three alleys converge into one, which then doglegs between a squeeze of assorted artisans' salesrooms (lanterns, metalwork and pottery) before exiting under an arch beside the Mouassine fountain and mosque (*see p78*).

Musée Lucien Viola

17 rue Sidi Ishak.
North of Place Rahba Kedima near the leather and carpets sections of the souks, this new museum is due to open at the end of 2007. Lucien Viola also owns the Galerie Rê (*see p150*) and promises to have a big collection of ancient Moroccan art, Berber textiles and even large carved wooden doors from Berber palaces of the Atlas. The museum will be on

Dyers' quarter.

three floors, have one permanent exhibition and some temporary ones. There will also be a coffee shop and gift shop. Sounds promising.

Ben Youssef Medersa

Place Ben Youssef (024 39 09 11). **Open** 9am-6.30pm daily. **Admission** 30dh. **No credit cards**. **Map** p73 & p251 D4.
A *medersa* is a Quranic school, dedicated to the teaching of Islamic scripture and law. This one was founded in the 14th century, then enlarged in 1564-5 by the Saadian sultan Abdellah El-Ghalib. It was given a further polishing up in the 1990s courtesy of the Ministry of Culture. Entrance is via a long, cool passageway leading to the great courtyard, a serene place centred on a water-filled basin. The surrounding façades are decorated with *zelije* tiling, stucco and carved cedar, all executed with restraint. At the far side is the domed prayer hall with the richest of decoration, notably around the mihrab, the arched niche that indicates the direction of Mecca. Back in the entrance vestibule, passageways and two flights of stairs lead to more than 100 tiny windowless students' chambers, clustered about small internal lightwells. Medieval as it seems, the *medersa* was still in use until as recently as 1962. The building stood in for an Algerian Sufic retreat in Gillies Mackinnon's 1998 film *Hideous Kinky*.

On foot Souk safari

Allow at least two hours.

From Jemaa El Fna, head off into the entrance of the souks opposite the **Café de France** and walk north between the spice and the egg market. Make your way through an arch that leads into the main spine of the souks – **rue Semarine**. This main street is straight and easy to follow. It passes stalls selling textiles, herbs and leather.

Rue Semarine eventually transforms itself into **Souk El-Kebir**. When wafts of varnish and wood shavings enter your nostrils you know that you have reached the furniture-making section and are at the end of the souks. Go left at the T-junction then immediately right and you should come onto a main road. The open square of the Place Ben Youssef is just ahead of you. Look for signs for the **Musée de Marrakech** (*see p77*). At the entrance to the museum is a pleasant café with parasols – a good place to have a mint tea and put your feet up.

The Museum of Marrakech has refreshingly cool rooms with evocative sepia ethnographic prints of Morocco as far back as the 1880s and a spacious main courtyard with what must be the biggest chandelier ever made.

Coming out of the museum you should see the **Medersa Ben Youssef** (*see p75*) on your right and the **Koubba** (*see p77*) on your left. The Medersa's elaborate wall carvings and beautiful proportions are striking. The Koubba is also worth seeing if only to gaze up from underneath its dome.

As you come out of the Koubba, take a left and walk away from the museum with the **Ben Youssef Mosque** on your right. Take the second left into the leather stalls (notice the 'Clinique du Ballon' which sells and repairs ancient rugby and soccer balls); walk through the **Souk des Babouches** and then turn right under an arch into **Souk Haddadin**.

You should come to a little mosque on your left. You then go through another arch and emerge into the open. Here you need to turn left into the **Souk des Teinturiers**. The street bends right and then left past the big mosque – the 16th-century **Mouassine Mosque** – this should be on your left. You then walk left at the Café Bougainvillea and keep going straight along the pleasant **rue Mouassine**. Walk past the baths and another little mosque on the right. You should see the attractive Café Les Delices de Ma Cousine on your right (a good place to take another break).

After passing yet another small mosque on your left, you should eventually come out of the souks under an archway and on to the triangular **Place Bab Fteuh**. Take the right fork here and you will find yourself on the northwestern corner of **Jemaa El Fna**.

Keep hugging the streets on the right and proceed down rue Koutoubia, packed with stalls of spices and dates. Walk past the Hôtel Les Jardins de la Koutoubia on your right and the slightly unsightly rear end of the Club Med on your left until you emerge in front of the stunning **Koutoubia Mosque**.

You can then turn back towards the Jemaa El Fna with the Place de Foucauld on your right. Viscomte Charles de Foucauld was an eccentric French aristocrat who toured Morocco at the end of the 19th century disguised as a rabbi and who later became a hermit in the Sahara. His bizarre life is described in *The Sword and the Cross* by Fergus Fleming.

By the time you have walked past the place de Foucauld and the rather smelly *calèches* on your right, you are back at the Jemaa El Fna again, and definitely deserve a drink.

Dar Bellarj
9 rue Toulat Zaouiat Lahdar (024 44 45 55).
Open 9am-6pm daily. **Admission** 15dh. **No
credit cards. Map** p73 & p251 D4.
North of the entrance to the Ben Youssef Medersa is
a large wooden door in the crook of the alley embla-
zoned with a bird's head: this is Dar Bellarj, the
'Stork's House', so called because it was formerly a
hospital for the big white birds. The stork is holy to
Marrakech. There are countless tales to explain its
exalted status, and the impression it gives of prayer-
like prostration when at rest. The most commonly
repeated is of a local imam, dressed in traditional
Moroccan garb of white *djellaba* and black robe,
drunk on wine, who then compounds the sin by
climbing the minaret and blaspheming. Shazam!
Man suffers wrath of God and is transformed into a
stork. Even before the arrival of Islam, an old Berber
belief held that storks are actually transformed
humans. To this day the offence of disturbing a
stork carries a three-month prison sentence.

Restored in the 1990s, Dar Bellarj now serves as a
local cultural centre hosting exhibitions, workshops
and performances. Unless you're lucky enough to
drop in on a happening there's little to see; the courtyard is attractive with seating and caged songbirds,
and sweet tea is offered to visitors, but you may
wonder exactly what it was you paid admission for.
And despite the posted opening hours, the big door
is sometimes firmly locked.

Koubba El-Badiyin
place Ben Youssef (024 39 09 11). **Open** *Apr-Sept*
9am-7pm daily. *Oct-Mar* 9am-6pm daily **Admission**
10dh. **Map** p73 & p251 C4.
Across from the Ben Youssef Mosque, set in its own
fenced enclosure and sunk several metres below the
current street level, is the Koubba El-Badiyin (also
known as the 'Koubba Almoravide'). It looks unprepossessing but its unearthing in 1948 prompted one
French art historian to exclaim that 'the art of Islam
has never exceeded the splendour of this extraordinary dome'. It's the only surviving structure from
the era of the Almoravids, the founders of
Marrakech, and as such it represents a wormhole
back to the origins of Moorish building history, presenting for the first time many of the shapes and
forms that remain the basis of the North African
architectural vocabulary. It dates to the reign of Ali
Ben Youssef (1107-43) and was probably part of the
ablutions complex of the original Ben Youssef
Mosque. It's worth paying the slight admission fee
to descend the brickwork steps and view the under-
side of the dome, which is a kaleidoscopic arrangement of a floral motif within an octagon within an
eight-pointed star.

Musée de Marrakech
*place Ben Youssef (024 39 09 11/www.museede
marrakech.ma).* **Open** 9am-6.30pm daily.
Admission 40dh. (60 dh for Museum, Koubba
and Medersa Ben Yousef). **No credit cards.
Map** p73 & p251 D4.

Inaugurated in 1997, the Musée de Marrakech is a
conversion of an opulent early 20th-century house
formerly belonging to a Marrakchi grandee.
Entering the outer courtyard, there's a pleasant café
off to one side and a crap bookshop opposite. Within
the museum exhibits rotate. We were impressed by
the collection of old sepia photographs of the city
from the early 1900s (Jemaa El Fna looked almost
as manic as it is today) and the ethnographic records
of Morocco's different peoples. But the star attraction is the building itself, particularly the tartishly
tiled great central court, roofed over and hung with
an enormous chandelier like the mothership from
Close Encounters of the Third Kind. The former
hammam is lovely and makes a fine exhibition space
for the prints and photos on show. If nothing else,
the museum is a cool refuge from the blazing heat.
Even the toilets are pleasant and clean. The three-
monument ticket for 60dh is good value but it normally specifies (rather pedantically) the order you
must visit the sights, and it's valid for one day only.

Mouassine

Although it's far from immediately apparent,
Mouassine is rapidly becoming the most
chic of Medina quarters. West of the main
souk area and north of Jemaa El Fna, it's
home to a growing number of smart boutiques,
interesting galleries and hip *maisons d'hôtes.*

Dar Cherifa.

Immediately on entering rue Mouassine from place Bab Fteuh is Beldi (*see p127*), a must-stop shop for the likes of Jean Paul Gaultier and sundry international fashion types. West of the junction with rue Ksour three elaborate brass lanterns above the alleyway mark the doorway of **Ksour Agafay**, Marrakech's own private members' club. If you ring the bell it's possible that staff might allow you in to look around – it's a well-restored 19th-century house with, unusually, the courtyard up on the first floor.

At the point where the street widens to embrace the walls of the **Mouassine Mosque** (which lends its name to the quarter and was erected in the 1560s by Saadian sultan Abdellah El Ghalib), a side street off to the west winds left then first right to reach a large wooden doorway with a signplate reading **Dar Cherifa**. Inside is a stunning late 16th-century riad with filigree stucco and beautiful carved cedar detailing. It operates as a gallery (*see p149*) and performance space, doubling as a café during the day.

Where rue Mouassine hits rue Sidi El-Yamami, a dim little archway under a sign

reading '*A la Fibule*' jogs left and right to the fantastical façade of the **Ministerio del Gusto** (*see p150*), an extraordinary gallery-cum-sales space executed in an architectural style that co-creator Alessandra Lippini describes as 'delirium'.

Following rue Sidi El-Yamami west leads to the city gate **Bab Laksour**, in the vicinity of which are the boutiques Kulchi (*see p127*) and Kifkif (*see p130*) and the Moroccan restaurants Ksar Es Saoussan (*see p98*) and Tobsil (*see p101*). In the opposite direction, a few paces east along Sidi El-Yamami is the **Mouassine fountain** with quadruple drinking bays, three for animals and one – the most ornate – for people. It's here that the character Louis Bernard is fatally stabbed in Hitchcock's 1955 version of *The Man Who Knew Too Much* – although not so fatally that he can't first stagger half a mile to Jemaa El Fna to expire in the arms of Jimmy Stewart.

Beside the fountain is an arched gateway beyond which is the **Souk des Teinturiers** (*see p75*). A couple of rooms within the gateway, above the arch, are now part of a boutique called Atelier Moro (114 place de Mouassine) run by Viviana Gonzalez of Riad El Fenn. It's a good place for buying funky decorative items, clothes, glass and bead work.

Further up the street are a couple of good examples of *fundouks*. A *fundouk* – in Marrakech – is the distant forerunner of the modern hotel. It was a merchant hostel, built to provide accommodation and warehousing for the caravan traders who had crossed the desert and mountains to the south to bring their wares into the marketplaces of Marrakech. A *fundouk* offered stabling and storage rooms on the ground floor, bedrooms off the upper galleries, and a single gated entrance to the street that was locked at night for security. Most of the city's surviving *fundouks* now operate as ramshackle artisans' workshops, such as the one at No.192 rue Mouassine. This *fundouk* also featured in the film *Hideous Kinky* as the hotel where Kate Winslet and daughters lodged. Up on the first floor, the 'room' numbers painted by the film production crew remain – Winslet's was No.38, the only one with a bright new door. Another grand *fundouk* across the street is thought to be the oldest surviving example of this building type in Marrakech.

SAINTS AND SHRINES

A few steps north of the *fundouks* is a cross-roads: go left for the Dar El-Bacha and Bab Doukkala (*see p80*) or right for the dyers' quarter (*see p75*), but only adherents of Islam should proceed straight ahead, according to a sign that reads 'Non Moslem interdit'.

Up this particular alley is the **Shrine of Sidi Abdel-Aziz**, resting place of one of the seven saints of Marrakech. Collectively known as 'El-Sebti', this group of holy men have been venerated for centuries as guardians of the city. Each has a nice new shrine erected by Sultan Moulay Ismail in the 18th century. All the shrines are within, or just outside, the walls of the Medina and once a year they are the focus of a seven-day *moussem* (pilgrimage).

Sidi Abdel-Aziz's shrine can be skirted, zigging east then north, then east and north again on to rue Bab Taghzout, which runs north to the renowned saintly resting place, the **Shrine of Sidi Bel Abbas**. En route is the stately Chrob ou Chouf – 'Drink and Look' – a monumental 18th-century fountain.

Soon after widening to accommodate a local bus stop and scrubby park, the street narrows again to squeeze through the ornate gateway known as **Bab Taghzout**, with its six-inch

thick wooden doors. This was one of the original Medina gates until the walls were extended in the 18th century to bring the shrine within the city.

Through the gateway and a few steps to the right is an even more elaborate arched gateway, executed in carved alabaster. Beyond is an arcade that was once lined with herbalists, faith healers and quack doctors here to minister to/prey on the sick and the ailing drawn to the tomb to bask in its saintly *baraka* (blessings). Such beliefs remain strong and the courtyard of the shrine – adorned with Marrakech's only sundial – is always filled with the crippled and infirm. If things don't work out, a shaded arcade on the south side harbours a decrepit gathering of largely blind characters, all of whom belong to a special sect of priesthood specialising in the ministering of last rites. The sanctuary itself is off limits; instead depart the courtyard on the western side where a large

The exorcist

Abdelhamid Oulhiad wears a grey wool rollneck, canvas khakis and a black donkey jacket. He looks every inch the young (late thirtyish), stylish modern Moroccan. It's only when he removes his shades to display nervously darting, red-rimmed eyes that a note of the other-worldly creeps in. Abdelhamid battles *jinn*.

Created from fire, the *jinn* are souls without bodies and a tendency towards malice. Belief in these troublesome spirits is widespread throughout Morocco, even in the most urbane of social circles. On the occasion of a death in the house, a run of bad luck, uncharacteristically antisocial behaviour or inexplicable illness in a loved one, worried parties seek out Abdelhamid. Practitioners like him can often succeed where more conventional methods fail. He tells of a case where a woman was inexplicably paralysed following the death of her husband. The doctors couldn't understand it until an exorcist discovered she was being held captive for sex by the spirit of her recently deceased partner. A cure was effected. Honest.

The worst of the *jinn* is one-eyed Aicha Kandicha, a female spirit with a donkey's tail who plagues men. But the types and varieties are legion, with one set that operates exclusively by day and a whole other army that appears only by night.

To do battle, Abdelhamid relies on the Koran and a complex hand-drawn reference chart that takes into account numerology and astrology to indicate which are the best days to fight and when it's expedient to lie low. There are also myriad incenses and compounds required in different measures for each and every situation.

Herbalist Abdeljabbar Ait Chaib on the Rahba Kedima at the heart of the Medina stocks most ingredients, from jars of leeches to dried chameleons, good for warding off the evil eye: toss it into a small wood-fired oven and walk around it three times. If the chameleon explodes, it's bye-bye evil eye. But if the chameleon melts, you're still in trouble.

And the little black scorpions? Nothing to do with black magic – they're good against haemorrhoids, apparently.

Mosques, muezzins, mourchidat

Marrakech has more than five hundred mosques. Indeed, a Marrakchi saying has it that 'at every step there is a mosque'. Since Muslims are instructed to pray five times a day there are five calls to prayer (*adan*) to remind the faithful. The basic call consists of the repetition of the phrases 'God is great' and 'Come to pray'. With *el-fajr* – the dawn prayer – comes the addition 'It is better to wake and pray than to sleep'. A sentiment you may not share when roused from sleep at 5am.

A muezzin can be a fully trained imam but doesn't have to be – the most important qualification for the job is that he has a good voice. Marrakech doesn't have recorded calls to prayer; in this city you get a real person every time, reciting from the minaret of his mosque.

Friday (*el-jomaa*) is the day of rest, and of prayer. Noon prayers on that day are the best attended of the week – be prepared for the muezzin to chant for up to 40 minutes beforehand. Friday prayers feature sermons from the mosque's imam. As part of its ongoing battle with Islamic radicalism, the state attempts to exert control over their content, with subjects supplied by the Ministry of Islamic Affairs.

In 2006 Morocco made history by creating the first female religious guides or *mourchidat* – again as part of the state's efforts to promote a liberal interpretation of Islam. Playing the government at its own game, some women members of the Islamist Justice and Charity Party attempted to become *mourchidat*, a cause of some embarrassment in government circles. The role of the *mourchida* includes conducting religious discussions, advising other women and working in the community. However they cannot actually lead prayers.

---

open plaza affords a photogenic view of the shrine's pyramidal green roofs.

Returning back through Bab Taghzout, a right turn leads down to the **Shrine of Sidi Ben Slimane El-Jazuli**, another of the patron saints of Marrakech. Active in the 15th century, he was an important Sufi mystic and his *Manifest Proofs of Piety* remains a seminal mystical text.

Dar El-Bacha

West of the Mouassine quarter and the city's holy shrines is the high-walled former residence of the most unsaintly Thami El-Glaoui, self-styled 'Lord of the Atlas' and ruler of Marrakech and southern Morocco throughout much of the first half of the 20th century; *see p12-23*. Known locally as **Dar El-Bacha** ('House of the Lord'), and also as Dar El-Glaoui, the residence is where the Glaoui entertained luminaries such as Churchill and Roosevelt, as well as the women his agents collected for him, scouring the streets for suitable prizes.

The complex dates from the early 20th century and is disappointingly dull to visit given its lurid past. Visitors pass through several mundane administrative chambers (the complex now belongs to the Ministry of Culture) into a large courtyard, overwrought with carved plaster and woodwork, and excessive tiling. A passage snakes through to a second courtyard, which once served as the Glaoui's harem. The decor is similarly ornate, with particularly ornate details around the column capitals. At the time of writing Dar El-Bacha is closed to visitors; dates for reopening have been repeatedly postponed.

Facing the side wall of the Dar El-Bacha is another property with pedigree – owned previously by the chamberlain of the Glaoui, later by French couturier Pierre Balmain ('dressmaking is the architecture of movement') and now the premises of Dar Moha (*see p97*), one of the finest restaurants in Marrakech.

Bab Doukkala

From Dar El-Bacha, rue Bab Doukkala runs due west for half a mile to the gate of the same name. At Nos.142-144 is Mustapha Blaoui (*see p132*), venue for some of the best shopping in the Medina.

The major monument round here is the **Bab Doukkala Mosque**, built in 1558 by the mother of the Saadian sultans Abdel-Malek and Ahmed El-Mansour. It's fronted by the Sidi El-Hassan fountain, now dry, fenced around and used as an occasional exhibition space. Across from the fountain, a small whitewashed building houses a 400-year-old hammam (men only) with a fantastic cedarwood ceiling in the reception area. Behind the fountain a faint hand-painted 'WC' signposts the city's oldest toilets, built at the same time as the Doukkala Mosque opposite. They're still in use.

The westernmost stretch of rue Bab Doukkala is the domain of the butchers and it verges on the macabre, with prominent displays of decapitated heads and mounds of glistening offal. Note that all the hanging bits of carcass display testicles: Moroccans don't eat female meat so butchers are mindful to prove the masculine provenance of their produce. The massive Almoravid gate of Bab Doukkala is now bypassed by a modern road that breaches the city walls. There's a petit taxi rank at the foot of the gatehouse.

The tanneries

To experience Marrakech at its most raw, not to mention most pungent, take a taxi to the place du Moqf and walk east along rue de Bab Debbagh to the tannery district. The tanners have been here since the city was founded and legend has it that they are descended from demons who lived under a black king. He condemned them to their vocation for failing to obey his rules. Some workers still believe that the tanneries are inhabited by *jinns* or spirits.

The tanners use hundreds of concrete vats to process the skins that are bought at the city's

markets. The treatment of the skins remains a pre-industrial process. First, hair and traces of flesh are removed. To do this the skins are soaked in vats of quicklime and water to bring the skins 'back to life'. They are then washed and pressed in other vats. After that the skins are placed in a vat of water and blood, which strengthens them. They are believed by some to gain a male and a female soul during the tanning process, which leads to their 'rebirth'. One of the workers separates and wrings the skins, which are suspended over one of the vats. In order to dye the skins, they are rubbed with pomegranate powder to colour them yellow. Olive oil is then used to make them shiny. Other traditional products, such as bark, saffron, henna and poppy are also used to dye the skins. The vats used to dye the skins are kept covered to prevent the sunlight from affecting the process. Stretched-out skins are then left to dry in the sun beside the tanneries. This whole complex process takes 20 days.

Many of the workers and their families live around the tanneries. The tanners were traditionally considered as being on the edges of society. Their skills are passed on through the male line. Apprentices are not allowed to perform some of the more difficult tasks, which are reserved for the master craftsmen. The work makes tanners prone to arthritis, and they often have to retire in their 40s, at which point their sons are inducted into the family trade.

The animal hides are mostly sheep and goat although cow and camel are sometimes used for bigger items. At one time antelope hide was tanned to order, but no more, and the trade in lion skins has dwindled since the last Atlas lion was shot dead in 1912.

The tanneries can be tricky to find but some loitering youth will always approach unaccompanied foreigners and offer his services as a guide. The tanneries fill large yards and, with rows of lozenge-shaped pools of various hues, look like giant paintboxes. However, closer up the bubbling pits are more like cesspools of floating, bubbling crud; the hides piled up beside look like rancid tripe. Pity the poor labourers who wade in the noxious fluids ladling the skins from one pit to another. Guides sometimes hand out sprigs of mint to hold under your nose to block out the reek of pigeon shit (used to soften the hides).

The results of the process can be seen and purchased at the leather shops near the gate, but you may prefer to get the hell out of the quarter and purge yourself in the nearest hammam. Taxis can be caught outside the Bab Debbagh (where a stair inside gives access to the roof of the gatehouse) on the route des Ramparts ringroad.

The tanneries.

The Kasbah & Mellah

Museums, palaces, tombs and the city's old Jewish quarter.

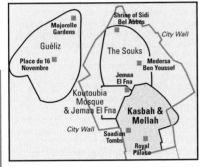

Almost since the founding of Marrakech, the area south of Jemaa El Fna has been the domain of sultans and their retinues. Today it houses the museum-palaces of the city. The present Royal Palace is built on the site of the earliest Almohad palaces and covers a vast area, equivalent to a whole residential quarter. Morocco's new king, Mohammed VI, a little more modest in his requirements, has had a much smaller residence built nearby. Neither of these two modern-day royal precincts is open to the public, but visitors are allowed to explore two 19th-century viziers' palaces, the Bahia and the Dar Si Said, as well as the impressive ruins of the Badii Palace. Also in the area is the Mellah, historically Marrakech's Jewish quarter.

Saadian Tombs

The pedestrianised **rue Bab Agnaou**, which runs south-west off Jemaa El Fna, is a honey pot for budget tourists, with banks, ATMs, moneychangers, téléboutiques, internet centres and numerous dodgy eateries. At the far end is the **Grand Tazi** (see p55), famed for decades as a roost for impecunious travellers and one of the few places in the Medina where it's possible to get a beer. South of the Tazi the street runs in the shadow of high walls: these are not the city walls, but a wall that formerly sectioned off the royal Kasbah (palace precincts) from the rest of the Medina.

The traditional entrance to the Kasbah is via the gorgeous **Bab Agnaou** (Gate of the Gnawa), named after the black slaves brought from sub-Saharan Africa. The gate was built on the orders of the Almohad sultan Yacoub

El-Mansour in 1185. It's one of the very few stone structures in this otherwise mudbrick city, and has weathered in such a way that the aged limestone now resembles heavily grained wood.

Across the street from Bab Agnaou is the original southern gate to the Medina, the **Bab Er Rob**, now filled by a pottery shop and bypassed by traffic, which exits through a modern breach in the walls.

A short distance inside the Agnaou gate is the **Kasbah Mosque**, constructed in 1190, again during the reign of Sultan Yacoub El-Mansour (hence its alternative name of El-Mansour Mosque). It has been renovated on numerous occasions since (most recently during the reign of Hassan II, father of the current king), but the cut-brick-and-green-tile decoration on the minaret is original. The plaza in front is usually busy with guide-led tourist groups. They're not here for the mosque, which, of course, they're forbidden to enter, but for what lies hidden in the lee of its southern wall: the **Saadian Tombs**.

In the early 1920s the French authorities noticed two green-tiled roofs rising above the shanty quarters. Inquiries made of the locals were met with evasive answers. The persistence of one curious official was eventually rewarded when he discovered a narrow, dark lane, wide enough for a single person, that ended in a tiny arched door. He pushed through to enter a courtyard garden and saw what apparently no infidel had ever seen before – the holy tombs of the Saadian sultans. According to the account in a 1928 travelogue, *The Magic of Morocco*, the Frenchman was then accosted by a wizened guardian who said, 'You have discovered our secret, but beware what you do with the knowledge. You cannot make it a mere show for your people to come and gaze at'. Well, tough luck, pal, because that's exactly what has happened: the tombs are possibly the most visited site in Marrakech.

Entrance is via that same constricted passage first 'discovered' 80 years ago and it gives access to an ancient walled garden, the use of which far predates the time of the Saadians. There are a great many early mosaic graves dotted around the shrubbery; the identity of those interned is long lost. Attention instead focuses on the three pavilions constructed during the reign of Saadian sultan Ahmed El-Mansour. Despite drawing so many visitors, it's far from spectacular, and the setting is so modest that it reminds one of an English parish churchyard.

First on the left is the Prayer Hall, which was not intended as a mausoleum but nevertheless holds numerous graves, mainly of Alaouite princes from the 18th century. Their resting places are marked by what look like marble offcuts from a mason's yard. Next to it is the Hall of Twelve Columns, a far more ornate affair with three central tombs surrounded by a dozen marble pillars. The tomb in the middle is that of Ahmed El-Mansour, flanked by those of his son and grandson. A third, stand-alone pavilion has ornate Andalucian-style entrance portals.

Exiting the tombs, a left turn on to rue de Kasbah eventually leads to the Grand Méchouar, or parade grounds of the Royal Palace, but the way is closed when the king is in town. Instead it's perhaps more interesting to duck into the warren of alleys behind the tombs, where a small square at the conjunction of four alleys hosts a morning market of fruit, vegetable, meat and fish vendors. A grander market – the **Marché Couvert** – is to the north-east of the Tombs, at the end of avenue Houmann El-Fetouaki, opposite the Badii Palace (*see below*).

Saadian Tombs

rue de Kasbah, Bab Agnaou (no phone). **Open** 8.30-11.45am, 2.30-5.45pm daily. **Admission** 10dh. **Map** p252 C8.

Badii Palace

Barely 400 metres east of the Saadian Tombs is the city's other great monument of that era, the **Badii Palace**. However, while secrecy preserved the sultans' mausoleums intact, the scale and ostentation of their triumphal residence marked it out for special attention and it survives only as a denuded ruin.

The palace was constructed during the reign of Sultan Ahmed El-Mansour (1578-1607), funded by wealth accrued through victories over the Portuguese. Walls and ceilings were encrusted with gold from Timbuktu (captured by El-Mansour in 1598), while the inner court had a massive central pool with an island, flanked by four sunken gardens filled with scented flowers and trees. At the centre of each of the four massive walls were four pavilions, also flanked by arrangements of pools and fountains. It took some 25 years for the labourers and craftsmen to complete the palace. Surveying the achievement, the sultan is said to have invited opinion from his fool and received the prophetic response that the palace 'would make a fine ruin'. And so it does. The sultan was spared that vision because barely were the inaugural celebrations over before the ageing ruler passed away. His palace remained intact for less than a century before the Merenid sultan, Moulay Ismail, had it stripped bare and the riches carted north for his new capital at Meknès.

The palace is approached via the open plaza of place des Ferblantiers and a canyon-like

The graves of 18th-century Alaouite princes in the **Saadian Tombs**.

Sightseeing

Badii Palace.

space constricted between two precipitous walls; the outer one was intended to keep the Medina at a respectful distance from the royal domains. The former main gate is collapsed and gone, and entrance is through a gaping hole in the fortifications directly into the great court. It's a vast empty space the size of a couple of football pitches, ringed around by pockmarked mudbrick walls that act as apartment blocks for pigeons and have stork nests along the battlements. The sunken areas that were once gardens still exist, as does the great dry basin that was the ornate central pool. On the west side are the ruins of the Pavilion of Fifty Columns; a small area of mosaic remains on the floor, but the colours are badly dulled by exposure to the elements.

In the south-east corner, a gate leads through to a newly reconstructed pavilion housing the **Koutoubia Mosque minbar** (20dh admission). This was the original minbar (stepped pulpit) in the city's great mosque. It was fashioned in the early 12th century by Cordoban craftsmen and the 1,000 decorative panels that adorn the sides supposedly took eight years to complete – the word 'ornate' falls somewhere short. It was removed from the mosque in the early 1960s for restoration and after a spell at the Dar Si Said Museum has ended up here. Next to the minbar pavilion are the excavated remains of troglodytic chambers and passages: a small underground labyrinth opened up for visitor exploration.

One of the palace bastions remains intact at the north-eastern corner of the great central court. Steps lead up to a rooftop terrace with fine views of the site and the surrounding quarter. You can also get up close and personal with the many nesting storks.

The palace comes back to life once a year when a giant screen is set up on the central island for the International Film Festival (*see p146*).

Badii Palace

place des Ferblantiers (no phone). **Open** 8.30-11.45am, 2.30-5.45pm daily. **Admission** 10dh; 20dh minbar pavilion. **Map** p252 C7.

The Mellah

Hugging the eastern walls of the Badii Palace are the narrow gridded alleys of the **Mellah**, the old Jewish quarter. The name translates roughly as 'Place of Salt', a reference either to the Jews' historic monopoly on the trade in mineral salts from the Atlas Mountains, or to their landing the job of salting the heads of decapitees before they were hoisted on spikes. Although the number of Jews in Marrakech is now negligible, evidence of Jewish heritage is abundant to anyone who knows where to look (*see p87* **Exodus**). Several houses in the neighbourhood have external balconies, which was peculiar to Morocco's Jewish population. Some have Hebrew letters on the metal grills above the doors and there's even an occasional Star of David.

Across the road from the Rose Garden, a green-painted arch leads through into the **Bab Es Salam Market**, also known to locals as the Jewish market. Following this south and east, past stalls of gaudy beaded necklaces (made in Hong Kong), bright pyramids of spices (the tallest of them are actually clever cardboard fakes), and windows of the lurid sweets known as Pâte Levy, leads deep into the Mellah. The streets here are some of the narrowest and poorest in

On foot Museums, palaces and tombs

Allow at least two hours.

Begin on the east side of Jemaa El Fna. Turn so that you can see the Café des Glaciers on your right and a small mosque on the left. Walk under an arch and head down the colourful rue **Riad Zitoun El-Kedim**. Pass Riad Jnane Mogador on your right and an alleyway that leads to Casa Lalla on your left. A pleasant place for a tea break is Dar Mimoun Salon de Thé on the left.

After this, walk under an arch and take a left; there should be a signpost for the Musée Dar Si Said. You will pass several shops selling traditional remedies. Turn left at the T-junction on to rue **Riad Zitoun El-Jedid**, passing a small mosque on the corner. Then almost immediately, take a sharp right under a small arch, then a right down Derb Si Said. This narrow street bends left and then right, taking you past the **Dar Si Said Museum** (*see p88*).

After the museum, walk straight ahead past some carpet shops and then take a right at the T-junction. Twenty metres further is the

entrance to the fascinating **Maison Tiskiwin** (*see p88*) – definitely worth a look inside.

Leaving the museum, walk under an arch that will bring you back on to rue Riad Zitoun El-Kedim and a pleasant little square. Go left past the Hammam Ziani and head towards the **Palais de Bahia** (*see p88*) whose courtyards and orange groves provide a welcome respite from the heat and dust.

For a short detour into the alleyways of old Jewish quarter, the **Mellah** (*see p84*), you can take an immediate left at the Palais de Bahia exit. Otherwise from the Palais de Bahia grounds you head into a square opposite and continue to walk in the direction of the Palais El-Badii. Notice the storks nesting on the old walls – they have lost their migratory instincts and stay in Marrakech all year round.

Very shortly afterwards you arrive in the place des Ferblantiers. Carry on through the **Bab Berrima** (Berrima Gate) to the **Palais El-Badii** (*see p83*). If you need a rest at this point, the **Kosybar** (*see p103*), on your left just before the gate, has a restaurant and roof terrace. When you re-emerge through Bab Berrima, turn left into another square and an open section of road with taxi ranks.

Keep left at this point, with the **Marché Couvert** on your right. Continue for about two hundred metres until the road kinks slightly to the left. This brings you to on to a long straight stretch of road with cafes on your left. Keep going for another five hundred metres or so, until you reach the end. Then turn left under an archway and walk for about a hundred metres towards some more arches. Turn left opposite Les Bains de Marrakech and walk for another hundred yards towards a large mosque. Follow the walls around to the entrance of the **Saadian Tombs** (*see p82*).

On exiting, retrace your steps, this time going through the double arches of **Bab Agnaou**. Turn right back on to **rue Oqba Ben Nafia**. Notice the walls of one of the king's many palaces on your left. Where the road forks, keep to the right, remaining on rue Oqba Ben Nafia. This turns into rue Bab Agnaou, and is the most direct route back to Jemaa El Fna, and will take about 10 minutes.

Life in the Mellah: **Bab Es Salam market**. *See p84.*

the Medina and in places crude scaffolding keeps the houses from collapsing.

At the heart of the quarter is a small square, **place Souweka**, now disfigured by a badly sited concrete building. At No.36 along the street that runs north just beyond the square is one of the Medina's three last working synagogues (once there were 29). It occupies a large hall off the open courtyard of a well-maintained community centre. Judging by the plentiful supply of new prayer books and other contemporary trappings, the synagogue is kept alive by remittances from Marrakchi Jews abroad, but the advanced age of the congregation suggests that money alone won't be enough to keep this community going.

On the very eastern edge of the Mellah is the extensive Miâara Jewish cemetery; the sheer number of modestly marked graves (tens of thousands) is probably the best remaining testament to the one-time importance of Jewish life in Marrakech.

Bahia Palace

On the northern edge of the Mellah is the **Bahia Palace**. If you've read Gavin Maxwell's *Lords of the Atlas* this place will mean much more to you but even if you haven't, its shady courtyards and blue mosaic walls make a pleasant break from the hot bustling streets outside. The palace was built principally by Bou Ahmed, a powerful vizier to the royal court in the 1890s and a man of 'no particular intelligence, but of indomitable will, and cruel' (*Morocco That Was*, Walter Harris; 1921). Entered via a long garden corridor, it's a delightful collection of paved courtyards, arcades, pavilions and reception halls with vaulted ceilings. The walls are decorated in traditional Moroccan zelije tiling, with sculpted stucco and carved cedarwood doors. The fireplace on your left as you enter is quite impressive too. The palace includes

Exodus

Talk about population shifts: according to the Paris-based Alliance Israélite Universelle, in 1905 there were 15,700 Jews living in Marrakech; best guess for a current total is 260, according to the keeper of one of three surviving synagogues.

Jews have been present in Morocco since Phoenician times. Later, protected by the walls and gates of their own quarter, and by the express patronage of the sultans (who valued their abilities in trade, linguistics and crafts), the Jews flourished as middlemen between visiting Christian merchants and local Muslims. Many of the latter viewed them with mistrust, especially in times of strife, but that didn't prevent the community from growing. However, from the end of the 19th century the pull of Zionism and the struggle for a homeland in Palestine (culminating in the creation of Israel in 1948) triggered mass emigration. King Mohammed V (who during World War II had resisted implementing the Vichy regime's anti-Semitic decrees) passed laws to prevent a mass exodus, fearing adverse effects on the economy. But Mossad, the Israeli secret service, smuggled out 18,000 Jews between 1958 and 1961. Arab-Israeli conflicts in 1956, '67 and '73 engendered such bad blood that even non-Zionists felt it expedient to relocate. Jews with money went to Canada, France and Israel. For many who arrived in the latter it was out of the frying pan and into the firing line –

they were settled on the northern border with Lebanon to absorb mortar and missile attacks. Those less well off sought refuge in the more cosmopolitan climes of Casablanca, where the remaining Jewish community now thrives as part of the upper middle classes. The only Jews to stay in Marrakech were those too poor to move on, hence the decrepit state of the Mellah today.

Maison Tiskiwin: home to artefacts from all over the Sahara.

extensive quarters that housed Bou Ahmed's four wives and twenty-four concubines.

On Bou Ahmed's death – probably poisoned by the sultan's mother, along with his two brothers – the palace was completely looted by Sultan Abdel-Aziz. Caravans of donkeys staggering under the weight of furniture, carpets and crates made their way the short distance from the Bahia to the Royal Palace. Between then and now it served as the living quarters of the French *résident généraux* (Edith Wharton stayed here at this time, described in her *In Morocco*; 1927) and it's still occasionally used by the current royal family.

Bahia Palace

Riad Zitoun El-Jedid (024 38 92 21). **Open** 8.45-11.45am, 2.45-5.45pm Mon-Thur, Sat, Sun; 8.45-11.30am, 3-5.45pm Fri. **Admission** 10dh; 5dh children. **Map** p253 D7.

Dar Si Said Museum

Connecting the Mellah with Jemaa El Fna (a distance of just under a kilometre) is **rue Riad Zitoun El-Jedid**. The name means the 'new olive garden road' but the only olive trees in the area these days are in the modern Rose Garden at the very southern end of the street.

Also down at this end is the Préfecture de la Medina and a narrow arch giving entrance to the Derb El-Bahia and **Maison Tiskiwin**. On display in this private house owned by the veteran Dutch anthropologist Bert Flint, is his fascinating collection of crafts and decorative arts from southern Morocco and the Sahara. He has donated all of these artefacts to the University of Marrakech but you can still see them at the Tiskiwin. The exhibition is designed to show Morocco's connection to sub-Saharan Africa and is a geographically laid-out collection that takes you on a journey across the Sahara, as if you were following an old desert trade route from Marrakech to Timbuktu. Exhibits include masks from as far afield as Mali and an entire Berber tent made of camel hair. This is one of Marrakech's hidden gems.

Following a couple of twists to the north is the **Dar Si Said Museum**, the former home of the brother of Ba Ahmed, builder of the Bahia. It's home to a large collection of crafts and woodwork. Among all the kitchen implements, weapons and musical instruments are numerous beautiful examples of carved cedar, rescued from the city's lost dwellings – among them, polychromic painted doors, window shutters and fragments of ceilings. There's also one room devoted to 'rural' woodwork that includes some primitively worked and painted Berber doors. Such items are very much in vogue with collectors these days and change hands for vast amounts of cash. The exhibits here are captioned in French only.

Also in the neighbourhood is **Riad Tamsna**, a restaurant of variable quality, a gallery, boutique and bookshop. It's also a beautiful building with a gorgeous central courtyard overlooked by high galleries. To find Riad Tamsna, coming along Riad Zitoun El-Jedid look for a small, shabby pâtisserie next to an arched entrance (it's on the right if approached from Jemaa El Fna); go down the arched passage, bear right and look for the black door with a No.23.

Dar Si Said Museum

Riad Zitoun El-Jedid (024 38 95 64). **Open** 9am-12.15pm, 3-6.15pm Mon, Wed-Sun. **Admission** 20dh. **Map** p253 D6.

Maison Tiskiwin

8 Derb El-Bahia, off Riad Zitoun El-Jedid (024 38 91 92). **Open** 9.30am-12.30pm, 3.30-5.30pm daily. **Admission** 15dh; 10dh children. **Map** p253 D6.

Guéliz

The other Marrakech.

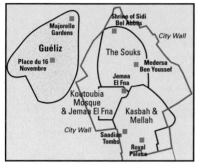

Guéliz (pronounced 'gileez') is the *nouvelle ville* or new town of Marrakech. Built during the French protectorate with some interesting modernist buildings, it is known for 1930s elegance but has recently been marred by new concrete blocks, tourist coaches and a McDonald's. Still, ladies who lunch promenade their poodles on quiet streets lined with orange trees, (fairly) respectable gents grab a beer at the Café Atlas (*see p119*), and local youths rev up their vespas on the street corners. Guéliz is where you find restaurants with airs and graces, pizza and pasta joints, and seedy bars with girls who try to catch visitors' eyes.

The rise of the riad hotel in the 1990s made the Medina the place to stay, and with an increasing number of decent restaurants there too, Guéliz has been pushed off the tourist map. But while the area is devoid of big sights, it does have a pleasant, unhurried atmosphere. This is the part of town where you can go to an art gallery, shop at fixed prices, or find a liquor store. It's a good break when everything has been getting just a little bit too Moroccan.

Things weren't always this way. Back in the 1970s it was the Medina that was run-down and few visitors ventured into the alleys away from the Jemaa El Fna. Foreigners would hang out in the Guéliz, with its broad avenues, European-style buildings, old-fashioned hotels and continental bistros. The big hangout was the rooftop bar of the Café Renaissance (now closed). The jetset dropped in on the Villa Taylor, while William Burroughs and Brion Gysin invoked demons in the Hotel Toulousain (still standing, just behind the site of the former Marché Central).

HOLY BEGINNINGS

The 'new city' came into being shortly after December 1913 – the arrival date of Henri Prost, the young city planner imported to assist in the schemes of French *résident général* Marshal Lyautey. One of Prost's early sketches shows how he took the minaret of the Koutoubia as his focal point and from it extended two lines: one north-west to the Guéliz hills; the other south-west to the pavilion of the Menara Gardens. In the pie slice between these lines (which have since become avenue Mohammed V and avenue de la Menara) is the original nucleus of the new European city.

One of the first buildings was the church, or *église* – a word that was corrupted into the name Guéliz. This wasn't the first church in Marrakech; in 1908 a French priest consecrated a house in the Medina near what is now the Dar Si Said Museum. A Christian cross fashioned into the wrought-iron grill over one of the windows survives as evidence. The priest, however, lasted nowhere near as long, murdered within two years of setting up shop.

The Guéliz *église* is now the Catholic **Church of St Anne**, barely a communion queue from the northern walls of the Medina. It is a modest affair with a bell tower very deliberately overshadowed by the taller minaret of a mosque built next door after independence.

PARKS AND AVENUES

One block over from the church is the **Jnane El Harti** park, originally laid out as a French formal garden and a zoo. In a 1939 essay titled 'Marrakech', George Orwell writes of feeding gazelles here and of not being able to look at the animals' hindquarters without thinking of mint sauce. The park was relandscaped recently and now boasts fountains, ponds and a children's play area with a big blue dinosaur.

The park's north-east corner connects with place du 16 Novembre, the hole in the middle of Guéliz's spider-web street pattern. Sadly, instead of developing as the grand *rondpoint* of Prost's vision, it has been disfigured by some plug-ugly structures, including a totalitarian central post office and two mammoth apartment blocks. Until the 1970s there were two lines of parking down the centre of the avenue, but the increase in traffic has done away with them. Shame, because standing in the middle of Mohammed V presents one of the city's best views: in one direction the Koutoubia minaret, sometimes with snowy Atlas mountains in the background; in the other a high rocky outcrop topped by the pink wall of a former French Foreign Legion fortress.

CENTRAL GUELIZ

The focal point of Guéliz used to be the Marché Central on avenue Mohammed V, and it was here that the expats and middle-class Marrakchis gathered for groceries, booze, flowers and gossip. However in a mystifying piece of town planning, it was demolished in 2005. It has been replaced by a much more sterile affair just east of the nearby place du 16 Novembre.

At the junction of avenue Mohammed V and rue de la Liberté is an elaborate colonial building with pavement arcades, art deco lines and Moorish flourishes. It dates to 1918 and is just about the oldest surviving building in Guéliz. This was the address (30 rue de la Liberté) of the city's first tourist office. A fading gallery of ancient hand-painted scenes of Morocco decorates the hallway.

The eastern stretch of rue de la Liberté is the local maid market, busy with poorly dressed women hanging around on the chance of some cleaning work. At the western end of the street, beyond the **Kechmara** bar (*see p119*) and where it meets rue de Yougoslavie, is a forgotten bit of Marrakech history: a narrow alley planted with mulberry trees and crammed with single-storey dwellings daubed in many colours (it may be the only non-pink street in Marrakech). This is the old Spanish quarter, a reminder of the city's once significant Hispanic population.

BRIGHT LIGHTS, LITTLE CITY

Towards the northern end of Mohammed V is place Abdel Moumen, which is about as close as this town gets to Piccadilly Circus. It's the hub of an area of cafés, bars, restaurants and nightclubs; it's even got neon. At **Café les Négociants** (*see p116*) grouchy uniformed waiters generate an air of efficiency while being brusquely indifferent to the customers. It's pleasing to find that almost 100 years on the ground rules laid by the French are still so lovingly adhered to. Across the intersection, the **Café Atlas** is the place for beer with added entertainments (*see p119*). North of the Atlas is the boarded-up building that was formerly the infamous Café Renaissance. From place Abdel-Moumen, it's a 20-minute walk to the **Majorelle Gardens** (*see p92*).

HIVERNAGE

South-west of place Abdel-Moumen, Guéliz peters out at the expanse of avenue Mohammed VI (formerly known, and still often referred to, as the avenue de France). Here, and to the south, is the area known as **Hivernage**. A showcase of colonial planning, it's a garden city for winter residence. On curving suburban streets, hidden in greenery, hotels sit next to modernist villas. In the shade of a well-groomed hedge, machine-gun toting soldiers indicate a royal in residence. There's an attractive little colonial-era **railway station**, which rises from its torpor a couple of times a day for the Casablanca train. A new but less charming station is under construction. The junction with avenue Hassan II is lorded over by the monumental **Royal Opera House**, designed by local star architect Charles Boccara. It's supposed to seat 1,200, but more than 14 years after it was begun the interiors have yet to be completed due to the spiralling costs. Here also sits the squat red mass of the **Palais des Congrès**, home to many an international incentive seminar. Constructed in 1989, it's a mammoth five-storey edifice used for the signing of GATT agreements in 1994. It has been mainly empty ever since, although it is used for the Marrakech Film Festival (*see p146*). Still, if you should find yourself in need of a couple of halls the size of a modest Baltic state, you know where to look.

Gardens

The desert city cherishes its green spaces.

In a hot, dusty city where the predominant colour is pink, it's a relief to contemplate water and see serene greens and blues. Some of the classic coffee-table and picture-postcard photographs of Marrakech are taken in two of the city's most famous gardens, the Menara and the Majorelle. These little urban oases – and others around the city – provide peace and calm away from the buzz of mopeds, the fumes of exhausts and the chatter of street hawkers. So should you start to feel that Marrakech is doing your head in, we recommend you escape to any of these tranquil spots.

Desert dwellers know how to manage water. When the Almoravids moved out of the Western Sahara to found Marrakech in the 11th century, they brought in water from the Ourika Valley by means of *khettaras*, long irrigation pipes made of baked mud, the remains of which can still be found in the Palmeraie on the outskirts of the city. They used the water to nurture *jnane* (market gardens) and *agdal* (walled private gardens), as well as abundant public gardens. They were eventually replaced by a system of artesian wells and reservoirs.

The **Menara Gardens**, for instance, go right back to the 12th century and the era of the Almohads, as do the royal **Agdal Gardens**. When the Saadian sultan Ahmed El-Mansour built the show-stopping Badii Palace in the late 16th century, visitors marvelled at its architecture, but more than anything they were awestruck by its multi-level gardens and 700 fountains.

Neither were gardens the preserve of royals. Wealthy merchants, judges, master craftsmen and petty officials dwelt in riads, townhouses built around courtyard gardens. These were usually designed symmetrically: four beds planted with trees, underplanted with perfumed flowers, and arranged around the all-important central fountain. The microclimate thus created provided shade, cooled the air, gave off sweet smells and encouraged songbirds.

All credit to the French, who continued the horticultural tradition under the Protectorate. In the *nouvelle ville* of Guéliz many of the boulevards are lined with jacaranda trees that bloom in electric blue each spring. Bougainvillaea and vines clothe the boundary walls of the villas and hibiscus flowers add spots of vibrant colour. Then there are the orange trees. The streets of Guéliz are lined with them. The combination of blue sky, pink walls, green leaves and orange fruit is a knockout; it's like walking through a landscape by Matisse. All this and free fruit too? But that would be just too perfect and the oranges are in fact too sour to eat or juice. Instead, the prize is the blossom, highly valued for its scent. Every year the rights to a city-wide harvest are bought up by a major international perfume company and armies of local women are sent out to lay sheets under the trees and start banging the hell out of the branches.

In recent years the municipality has embarked on a scheme to green the city even more. Large-scale planting of trees and flowers along the airport and Medina ring roads has already been completed and the ramparts are now surrounded by beds of roses, hibiscus and jasmine. The **Jnane El Harti** park (*see p89*) in Guéliz has been completely replanted and re-landscaped, as has the **Arset Abdelsalam** on the edge of the Medina.

PUBLIC GARDENS

Besides the gardens described in this chapter, there are several other public gardens within the ramparts of the Medina. Most notable is the massed greenery of the place de Foucault, between Jemaa El Fna and the Koutoubia Mosque. It's a tight triangle of great palms soaring above the surrounding buildings, with benches at their bases. In spring these gardens are full of Candidum lilies.

Over the far side of the mosque are the Koutoubia Gardens, planted heavily with roses that are seemingly permanently in flower. Roses flourish in this climate, impervious to the heat of summer. Carefully shaped topiary hedges fringe the pathways.

To the north, flanking main avenue Mohammed V, is the **Arset Abdelsalam**, an extensive area of scrubby lawns, palms and pathways that are a favourite with promenading couples and civil servants from the town hall (Hôtel de Ville) opposite enjoying an open-air afternoon siesta. The park has recently been given a 21st-century upgrade, with shopping kiosks and public internet booths sponsored by Maroc Télécom.

Agdal Gardens.

Agdal Gardens

Laid out in 1156-7 by the Almohads, the royal
Agdal Gardens are several hundred years
older than those most celebrated of Islamic
gardens at the Alhambra. They cover a vast
16 hectares (40 acres) stretching south for a
couple of kilometres from the back door of
the Royal Palace. At the centre of the Agdal
is a massive pool, the Sahraj El-Hana, so large
that the sultan's soldiers used it for swimming
practice. In 1873 Sultan Mohammed IV
drowned in it while boating with his son;
the servant who managed to swim to safety
was executed on the spot for failing to save
his lord. The rest of the area is divided into
different kinds of orchards and gardens,
including an orange grove, vineyards, areas
of pomegranates and figs, masses of walnut
trees and palm groves. There are several
ornamental pavilions, and it's possible to climb
on to the roof of one of them, the Dar El-Hana,

beside the pool, for an impressive view of
the gardens and the High Atlas beyond.
    To get to the Agdal take the path off the
south-western corner of the Méchouar Intérieur
(see map p253 D9).

Agdal Gardens
Open usually on Fri & Sun; closed if the king is
in residence at the Royal Palace. **Admission** free.
Map p253 D5/E5.

Majorelle Gardens

Now privately owned by Yves Saint Laurent
– but open to the public – the gardens were
created in the 1930s by two generations of
French artists, Jacques and Louis Majorelle.
Although small in scale and out on the edge
of the New City, the glamour of the YSL
connection ensures that the gardens are usually
packed well beyond comfort by coachloads of
visitors. The juxtaposition of colours is striking;
plants sing against a backdrop of the famous

east along boulevard Mohammed Zerktouni) or take a *petit taxi*. Note that picnics, children and dogs are not allowed; it's a shame that the prohibitions don't extend to coach parties.

Majorelle Gardens

avenue Yacoub El-Mansour, Guéliz (no phone). **Open** 8am-5.30pm daily. **Admission** 30dh; *Museum of Islamic Art* 15dh. **Map** p254 C1.

Mamounia Gardens

The world-famous Mamounia Hotel takes its name from its gardens, the Arset El-Mamoun, which predate the hotel by more than a century. They were established in the 18th century by Crown Prince Moulay Mamoun on land gifted to him by his father the sultan on the occasion of his wedding. A central pavilion served as a princely residence, occasionally lent out to visiting diplomats. Ten years after the imposition of French colonial rule in Morocco, the gardens were annexed and a 100-room hotel built on the site. Happily, the gardens remain. They're designed in a traditional style, on an axis, with walkways, flowerbeds, orange groves and olive trees and attended by 40 gardeners who, twice a year, plant 60,000 new annuals. Non-guests can visit – in the context of a buffet lunch at the poolside Trois Palmiers restaurant or afternoon tea at one of the terrace cafés. Dress smartly (no jeans or shorts) or you risk being sent packing. The Mamounia was closed for major renovations at the time of writing, due to open in late 2007 or early 2008.

Mamounia Gardens

Mamounia Hotel, avenue Bab Jedid, Medina (024 38 86 00/www.mamounia.com). **Open** no set hours; hotel closed at time of writing. **Admission** non-guests should have lunch, drink or tea at the hotel. **Map** p252 A6/7.

Menara Gardens

Coming in to land at Aéroport Marrakech Menara, alert passengers may notice a large rectangular body of water to the east. This is the basin of the gardens from which the airport takes its name. They've been there since around 750 years before man took to the air – like the Agdal, the Menara Gardens were laid out by the Almohads in the 12th century. Later they fell into neglect and their present form is a result of 19th-century restoration by the Alouites. The highly photogenic green-tile-roofed picnic pavilion that overlooks the basin was added in 1869. Climb to the upper floor for a wonderful view over the water or, better still, stroll around to the opposite side for the celebrated view of the pavilion against a backdrop of the Atlas.

Majorelle blue, offset with soft yellows and terracottas. Bamboo groves rustle in the soft breeze and great palms tower over all, sheltering huge ancient cacti. Rills lead into pools floating with water lilies and flashing with golden carp, terrapins paddle languidly and frogs croak. Great pots overflow with succulents and birds sing. For the botanically curious, everything is clearly labelled.

Jacques Majorelle's former studio has been turned into a fine little **Museum of Islamic Art**, recently renovated and reorganised to display a collection of traditional jewellery, fine embroidery, illuminated manuscripts, carved wooden doors and Majorelle lithographs of the High Atlas. Air-conditioned and dimly lit, the museum is a welcome refuge from the intensity of light and colour outside; exhibits have English labelling. Beside the museum is a small boutique selling books, T-shirts, leather goods, babouches, pottery, cushions…

To get to the garden walk from central Guéliz (it's about two kilometres, or just over a mile,

Sightseeing

Sun sets on the **Menara Gardens**.

Great ancient carp live in the basin; buy some bread, toss it in and watch the water churn as the fish go into a feeding frenzy.

The bleachers that disfigure the view are there to accommodate the evening audiences for the 'Marvels and Reflections' sound and light show, which four nights a week presents the history of Morocco via the medium of contemporary dance and fireworks (which to us seems a bit like presenting Beethoven's oeuvre in mime). The show takes place year round apart from January and February. The ticket office is at the entrance to the gardens.

To get to the Menara Gardens take a *petit taxi*, which should cost about 30dh from just about anywhere in the Medina. They'll try to charge you more coming back.

Menara Gardens

avenue de la Menara, Hivernage (024 43 95 80).
Open 5am-6.30pm daily. *Marvels and Reflections* box office 9am-8pm daily; show 9.45pm Wed-Sat. **Admission** free; picnic pavilion 15dh. *Marvels and Reflections* 250dh.

The Palmeraie

Legend has it that the huge Palmeraie north-west of the Medina was born of the seeds cast away by date-chomping Arab warriors centuries ago. A nice story but it fails to accord due credit to the clever minds that designed an underground irrigation system to carry melted snow water all the way from the High Atlas and enable a palm oasis of several hundred thousand trees. The ancient *khettra* system now has only historical curiosity value because the water supply is guaranteed by several reservoirs and a network of artesian wells.

It's not what you'd call a pretty oasis: many of the palms are worse for wear and the ground is dry, dusty and lunar-like. Even so, this is probably the most prime real estate in all North Africa. Ever since the 1960s, when King Hassan II first granted permission for it to be sold, Palmeraie land has been the plot of choice for the rich. This is the Beverly Hills of Morocco. Land is available only in parcels of more than one hectare and buildings must not interfere with the palms. Narrow lanes slalom between copses, occasionally squeezing by high walls surrounding the typically massive grounds of very discreet residences.

Other than pricey accommodation, there isn't much to see in the Palmeraie (ramshackle villages, grazing camels, building sites). You might venture out here for a combination lunch and swim at Nikki Beach (*see p112*). It's also a good area for cycling. The ideal half-day ride is to head east out of town along the main route de Fes and take a left on to the route de Palmeraie (look for signs for the Tikida Gardens hotel), which winds through the oasis to exit north of the city on the Casablanca road. For details of where to hire bikes, *see p226*.

Eat, Drink, Shop

Restaurants & Cafés

Cushions, couscous and a dash of French flair.

Tradition with a twist is the flavour at decadent **Dar Moha**. *See p98.*

Eat, Drink, Shop

As Marrakech continues to boom, and more and more westerners jet in from an increasing variety of locations, the number of dining establishments is growing in quantity, quality and variety. French kitchens are still the most common after Moroccan, but the city also has a number of good Italian places, established Thai and Indian restaurants, and a couple of recently added Japanese options complete the picture.

As for Moroccan food, there's good news and bad news. On the plus side Morocco does have its own distinctive cuisine, quite different from the rest of North Africa, and this can be sampled in all price ranges. The bad news is, as served in restaurants, it's often very limited in scope: tagine or couscous, couscous or tagine, with a *pastilla* or some *briouats* thrown in. It is also mostly served in inflexible menu deals, where you pay for the whole lot even if you don't want to eat it all (*see p107* **The Moroccan menu**). Eating in showy surrounds, where the whole

dining experience is conceived as a kind of orientalist *Gesamtkunstwerk*, adds some variety around the edges (*see p100* **Putting on a show**), but one is often left wishing that a little more imagination went into the food, and a little less into the cushion covers.

Morocco is a poor country, where meat is regarded as a luxury. Moroccans don't 'get' vegetarians. The standard menu will usually include a *salade marocaine* – a selection of small, single-vegetable dishes, each separately prepared and spiced – and this can be a treat, but otherwise it's a boring old *couscous de légumes* (usually boiled peas and carrots). Prospects brighten, though, if you warn the restaurant of your arrival in advance.

❶ Purple numbers given in this chapter correspond to the location of restaurants on the street maps. See pp250-254.

It's worth remembering that many riads and rented houses have arrangements with cooks – and Moroccan home-cooking can put many restaurants to shame. You will have to order in advance, but sometimes you can specify the kind of thing you want, and direct where it gets served – on your terrace, in the courtyard, even up on the roof.

Alcohol is served in most of the better restaurants, but rarely in those at the cheaper end of the market. Where you can get a drink, we've noted the fact in our listings. Moroccan wines can be surprisingly good. For more on Moroccan wine and beer, see *p117*.

RESERVATION AND PAYMENT

Other than at the cheapest places, it is always a good idea to make reservations. The hotel concierge or the staff at your riad will be happy to take care of this.

Prices vary from the unbelievably cheap (a handful of dirhams for a full meal at **Restaurant Toubkal**, *see p99*, or **Chez Chegrouni**, *see below*, for example) to the affordably expensive (700dh per head at **Dar Yacout**, *see p98*). On average, expect to shell out around 200dh (roughly £10/$20) per head for dinner with wine. It is customary to leave a tip of around ten per cent, although in more upmarket restaurants service is often included in the bill.

While many places display the symbols of major credit cards, management will commonly claim that the machine is broken. If you insist and are willing to endure a 20-minute stand-off, the machine may miraculously start working again, but it's easier to make sure that you carry enough cash. American Express is particularly unpopular on account of hefty surcharges.

Restaurants

Medina

Moroccan

Argana

Jemaa El Fna (024 44 53 50). **Open** 5am-11pm daily. **Main courses** 40dh-80dh. **No credit cards**. **Map** p250/252 C5 ❶

A no-frills (plastic tablecloths, garden furniture) eaterie on the edge of Marrakech's mayhemic main square, Argana's formula of pack-'em-in seating, canteen catering and ringside views makes it a big hit with tour groups. Stairs at the back of the ground-floor café (good ice-cream) lead up to two floors of restaurant terrace. Choose from a trio of three-course set menus (90dh, 100dh or 140dh), or

order à la carte from a basic menu (in English) of salads, ten kinds of tagine, or meat from the grill. The quality is so-so, but portions are large. It makes for a good lunch spot, but the views are best at dusk.

Chez Chegrouni

Jemaa El Fna (065 47 46 15). **Open** 6am-11pm daily. **Main courses** 25dh-60dh. **No credit cards**. **Map** p250/252 C5 ❷

Everybody's favourite cheap restaurant in the Medina, Chegrouni has a first-floor dining-room and a rooftop terrace with a partial view of the Jemaa El Fna, as well as the ground-floor terrace – a great vantage point for watching locals sweep in and out of the square by foot or on mopeds. Chegrouni is clean, well run and deservedly popular with both Marrakchis and tourists. All the usual dishes (salads, grills, couscous and tagines) are served briskly, accompanied by big baskets of fresh bread. Note to vegetarians: there is no meat stock in the vegetable couscous, while the vegetable soup is excellent. The menus are in English and glasses on the tables contain paper napkins on which you scribble your order and then hand it to a waiter; it returns at the end as your bill.

The best Restaurants

For fine Moroccan

Al Fassia (*see p105*); **Dar Moha** (*see p98*); **Le Tanjia** (*see p100*); **Maison Arabe** (*see p98*); **Tobsil** (*see p101*).

For eating on a budget

Chez Chegrouni (*see p97*); **Jemaa El Fna** (*see p69*); **Restaurant Toubkal** (*see p99*).

For light lunching

Bagatelle (*see p106*); **Café du Livre** (*see p116*); **Jardins de la Koutoubia** (*see p103*); **Terrasses de l'Alhambra** (*see p105*).

For Gallic gastronomy

La Villa (*see p111*); **Pavillion** (*see p104*); **Sur une Ardoise** (*see p109*).

For outdoor dining

Alizia (*see p110*); **Bô-Zin** (*see p112*); **L'Abyssin** (*see p111*); **Pizzeria Venezia** (*see p104*); **Rôtisserie de la Paix** (*see p109*).

For seeing and being seen

Comptoir (*see p111*); **Crystal** (*see p112*).

For something without meat

Casanova (*see p106*); **Narwama** (*see p103*); **Salam Bombay** (*see p109*); **Tatchibana** (*see p105*).

Dar Moha

81 rue Dar El-Bacha (024 38 64 00/www.dar moha.ma). **Open** noon-3pm, 7.30pm-late Tue-Sun. **Set meals** 220dh lunch; 420dh dinner (drinks not included). **Credit** AmEx, MC, V. **Alcohol served**. **Map** p250 B4 ❸

Owner Moha Fedal is the closest thing Marrakech has to a home-grown celebrity chef. He learned his trade over 14 years in Switzerland and the result is a kind of Moroccan fusion cuisine – traditional dishes with a twist. We recommend sampling a standard tagine or couscous elsewhere first, then coming here to delight in the difference. Both lunch and dinner are set-course affairs but there is some choice of dishes. Service is good; gregarious Moha is often found flitting from table to table, and the gnawa musicians who play nightly are among the best we've encountered in Marrakech restaurants. Book well in advance, and try to get a table outside by the pool – the interior is dull by comparison. **Photo** *p96*.

Dar Yacout

79 rue Ahmed Soussi, Arset Ihiri (024 38 29 29). **Open** 7pm-1am Tue-Sun. **Set meal** 700dh dinner. **Credit** AmEx, DC, MC, V. **Alcohol served**. **Map** p250 B3 ❹

Yacout's fame rests more on its style of decor and performance than it does on the food. The building is all show, a madcap mansion designed by Bill Willis, complete with flowering columns, candy striping and fireplaces in the bathrooms, topped off by a yellow crenellated rooftop terrace. Guests are led up to the latter on arriving or invited to take a drink (included in the price, so feel free) in the first-floor lounge, before being taken down, past the swimming pool and across the courtyard, to be seated for dinner at great round tables, which are inset with mother-of-pearl. On comes the food, delivered with maximum pomp by teams of costumed waiters, course after course, quickly passing the point where you'd wish it would stop. It's perfectly adequate stuff, but you wouldn't come here just for the cooking. Reservations are essential. *See also p100* **Putting on a show**.

Ksar Es Saoussan

3 Derb El-Messaoudyenne, off rue des Ksour (024 44 06 32). **Open** 8pm-1am Mon-Sat. **Set meals** 350dh, 450dh, 550dh. **Credit** MC, V. **Alcohol served**. **Map** p250/252 B5 ❺

Yet another historic house/fixed menu combination, but one possessed of a peculiar old-world charm. The tone's set by the elderly French gent who greets guests with an invitation to ascend to the roof for the fine view of the Koutoubia. Then back down to be seated in silk-cushioned corners with gentle piano concertos filling the space where other diners' conversation would be (the number of covers barely reaches double figures). Tall Africans take the orders from a choice of three set dinners; all but the most ravenous should be satisfied by the three-course 'petit' option (350dh), which comes with aperitif, a half-bottle of wine and bottled water.

Maison Arabe

1 Derb Assehbe, Bab Doukkala (024 38 70 10). **Open** 7-11pm daily. **Set meals** 350dh (drinks not included). **Credit** MC, V. **Alcohol served**. **Map** p250 A4 ❻

Other than the address, the house restaurant of the hotel of the same name (*see p44*) has no connection to the original and legendary Maison Arabe. But the food is commendable and, as with the hotel, the surroundings are beautiful. The setting comprises a grand dining room under a brilliant blue-hued Persian-style ceiling. The heavily draped tables are generously spaced and discreetly attended by liveried staff. In fact, the place feels more like an exclusive private club than a restaurant – if you want to glam it up, this is a good place to do so. The restaurant offers a *prix fixe* menu but there are choices between some wonderful tagines (including the excellent lamb and pear) and several different kinds of couscous. Lighter European dishes are served at the bar. Afterwards, take tea or coffee in the charming courtyard which features a trompe l'oeil façade. Reservations are recommended.

Marrakchi

52 rue des Banques, Jemaa El Fna (024 44 33 77/www.lemarrakchi.com). **Open** 11.30am-11pm daily. **Main courses** 100dh-160dh. **Credit** MC, V. **Alcohol served. Map** p250/252 C5 **7**

There are two pluses to this place: one is the location, on the edge of Jemaa El Fna, which is laid out panoramically beyond the wrap-around windows. The second is that it serves Moroccan food à la carte – although there are also set menus. Skip the claustrophobic first-floor salon with its heavy Fes tiling and continue up to the top-floor, made luscious with dusky-pink tablecloths, maroon tableware and a billowing ceiling of swagged black material. The lighting is dim and the black-clad staff charming. The menu holds no surprises (tagines and couscous) but the food is good, and there's a list of local wines.

Palais Soleiman

Route de Fès, Kaa Machraa (024 37 89 62/ www.palais-soleiman.com). **Open** 7.30pm-1.30am Mon-Sat. **Set meal** 485dh. **Credit** AmEx, V. **Alcohol served. Map** p250 C1 **8**

This serious 19th-century palace, owned by the Segueni family from Casablanca, opened as a restaurant in June 2006 after years as a private event location. It's a truly spectacular setting, with tables scattered around an immense and beautifully lit courtyard. Decorative highlights include huge pillars and fine tiling and woodwork, topped off by antique chandeliers. The whole place is covered by a clear electric retractable roof. The experience is a bit like eating on the set of a Bond film; you half expect a missile to rise from the central fountain and soar off into the night. The traditional Moroccan food is fine, if a little pricey (and wine comes extra), but you get whatever you're given and the setting remains the main reason to visit. Entertainment is provided in the form of alternating gnawa and arabo-andalucian musicians. There are also occasional piano recitals.

Restaurant Toubkal

48 Jemaa El Fna (024 44 22 62). **Open** 7am-11pm daily. **Main courses** 18dh-50dh. **No credit cards. Map** p252 C6 **9**

Ksar Es Saoussan.

Putting on a show

As the nightly pageant of the Jemaa El Fna unfolds, with people taking their seats at food stalls while musicians and storytellers begin to draw the crowds, two essential elements come together: dining and entertainment. And as it is at the city's iconic heart, so it goes in more secluded dining spots. At the high end of Moroccan traditional dining – as well as in the middle range inhabited by tour groups being force-fed an 'authentic' experience – it's almost impossible to separate the business of serving up a good meal from the business of putting on a show.

First, the set-up. You negotiate dark twists of the Medina, uncertainty creeping in as you seek your elusive destination – can it really be right down here? Then, the reveal. A door like any other opens on to some truly sumptuous interior: think intricate tiling and tinkling fountains, piles of cushions and lots of candles, a scattering of rose petals and a starry sky above an open courtyard.

At **Palais Soleiman** (*see p99; pictured*) you can literally eat in a palace. The tables are scattered around an enormous but subtly lit courtyard. Other restaurants in grand historic buildings include **Ksar Es Saoussan** (*see p98*), **Tobsil** (*see p101*), **Pavillion** (*see p104*) and **Narwama** (*see p103*).

Big with backpackers from the budget hostels off nearby Riad Zitoun El-Kedim, but also popular with Marrakchis, Toubkal is the next to last stop on the restaurant chain, just above eating al fresco at the food stalls on Jemaa El Fna. The prices are the main draw. The Toubkal does some of the cheapest tagines around (25dh); couscous dishes cost between 18dh and 30dh and brochettes, chicken and lamb served with fries are all around 25dh. The premises are as basic as it gets, with plastic furniture and plastic tablecloths, but the wildlife is real. Chiller cabinets at the rear sell basic grocery-style provisions including yoghurt, packets of biscuits, cheese, chocolate and juice to take away.

Le Tanjia

14 Derb J'did, Mellah (024 38 38 36/www.letanija. com). **Open** 10am-1am daily. **Main courses** 130dh-180dh dinner. **Credit** MC, V. **Alcohol served. Map** p253 D7 ❿

This new Moroccan à la carte venture by the owners of the successful Marrakchi (*see p99*) occupies a house on the edge of the Mellah, with a comfortable bar on the ground floor lit by candles and chandeliers, and a variety of dining spaces on the balconies and terraces above. It's named after a local speciality (a *tanjia*, like a tagine, is a kind of cooking pot) and there are both chicken and beef *tanjias* on the menu, but the real gastronomic selling-point is the

Eat, Drink, Shop

And now, on comes the food – usually in impossible amounts. The custom of serving ostentatiously large portions stems from a tradition of generous hospitality. It's all part of the show. In the extravagant Moroccan burlesque that is **Dar Yacout** (see p98), three costumed waiters deliver each dish in a choreographed routine. One carries it in on a sort of wicker stand, another whisks off the conical lid, a third lifts out the pot and puts it on the table.

Finally there is the actual entertainment: an arabo-andalucian musician strumming an oud, gnawa guys with a guimbri and castanets, a whole bunch of drummers.

As course follows course, the music gets louder. And in some places, such as **Comptoir** (see p111) or **Jana** at Pacha (see p112), belly dancers will eventually appear.

But the culture of dining as show isn't limited to traditional places. **Narwama**, in a wonderful old mansion with tables ranged around a mad fire-and-water feature, serves Thai food but has a very Moroccan sense of fun. And even at **Crystal** (see p112) at Pacha, the most avant-garde menu in town is accompanied by musicians prowling the tables, and a glass wall to the kitchen that transforms the chefs at work into yet another piece of theatre.

mechoui (360dh for two), a lamb barbecue dish that in most places has to be ordered a day in advance, but here can be had on the spot. There's a light international menu at lunch, tea and shisha on the terrace in the afternoon, and belly dancers and musicians every night.

Tobsil

22 Derb Abdellah Ben Hessaien, Bab Ksour (024 44 40 52). **Open** 7.30-11pm Mon, Wed-Sun. **Set meal** 580dh. **Credit** MC, V. **Alcohol served**. **Map** p250/252 B5 ⑪
Considered by some to be Marrakech's premier Moroccan restaurant, Tobsil offers a lesson in local

gastronomy. There is no menu. On being led by a uniformed flunkey to the door (the place is otherwise impossible to find), diners are greeted by owner Christine Rio, then seated either downstairs in the courtyard or upstairs in the galleries. And then the endurance test begins. Aperitifs (included in the price of the meal, as is the wine) are rapidly followed by a swarm of small vegetarian meze dishes. Then comes a pigeon pastilla, followed by a tagine, then a couscous dish, and finally fruit and tea or coffee accompanied by an array of cakes or pastries. Everything is delicious but you need a very good appetite to manage it all. Reservations (and a doggy bag) are recommended.

Recline and conquer: lounging around at **Narwama**.

International

Foundouk
55 rue du Souk des Fassi, Kat Bennahïd (024 37 81 90/www.foundouk.com). **Open** noon-midnight Tue-Sun. **Main courses** 110dh-170dh. **Credit** AmEx, MC, V. **Alcohol served**. **Map** p251 D4 ⑫
The rutted trench of a street that leads to this restaurant appears so unpromising that many probably turn back. Those who locate the two lanterns marking the door enter into a gorgeous courtyard space with creamy leather seating around a flower-filled sunken water tray. A massive spindly chandelier hangs above, looking like something from one of Tim Burton's skewed fantasies. Softly glowing side rooms are filled with plush sofas and armchairs; one holds a tiny bar. There is more dining space upstairs at candlelit tables ranged around a gallery open to the sky most of the year. French-Moroccan food (couscous and tagines are on the menu alongside modern French dishes) is served by nattily dressed waiting staff, but the menu is doggedly inflexible. It's generally good, though not everything lives up to the surroundings. Highlight of our recent meal was the puddings, particularly a luscious pistachio crème brûlée. Stick to the simple stuff and leave experimentation to the expert bar staff. Drinks are ideally sipped on the roof terrace beneath the stars.

Jardins de la Koutoubia
26 rue de la Koutoubia (024 38 88 00). **Open** 12.30-4pm, 7.30-10.30pm daily. **Main courses** 100dh-210dh. **Credit** MC, V. **Alcohol served**. **Map** p250/252 B5 ⑬

The poolside grill at this luxury hotel (*see p43*), just a few minutes' walk from the Jemaa El Fna, is a fine spot for a peaceful lunch serenaded by birdsong. The setting is a spacious central court with trees and shrubbery flanking a rectangle of blue water. Choose from a simple but intelligent menu of salads, hearty sandwiches and dependable standards such as chicken with pasta or a mixed grill.

Kosybar
47 place des Ferblantiers (024 38 03 24). **Open** *meals* noon-2.30pm, 7.30pm-11pm; *drinks only* 2.30pm-7.30pm Tue-Sun. **Main courses** 70dh-150dh. **Credit** MC, V. **Alcohol served**. **Map** p252 C7 ⑭
The decor is funky Moroccan, and there are tables on the ground and first floors as well as the roof; it's not unlike the Foundouk (*see above*) in style, but a bit smaller. The place belongs to the son of the owner of some of Morocco's best wine estates, so it won't come as a surprise to learn that the list here includes a number of rarities and the cellar has quite a few others that are not listed. The menu features a number of appealing fish and meat dishes, and there is also a skilled sushi chef, who produced an excellent selection of very fresh sushi and sashimi on a recent visit. At weekends a piano player accompanied by drumming creates a great atmosphere. The other entertainment is watching the storks nesting in the ruins of the Badi Palace opposite.

Narwama
30 rue de la Koutoubia (024 44 08 44). **Open** 7pm-1am daily. **Main courses** 150dh-320dh. **Credit** MC, V. **Alcohol served**. **Map** p250/252 B5 ⑮

Opened in early 2005, Narwama was the city's first proper Thai restaurant. It's a fun place. The setting is the central courtyard of a palatial 19th-century residence tucked down an alley behind the Jardins de la Koutoubia hotel. It's an enormous space that, with its plastic-sheeted roof and potted palms, pastel hues and global lounge music, feels like a Buddha Bar night in some orientalist conservatory. Some intimacy is offered in a smaller rear room with fantastic old painted ceilings and a couple of curtained *diwans*. The kitchen doesn't have the courage of its convictions and the Thai dishes (prepared by a team from Bangkok and mostly pretty good) are supplemented by a miscellany of Moroccan and international standards. If you're not hungry, it's possible just to settle down for a cocktail or two in the spacious bar. If it's not in operation, ask a waitress to turn on the fire-shooting, water-spewing feature at the centre of the room. It reflects the restaurant's name, which means 'fire and water'. **Photo** *p103*.

Pavillion

Derb Zaouia, Bab Doukkala (024 38 70 40). **Open** 7.30pm-midnight Mon, Wed-Sun. **Main courses** 140dh-270dh. **Credit** AmEx, MC, V. **Alcohol served**. **Map** p250 A4 ⑯

The setting is superlative: the courtyard of a splendid old house where tables are squeezed under the spreading boughs of a massive tree. Several small salons provide for more intimate dining. The day's menu is scrawled out on a white board presented by the waiter. Offerings change regularly but expect the likes of *agneau*, *canard* and *lapin*, all exquisitely presented with seasonal veg and rich wine sauces. The staff can be supercilious, but otherwise this is a classy affair. The restaurant is a little difficult to find, but if you can locate the alley leading to the Maison Arabe (well signposted), then Pavillion is 100 metres north, tucked down the next alley but one. Reservations are recommended.

Pizzeria Venezia

279 avenue Mohammed V (024 44 00 81). **Open** noon-3pm, 6pm-midnight daily. **Main courses** 60dh-150dh. **Credit** MC, V. **Map** p250/252 B5 ⑰

It's worth eating at the Venezia at least once, if only for the view: it occupies a rooftop terrace opposite the Koutoubia minaret and overlooking Mohammed V with its shoals of darting mopeds. Although it's only a pizzeria, freshness and quality of ingredients is the priority here, so the wood-oven cooked pizzas are good. The menu also stretches to salads and meat dishes, including a good fillet steak in a green peppercorn sauce. On Friday and Saturday there's a self-service buffet with an enormous choice including vegetable dishes and puddings. Although no alcohol is served you are allowed to BYO.

Portofino

279 avenue Mohammed V (024 39 16 65/www. portofinomarrakech.com). **Open** noon-11pm daily. **Main courses** 45dh-180dh. **Credit** MC, V. **Map** p250/252 B5 ⑱

Al Fassia.

At street level below the Pizzeria Venezia, this big, modern rival to its upstairs neighbour is increasingly favoured by Marrakchis who like a good pizza but don't need a view of the Koutoubia to go with it. The menu also includes a range of pasta dishes and steaks, and a very good selection of fish. There's almost too much space here, so there's rarely any trouble finding a table – actually the place can get a bit draughty when empty. We wish staff would change the boring pop music.

Tatchibana

38 Derb Bab Ksiba (024 38 71 71/www. tatchibana.com). **Open** 7.30-10.30pm Tue; noon-2.30pm, 7.30-10.30pmWed-Sun. **Set meals** 160dh, 180dh, 325dh. **No credit cards. Alcohol served.** **Map** p252 B9 ⑲

The German owner has worked hard to make this old Kasbah house look Japanese – to the point where it can be disorientating to walk into its comfortable, clean-lined interior, all latticed screens and simple wood surfaces. Its Moroccan aspects reveal themselves on closer inspection – lampshades that would be paper in Tokyo are here made of camel-skin. The food is similar: Japanese ideas with local ingredients. It's all tasty and well-prepared, even if it bears only a vague resemblance to the Japanese food you'll have eaten elsewhere. The tempura served with lemon, salt and green tea powder is particularly good, and the kiwi sorbet memorable. There are three menus, one vegetarian.

Terrasses de l'Alhambra

Jemaa El Fna (no phone). **Open** 8am-11pm daily. **Main courses** 50dh-100dh. **No credit cards.** **Map** p250/252 C5 ⑳

A clean, smart, French-run café-restaurant on the east side of the main square (across from the landmark Café de France). The ground floor and patio is a café for drinks and ice-cream; the first floor with terrace is for diners; the top-floor terrace is for drinks (non-alcoholic). The menu is brief – salads, pizzas and pasta, plus a few desserts, ice-cream and milkshakes – but the food is good. If you're new to Marrakech, it's somewhere you can eat and feel confident that your stomach will hold up. Settle in aircon comfort indoors or slow roast in the open air overlooking the madness of Jemaa El Fna.

Guéliz

Moroccan

Al Fassia

55 boulevard Zerktouni, Guéliz (024 43 40 60/ alfassia@menara.ma). **Open** noon-2.30pm, 7.30-11pm daily. **Main courses** 100dh-150dh. **Credit** MC. V. **Alcohol served. Map** p254 B2 ㉑

One of the few posh Moroccan restaurants in town that allow diners to order à la carte, Al Fassia is also unique in being run by a women's co-operative – the chefs, waiting staff and management are all female.

It recently moved from avenue Mohammed V into this quieter location, where excellent versions of Moroccan standards are served in a sober dining-room with traditional touches, or in a pleasant courtyard garden. It's a classy place. We'd come here for the Moroccan salad alone, but there are also ten tagines, five couscous dishes and a couple of pastillas, all in very un-ladylike portions. Reservations recommended. **Photo** *p104*.

International

Bagatelle
101 rue de Yougoslavie (024 43 02 74). **Open** noon-2pm, 7-11pm Mon, Tue, Thur-Sun. **Main courses** 70dh-100dh. **Credit** MC, V. **Alcohol served. Map** p254 A2 ㉒
In business since 1949, Bagatelle is a charming relic of the last days of French rule. There's a spacious salon indoors but the place to be is the open-air patio, with shade provided by vine-trailed trellising that for part of the year bows under the weight of the ripening grapes. The menu is old-school bistro: salads and standard entrecôtes, escalopes and fillets, veal, kidneys and calf's liver. These are supplemented by a few Moroccan dishes and a typed page of daily specials. Waiters wear black bow ties and waistcoats; a sound system wafts smoky-voiced chanson. The place is particularly popular with lunching mademoiselles on time out from raiding the nearby boutiques, examining purchases over oysters and a bottle of Gris Guerrouane. **Photo** *p109*.

Bar L'Escale
Rue de Mauritanie (024 43 34 47). **Open** 11am-10.30pm daily. **Main courses** 35dh-80dh. **No credit cards. Alcohol served. Map** p254 B2 ㉓
It's primarily a bar (*see p118*), but L'Escale's also a good place for a quick, cheap lunch – unless you're a vegetarian. The humble house special is grilled chicken, leg (*la cuisse*) or breast (*le blanc*), which comes with a tomato and onion salsa and a basket of bread for mopping up. What more could you want? The spicy merguez sausages are also good. There's a back room specifically for dining but prime seating is at one of the six sun-shaded tables out on the pavement.

Casanova
221 avenue Yacoub El-Mansour, Guéliz (024 42 37 35/ristorantecasanova@menara.ma). **Open** noon-3pm, 8-11pm daily. **Main courses** 120dh-150dh. **Credit** MC, V. **Alcohol served. Map** p254 C2 ㉔
Housed in one of the splendid modernist villas that are scattered around Guéliz, this Venetian-run restaurant (though, surprisingly, with a Moroccan chef) serves up Italian food to international standards. The surroundings are unpretentious and comfortable, though cultural overload is sometimes reached with both televisions showing Serie A football and a pianist knocking out (by Marrakech standards) relatively uncheesy interpretations of 'Feelings' and 'Windmills of Your Mind'. The menu

includes home-made pasta and familiar grill standards as well as specials such as pappardelle with wild boar and some interesting salads. There's also a good wine list and a nice selection of digestifs.

Catanzaro
42 rue Tarek Ibn Ziad (024 43 37 31). **Open** noon-2.30pm, 7.30-11pm Mon-Sat. **Main courses** 50dh-130dh. **Credit** MC, V. **Alcohol served. Map** p254 B2 ㉕
It's a simple, rustic-styled neighbourhood French-run Italian (red-checked tablecloths, faux-woodbeam ceiling) with a homely air and reliable cooking, but Catanzaro is one of the most popular eateries in town. White-hatted chefs work an open kitchen with a big wood-fired oven turning out excellent thin-crust pizzas. Alternatives include various grills and steaks, with a good selection of salads and a good choice of wine by the bottle or half-bottle. The dessert list includes a tiptop crème brûlée. Customers all seem to be regulars – most are greeted by name as they arrive – and, although the place seats 60 or more, reservations are recommended in the evenings. It's easy to find: one street back from avenue Mohammed V, behind the site of the old Marché Central.

Le Guépard
Residence Al Mourad, avenue Mohammed V, Guéliz (024 43 91 48). **Open** 11am-5pm, 6pm-1am Tue-Sun. **Main courses** 120dh-160dh. **Credit** V. **Alcohol served. Map** 254 B3 ㉖
Opened in June 2006, this restaurant and bar decorated in faux African colonial style (leopardskin upholstery, pictures of gorillas) has quickly become one of the most fashionable spots in Guéliz. Many will find it of more use for a drink than a meal – chef Laurent Agredano's menu is full of over-rich dishes leaning heavily on foie gras and caviar – but the light lunch menu (50dh-80dh) is useful, and the croque monsieur (60dh) is probably the best in town.

Jacaranda
32 boulevard Mohammed Zerktouni (024 44 72 15/ www.lejacaranda.ma). **Open** noon-3pm, 6.30-11pm daily. **Main courses** 110dh-150dh. **Credit** MC, V. **Alcohol served. Map** p254 A2 ㉗
With large picture windows looking on to the traffic tango of place Abdel-Moumen, Jacaranda is the place for an urban dining experience. Inside it's hardly less busy: a crush of furniture, chintzy table settings and assorted paintings spill down from the mezzanine gallery cluttering all available wall space. Despite the frenzy, it has a friendly and comfortable atmosphere. The kitchen specialises in *cuisine française* with plenty of *viande* and *poisson*, but it's hardly haute cuisine and as such is a bit overpriced. However, decent value is offered by a lunchtime two-course *menu rapide* at 85dh or the *menu tourisme*, three courses for 105dh. In the evenings there's a *menu du marché* for 180dh. In addition to beer and wine, the tiny bar counter stretches to aperitifs and a small selection of cocktails.

The Moroccan menu

Moroccan cuisine is practical and unfussy. Dishes have evolved from Persia via the Arabs, from Andalucía with the returning Moors and from the colonial French – but the overriding principle is to throw all the ingredients into a dish and then leave it to cook slowly.

Prime exhibit is the national dish of **tagine**. It's essentially a slow-cooked stew of meat (usually lamb or chicken) and vegetables, with olives, preserved lemon, almonds or prunes employed for flavouring. The name describes both the food and the pot it's cooked in – a shallow earthenware dish with a conical lid that traps the rising steam and stops the stew from drying out.

The other defining staple is **couscous**, which is again the name of the basic ingredient (coarse-ground semolina flour)

and of the dish; the slow-cooked grains are topped with a rich meat or vegetable stew, not unlike that of a tagine. It's a main course, not a side dish.

Don't expect a menu in most upmarket traditional Moroccan restaurants. Once customers are seated, the food simply arrives. First thing will be a selection of small hot and cold dishes, called **salade marocaine**, actually carrots, peppers, aubergine, tomatoes and the like, each prepared differently, as well as diced sheep brains and chopped liver. Next, **briouettes** – little envelopes of paper-thin ouarka (a bit like filo) pastry wrapped around ground meat, rice or cheese and deep fried. Next, **pastilla** (or b'stilla), which is ouarka pastry filled with shredded pigeon or chicken, almonds, boiled egg and spices, baked then dusted with cinnamon and powdered sugar. Next, a tagine of lamb or chicken. Following that, a couscous of chicken or lamb. Next, dessert of flaky pastry drizzled with honey and piled with fruit. Next, indigestion and the beginnings of a pronounced aversion to all foodstuffs delivered in pottery dishes with conical lids. All the above is delivered with Moroccan wine and finished off with mint tea and, gawd help us, more pastries.

To be frank, the set-menu dining experience can seem like being a duck on a foie gras farm. That a great portion of the excessive mounds of food is inevitably sent back to the kitchen almost untouched seems supremely wasteful as well as offering the diner poor value for money. Uneaten food is distributed to the poor but perhaps you might appreciate being able to make your own choices as to how you dispense your charity.

A la carte menus of Moroccan food are available in only a few blessed places, notably **Al Fassia** (*see p105*) in Guéliz, **Marrakchi** (*see p99*) on Jemaa El Fna and **Le Tanjia** (*see p100*) on the place des Ferblantiers.

Eat, Drink, Shop

Kechmara

3 rue de la Liberté (024 42 25 32). **Open** 7am-midnight Mon-Sat. **Set meals** 80dh, 100dh, 120dh. **Credit** MC, V. **Alcohol served**. **Map** p254 B2 ㉙

Its name a reversal of 'Mara-kech', this is a hip young café-bar-restaurant. The stylish decor is all white and clean-lined with chrome fittings and white moulded plastic chairs. Lunch and dinner are a *prix fixe* continental menu; choice is limited (soup, salads, meat in sauces, grills and desserts) but the food is generally excellent and well presented. There is absolutely nothing here for vegetarians, however. The drinks menu includes *bière pression* at a reasonable 25dh and a good line-up of cocktails to be drunk at the bar counter or, better still, up on the fine first-floor terrace – which makes Kechmara one of the few places in Marrakech where you can legitimately booze al fresco.

Pizzeria Niagra

31 Centre Commercial El-Nakhil, route de Targa (024 44 97 75). **Open** 12.15-2.15pm, 7.15-11pm Tue-Sun. **Main courses** 50dh-150dh. **Credit** MC, V (over 150dh only). **Alcohol served.** **Map** p254 A1 ❷
One of three adjacent pizza joints five minutes' walk north of central Guéliz on the road out to the French Lycée, and easily the best (although neighbouring Pizzeria Exocet shades it in the name stakes). An excellent menu of far more than just pizza (pasta, escalopes, steaks, fillets and 14 different salads) at cheap prices ensures that the place is packed almost every lunch and dinner – the latter often quite boozy given that beer and wine are sold at almost supermarket prices. With pink and chintzy decor, it's far from being an event restaurant, but if you lived in Marrakech then Niagra would probably become a much-loved local.

Rôtisserie de la Paix

68 rue de Yougoslavie (024 43 31 18). **Open** noon-3pm, 6.30-11pm daily. **Main courses** 60dh-180dh. **Credit** MC, V. **Alcohol served.** **Map** p254 B2 ❸
Flaming for decades, the 'peaceful rôtisserie' is a large garden restaurant with seating among palms and bushy vegetation. Simple and unpretentious, it's utterly lovely whether lunching under blue skies (shaded by red umbrellas) or dining after sundown when the trees twinkle with fairy lights. (In winter, dining is inside by a crackling log fire.) Most of the menu comes from the charcoal grill (kebabs, lamb chops, chicken and merguez sausage) but there are also delicacies such as quail, and a selection of seafood. We recommend the warm chicken liver salad, listed as a starter but easily a meal in itself.

Salam Bombay

1 avenue Mohammed VI (024 43 70 83). **Open** noon-2.30pm, 7pm-12.30am daily. **Main courses** 80dh-180dh. **Credit** DC, MC, V. **Alcohol served.**
Not only was this Marrakech's first Indian restaurant, it was also the first in Morocco, set up by four guys from Madras who already had a successful Indian restaurant in Toulouse. They've adapted to local sensibilities by going over the top with the design – it's all very big, ornate and pink, and there's a row of painted elephant heads studding the roadside wall. The serving girls wear shimmery *kurtas* and *bindis* dot their foreheads but they're all Moroccan and the biriyani is served in a *tanjia* clay pot. The Rajasthani chefs have been careful to tone down the spicing to the extent that anyone familiar with Indian food as eaten in India (or even the UK) is liable to find their curries a little bland. The wide-ranging menu is heaven for vegetarians, though.

Sur une Ardoise

Route de Targa, camp El-Ghoul (024 43 02 29). **Open** noon-2.30pm, 8-10.30pm Mon-Sat. **Main courses** 80dh-130dh. **Credit** MC, V. **Alcohol served.** **Map** p254 A1 ❸

The French connection: **Bagatelle** is a throwback to colonial times. *See p106.*

Eat, Drink, Shop

Café des Epices. *See p112.*

Since late 2005, this classic French brasserie has been serving an unpretentious daily-changing bistro-style menu, presented to the diner, as the name suggests, 'on a blackboard'. The airy interior is in a blocky, art deco style with grey walls leavened by Jacques Tati film posters. Ignore the pink buildings over the road and you could imagine you were in Paris. Service is brusque but intelligent and the kitchen is flexible, though the food can be hit and miss, veering from excellent to indifferent. Still, it's a reliable place for a solid, simple meal and the only real downside is the irritating noise in the background that might happen to be music, if anyone turned up the volume.

Trattoria de Giancarlo
179 rue Mohammed El-Bekal (024 43 26 41/www. latrattoriamarrakech.com). **Open** 7.30-11.30pm daily. **Main courses** 110dh-270dh. **Credit** AmEx, MC, V. **Alcohol served**. **Map** p254 A2 ㉒
Just about clinging on to its reputation as Marrakech's finest Italian restaurant, Trattoria serves good food in enchanting surroundings. The Felliniesque interiors (lush, occasionally lurid and more than a little louche) are designed by local legend Bill Willis and are a delight – in fact, they are alone worth a visit. The best tables are those overhung by oversized greenery out on the tiled garden terrace. The latter is situated beside a large luminous pool. In the evening the place is lit by lanterns and candles to ridiculously romantic effect. While the menu is hardly extensive, it holds plenty of broad appeal (a variety of salads, several vegetarian pastas, and an array of meat and seafood dishes). Service is excellent verging on obsequious: 'Would sir like his beer with a head or without?' Reservations are recommended.

Hivernage

International

Alizia
Corner of rue Ahmed Chouhada Chawki (024 43 83 60). **Open** noon-2.30pm, 7-11pm daily. **Main courses** 80dh-180dh. **Credit** MC, V. **Alcohol served**. **Map** p254 C4 ㉝
Presided over by Madame Rachida, who learned her English in Bayswater, this is an intimate and well-established Italian-flavoured venture popular with the old-school expat crowd. As well as pizzas, pastas, fillets and steaks, it serves wonderful fish dishes, such as a starter salad of small red mullet fillets flamed in balsamic vinegar, followed by fillet of John Dory served in a prawn bisque sauce. Ask about the special of the day – a roll of plaice stuffed with salmon and spinach on a recent visit. Save room for the dessert selection, one of the best in town. There's a decent wine list too. Although the pitch is upscale, prices are reasonable and the atmosphere relaxed, especially in the bougainvillea-draped garden.

the Hivernage, decorated with warm accents by Léon L'Africain, and with a roof that opens to the sky in summer. There's a lot of choice in the three-course French menu (five starters, five mains, six desserts) and it's solid, sensible stuff: well-presented with an eye for detail and all very decent for the price. The place was still finding its feet when we visited in early 2007, but looked to have got the formula right.

Palmeraie

Palmeraie is a long way to travel for lunch unless you're actually staying out here or have an ulterior motive; for instance, L'Abyssin is attached to **Palais Rhoul** (*see p164*), popular for its fantastic hammam. And the food at **Nikki Beach** is secondary to its stunning swimming pools.

International

L'Abyssin
Palais Rhoul, route de Fès, Dar Tounsi (024 32 85 84/www.palaisrhoul.com). **Open** 8-11pm Mon, Wed-Sun. **Main courses** 95dh-220dh. **Credit** MC, V. **Alcohol served**.
The garden restaurant of the Palais Rhoul, a unique and surreal retro-modern villa on the edge of the Palmeraie, L'Abyssin is no more than a series of gauzy, open-fronted white pavilions set around a central slate basin. The place is all very low slung, with white sofas, lounging platforms and plump cushions. White-costumed staff waft across lawns under brilliant blue skies. It's somewhat reminiscent of some cultish retreat for the fabulously rich and misguided. The handwritten chalkboard menu is French but it stretches to include tagines, pasta and a 'maison burger'.

Nikki Beach
Royal Golf Palace, Circuit de la Palmeraie (024 36 87 27/nordine@nikkibeach.com). **Open** 10.30am-7pm daily. **Main courses** 110dh-250dh. **Credit** AmEx, MC, V. **Alcohol served**.
In the grounds of the Royal Golf Palace but independently managed, Nikki Beach is total Miami. It's a series of aqua-blue swimming pools surrounded by sun-shaded seating. Further back from the water are massive loungers like four-poster beds, and a host of plushly sofa'd little enclaves. There's an Indonesian-ornamented bar/ servery and a swim-up bar at the centre of the largest pool. Lunch is served from a menu of salads (delivered in immense bowls), room service staples (cheeseburger, club sandwich) and meat grills (lamb chops, *brochettes de poulet*). Bring your swimsuit for a post-prandial splash before taking to a recliner with a cocktail. It's a place to spend a whole afternoon and kids love it. There is a 200dh entry fee to cover pool use but some riads have an arrangement for their guests to get in free: ask.

Comptoir
Avenue Echouada (024 43 77 02). **Open** 4pm-1am Mon-Thur, Sun; 4pm-2am Fri, Sat. **Main courses** 100dh-220dh. **Credit** MC, V. **Alcohol served**. **Map** p254 C4 ③④
Inevitably Comptoir's exotic-East-meets-moneyed-West style has become diluted by overexposure. What began as a hangout for hipsters, fashionistas and models now seems to cater largely for coach parties from Club Med. The menu is divided between *saveurs d'ici* (Moroccan) and *saveurs d'ailleurs* (French), a smart move to satisfy both the visitor fresh off the plane and those who've already done one tagine too many. Food quality varies wildly, though. What's constant is an ebullient party atmosphere, aided by a four-piece of elderly fez-wearing musicians and brought to a raucous climax each Friday and Saturday evening with the arrival of a troupe of belly dancers. Audience participation is encouraged. You have been warned.

La Villa
Avenue Kennedy (024 42 19 69). **Open** 8-11pm Mon; noon-2.30pm, 8-11pm Tue-Sat. **Set meal** 250dh. **Credit** MC, V. **Alcohol served**. **Map** p254 B4 ③⑤
Chef Didier Beckaert came to Marrakech from Lille, bringing with him a good reputation and the intention of presenting 'affordable gastronomy'. This he has been doing since late December 2006, in a comfortable tented dining area on the edge of

Eat, Drink, Shop

Sweet things at **Amandine**. *See p115.*

(alternately a violinist and a saxophonist) prowling the tables and playing to a click track, plus a big glass wall beyond which the chefs can be seen at work. Both add life to a space otherwise filled with trendy folk sampling strangely geometrical dishes. The volume of the former doesn't aid communication with the young, good-looking waiting staff, many of whose English is poor. After dinner, have a drink in the opulent red and gold chill-out room, or head straight to the dancefloor to work it all off.

Cafés

Thanks to the French, Marrakech has a legacy of continental cafés for croissants and pastries, as well as ubiquitous oversweetened green mint tea and thick gritty coffee. They open early for breakfast and close early too.

Further afield

International

Bô-Zin

Km3.5, route de l'Ourika, Douar Lahma (024 38 80 12/www.bo-zin.com). **Open** 8pm-1am daily. **Main courses** 110dh-250dh. **Credit** AmEx, MC, V. **Alcohol served**.

It's a way out of town (a 15-minute taxi ride from the Medina) but Bô-Zin is worth travelling for. It's a smart and stylish international restaurant of the kind that people dress up for (when the waiting staff are as good-looking as they are here, then the customers are obliged to make an effort). There are several sprawling rooms, each filled with a variety of bars, fireplaces, potted plants and heavy drapes. The place everyone wants to be, however, is the glorious and spacious rear garden. The menu is brief but wide-ranging, taking in Moroccan, Thai and an international miscellany. If the food doesn't quite live up to the surrounds, it's still a cut above most of the competition. The music can be good, too, depending on the DJ, but is sometimes loud enough to render conversation difficult.

Crystal at Pacha

Boulevard Mohammed VI, Zone Hotelière de l'Aguedal (024 38 84 80/www.pachamarrakech.com). **Open** 8-11pm daily. **Main courses** 160dh-230dh. **Credit** AmEx, MC, V. **Alcohol served**.

One of two restaurants at the self-styled 'largest club in Africa' (the other is called Jana, serving Moroccan food in absurdly raucous surrounds), Crystal is a 'lounge restaurant' serving an experimental and slightly pretentious European and 'modern Moroccan' menu devised by Alain Ducasse. It's a huge room decorated in the kind of global style popular in chic new London hotels, with live musicians

Medina

Café des Epices

75 Rahba Kedima (024 39 17 70). **Open** 8am-8pm daily. **No credit cards. Map** p250/252 C5 ③⑥

Marrakech was crying out for a place like this: a spot in the souks to sit down in pleasant surroundings and refresh with a soft drink or light snack. In a small building overlooking the spice souk, there's a ground-floor terrace, a first-floor salon for lounging and tables on the roof. The decor is simple, the staff young and friendly, there's Wi-Fi and good music. A basic menu comprises tea and coffee, salads and sandwiches, juices and sodas. The only problem is its popularity. **Photos** *p110.*

Café de France

Jemaa El Fna (no phone). **Open** 6am-11pm daily. **No credit cards. Map** p250/252 C5 ③⑦

The most famous of Marrakech cafés is these days distinctly grotty, but it boasts a prime location and terrace fronting right on the main square. No one knows exactly how old the place is but it crops up in Peter Mayne's *A Year in Marrakesh*, written in the early 1950s. It remains a prime meeting place for travellers and locals with business in the Medina: assorted Morocco guidebooks and copies of the day's Arabic-language press are present in about equal numbers. Neither category is favoured and prices are posted ensuring fair trade for all.

Pâtisserie des Princes

32 rue Bab Agnaou (024 44 30 33). **Open** 5am-11.30pm daily. **No credit cards. Map** p252 C6 ③⑧

A weak-kneed wobble from Jemaa El Fna, this offers gloriously icy air-conditioning in a dim coldstore of a back room. It may sound gloomy but, the hotel pool aside, there's no better retreat on a sweltering afternoon. The front of house is taken up by glass cabinets filled with fine cakes and pastries, to be accompanied by cappuccino, English tea, orange juice or shakes. There's a large salon upstairs.

Square meals

As the sun sets on central Jemaa El Fna, the stew of musicians, snake charmers, dancers, dentists and herbalists shift their pitches to accommodate the early evening arrival of massed butane gas canisters, trestle tables and tilly lamps. With well-practised efficiency, it takes only an hour to set up 100 food stalls in tightly drawn rows, with benches for diners, strings of lights overhead and masses of food banked up in the middle. Stallholders fire up the griddles and the smoke drifts and curls to create a hazy pall over what must be one of the world's biggest open-air eateries.

Most stalls specialise in one particular dish, and between them they offer a great survey of Moroccan soul food. Several places do good business in ladled bowls of *harira* (a thick soup of lamb, lentils and chickpeas flavoured with herbs and vegetables). Similarly popular are standbys of grilled *brochettes* (kebab), *kefta* (minced, spiced lamb) and *merguez* (spicy sausage; stall No.31 apparently sells the best in all Morocco). Families perch on benches around stalls selling boiled sheep heads, scooping out the jellyish gloop inside with small plastic forks. Elsewhere are deep-fried fish and eels, bowls of chickpeas drizzled with oil, and mashed potato sandwiches, while a row of stalls along the south side have great mounds of snails, cooked in a broth flavoured with thyme, pepper and lemon. Humblest of the lot is the stallholder selling nothing more than hard-boiled eggs.

Menus and prices hang above some of the stalls, but not everywhere. It's easy enough to just point, and prices are so low that they're hardly worth worrying about. Etiquette is basic: walk around, see something you like, squeeze in between fellow diners. Discs of bread serve instead of cutlery. For the thirsty, orange juice is fetched from one of the many juice stalls that ring the perimeter of the square.

The food is fresh and prepared in front of the waiting diners, so you can actually see the cooking process. Few germs will survive the charcoal grilling or boiling oil; plates and dishes are a different matter. The single same bucket of water is used to wash up all night, so play safe with your stomach and ask for the food to be served on paper.

Eat, Drink, Shop

Restaurant **Le Marrakchi** الـمـراكـشي

Moroccan Restaurant
Marrakech

A legend dary table with
panoramic view on the famous
Jemaa El Fna Square.
Belly Dancers Show.

Moroccan Cuisine
Restaurant from noon to 1:00 am

Place Jamaa El Fna - 52, rue des Banques 40000 Marrakech
Tél. : +212 (0) 24.443.377 Fax : +212 (0) 24.449.042
E mail : lemarrakchi@gmail.com - www.lemarrakchi.com

Guéliz

Amandine

177 rue Mohammed El-Bekal (024 44 96 12). **Open** 6am-11pm daily. **No credit cards**. **Map** p254 A2 ❸
Amandine comes in two parts: there's the smart pâtisserie with a long glass display cabinet layered with continental-style cakes and pastries and a few chairs and tables in front; or next door there's a proper café space with a high bar counter, fewer cakes and far more atmosphere. Both spaces are air-conditioned but we prefer the café, where efficient table service provides the usual coffees and (mint) teas, plus a mix of hot savouries and things like croissants and French toast.

Boule de Neige

Corner of rue de Yougoslavie, off place Abdel-Moumen (024 44 60 44). **Open** 5am-11pm daily. **No credit cards**. **Map** p254 A2 ❹
Don't come particularly for the coffee or food, but do come for a look. The large room is a fetching mint green and pink, with tables laid out canteen style. There's a food counter at one end with things shiny, gelatinous and best left well alone. There's also a breakfast menu but it baffles the staff if you order from it. Instead, nip next door to the Pâtisserie Hilton and bring something back – this is permitted, even encouraged. Then settle in and watch the sitcom-like spectacle of staff chasing cats chasing other cats dodging men eyeing single girls… Huge fun.

Café du Livre

44 rue Tarek Ibn Ziad (024 43 21 49). **Open** 9.30am-9pm Mon-Sat. **Credit** MC, V. **Alcohol served**. **Map** p254 B2 ❹
So quickly did Sandra Zwollo's bookshop café become a key hangout for anglophone expats, it's hard to believe that nothing like it existed before. It's a comfortable first-floor space (accessed from the courtyard of the Hotel Toulousain) with (mostly second-hand) books at one end and café tables at the

other. Breakast is served until 11.30am, high tea from 4pm to 6pm, and an all-day menu including a handful of dishes devised by celebrity chef and erstwhile Marrakech resident, Richard Neat. Popular attractions include the excellent traditional hamburgers and the lemoniest lemon tart this side of the Mediterranean.

Café les Négociants

Place Abdel-Moumen, avenue Mohammed V (024 43 57 82). **Open** 6am-11pm daily. **No credit cards**. **Map** p254 A2 ❹
Far classier than the endearingly sleazy Café Atlas, which it faces across the road, Les Négociants is a Parisian boulevard-style café with acres of rattan seating and round glass-topped tables crowded under a green-and-white striped pavement awning. We like it for breakfast: café au lait, orange juice and croissants, plus the papers from the international newsagent across the road.

Hivernage

Table du Marché

Corner of avenue Echouda & rue du Temple (024 42 12 12). **Open** 7am-11pm daily. **Credit** MC, V. **Map** p254 C4 ❹
Attached to the Hivernage Hotel & Spa, the Table du Marché is a dependable French-style pâtisserie and café with outdoor patio seating. The view isn't up to much – it's of the massed balconies of the Sofitel opposite – but the wickerwork furniture is attractive and the maroon canopies offer welcome shade from the sun (there are just a handful of seats in the air-conditioned interior). The tarts, croissants and breads are excellent, coffee comes coffee flavoured (which isn't always the case in Marrakech), and there are sandwiches and panini. While it's off-route for most visitors, the local middle classes have taken to the place, driving over to exit with a baguette tucked under one arm.

Café du Livre.

Bars

Marrakech takes on bar culture.

Tinkling the ivories at the **Piano Bar**. *See p117.*

If bar-hopping is your consuming passion, then Marrakech is probably not your ideal holiday destination. That said, it has more watering holes than you might expect to find in an Islamic city. If you really want a drink, it's not too hard to find one, and many of the options are actually quite entertaining. At one end of the drinking spectrum are insalubrious, beery Moroccan dives where most women won't feel especially comfortable; while at the other end are smart bars in hotels and restaurants, which are pretty much off-limits to locals. In between there's a scattering of lounge bars with cocktail menus.

The Qur'an strongly cautions against the consumption of 'substances that cloud the mind', which has generally been understood to mean 'intoxicants': in other words, lay off the booze. But the reality is that attitudes towards drink are more ambiguous. Morocco has prohibitions against alcohol (including, notably, that it shouldn't be drunk in public) but not against its production or sale. Which is handy when it's the authorities that produce over half of the country's booze. Sales of beer,

wine and spirits generate several millions of dirhams annually in profit for the largely state-owned alcohol industry.

Generally speaking, Moroccans aren't that fussed about alcohol. Many of them like a drink, but even those who abstain aren't overly censorious of others who don't. Anyway, the comparative expense of wines and spirits means that their consumption is largely limited to the moneyed – and more liberal – upper-middle classes and mostly confined to pricey restaurants. The handful of local bars that there are, which serve only beer, typically draw their clientele from the less salubrious side of life (*see p118* **Bad boys and beer bottles**).

Most importantly, beware the holy month of Ramadan, when all bars other than those in hotels close for the duration: for dates, *see p234* **Islamic holidays**.

> ❶ Pink numbers given in this chapter correspond to the location of each bar as marked on the street maps. *See pp250-54.*

BEER AND WINE

Beer comes in both local and foreign brands. Flag and Flag Spéciale are brewed in Tangier, Stork comes from Fes, and Casablana is marketed as 'the legendary beer from the legendary city'. Otherwise, it's usually Heineken. Chilled, the local stuff is perfectly drinkable and sells by the bottle for anything from 12dh to 40dh.

Local wines are decent if undistinguished. Reds predominate and the best are Cabernet du Président or Domaine de Sahari. The best white is probably Sémillant or Coquillages. Local rosés can be good on a hot day; try the Gris Guerrouane.

Cocktails are a relatively new phenomenon. Marrakech is just beginning to get the hang of them but menus still contain some eccentric combinations and don't expect everything to be expertly shaken.

Medina

The sale of alcohol in the Medina, with its seven saintly shrines, is heavily restricted. It's practically impossible to get a licence. A few restaurants have persevered and are able to offer drinks to diners, but bars are an absolute no-no, except in the 'international zones' that are hotels.

Alanbar

47 rue Jebel Lakhdar, Bab Laksour (024 38 07 63). **Open** 8pm-2am daily. **Credit** DC, MC, V. **Map** p250 B4 ❶

Inspired by waning Parisian fashion haunt the Buddha Bar, Alanbar tops a grand flight of stairs with a glowing HR Geiger goddess. It also features a baronial fireplace, a grand piano in the corner and a basement palm-court dining area, all of which are rendered completely insignificant by the sheer scale of a place that has the ungainly size, atrium-style layout and acoustics of a shopping mall. You could march the entire population of Liechtenstein inside here and still feel agoraphobic. But it does boast what may just be the best-stocked bar in town and you are always guaranteed to get a table (several if you like).

Le Club

Maison Arabe, 1 Derb Assehbe, Bab Doukkala (024 38 70 10/www.lamaisonarabe.com). **Open** 3-11pm daily. **Credit** MC, V. **Map** p250 A4 ❷

Le Club is a Moroccan take on the gentleman's lounge, with leather-panelled walls, club chairs, scatterings of tribal rugs, a fire in the hearth (very welcome in winter, let us tell you) and imposing big-game oils (elephant in oils), plus sculpture (a wood-carved African lady breastfeeding). It could be the bar at the Swaziland Royal Links. If this sounds a bit hokey, it's actually very comfortable and further redeemed by a bar counter that's sized

to mean business and that delivers better-than-competently mixed drinks (cocktails 70dh). Local and imported beer by the bottle is 40dh to 60dh.

Grand Tazi

Hotel Grand Tazi, corner of avenue El-Mouahidine and rue Bab Agnaou (024 44 27 87). **Open** 7-11pm daily. **No credit cards. Map** p252 C6 ❸

The Tazi's a godsend – the only place in the central Medina where the weary and footsore can kick back with a cheap beer. There's no real bar as such, just a sofa space off to one side of the lobby (and a large empty room beyond that) where accommodating waiters will fetch a cold one for anybody who succeeds in snaring their attention. You don't have to be a resident, just not too fussy about the company you keep or addicted to quality furnishings. Fellow drinkers tend to be young locals in leather jackets and budget travellers swapping stories of loose bowels amid the dunes of Merzouga.

Narwama

30 rue de la Koutoubia (024 44 08 44). **Open** 8pm-12.30am daily. **Credit** MC, V. **Map** p250/252 B5 ❹

Narwama is primarily a restaurant (*see p103*), in a palatial 19th-century residence tucked down an alley behind the Jardins de la Koutoubia Hotel. But proprietor and all-round nice guy Ali Bousfiha has also developed the front-of-house bar as a stand-alone entity. Painted a midnight blue, it has comfortable seating, a long cocktail menu and a bearable lounge-core soundtrack, all of which you can enjoy with no obligation to eat. Plans for further expansion – a 'long bar' is envisaged – now seem to be afoot.

Piano Bar

Hotel les Jardins de la Koutoubia, 26 rue de la Koutoubia (024 38 88 00). **Open** 5pm-midnight daily. **Credit** AmEx, DC, MC, V. **Map** p250/252 B5 ❺

A modest space in red and gold, the piano bar is just off the lobby of this conveniently located hotel – a mere stumble from the Jemaa El Fna. From 7pm to 11pm there is music, and the quality of your drinking experience will partly depend on how well you take to whoever is at the actual piano. Otherwise, the bar is well stocked, the experienced staff knows how to mix a cocktail and the counter is a fine place for perching. Drinks aren't cheap (50dh-100dh) but there's no dress code, and if the current pianist insists on singing with tons of echo and a cheesy percussion track, you can always take your drink out to the poolside terrace and contemplate the sky instead of the cigar selection.

Guéliz

The area for vaguely disreputable local bars, most a short stumble from place Abdel-Moumen.

Afric'n Chic

6 rue Oum Errabia (061 43 04 45/www.africn chic.com). **Open** 6pm-1am daily. **Credit** AmEx, MC, V. **Map** p254 C3 ❻

Eat, Drink, Shop

Bad boys and beer bottles

The story goes that figures released by the Moroccan government showed an astonishing fact. Tourists were found to be drinking, on average, no less 30 litres of alcohol a day. Moroccans tell you this with a smile, and the joke is the official fiction that beers are brewed and spirits imported solely for the consumption of foreigners.

Moroccan bars – as opposed to hotel bars or European-style bars – have to keep a low profile. There aren't many, they don't advertise, and they are often tucked in obscure side streets. In Marrakech that means on and around the northern end of rue Mohammed El-Bekal in Guéliz, in the vicinity of the Cinema La Colisée.

Even when you find one, there's nothing to see from outside. Windows will be opaque and the entrance kinked so you can't peer within. This is as much to shield the clientele from prying gazes as it is to protect the passer-by from depravity. But most of all it's so everyone can pretend that nothing as disreputable as beer-drinking is really going on.

Don't be deterred by the unwelcoming exterior but expect few frills inside. Basic furniture. Even more basic toilets. Nothing on sale but beer, except maybe a dusty bottle of Ricard somewhere. A couple of old posters on peeling walls. Uncollected empties crowding unwiped tabletops. Lots of drunken guys in jellabas. And no women, unless they're whores or tourists.

Nobody will mind you wandering in, though there can be a disconcerting absence of middle ground between everyone studiously ignoring you, and everyone trying to buy you a beer. Some places are raucous and jostly; others are quiet and concentrated. But either way, people are mostly too busy drowning their sorrows to bother about bothering you.

Two things shape the atmosphere. The first is a sense of camaraderie. The business of beer-drinking is the province of defiant reprobates, united in their shared sense of marginality. The second is a sense of enormous frustration – with sex, with poverty, with whatever. These places are about drinking enough to forget about it for a while, and they can teeter on a manic edge, feeling like they might kick off at any moment. But they can also have an almost joyful, all-in-this-together kind of quality.

Moroccan bars don't all double as hooker hangouts, but many in Marrakech do. It obviously makes sense to the authorities for the disreputable business of prostitution to cohabit with the disreputable business of beer-drinking, the better to keep an eye on it all. Non-Moroccan women, accompanied by men, will be left alone but may still feel uncomfortable. The whores in these places are mostly ageing and sad, but they can be as cheerful as the next guy once they've got enough beer inside them.

Taking the fashion for all things 'African' to a raucous extreme, this is a big space with a party atmosphere. There's a small stage for occasional live music, lots of sub-Saharan figurines, and a crowd of nattily dressed young men, along with middle-aged beer drinkers and good-time girls clustering around tables and massing at the long, busy bar. Flag beer, unusually, on tap.

Bar L'Escale

Rue de Mauritanie (024 43 34 47). **Open** 11am-10.30pm daily. **No credit cards.** Map p254 B2 **❼**

The menu claims that L'Escale opened in 1927; the window says it was '47. Either way, most of the customers look as if they've been settled in place since opening night. Most nurse bottles of Flag Spéciale, half an eye on the big, boxy wall-mounted TV, while engaging in sporadic chat with the red-jacketed, grey-haired old gent who patrols the big, bare paddock behind the high bar counter. Though all male – or perhaps because it is all male – Bar L'Escale is a totally non-threatening environment (although hygiene freaks might have a tough time of it). Beers can be taken out to the pavement tables and there's food in the form of grilled meats (see *p106*).

Café Atlas

Place Abdel-Moumen, avenue Mohammed V (024 44 88 88). **Open** 8am-10pm daily. **Credit** MC, V. **Map** p254 A2 ❽

You used to be able to take your beer at one of the outside tables but this is no longer the case. Its role as a rendezvous for foreign gents and local gigolos does Café Atlas few favours, but obviously uninterested parties are left alone. A beer costs 13dh-20dh depending on the mood of the waiter, and patrons are also offered the chance to purchase anything from peanuts to lotto cards to carpets by itinerant salesmen. Leaving your cigs in view on the table invites a steady stream of supplicants, including those boys in their snug white trousers.

Chesterfield Pub

Hotel Nassim, 1st floor, 115 avenue Mohammed V (024 44 64 01). **Open** 9am-1am daily. **Credit** MC, V (min 200dh). **Map** p254 B2 ❾

Also known as the 'Bar Anglais', though there's nothing particularly English about this vertically challenged little first-floor hotel bar. A tiny lounge is cast in an eerie glow by a luminously underlit pool on the other side of a glass wall, while a larger back bar is an equally twilit gents' hangout, heavy with a fug of cigarette smoke. In between is a polished mahogany counter area dispensing bottled and draught beers, spirits and cocktails at reasonable cost. Best of all is the open-air, pool-side patio – a popular Friday night-meet-up venue for expats on the razz.

Le Guépard

Residence Al Mourad, Avenue Mohammed V (024 43 91 48). **Open** 11am-5pm, 6pm-1am Tue-Sun. **Credit** V. **Map** p254 B3 ❿

After opening in June 2006, this restaurant and bar decorated in faux African colonial style (leopardskin upholstery, pictures of gorillas) quickly became one of the most fashionable spots in Guéliz. With its outdoor tables and indoor saloon, we find it of more use for a drink than a meal. Chef Laurent Agredano's menu is full of rich dishes leaning on foie gras and caviar, but if you feel like a snack, the croque monsieur (60dh) is probably the best in town.

Kechmara

3 rue de la Liberté (024 42 25 32). **Open** 7am-midnight Mon-Sat. **Credit** MC, V. **Map** p254 B2 ⓫

A café by day and restaurant by night, Kechmara also functions well as a lively and convivial bar. There's a long bar counter to the right as you enter with a tap for *bière pression*, back shelves lined with spirits and bar stools for perching. The menu lists long drinks and cocktails and things seem to have improved since the time we ordered a gin and tonic and it arrived without the gin. There's also a spacious roof terrace where drinks are served. *See also p107.*

Le Lounge

24 rue Yougoslavie (024 43 37 03). **Open** 9pm-1am Mon-Sat, 6pm-1am Sun. **Credit** MC, V. **Map** p254 A2 ⓬

Just north of place Abdel-Moumen on a short stretch of pedestrianised street, Le Lounge is a small bar-restaurant. While a simple Moroccan and international menu (main courses 70dh-130dh) is served downstairs, beers and cocktails are imbibed on the big sofas and throne-like armchairs of an orange-accented mezzanine. Naturally, the music is lounge-like – a selection of ironically tasteful cover versions

Kechmara.

Eat, Drink, Shop

on our last visit. The small outdoor terrace where you were once allowed to drink seems to have been banished, but may yet reappear.

El-Moualamid Bar

Hotel El-Moualamid, 6th floor, avenue Mohammed V (024 44 88 55). **Open** 5pm-2am daily. **No credit cards. Map** p254 A2 ⑬

It has all the charm of a Mongolian bus station waiting room – with added drunkenness – but the beer is cheap and there are great views from the outdoor terrace (six floors up) south down Mohammed V to the Koutoubia minaret. A resident band with a frightening way with a synth brings the elderly boozy males to their unsteady feet, while the hard-faced local 'ladies' patiently bide their time. On the right night it could pass for fun. To ascend to these tawdry heights, enter the uninviting corner bar just north of place Abdel-Moumen and take the lift.

Montecristo

20 rue Ibn Aicha (024 43 90 31). **Open** 8pm-2am daily. **Credit** AmEx, MC, V. **Map** p254 A1 ⑭

On the ground floor is the Bar African, a world music venue, where French musicians indulge in interminable twiddly solos. Upstairs is where a smart set of foxy chiquitas and macho hombres slink and strut to samba and salsa. Off to the side of the dancefloor is a small area of non-ergonomic seating, made all the more uncomfortable by the inevitable crush of bodies. For elbow room and aural respite head up to the cushion-strewn rooftop terrace, which is peaceful and pleasant until the drinks menu arrives and you note that a crappy little bottled beer goes for an outrageous 70dh (almost five of your English pounds).

Musica Bar

Boulevard Mohammed Zerktouni (no phone). **Open** 7pm-midnight daily. **No credit cards. Map** p254 B2 ⑮

Its gaping black hole of an entrance, signed with a desultory scrawl of neon, looks as if it belongs on the Reeperbahn. But the Musica Bar isn't as classy as that. Enter – if you dare – into a huge tiled hall of swimming pool acoustics that nightly reverberates to the mad cacophony of a five- or six-piece mini Arab orchestra. Fuelled by cheap bottled beer, punters are too far gone to dance but they bang their hands on the tabletops and wail along with the chorus. Downstairs is a nightclub of sorts that kicks off as the bar closes, but we're not that brave.

Samovar

133 rue Mohammed El Bekal (no phone). **Open** 7pm-2am daily. **No credit cards. Map** p254 A3 ⑯

Possibly the most raucous saloon in town. Two rooms heave with a crush of slurry young men in cheap leather jackets, rambling old soaks and ageing prostitutes. Every table teeters beneath the weight of squadrons of Stork empties. Body contact is frequent, unavoidable and occasionally opportunistic. It's a place where 'too much to drink' is the

natural state of being and the underlying threat of violence is periodically realised before being quickly smothered by laconic bar staff. You don't want to go to the toilets. Visit, if you will, and take a walk on the Marrakech wild side, but don't come crying to us afterwards.

La Strada

90 rue Mohammed El Bekal (061 24 20 94). **Open** 7pm-2am daily. **No credit cards. Map** p254 A3 ⑰

By day this is a local take on a pizza restaurant, but by night the oven goes cold, the heavy drapes are drawn across the windows and place settings are pushed aside to accommodate steadily growing collections of empty bottles. Upstairs is a small air-conditioned lounge with cushioned seating, which is where the 'ladies' hang out. We feel safer staying down on the ground floor, watched over by a grimacing, bare-chested Anthony Quinn in a large, framed film poster of Fellini's *La Strada*.

Hivernage

All the neighbourhood's big hotels come complete with a couple or more bars – and that's as much as we need to say about them.

La Casa

Hotel El Andalous, avenue Président Kennedy (024 44 82 26/www.elandalous-marrakech.com). **Open** 8pm-2am daily. **Credit** MC, V. **Map** p254 B5 ⑱

A bar that thinks it's a club, La Casa mixes food, music and dance to great effect. It is primarily a bar, dominated by a huge central serving area, surrounded on all sides by table-led seating. Above the counter hangs a giant rig of multicoloured lights fit for a Pink Floyd gig. Much flashing and strobing occurs in accompaniment to a heavy Arab/Latin beats soundtrack. There's no dancefloor, but then there's none needed, as everyone just lets go where they are. About the stroke of midnight expect an 'impromptu' performance of dancing from the chefs in the corner kitchen area. Berber columns cloaked in purple drapes and characters from the ancient Tifinagh alphabet highlit in ultraviolet add the thinnest veneer of Moroccan theming.

Comptoir

Avenue Echouada (024 43 77 02). **Open** 4pm-1am Mon-Thur, Sun; noon-1am Fri, Sat. **Credit** MC, V. **Map** p254 C4 ⑲

Marrakchi socialites will tell you that Comptoir is sooo over, but on the right night it's still the best party in town. From the outside it's a well-behaved little villa on a quiet residential street, but inside the place buzzes with dressed-up diners (*see p111*) on the ground floor, while upstairs is a sizeable lounge filled each weekend night to within a whisper of health and safety violations. The crowd is a mix of good-looking locals, sharper expats and wide-eyed tourists delighted to have stumbled on the Marrakech they'd always heard about. Drinks are pricey but the nightly belly-dancers are hilarious.

Shops & Services

Variety is the spice of life in the city's bustling souks and shops.

Marrakech has always been, in one sense or another, about shopping. For centuries, its growth and prosperity hinged on its position at the confluence of ancient trade routes. Merchants dealt with goods arriving from across the Sahara, while caravans stocked up before making the long journey south. It's long been the main market town not just for the High Atlas and the plain of Hauoz, but for the whole of southern Morocco.

The trade in ostrich feathers may no longer be brisk and there aren't any slaves on sale these days, but shopping remains way up there on the Marrakech list of things to do. Rightly so, for to avoid the haggle and hustle of the souks, or to peer at all the products of artisanal Marrakech merely as if they were exhibits in a museum, would be to miss out on the city's central activity and liveliest culture.

There's no doubt that this is a great place to shop, with both beautiful and bizarre potential purchases to be looked at and possibly lugged home. The souks are commerce at its most intoxicating – a riot of strong colours, seductive shapes and rampant exoticism. The first impulse is to embark on a mass shop for a Moroccan makeover back home. Fine, but be

aware that back in more drizzly and mundane surrounds, those bright oranges and reds just look garish, the brass lanterns are the height of tack, and the curly yellow slippers are likely to end up at the back of your wardrobe.

Still, the artisans of Marrakech do their best to knock out things that might prise open Western wallets, and stay tuned to trends in interior decor. Good buys include fashion accessories, fabrics, spices, natural oils and pottery. But there's also plenty of fun to be had in considering a few less conventional purchases. A mother-of-pearl inlaid dowry chest? A pair of shoulder-high brass candlesticks? Obscure musical instruments? Magic supplies? Mummified baby alligator?

Above all else, shopping in Marrakech can be an absolute hoot – and you wouldn't be human if you didn't go home with a few utterly unnecessary items.

SHOPPING THE SOUKS

The vast bazaar that spreads north of Jemaa El Fna is actually a coalescence of different markets, most specialising in one kind of item (for map, *see p73*). General handicrafts shops are scattered everywhere, but particularly on

Marché Couvert. *See p132.*

the two main souk streets of rue Mouassine and rue Semarine. An intrepid spirit brings its rewards, as the closer you remain to the Jemaa El Fna, the higher the prices.

Most shops are tiny holes in the wall with lone owners keen to attract business. It's essential to saunter purposefully, avoid eye contact and remain deaf to overtures of 'Just for looking' and 'I give you Asda price!' Any hesitation or sign of fatigue will be punished by insistent offers of tea and assistance.

Debate rages on the issue of guides. Yes, they can zero in on the shops selling the items that you're looking for, and yes, they can haggle on your behalf, but wherever they lead it ends in a commission and that goes on your bill.

A new breed of 'personal shoppers', many of them European expats, can better understand what you're after, sort out the quality from the tat, and lead you to places they think you'll find interesting, working outside the traditional kick-back system. The best of them charge around €200 a day for this service, so it's only worth considering if you have some very serious shopping in mind. And beware, many old-school guides are now also billing themselves as 'personal shoppers'.

Katie Lawrence

067 96 69 69. **Rates** €120 each per day (without transport), 2-4 people. **No credit cards**.

Laetitia Trouillet

074 21 72 28/www.lalla.fr. **Rates** €250 per day (incl transport); €170 half day (4 hrs). **No credit cards**.

THE HASSLE OF HAGGLING

It's a drag, but when shopping in the souk haggling is expected, even demanded. There are no hard and fast rules as to how to do it, but when you've spotted something you want it's smart to do a little scouting around and get a few quotes on the same or similar item at other stores before making your play. Don't feel you need to go through the whole silly charade of offer and counter-offer like in some B-movie dialogue; simply expressing interest then walking away on being told the price is usually enough to bring about some fairly radical discounting.

Otherwise, to avoid having to haggle, try shopping at either the **Centre Artisanal** or **Ensemble Artisanal** (for both, *see p124*), both of which have fixed prices.

BEYOND THE SOUKS

Some of the best shopping lies outside the Medina, up in the *nouvelle ville* of Guéliz. On and around avenue Mohammed V are plenty of smart and sophisticated little boutiques, stocking exclusive designer items and one-offs

superior in style and quality to anything found in the souks – and without the hassle of hard sell, haggling and yet more mint tea.

Committed shoppers might also venture out to the **Quartier Industrielle** at Sidi Ghanem, where there are factory showrooms and the ateliers of various designers. *See p131* **The industrial revolution**.

OPENING HOURS

Just as prices are highly elastic, so are hours of business. We've done our best to extract from recalcitrant shop owners the times they're likely to be open and trading, but it's all a bit *inshallah* (God willing). A chance meeting with a colleague in the street, and the *fermé* sign can stay in place all morning. As a rule of thumb, the working day stretches from around 9am to 7pm, with a break of a couple of hours for lunch and a snooze. Shops in the souk will often close on the Muslim holy day of Friday, at least for the morning; shops in Guéliz take Sunday off. Some places take both. During Ramadan (for dates, *see p234*) it's even more unpredictable, but there's a general shift for businesses to open and close later.

PAYMENT

Generally speaking, it's dirhams only. Some shops are authorised to take euros, pounds sterling or US dollars, particularly in the more heavily touristed places. But this won't be self-evident and the only way to find out is by asking. Many shops purport to take credit cards, but actually would much rather not. Payment by plastic also often incurs a five per cent surcharge (to cover processing costs). If you find yourself short of cash, shops are often prepared to deliver to your hotel and accept payment on receipt.

Note that there are no added taxes, and hence nothing to be claimed back.

BRINGING IT ON HOME

Lots of shops offer a shipping service for foreign visitors. Beware. Tales of goods last seen somewhere in Marrakech are legion. Unless it's a container load, the best advice is to take charge of transporting purchases home yourself. The most straightforward option is to bite the bullet and pay the excess baggage fee. On British Airways this is about 100dh per kilogram. **Worldsoft** is a reliable *transitaire* in Daoudiate; it charges around 15dh per kilo to London, plus 800dh per shipment to cover paperwork. Alternatively, go to the main post office on place du 16 Novembre in Guéliz, *see p233*.

---

❶ Orange numbers given in this chapter correspond to the location of shops marked on the Souks map. *See p73*.

There is a levy of between five and 15 per cent payable on anything above the 2,300dh duty-free customs allowance.

Worldsoft
26 avenue Allal El Fassi, Daoudiate (024 31 05 55). **Open** 8.30am-12.30pm, 2.30-6.30pm Mon-Fri; 8.30am-12.30pm Sat. **No credit cards**. **Map** p250 C1.

One-stop shopping

In addition to places listed below, there's a small Western-style supermarket in Guéliz on avenue Abdelkarim El Khattabi, just south of the junction with avenue Mohammed V.

Aswak Assalam
Avenue du 11 Janvier, Bab Doukkala (024 43 10 04). **Open** 8am-10pm daily. **Credit** MC, V. **Map** p250 A2.
Across from the *gare routière* at Bab Doukkala, this decent-sized *supermarché* offers the closest good grocery shopping to the Medina. There's no booze here though – the owner's a religious man. It has less choice than Marjane (*see below*) and is pricier, but it's also much more convenient for anyone without a car.

Marjane
Route de Casablanca, Semlalia (024 31 37 24). **Open** 9am-10pm daily. **Credit** MC, V.
How did Marrakech manage before Marjane? This massive *hypermarché* is the utimate shopping destination for the city's middle and upper classes. It combines a supermarket (food and booze, clothes, household items, electronics, white goods, CDs, computers) with a Kodak Express Lab, McDonald's, Lacoste, Yves Rocher and Caterpillar franchises, plus banks, Méditel and Maroc Télécom, and a pharmacy. The alcohol department has its own checkout and a separate exit; if buying booze, assemble your other purchases first. Marjane is about 8km (five miles) north of town; a *petit taxi* will get you out here for around 30dh each way.

Antiques

Antique is a manufactured style here, and few things in Marrakech are as old as they might appear. Fraud is widespread too. Buy it because you like it, and if one day you discover it really was as old as the vendor claimed, then that's an added bonus.

Bric-a-brac shops offering old but less exalted items are scattered around the souk. On rue Sidi Ishak, the lane leading north from the east side of Rahba Kedima, the spice market, there are three where it skirts around the mosque, and a fourth as it passes through a short tunnel. There's another on the same road south of Rahba Lakdima, a short walk down on the right, and one or two on rue Sidi El-Yammami, just east of the Mouassine

fountain. Expect a mad jumble of old cameras, cigarette lighters, advertising signs, teapots, toys, doorknobs, enamel badges and picture frames, among which a few treasures can sometimes be found.

Amazonite
94 boulevard El Mansour Eddahbi, Guéliz (024 44 99 26). **Open** 9.30am-1pm, 3.30-7.30pm Mon-Sat. **Credit** AmEx, MC, V. **Map** p254 B2.
This is a cramped, three-storey repository of all manner of objets d'art, top quality Berber jewellery, early 20th-century oil paintings (displayed in the basement), a stunning collection of ancient silk carpets, plus miscellaneous ethnic trappings, including old marriage belts. A place for serious buyers in search of rare finds. Ring the doorbell for entry.

El Badii
54 boulevard Moulay Rachid, Guéliz (024 43 16 93). **Open** 9am-7pm daily. **Credit** AmEx, MC, V. **Map** p254 A2.
Two floors of museum-quality antiques, handpicked by owners Najat Aboufikr and his wife, featuring a dazzling array of gold and silver jewellery, unusual lamps, carved Berber doors, ornate mirrors and a huge choice of carpets. In pride of place are ancient ceramics from Fes, in traditional yellow and cobalt blue. They display photos of Brad Pitt, Tom Cruise and Hillary Clinton browsing here, but the fixed prices and warm welcome are for everyone.

Bazaar Ikhouan
15 Marché Sidi Ishak, off rue Sidi Ishak, Medina (024 44 36 16). **Open** 10am-7pm daily. **Credit** AmEx, MC, V. **Map** p73 ❶
Just how unique most of these pieces is open to debate – antiquity is in the eye of the beholder. Anyway, curious excavators can sift through piles of tarnished jewellery, dull-bladed daggers, trays and teapots, greening brass lanterns, fancy-headed walking sticks, silver Koranic carry-cases, gunpowder flasks and ivory-handled muskets. Owner Khalid is a real charmer and speaks fluent English.

De Velasco
4 rue le Verdoyant, avenue Hassan II, Guéliz (024 43 03 27). **Open** 9am-1pm, 3-8pm daily. **Credit** AmEx, MC, V. **Map** p254 B3.
Adolfo de Velasco was a kaftan designer and colourful raconteur who, until a few years ago, held court in a Mamounia boutique, fitting splendid one-off kaftans to royals and flogging a few *objets* on the side. Now Adolfo has gone to the great salon in the sky, the shop still bearing his name has moved to Guéliz. There's still a rack of kaftans in the back, but mostly it's an ornate orientalist clutter of outsize vases, lacquer cabinets, silver rhinos, chaises longues, paintings of souks, ceramic leopards and the occasional mounted pair of tusks – everything you might need to furnish a camp fantasia of the colonial era. It's pricey stuff and not much fun to browse; charmless staff pursue in packs.

MOHA

5 Laksour Sabet Graoua, Mouassine, Medina (068 94 90 97). **Open** 9am-8pm daily. **No credit cards.** **Map** p73 ❷

One of several objets d'art shops around Mouassine, this place offers a good selection of choice, if not always particularly old, doors, large vases, armoires and chests. Moha himself speaks English and will happily hold court in his modest showroom and serve mint tea while discussing purchases. He also has a second shop nearby.

Mustapha Latrach

7 Souk Labbadine, Medina (061 74 34 58). **Open** 9am-7pm daily. **Credit** MC, V. **Map** p73 ❸

The amiable Mustapha Latrach runs this small shop, located near the slipper souk. It's filled with authentic antique teapots, including quite a few with old English hallmarks – highly collectible and becoming ever-harder to find. Prices start at around the 1,000dh mark.

L'Orientaliste

11 & 15 rue de la Liberté, Guéliz (024 43 40 74). **Open** 9am-12.30pm, 3-7.30pm Mon-Sat; 10am-12.30pm Sun. **Credit** MC, V. **Map** p254 B2.

A small street-front boutique and a huge basement space hidden round the corner make up L'Orientaliste. The former is stuffed with piles of inexpensive items – Fès ceramics, filigree metal containers, painted tea glasses, scented candles and perfume bottles, some filled with essences. The latter is crammed with pricey antique furniture, early 20th-century Moroccan paintings and engravings, and leatherbound notebooks with original watercolours.

La Porte d'Orient

6 boulevard El Mansour Eddahbi, Guéliz (024 43 89 67). **Open** 9am-7.30pm Mon-Sat. **Credit** AmEx, MC, V. **Map** p254 A2.

The most mind-blowing of shopping experiences occurs when a door at the rear of this modest shop is opened to a back room, revealing a space of warehouse-like proportions. The enormous room houses an impressive panoply of Berber jewellery, ancient carved doors of fantastic size and patterning from Fès and Meknès, irridescent lanterns, beautiful glass cases of illuminated manuscripts and gilded lion thrones. The only thing you won't find is too many bargains. English is spoken.

Tinmel

38 rue Ibn Aicha, Guéliz (024 43 22 71). **Open** 9am-7.30pm Mon-Sat. **Credit** AmEx, MC, V. **Map** p254 A2.

A highly browseable mini-museum of Islamic art with a staggering variety of antiques: aged silver swords, Touareg earrings and pendants, 18-carat-gold jewellery from the early 20th century, colossal bronze lanterns that once adorned palaces, decorative oil jars, mirrors with cedar and camel-bone frames, silk-embroidered camel-skin bags and a variety of marble fountains. Don't miss the exquisitely crafted backgammon tables displayed upstairs.

Arts & handicrafts

Almost every store in the souk is a handicrafts store of some description, but for anyone pushed for time, the huge **Centre Artisanal** and **Ensemble Artisanal** are good one-stop options. For other stores selling similar, *see p133* **Home accessories.**

Centre Artisanal

7 Derb Baissi Kasbah, off rue de Kasbah, Medina (024 38 18 53). **Open** 8.30am-8pm daily. **Credit** AmEx, MC, V. **Map** p252 B8.

Don't let the humble entrance fool you – this is the closest thing to a department store in Marrakech, albeit a department store selling nothing but handicrafts. It's the ultimate souvenir store, with everything from trad clothing (*babouches, jellabas,* kaftans) to jewellery, and home furnishings to carpets. Prices are fixed at slightly above what you would pay in the souk, but this at least does away with tiresome haggling. The stalker-like behaviour and rudeness of the sales assistants can irritate.

Chez Climou et Ahmed

2 Souk Lebbadine (070 94 94 00). **Open** 9am-8pm daily. **No credit cards. Map** p73 ❹

Using a small, rudimentary lathe that he spins with his bare feet, Ahmed carves chess pieces from cedar, olive and lemon wood. His designs are pleasingly solid and simple, the black pieces created using burnt olive oil as a stain. He also sells boards and other woodcraft items, but only makes the pieces himself – a process well worth watching.

Ensemble Artisanal

avenue Mohammed V, Medina (024 38 67 58). **Open** 8.30am-7.30pm daily. **Credit** AmEx, MC, V. **Map** p250/252 A5.

The second major tourist stop after photo ops at the Koutoubia, the EA is another state-sponsored crafts mini-mall like the Centre Artisanal described above – but far more popular because of its central location. All the artisans selling within are purportedly here by royal appointment, selected as the best in their field (a licence therefore to charge higher prices, which are completely non-negotiable). Expect everything from fine embroidered table linen (first floor at the back) to jewellery, clothing, lamps and even knock-off European handbags.

Beauty

Branches of **Yves Rocher** (*see p139*) are scattered across Marrakech, offering reasonably-priced hair and beauty products as well as facials and beauty treatments. For salons and hairdressers, *see p139*.

Nectarome

BP 142 Tnine Ourika, Haouz (024 48 24 47/ www.nectarome.com). **Open** 9am-5pm daily. **No credit cards.**

Discover the healing properties of plants in the gardens at **Nectarome**. *See p124.*

On the outskirts of the village at the foot of the Ourika Valley (*see p201*), this walled compound contains an organic garden full of aromatic and medicinal plants, plus a small shop selling natural products made with their essential oils. First you're invited to take a tour of the gardens, where the properties of plants are explained. Afterwards, browse the selection of soaps, shampoos and bath, massage, skin treatment and aromatherapy oils. Call ahead to book a foot bath (70dh) or foot massage (300dh), and also for a better chance of getting an English-speaking guide. If you can't manage the 37km drive down here, Atelier Moro (*see p133*) stocks a small selection of Nectarome products.

La Savonnerie
Marché Central, rue Ibm Toummert, Guéliz (068 51 74 79/rambad5@yahoo.com). **Open** 9.30am-7pm Mon-Thur, Sat; 9.30am-2pm Fri, Sun. **No credit cards. Map** p254 B2/C2 .
Among the horse butchers and grocers of the new Marché Central, this soapmaker's stall is a fragrant highlight. As well as colourful bars and lozenges of soap, with a variety of scents such as almond, rosemary, orange, musk or green tea, the owner also sells terracotta soap dishes to put them in.

Carpets

For an idea of the best places to shop for carpets and how much to pay *see p136* **Shopping the souk**.

L'Art de Goulimine
25 Souk des Tapis, Medina (024 44 02 22). **Open** 9am-6.30pm daily. **Credit** AmEx, MC, V. **Map** p73 ❺
For something a little different, Rabia and Ahmed are two young dealers specialising in Rhamana carpets from the plains north of Marrakech. They have a small showroom displaying choice pieces downstairs from the main sales space, where you'll find plenty of all the more usual carpet types at competitive prices.

Bazaar du Sud
117 Souk des Tapis, Medina (024 44 30 04). **Open** 9am-7pm daily. **Credit** AmEx, MC, V. **Map** p73 ❻
This place has possibly the largest selection of carpets in the souk, covering all regions and styles, new and old. The owners say they have 17 buyers out at any one time scouring the country for the finest examples. Although considerable effort goes into supplying collectors and dealers worldwide, sales staff are just as happy to entertain the novice. Prices range from 2,000dh to 350,000dh. Ask for Ismail, who speaks perfect English.

Bazaar les Palmiers
145 Souk Dakkakine, Medina (024 44 46 29). **Open** 9am-7pm Mon-Thur, Sat, Sun. **Credit** AmEx, MC, V. **Map** p73 ❼
Hamid is a fourth-generation carpet dealer. His passion is carpets from the High Atlas, characterised by their beautiful colouring. Pieces here take in the old and not-so-old, with prices starting at an

affordable 100dh (although all that gets you is a cushion). He speaks English, and is happy to expound on his favourite subject over a glass of mint tea.

Tapis Akhnif
6 rue Mouassine, Medina (024 42 60 96). **Open** 9am-8pm daily. **Credit** MC, V. **Map** p73 ③
A small family business, run by a father and his two sons, Akhnif offers a wide array of carpets, raffia and wool rugs, pillow cases and pouffes, without any sales hassle. Prices are fair, and there's good café au lait on request.

Fashion

A word of warning: what wears well in Marrakech won't necessarily have the same glamour in inner London or downtown NYC. Kaftans suit souks not subways.

Accessories are another matter, and there are some fun bags, belts and jewellery pieces to be found. Apart from the shops listed here, **Atelier Moro** (*see p133*) and **Miloud Art Gallery** (*see p135*) also stock both garments and accessories.

Akbar Delights
45 place Bab Fteuh, Medina (071 66 13 07). **Open** 10am-1pm, 3-7.30pm Tue-Sun. **Credit** AmEx, MC, V. **Map** p73 ⑨
This extremely upmarket French-owned boutique specialises in luxury clothing and textiles from Kashmir, with some items made to their own designs.

Bazaar les Palmiers. *See p125.*

The tiny space is crammed with embroidered tops and dresses, cotton robes, silk shawls and scarves, plus shimmery, golden shoulder bags. The only made-in-Morocco items are some extraordinary brocaded *babouches*. The most recent innovation is bags made from mink. A new showroom recently opened on the rue de la Liberté in Guéliz, as some of their extremely well-heeled customers (members of the royal family among them) may baulk at an excursion to the Medina. The new space stocks more home linens and a wider selection of clothing than you'll find in the Medina, and is open by appointment; call the owner to arrange a visit (071 66 13 07, rue de la Liberté, Imm 42C, apartment 47, just past Atika Shoes).

L'Art de la Couture
42-44 rue Rahba El Biadyne (024 44 04 87/061 34 40 26). **Open** 9am-1pm, 3-7.30pm daily. **Credit** AmEx, MC, V. **Map** p73 ⑩
It looks nothing from the outside – nor within, for that matter – but this tiny shop sells wonderful classic coats and jackets for men and women, and has made to order for the queen. Cuts are simple, with embroidered details in subtle colours. The best garments are made from B'zou wools, the speciality of a small mountain town. Prices start at 1,000dh and custom orders take two weeks (shipping overseas available). Coming from Derb Dabbachi, look for a modest light-pine frontage on the right with an AmEx sticker on the glass.

Beldi
9-11 Soukiat Laksour, Bab Fteuh, Medina (024 44 10 76). **Open** 9.30am-1pm, 3.30-8pm daily. **Credit** MC, V. **Map** p73 ⑪
Toufik studied fashion in Germany and now, back in Marrakech, he and his brother Abdelhafid have transformed the family tailoring business into what is probably the most talked-about boutique in town. They offer both men's and women's ranges in the most beautiful colours and fabrics, fashioned with flair and an eye to Western tastes. Beautiful velvet coats lined with silk start at around 1,600dh; men's shirts in fine linen cost from 400dh. Collections change seasonally.

Costumes 1001 Nuits
97 Souk Semarine (061 87 26 87). **Open** 8am-8pm daily. **Credit** MC, V. **Map** p73 ⑫
In a prime position on a busy corner, Abdelaziz Elouissi's shop specialises in beautiful vintage kaftans and *jellebahs* for men and women, all from Marrakech and some of them over a century old. In addition to the stock displayed in his small shop, he has still more stashed nearby, and will hurry off to find other examples of whatever you seem to want. Prices start at around 500dh, but can climb very high for more elaborate pieces.

Eva/Adam
144 Souk El Hanna, Medina (024 44 39 69). **Open** 10am-12.30pm, 3.30-6.30pm Mon-Thur, Sat, Sun. **Credit** AmEx, MC, V. **Map** p73 ⑬

Dress up at **La Maison du Kaftan Marocain**.

No high fashion or class cuts, just practical and genuinely comfortable warm-weather clothes in neutral colours. Made from cotton and lightweight wool, the styles are loose fitting yet elegant. It's the kind of stuff you might actually wear on a day-to-day basis, and prices are reasonable enough. To find it, walk north up Souk El Attarin just past the entrance to the mosque on the left. Look to the right for the word 'Lacoste' painted on a whitewashed arch: Eva/Adam is first on the right, with barely more than a door by way of shop frontage.

Au Fil d'Or

10 Souk Semmarine, Medina (024 44 59 19). **Open** 9am-1pm, 2.30-7.30pm Mon-Thur, Sat, Sun; 9am-1pm Fri. **Credit** AmEx, MC, V. **Map** p73 ⑭

It's almost indistinguishable from the multitude of small stores that surround it, but Au Fil d'Or is worth honing in on for the finest quality *babouches* and wool *jellabas*, plus fantastic own-label hand-stitched shirts (400dh) in gorgeous deep hues, and finely braided silk-lined jackets (2,200dh) – just the thing should one be invited to the palace. Note that the bulk of the stock is kept in the cellar-like space downstairs, accessed via a trapdoor behind the counter. Watch your head (and your spending).

Intensité Nomade

139 avenue Mohammed V, Guéliz (024 43 13 33). **Open** 9am-12.30pm, 3-7.30pm Mon-Sat. **Credit** AmEx, MC, V. **Map** p254 B2.

IN features owner-designer Frédérique Birkemeyer's own chic 'nomad' line of colourful kaftans, suede skirts, comfy raffia slippers, men's cotton shirts, leather jackets and a host of relatively inexpensive accessories. Pickings are mixed, but the place draws a glitzy local clientele, poking around the racks for casual prêt à porter.

Kulchi

1 rue des Ksour, Bab Laksour, Medina (no phone). **Open** 9.30am-1pm, 3.30-7pm Mon-Sat. **No credit cards**. **Map** p250/252 B5.

Florence Taranne's small boutique stocks a quirky hand-picked collection of boho Moro chic, including leather shopping bags with the *khamsa* ('hand') motif, lovely ruffly silk dresses as well as chiffon blouses in flowery prints by Spanish designer Lola, T-shirts by Hassan Hajjaj, Zina-label plastic shopping bags with brightly coloured flower designs and delicate jewellery, including rose petals laminated as earrings. It's pricey, at around 1,200dh-1,600dh for a silk and chiffon blouse, although you can find the odd bargain kaftan for 65dh or less. Our biggest beef is that most of the clothes are too small around the bust and would suit only Kate Moss or Sienna Miller – both of whom have been seen here. The store was closed for a while, but recently reopened.

La Maison du Kaftan Marocain

65 rue Sidi El Yamami, Medina (024 44 10 51). **Open** 9am-7.30pm daily. **Credit** AmEx, MC, V. **Map** p73 ⑮

La Maison may have the unloved, run-down look of a charity shop, but it also has the widest selection of Moroccan clothing for men, women and children in the souk, housed in what sustained exploration reveals to be a vast mausoleum of a place. Stock ranges from *pantalon turque* (traditional men's trousers) to beautiful velvet jackets and vintage kaftans that go for 20,000dh. Scouts for international fashion houses often drop by to place orders and look for inspiration.

Marrakech Maille Sarl

69 boulevard El Mansour Eddahbi, Guéliz (024 43 95 85). **Open** 8am-1pm, 3-7pm Mon-Sat. **No credit cards**. **Map** p254 B2.

A well-kept secret among Moroccan royalty and the chic wives of diplomats, this small and unprepossessing boutique contains some very wearable clothes which will also make that all-important transition home to a colder climate. In winter, the owner and designer Khadija Daaraoui stocks lovely woollen shawls and scarves, quality wool and mohair suits and *jellabas* in natural fibres. In summer, expect lightweight cotton T-shirts in all colours (think John Smedley) and cotton and linen skirts, trouser suits and kaftans. Classic.

Miloud El Jouli

6-8 Souk Smat El Marga, off Souk El Kebir, Medina (024 42 67 16). **Open** 9am-7.30pm daily. **Credit** MC, V. **Map** p73 ⑯

Eat, Drink, Shop

Join buyers from boutiques in Chelsea and New York's Upper East Side to rifle through patterned *babouches*, vibrantly coloured shirts and blouses in Indian silks, silk and dyed-leather sequinned handbags, beaded belts with heavy silver buckles and *jellabas*. Some of the wares are Miloud's own designs, some cleverly-crafted local copies of high-fashion pieces, as in the Hermès sandals that fill one shelf. Prices are less than you'd pay back home, but not that much less. Miloud has now applied this same approach to homewear and furnishings at Miloud Art Gallery (*see p135*). Souk Smat El Marga is in the Kissaria, the third narrow alley from the northernmost end of Souk El Kebir.

Mysha & Nito

rue Sourya, corner rue Tarik Ibn Ziad, Guéliz (024 42 16 38/www.mysha-nito.com). **Open** 9am-1pm, 3.30-8pm, Mon-Sat. **Credit** MC, V. **Map** p254 B2.
On the ground floor you'll find womenswear by 12 local designers (11 Moroccan, one Belgian). The focus is kaftans and *jellebahs*, reinvented as evening-wear in a variety of fabrics – including chiffon, gingham, simulated leather and imitation snakeskin – and priced anywhere between 1,000dh and 25,000dh. There are also T-shirts, bags, slippers and belts for those on a smaller budget. Downstairs is an assortment of antiques and sculpture.

Fashion accessories

For bags belts and the like try **Kulchi** (*see above*), **Miloud El Jouli** (*see above*) and **Atelier Moro** (*see p133*); for scarves, shawls and mink bags visit **Akbar Delights** (*see p126*).

Michi

19-21 Souk Lakchachbia, Medina (061 86 44 07/ aitelaloud2001@yahoo.fr). **Open** 9am-7pm daily. **No credit cards**. **Map** p73 ⑰
Owned by a Japanese-Moroccan couple, this small shop near the slipper souk has a small but appealing selection of well-made Moroccan items, chosen with a Japanese aesthetic. These include simple slippers and jewellery, delicate wooden spoons and spatulas, and raffia shoes from Essaouira.

Jewellery

Most of the jewellery for sale in Marrakech is ethnic in either inspiration or origin. Favoured materials are silver, amber and beads, and pieces tend towards the heavy and chunky.

Bazaar Atlas

129 boulevard Mohammed V, Guéliz (024 43 27 16). **Open** 9.30am-1pm, 3.30-7.30pm Mon-Sat; 9.30am-1pm Sun. **Credit** MC, V. **Map** p254 B2.
This small but eye-catching boutique in central Guéliz comprises one room lined from floor to ceiling with cabinets full of jewellery: antique, antique-styled, ethnic (Berber and Touareg) and modern. In

Bunches of beads at **Boutique Bel Hadj**.

among it all is a smattering of odd gift items, including ceramics, tiny silver pill boxes and sculpted gazelle-horn and camel-bone ink wells and letter openers. The owner speaks fluent English.

Bellawi

Kessariat Lossta No.56, off Souk El Attarin, Medina (024 44 01 07). **Open** 9am-7pm Mon-Thur, Sat, Sun. **Credit** MC, V. **Map** p73 ⑱
Abdelatif, owner of this closet-like jewellery store, is brother to the famed Mustapha Blaoui (*see p135*). Here, there's just about room for Abdelatif, his workbench and one customer. The walls are hung with beads clustered like bunches of berry fruits, along with a fine selection of traditional Moroccan-style silver bangles, necklaces and rings set with semi-precious stones. The shop is along the same narrow passage as Eva/Adam (*see p126*). There's no sign in English, but just ask for Abdelatif. Everyone knows him – he's been here for over 40 years.

Boutique Bel Hadj

22-33 Fundouk Ourzazi, place Bab Fteuh, Medina (024 44 12 58). **Open** 9am-8pm daily. **Credit** AmEx, MC, V. **Map** p73 ⑲
The landmark Café Argana on Jemaa El Fna occupies the south-west corner of an old *fundouk* (merchants' inn); walk right round the corner and into place Bab Fteuh and you'll find Mohammed Bari's shop, which is piled high with a mad assortment of bits and pieces of jewellery, old and new.

The range and quality are impressive, prices are fair and Mohammed will never knowingly try to foist off the new as antique.

El Yed Gallery

66 Fhal Chidmi, rue Mouassine, Medina (024 44 29 95). **Open** 9.30am-12.30pm, 1.30-6.30pm Mon-Sat. **Credit** AmEx, MC, V. **Map** p73 ⑳

Opposite the side of the Mouassine Mosque, El Yed is a real collectors' haunt, specialising in beautiful antique Moroccan jewellery and pottery. Much of it comes from the deep south, and it's not for the delicate of frame – bracelets look like great silver sprockets and the favoured stone is amber by the hunk. The owner speaks English and is highly knowledgeable about his stock. He's happy to discuss details and provenance, but probably less willing to talk prices, which are fixed and expensive.

Leather

For more on buying leather bags in Marrakech, *see p136* **Shopping the souk**.

Chez Said

155 Souk Chkairia, Medina (024 39 09 31). **Open** 9.30am-7.30pm daily. **Credit** MC, V. **Map** p73 ㉑

Said specialises in fashionable leather bags, decorated with coins or beads, or just a simple metal disc on the front. Designs come in both modern and vintage styles. The leather is either au natural or dyed; when the latter, colouring is properly fixed and doesn't come off on your clothes. Said speaks English, and also sells his bags in bulk to certain well-known stores in the UK.

Galerie Birkemeyer

169 rue Mohammed El Bekal, Guéliz (024 44 69 63). **Open** 8.30am-12.30pm, 3-7.30pm Mon-Sat; 9am-12.30pm Sun. **Credit** AmEx, MC, V. **Map** p254 A2.

A long-established haunt for leather goods, from handbags and luggage to shoes, jackets, coats and skirts, with a sportswear section of international designer labels. The sales assistants aren't particularly helpful, and founder Ms Birkemeyer no longer

has anything to do with the place (she now owns Intensité Nomade, *see p127*), but you still might stumble across a good bargain, such as a beautifully crafted purse for 600dh.

Place Vendome

141 avenue Mohammed V, Guéliz (024 43 52 63). **Open** 9am-12.30pm, 3.30-7.30pm Mon-Sat. **Credit** AmEx, MC, V. **Map** p254 B2.

Owner Claude Amzallag is known for his custom-designed buttery leather and suede jackets, and sleek line of handbags and wallets, which come in every colour from forest green to hot pink. The suede shirts for men and stylish luggage are also big hits with the fortysomething crowd.

Shoes

If it's slippers you're after, check out **Art Ouarzazate** (*see p138*), **Au Fil d'Or** (*see p127*) and **Akbar Delights** (*see p126*), as well as **Haj Ahmed Oueld Lafram** (*see 131*).

Atika

35 rue de la Liberté, Guéliz (024 43 64 09). **Open** 8.30am-12.30pm, 3-7.30pm Mon-Sat. **Credit** MC, V. **Map** p254 B2.

This is where well-heeled residents and enlightened tourists flock for stylish and affordable men's and women's ranges – everything from classic loafers to natural leather sandals and stylish beige canvas mules. Prices start at 300dh and rarely go beyond 750dh. It also carries children's shoes and a small selection of handbags. There's a second branch a few hundred metres south at 212 avenue Mohammed V.

Cordonnerie Errafia

Riad Zitoun El Jedid, Medina (mobile 062 77 83 47). **Open** 9am-1pm, 3-9pm daily. **No credit cards**. **Map** p253 D6.

In a little workshop opposite the Préfecture de la Medina, artisan Ahmed cobbles together classic loafers out of raffia for gents, with more extravagantly coloured and cut stylings for women. Given three or four days, he can also make to order.

Resourceful *babouche*-makers can get inspiration anywhere.

The industrial revolution

Perhaps you're wondering where the beautifully glazed bowl in your riad came from – or those sumptuously coloured candles, or the soft cotton bedsheets you slept in last night. Ask, and they'll probably tell you. But if it wasn't sourced at **Mustapha Blaoui** (see p135), chances are it came from one of the workshops, ateliers and factories out in the Quartier Industriel of Sidi Ghanem.

About eight kilometres (five miles) north of town, this isn't the most romantic of locations. Sure, there's a palm tree or two and the buildings are still pink – even the giant works at the quarter's northern end. But this old industrial and warehousing area, built on an ordered, linear street pattern, offers space that can't be found in the Medina or Guéliz. As a result, more and more Marrakech-based designers are establishing studios and showrooms here.

By car or taxi, follow the Casablanca road, then turn left at the McDonalds on to the Route de Safi. After you've crossed the railway tracks, take the second left and then turn right at the big, square intersection. You are now on the long, nameless thoroughfare where most of the interesting places can be found. We'd recommend stopping off at **Café Cosaque**, on the left at No.280, and picking up one of the free advertising maps of the area that are usually lying around. Over a coffee, plan which of the many showrooms you want to visit. Here are some highlights – all of which accept Mastercard and Visa.

Amira (No.277, 024 33 62 47, www.amira bougies.com, open 9am-1pm, 2.30-6pm Mon-Sat) is just a few doors away from Café Cosaque. Candles are a key ingredient of the Moroccan night, and Amira make the best ones. They come in all shapes and colours:

giant orange or purple cubes, candles that can also be used as vases, knee-high stripy cylinders and candles within candles. Prices start at around 500dh.

Back up the road at No.322 is **Akkal** (024 33 59 38, www.akkal.net, open 8am-6pm Mon-Sat, 9.30am-6pm Sun), whose pottery factory produces modern takes on classic Moroccan shapes, from tajines to tea glasses, as well as pick 'n' mix dinnerware, mostly in fantastically rich colours. They change the range every year, but keep older designs in stock so that broken pieces can be replaced.

Directly upstairs from Akkal is the showroom of **Via Notti** (024 35 60 24, open 9am-6pm Mon-Sat). It's full of wonderful Egyptian cotton bedlinen, all in pure white embellished with simple, coloured embroidered detailing. You can specify colours with an order, and they can also do calligraphic embroidery to your specifications. Big white towels and towelling bathrobes round off the range.

Right down the other end of the road at No.16 is **Fan Wa Nour** (024 33 69 60, open 2-6pm Mon, 9am-6pm Tue-Sat). This is the showroom of Belgian designer Marc Vanden Bossche, who uses Moroccan craft methods and materials to reinvent everything from vases and lamps to sofas and storage systems, handbags and belts. There's also work by the Carlo Cumini and Michel Durand Meyrien, and an assortment of retro items.

Be warned that it's a long walk from one end of this street to the other. If you take a taxi out here, you won't want to let it go – it's not easy to find another one in these parts. If you ask a driver to wait or to shuttle you from shop to shop, agree an hourly rate; 50dh-60dh is a fair price.

Haj Ahmed Oueld Lafram

51 Souk Smafa (024 44 51 27). **Open** 10am-6.30pm Mon-Thur, Sat, Sun. **No credit cards.** **Map** p73 ㉒
Most of the souk's slipper shops are much of a muchness – look into one and you've pretty much seen them all; the same styles pop up again and again. But Haj Ahmed Oueld Lafram offers a selection of *babouches* in a variety of styles from all over Morocco – embroidered leather ones from Tafraoute, for example – and in a variety of materials that include the likes of dyed goat fur, Italian horse leather and python skin. They're not the cheapest, but the quality is excellent.

Florists

In addition to the places listed below, a corner of the Marché Central (see p132 **Market forces**) is given over to florists.

Vita

58 boulevard El Mansour Eddahbi, Guéliz (024 43 04 90). **Open** 8.30am-12.30pm, 3-7.30pm Mon-Sat; 9am-1pm Sun. **No credit cards.** **Map** p254 A2.
A Western-style florist and garden centre with a decent stock of cut flowers and ready-made bouquets. It also does delivery (local and Interflora), and sells potted plants, seeds and compost.

Market forces

Away from the souks' main lanes of concentrated commerce are several other markets that are worth investigating.

In the old Jewish quarter of the Mellah there's the **Bab Es Salam market** (map p253 D7) one block east of the place des Ferblantiers. It's very much a local affair, with traders selling fruit and vegetables, herbs and spices. Nearby, on the south side of avenue Houman El-Fetouaki is the **Marché Couvert** (map p253 C7), another working market supplying fresh produce, meat and fish to the kitchens of the homes of the southern Medina.

At the opposite extreme, in all senses, is the **Souk El-Khemis** (map p251 D2). At the northern end of the Old City, just inside the Bab El-Khemis gate, it's as much rubbish dump as market. A last chance saloon for manufactured goods, stalls here can be no more than a blanket spread with a pitiful heap of cast-offs – single shoes, a box of rusted bicycle gears, a bag of unravelled audio cassettes. But it's also a legendary treasure trove of architectural salvage. Palmeraie villas have been kitted out at the Souk El Khemis, and when the Mamounia underwent its last refit, the discarded sinks, fittings and even carpets all turned up here.

The **Marché Central** (map p254 B3) in Guéliz has moved from its old spot on avenue Mohammed V to an off-the-beaten-track location on rue Ibn Toummert, just behind place du 16 Novembre. It's still the place for horse butchers, florists and grocery shops that sell European breakfast cereals, biscuits, cheeses and booze, but it's lost a lot of its life and custom.

A kilometre north-east, just off avenue Yacoub El Mansour and in the neighbourhood of the Majorelle Gardens, is the city's **Wholesale Market** (map p254 C1). Operating from seven to ten each morning, it's where farmers from outlying villages bring crates of produce. At press time, however, plans were being announced to move it further out of town, and the city's fruit and veg merchants were threatening a strike.

Finally, back in the souks, just south of Rahba Kedima is **Souk Lagzhel** (map p250 C5). The site of the old slave market, it's now home to a second-hand clothes market. The piles of old garments spread out on the ground don't look like very much, but many boast of wonderful finds here. Arrive early in the day.

Marché Couvert.

Food & drink

The greatest range of food and drink is found at **Aswak Assalam** and **Marjane** (see p123). For fresh fruit and veg there's the **Marché Couvert** and **Bab Es Salam** market in the Medina, and the new **Marché Central** in Guéliz.

Entrepôt Alimentaire
117 avenue Mohammed V, Guéliz (024 43 00 67).
Open 8am-noon, 3-10pm Mon-Sat; 8am-noon Sun.
No credit cards. Map p254 B2.

This dusty little place may appear disorganised, but it does have one of the best selections of wine (Moroccan and French) in town. If you can't see what you're looking for, ask.

Jeff de Bruges
17 rue de la Liberté, Guéliz (024 43 02 49).
Open 9am-1pm, 3.30-8pm Mon-Sat. **Credit** MC, V.
Map p254 B2.

Not real Belgian chocolates, but still the best chocolates in Marrakech. They make a great gift if you're invited to dinner at a local home (Moroccans are notoriously sweet-toothed), but don't expect to get

Eat, Drink, Shop

a share because they'll be hoarded away for later. There's also a branch at Marjane (*see p123*).

Yacout Services

2 rue Yakoub El Marini, Guéliz (024 43 19 41). **Open** 8am-9pm daily. **No credit cards.** **Map** p254 B3.

Just south of place du 16 Novembre in Guéliz and not far from the church, Yacout is a fantastically well-stocked mini-market thats incorporates a basement store devoted to booze – local and imported wines, beer and spirits. Next door is a shop selling own-made pasta.

Home accessories

By which we mean crystal, china and pottery, furnishings and drapes, lanterns and candles, gee-gaws, leather pouffes and knick-knacks. In this city of a 1,001 interior designers, 'home accessories' has to be just about the biggest business in town. *See also p131* **The industrial revolution**.

African Lodge

1 rue Loubnane, Guéliz (024 43 95 84/laurence corsin@yahoo.fr). **Open** 10am-1pm, 3-7.30pm Mon-Sat. **Credit** AmEx, MC, V. **Map** p254 B2.

'African', as opposed to North African, style is currently the fashionable thing in Marrakech, and unique furniture pieces by designer Laurence Corsin, whose shop this is, have started to appear in many a restaurant and riad. There's a selection of his work downstairs, along with sub-Saharan ornaments and figurines. Much of Corsin's work is in metal; we liked the shelves and tables fashioned out of old bedsprings, like a high-style version of those toys made from old olive oil or sardine cans. A small mezzanine hosts a colourful cornucopia of knick-knacks from around the world, including lacquer-bound Japanese photo albums, Chinese thermos flasks, Lebanese jewellery and an assortment of crockery.

Atelier Moro

114 Place de Mouassine, Mouassine (024 39 16 78/ 060 54 35 20/ateliermoro@menara.ma). **Open** 9am-1pm, 3-7pm Mon, Wed-Sun. **Credit** AmEx, MC, V. **Map** p73 ㉓

This L-shaped first-floor space by the Mouassine fountain contains a cool, eclectic selection of homeware, clothes, accessories and carpets chosen by Viviana Gonzalez of Riad El Fenn (*see p43*). Some of the clothes are designed by Viviana herself and a few other items are from her native Colombia, but most of the stock is Moroccan, often the work of nameless artisans that would otherwise be lost in the souks. There's everything from inexpensive hand-made scissors and Tuareg cutlery to pricey rugs, lamps made from ostrich eggs and suede or Egyptian cotton tops. The door is to the west of the fountain, just right of the arch that leads into the Souk des Teinturiers. Ring for entry.

Cherkaoui

120-122 rue Mouassine, Medina (024 42 68 17). **Open** 8.30am-7.30pm daily. **Credit** AmEx, MC, V. **Map** p73 ㉔

Opposite the Mouassine fountain is this glittering Aladdin's cave, full of everything imaginable in the way of home decoration Moroccan-style (with the exception of carpets). The proprietors, one local (Jaoud) and one German (Matthias), use their own local artisans, working in various media including wood, leather, metal and clay, to supply the store. Customers include the famed restaurant Dar Yacout (*see p98*) and the Hotel les Jardins de la Koutoubia (*see p41*). Any piece can be made up in eight weeks, and shipping can be arranged.

Founoun Marrakech

28 Souk des Teinturiers, Medina (024 42 62 03). **Open** 10am-7pm daily. **Credit** AmEx, MC, V. **Map** p73 ㉕

This is the place to come if you want a lantern (*founoun*) of quality. At first glance it's tiny, but walk through to the back room to find an impressive choice of truly beautiful things. Ask owner Rachid El-Himel to take you through to the workshop; here, a team of men and young boys hammer and cut at sheets of copper, fashioning the goods to stock the shop. To find it, walk east past the Mouassine fountain then through the arch, and it's the first lantern shop on the left.

Kifkif

8 rue des Ksour, Bab Laksour, Medina (061 08 20 41). **Open** 9.30am-7.30pm daily. **No credit cards.** **Map** p250/252 B5.

A quality knick-knack shop with an eclectic array of goods, including unique bangles, belts, earrings and other accessories, little towelling dressing gowns for kids, embroidered napkin sets and own-designed glasses, electric lights, vases and table decorations. Stephanie is the owner, and almost everything she stocks is made in Morocco. Some things are too expensive, like the set of Momo's Arabesque CDs at 350dh (buy the bootleg in Jemaa El Fna), but others, like the charming white cotton baby romper suits at 100dh a throw, or the attractive beaded cigarette lighter covers for tabletops, are good value. There is also a branch in Essaouira (*see p187*).

Lun'art Gallery

24 rue Moulay Ali, Guéliz (024 44 72 66). **Open** 9am-12.30pm, 3.30-8pm Mon-Sat. **Credit** AmEx, MC, V.

Eclecticism reigns supreme at this rather odd gallery and Moro curio shop. It has a garden space showcasing wrought-iron garden furniture and heavy mosaic tables, while indoors is a mixture of modern paintings by Moroccan artists, traditional pottery, *tadelakt* lamps, bric-a-brac and the odd curveball such as cinema costume accessories (for example, neckties left over from the filming of Scorcese's *Kundun*). Prices are reasonable.

Eat, Drink, Shop

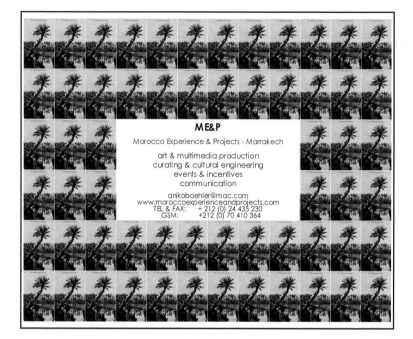

Miloud Art Gallery

48 Souk Charatine (024 42 67 16/070 41 76 61).
Open 9am-8pm daily. **Credit** AmEx, MC, V.
Map p254 A2.

This new venture, opened by Miloud El Jouli in early 2007, is a one-stop shop for competitively priced versions of modern Moroccan design – essentially knock-offs of the kind of thing you might find in places such as Yahya Creation (*see p136*) or Akkal (*see p131* **The industrial revolution**). A generous space is packed with large furniture pieces and smaller, more transportable items to take back home. Armchairs and coffee tables, ceramics and textiles, pouffes and picture frames are all specially made and of good quality. There's also a selection of kaftans and handbags from Miloud El Jouli's other shop (*see p127*). With no shop front, this place can be hard to find; call to arrange a visit.

Mustapha Blaoui

142-144 Bab Doukkala, Medina (024 38 52 40).
Open 9am-8pm daily. **Credit** AmEx, MC, V.
Map p250 B4.

This is the classiest, most beloved 'best of Morocco' depot in town. It's a warehouse of a place; crammed, racked, stacked and piled with floor-to-ceiling irresistibles – lanterns, dishes, pots, bowls, candlesticks, chandeliers, chests, tables and chairs… If Mustapha doesn't have it, then you don't need it. He supplied a lot of the furnishings for both the Villa des Orangers (*see p41*) and the nearby Riad Noir d'Ivoire (*see p47*). Even people who don't own a hotel will find it almost impossible to visit here and not fill a container lorry. Added to which, Mustapha is a real sweetheart, his staff are ultra-helpful and shipping here is a cinch.

Scènes de Lin

70 rue de la Liberté, Guéliz (024 43 61 08). **Open** 9.30am-12.30pm, 3.30-7.30pm Mon-Sat. **Credit** MC, V. **Map** p254 B2.

A chic fabric store that specialises in linens, and also offers a huge range of brilliant hues in striped woven cloth or delicate pastel organdie. Any combo can be ordered for custom-made curtains, tablecloths or place settings. There's plenty of other top quality stuff besides, including luxurious fringed hammam towels, cushions with Fès embroidery, natural essential oils (including argan oil) and unusual contemporary lamps. Downstairs is a small selection of Moroccan couture.

Furniture

For something in a traditional vein, pay a visit to **Mustapha Blaoui** (*see above*). For something a little more unique, look at the work of Thierry Isnardon at **La Medina** (*see above*).

Ministerio del Gusto

22 Derb Azouz El Mouassine, off rue Sidi El Yamami, Medina (024 42 64 55). **Open** 9.30am-noon, 4-7pm Mon-Sat. **Credit** MC, V. **Map** p73 ㉖

The Ministero is HQ to ex-*Vogue Italia* fashion editor Alessandra Lippini and her business partner Fabrizio Bizzarri. It's a surreal space – a sort of Gaudí goes Mali with a side trip to Mexico. As well as filling the role of informal social centre for friends and assorted fashionistas and creatives blowing through town, the two floors also act as an occasional gallery (*see p150*) and a showcase for funky 'found' objects (sourced from house clearances) such as African-inspired furniture, Eames chairs and Bernini glassware.

Glassware

Myriam Roland-Gosselin

6 route de l'Aeroport (024 36 19 88). **Open** by appointment only. **No credit cards.**

Roland-Gosselin has a studio in a tranquil garden just off the airport road, where she makes delicate hand-blown glass objects for the home. Her collection, exhibited in an adjacent showroom, consists of vases, tumblers, bowls, bells, wine glasses, candle holders and small lamps. Colour schemes range from neutral to warm ambers and oranges that bring to mind fiery Moroccan sunsets. Purchases are packaged in her lovely signature boxes. A selection of her work is also on sale at the boutique at the Villa Des Orangers (*see p41*).

Metalwork

Artisanat Berbère

33 Souk El Attarin, Medina (024 44 38 78). **Open** 9am-8pm daily. **Credit** MC, V. **Map** p73 ㉗

A charmingly dusty old place, filled with heaps of largely useless items fashioned from brass, copper, pewter and other pliable metals. There are lots of trays, pots and lamps on offer, plus ancient flat irons and giant sculpted animals. And you've got to love a place that promises 'small margin profit' on its business card.

Dinanderie

6-46 Fundouk My Mamoun, Mellah (024 38 49 09). **Open** 8am-8pm Mon-Sat. **Credit** MC, V. **Map** p253 D7.

Moulay Youssef is one of the country's handful of elite artisans. If you need something extravagant wrought from metal – and if you have the money – then Moulay is your man. The bulk of his work is made to order, but adjacent to his workspace is a crowded gallery of smaller pieces. A little difficult to find, the Dinanderie atelier fills an alley immediately west of the small rose garden across from the place des Ferblantiers.

Mohammed Ouledhachmi

34 Souk El Hararin Kedima, Medina (066 64 41 05). **Open** 9am-6pm Mon-Thur, Sat, Sun. **No credit cards. Map** p73 ㉘

Mohammed does copper – copper trays, copper pots, copper kettles, copper you-name-it. Some of the

Eat, Drink, Shop

Shopping the souk

Every city has that something that you just have to pick up before you leave. Marrakech has numerous must-buys. Here's our checklist of the standard purchases:

Argan oil

Morocco's famed argan oil is rich in vitamin E and essential fatty acids. It lowers cholesterol levels, unblocks arteries, relieves rheumatic joint pain, reduces scars and wrinkles, whitens your smile, makes you horny and pays off your mortgage – or so they say. The miraculous stuff is available at 'Berber pharmacies' (herbal shops) in the souk. What you buy in such places is OK as a massage oil but should not be ingested. It's likely to have been cut with some other inferior oil, like cooking oil. For argan oil to use as a food dressing you need to go to a reputable outlet (*see below*). You may pay a little more at these places but you can be sure of the provenance and quality of the product.

The average price for argan oil in Marrakech is around 150dh a litre, but you can pay more for fancy packaging. You'll find it cheaper if you're going to Essaouira or Taroudant.

● The quality stuff is available at **Marjane** (*see p123*) or **Scènes de Lin** (*see p135*).

Babouches

Babouche-buying is not as straightforward as it seems. The slippers come in leather, nubuck, suede or sabra (which looks like silk but is actually a kind of viscose). The sole will be leather, plastic or rubber and can be sewn on (good) or glued (not good). Yellow is the traditional Moroccan fave but *babouche* come in all colours as well as round-toed or pointy, with or without sequins, embroidered or not furry or stripey – you name it, someone does it.

Prices vary, but expect to pay around 50dh for fake leather *babouche* with glued soles up to around 150dh for a pair of the all-leather, stitched-sole variety.

● Available from just about everywhere but the obvious place to go is the **Souk des Babouches** (*see map p73*).

Carpets

There's one simple rule when it comes to carpets: buy it because you like it, not because you've been told it's worth money. The seller was probably lying: very few carpets are antique. And ignore claims that a carpet is made of cactus silk. It's most likely not: genuine cactus silk carpets cost ten times as much as normal ones. What is sold as cactus silk is usually viscose.

When you see a carpet that you like, bear in mind that you are unlikely to find its double in another shop as most are unique. And don't be afraid of not buying after having a guy unfurl two dozen specimens for you: it's his job and anyway carpets have to be unrolled now and then to let them breathe a little.

Carpets come in three standard sizes with standard prices, although there are modifying factors of age, quality and type. As a rule of thumb, something one metre by 1.5 metres should cost around 1,500dh; a carpet 1.5 metres by 2.5 metres will go for around 2,500dh; and one two metres by three will set you back somewhere around 4,500dh-5,000dh.

● The main places to buy carpets are along rue Mouassine (try **Tapis Akhnif**, *see p126*) and rue Semarine and in the Souk des Tapis off the Rahba Kedima, which is where you'll find **L'Art de Goulimine** (*see p125*) and **Bazaar du Sud** (*see p125*).

Ceramics

The local style is plain terracotta glazed in bright colours. As an alternative to the standard hard enamel finish (done here

pieces are new, but the bulk of the stock is older and sometimes includes pieces by well-known metalsmiths whose work is prized by collectors. To find the shop, head north up Souk El Attarin and take the second right after passing the entrance to the mosque on your left.

Yahya Creation

49 passage Ghandouri, off rue de Yougoslavie, Guéliz (024 42 27 76/www.yahyacreation.com). **Open** 10am-12.30pm, 2.30-7pm Mon-Sat. **Credit** MC, V. **Map** p254 A2.

Yahya Rouach's mother is English and Christian, his father is a Jew from Meknès, and he's a Muslim convert brought up in the UK and now resident in Marrakech. He designs extraordinary items, such as lanterns, torches and screens, all made from finely crafted metals. His pieces are unique, often stunning one-offs. Most of them are big too: conversation pieces for a chic sheikh's Dubai penthouse, perhaps. This arcade outlet is a showroom rather than a shop, where customers drop in to place commissions, joining a client list that includes Harrods and Neiman Marcus.

with startling colours), there's also *tadelakt* effect, which is smooth and satiny to the touch with more subdued tones of mustardy yellows, minty greens and burgundy.

Price for the standard enamel finish start at around 30dh (ashtrays and bowls) rising up to 200dh for large platters. *Tadelakt*-style pottery is more expensive, ranging from 50dh for a candleholder up to 400dh for a table lamp.

● Available everywhere but particularly in and around the Souk des Teinturiers (try **Création Chez Abdel**, *see below* and along the lower part of rue Mouassine (notably **Caverne d'Ali Baba**, *see below*). For superior quality visit **Akkal** (*see p131* **The Industrial Revolution**). The cheapest option is to shop at the sprawling, open-air **pottery market** just outside the south-eastern Medina gate of Bab Ghemat (see map p253 F6).

Lanterns

Styles range from traditional North African, inspired by the hanging lanterns found in mosques, to the art deco and avant garde – including tall, curly ones made out of decorated goatskin. The cheapest are those made of tin, which is often rusted for colour. The price increases with the addition of glass, patterned or plain (the latter is known as Iraki glass, and is more expensive than the patterned sort because it's better quality). Brass and copper lanterns are a bit more expensive but generally better finished, harder wearing and more easily integrated into a modern interior.

Prices range from around 30dh to 300dh for tin, and from 100dh to 500dh for copper and brass.

● Available in the **Souk des Ferroniers** or the **Souk des Dinandiers** (for both, *see map p73*) and at **Founoun Marrakech** (*see p133*).

Leather bags

Marrakech is good for quality leather, much of which ends up being fashioned into shoulder bags and travel luggage. But be careful: some of the work is shoddy and you can end up with a bag that leaves its contents stinking like a cowshed or transfers its colour to your skirt or trousers (rub the bag with a wet tissue before buying).

Also popular are vintage shoulder bags, often decorated with aged metal coins and copper discs. These sell for between 200dh and 400dh, or you can get modern copies for less.

Contemporary handbags go for anywhere from 150dh to 300dhs, while travel luggage starts at around 400dh and up to 800dh, depending on the size.

● Available from the northern end of the **Souk El Kebir** (*see map p73*) in the alleys of the Kissaria or, for something more modern and stylish try **Miloud El Jouli** (*see p127*).

Pottery

For general information on buying pottery, *see p136* **Shopping the souk**. *See also p131* **The industrial revolution** for **Akkal**.

Caverne d'Ali Baba

17A Fhal Chidmi, Mouassine, Medina (024 44 21 48). **Open** 9am-8pm daily. **Credit** MC, V. **Map** p73 ㉙

This huge shop is stocked with an incredible array of goods in all imaginable colours, from egg cups

to lamp bases . In fact, just about any pottery trend that has hit the Medina will very quickly be copied and put on sale here. Especially attractive are the *tadelakt*-finish items, which have an almost soft, leather-like appearance.

Création Chez Abdel

17 Souk des Teinturiers, Medina (024 42 75 17). **Open** 9am-9pm daily. **No credit cards**. **Map** p73 ㉚

Another good outlet for *tadelakt* pottery, this small shop is packed from floor to ceiling with simple shapes in rich, luminous colours. There are great bowls and lamps, but also lighter and more portable items such as candlesticks and ashtrays. Quality is excellent and prices are reasonable. There's no name on the shop so it can be difficult to spot – walk east past the Mouassine fountain and there's a sharp right, then a left; Abdel's is behind the pine-framed door on the right.

Chez Aloui

52 rue des Ksour, Mouassine, Medina (062 08 48 71). **Open** 9am-8pm daily. **No credit cards.** Map p73 ③①

A great place to look for ceramics in a variety of styles including Berber (which looks very African, with bold, clean shapes) and both old and new pieces from Safi, one of Morocco's main pottery-producing centres. Our favourites are the traditional green ceramics from Tamegroute near Zagora. The green glaze never comes out quite the same, so each piece is unique. Some of the plates and bowls are marked with a spiral motif, the Berber circle of life.

Textiles

Art Ouarzazate

15 rue Rahba Kedima, Medina (067 35 21 24). **Open** 10am-6.30pm daily. **Credit** MC, V. Map p73 ③②

A small sparsely stocked shop, but with an interesting stock, including beautiful throws hand-woven from agave fibres. Colours are jewel-like and prices pretty reasonable. There are also old kaftans and *jellabas*, and *babouches* made of silk (about 200dh a pair). Mohammed speaks English, and you can accept his offer of tea without feeling cornered into buying.

Chez Brahim

101 Rahba Lakdima, Medina (024 44 01 10). **Open** 9.30am-6.30pm daily. **Credit** AmEx, MC, V. Map p73 ③③

Brahim offers an almost overwhelming selection of fabulous Moroccan textiles, with a collection that covers all regions and styles. Many of his textiles are antique, and hard to find elsewhere. Visiting Chez Brahim is rather like going to a museum where everything is for sale; prices are steep, but these are collectors' pieces.

Chez Moulay Youssef

Souk El Kchachbia, off rue El Hadadine, Medina (024 44 34 01). **Open** 10am-8pm daily. **No credit cards.** Map p73 ③④

One of our favourite shops in the souk, Moulay Youssef does beautiful, richly coloured and stripy bedspreads in sabra, cotton or raffia. There are also homeware items such as jewellery boxes, napkin rings and pillow cases, plus fashion accessories like belts and hand-embroidered bags. It isn't the easiest place to find, but if you can locate the general neighbourhood, just ask – everybody round here knows Moulay Youssef.

Bookshops

Marrakech is not a literary city, and reading matter in any language is scarce. Beyond the places listed below, the **Musée de Marrakech** (*see p77*) has a bookshop, but it never seems to contain much of interest.

ACR Libraire d'Art

Immobelier Tayeb, 55 boulevard Mohammed Zerktouni, Guéliz (024 44 67 92). **Open** 9am-12.30pm, 3-7pm Mon-Sat. **Credit** MC, V. Map p254 B2.

ACR is a French publishing house, notable for its lavish art books. The company is seemingly dedicated to photographing every last mud brick and orange blossom in Marrakech and publishing the results in a series of coffee-table volumes. Get them all here, along with other (non-ACR) titles on the art and architecture of Morocco and the Islamic world, guides, cookery books and art cards. What little English-language stock the shop used to have seems to have disappeared. You'll find some Acr books for sale at the Musée de Marrakech bookshop.

Café du Livre

44 rue Tarik Ben Ziad, Guéliz (024 43 21 49). **Open** 9.30am-9pm Mon-Sat. **Credit** MC, V. Map p254 B2

The only English-language bookshop in town has a reasonably good stock of second-hand books and a small selection of new books about Morocco. It also occasionally hosts readings and signings – John Hopkins, a Tangier resident through the 1960s and 1970s, was a recent guest, signing copies of his novel, *All I Wanted was Company*. Bibliophiles should be thankful for the café component of the operation (*see p116*), not only because of the excellent light meal it serves up, but also because without it the book business wouldn't survive. While anglophone expats exchange gossip over coffee and lemon tart, the book side of the premises often has a few laptop-toting Moroccan students, making the most of the free Wi-Fi internet. The shop's entrance is in the courtyard of the Hotel Toulousain.

Librairie Chatr

23 avenue Mohammed V, Guéliz (024 44 79 97). **Open** 8am-1pm, 3-8pm Mon-Sat. **Credit** MC, V. Map p254 A2.

These days Librairie Chat is mainly a stationers, the long bar counter perpetually swamped by short-trousered fiends in search of marker pens and note-books. However, there is a large back room where a heavy patina of dust fogs the titles of what's mainly Arabic and French stock. A single shelf represents the English-language world, and much of what it contains is heavier on pictures than words.

Librairie Dar El Bacha

2 Rue Dar El Bacha, Medina (024 39 19 73). **Open** 9am-1pm, 3-7pm daily. **No credit cards.** Map p250 B4.

This small shop mostly stocks coffee table books about Morocco and Marrakech, but there's also a decent selection of guide books and reproductions of old tourist posters.

Maktabet El Chab
rue Mouassine, Medina (024 44 34 17). **Open** 8.30am-8.30pm daily. **No credit cards. Map** p73 ㉟
Aka the 'FNAC Berbère' bookshop, this corner kiosk claims to be 'La première librairie à Marrakech', founded in 1941. Stock is pitifully limited, but full marks for perseverance.

Music

There are stalls selling cassettes and CDs among those of the juice sellers on the Jemaa El Fna. Others can be found in the southernmost crook of the souk – turn into the passage that runs west from the Terrasses de l'Alhambra as if you're heading towards the egg market, then take the first left. Stock doesn't vary much, so choose a stall where you feel comfortable hanging around and listening to a few things.

It may all seem impenetrable at first, but stallholders will be happy to play whatever ignites your curiosity. Good buys include percussive bellydance music, live gnawa recordings from the Festival d'Essaouira, Algerian rai and Tuareg blues from the Sahara. Most of this stuff is pirated, so prices are low. You shouldn't pay more than 20dh-40dh per CD. One stall on the west side of rue Bab Agnaou has a posted fixed price of 15dh.

Newsagents

The two best newsstands are both on avenue Mohammed V in Guéliz: one on the corner of rue de Mauritanie, the other two blocks north beside the tourist office, just off place Abdel Moumen. There's also a decent newsstand outside the Hotel CTM on Jemaa El Fna.

Services

Beauty & hair salons

Sun cream is available at pharmacies (*see below*), but the choice is better at **Marjane** (*see p123*).

Salon Jacques Dessange
Sofitel Marrakech, rue Harroun Errachid, Hivernage (024 43 34 95). **Open** 10am-8pm daily. **Credit** MC, V. **Map** p254 C5.
A French hairdresser, formerly at the Meridien, with a growing reputation among the moneyed set.

L'Univers de la Femme
22 rue Bab Agnaou, Medina (024 44 12 96). **Open** 9am-1pm, 3-8pm Tue-Sun. **Credit** MC, V. **Map** p252 C6.

All manner of beauty treatments are available here. The pleasant surroundings are perfect for pampering at affordable prices.

Yves Rocher
13 rue de la Liberté, Guéliz (024 44 82 62). **Open** 9am-1pm, 3-7pm Mon-Sat. **No credit cards. Map** p254 B2.
This French beauty chain has several sites, but the rue de la Liberté branch is the easiest to find. All offer moderately priced beauty products, as well as manicures, pedicures, facials and epilation.

Herbalists

For an explanation of what a dried lizard can do for you, *see p79* **The exorcist**.

Rahal Herbes
43-47 Rahba Kedima, Medina (024 39 14 16). **Open** 9am-8pm daily. **No credit cards. Map** p73 ㊱
The west side of Rahba Kedima is lined with herbalists and 'black magic' stores; we recommend Rahal for owner Abdeljabbar's fluency in English and wickedly dry sense of humour.

Pharmacies

Pharmacie Centrale
166 avenue Mohammed V, corner of rue de la Liberté, Guéliz (024 43 01 58). **Open** 8.30am-12.30pm, 3.30-7.30pm Mon-Thur; 8.30am-noon, 3.30-7.30pm Fri; 8.30am-1pm, 3.30-7.30pm Sat. **Credit** MC, V. **Map** p254 B2.
The most conveniently central pharmacy in the New City. On the door is a list of the city pharmacies which are on 24-hour duty that particular week.

Pharmacie du Progrès
Jemaa El Fna, Medina (024 44 25 63). **Open** 8.15am-12.30pm, 2.15-6.30pm daily. **No credit cards. Map** p73 ㊲
Knowledgeable, qualified staff will advise on minor ailments and suggest medication. English is spoken.

Photography

There's also a Kodak Express lab at the **Marjane** *hypermarché (see p123)*.

Ikram Photo Lab
Centre Kawkab, 3 rue Imam Chafii, Guéliz (024 44 74 94). **Open** 9am-noon, 3-9pm Mon-Sat. **Credit** MC, V. **Map** p254 B3.
A smart Fuji lab near the Jnane El Harti, offering 24-hour print processing, plus slide and video services.

Wrédé
142 avenue Mohammed V, Guéliz (024 43 57 39). **Open** 8.30am-12.30pm, 2.45-7.30pm Mon-Sat. **Credit** MC, V. **Map** p254 B2.
Staff are friendly and the quality of processing is fine. Slide film is sent to Casablanca and returns in three days. Staff speak some English.

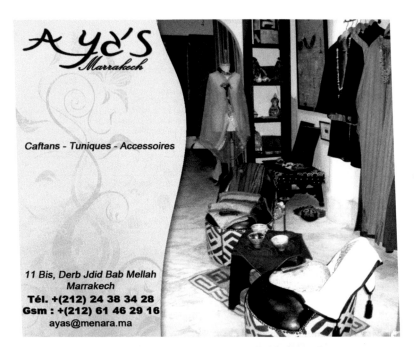

Arts & Entertainment

Children

Snake charmers, souks and friendly locals keep children entertained.

Marrakech is not an obviously child-friendly town. There's virtually nothing in the way of entertainment dedicated to children, and the concept of children's menus or highchairs in restaurants is unknown. That said, they should have a memorable holiday here.

For one thing, children are universally adored in Marrakech. It's not unusual for a businessman talking on a mobile phone to stop to smile at a cute kid. There may even be overzealous kissing and hugging of your baby. People generally tend to be very tolerant of other people's kids, and unruly behaviour that in other countries would inspire stern looks is here more likely to inspire indulgent cooing.

Moroccan families tend to be large, and entertainment comes in the form of brothers, sisters, myriad cousins and neighbours' children. They're allowed the freedom to play in the street. The risks of scrapes and bumps aside, Marrakech is extremely safe, particularly in the traffic-free Medina, and there are few crimes against children.

For many families the hottest outing is to Marjane (*see p123*), the hypermarket, where kids can gaze wide-eyed at the shelves of toys. Likewise, petrol stations are a popular place to take little boys (really), and anything with a playground such as McDonald's (*see p144*) is swamped when school's out.

SIGHTSEEING

Sightseeing with very young children is difficult, particularly in the Medina. The heat can be hard on kids, especially in summer months when temperatures can reach over 40°C (104°F). Avoid the middle of the day, when the sun is at its strongest. Be sure to take the usual precautions: light, loose cotton clothes, sun hats, high-factor sun cream and plenty of fluids.

Apart from cafés, there are few parks or other places to take a break from walking, and amenities such as toilets and washrooms are scarce. It's worth making use of toilets in hotels and restaurants wherever possible, and carrying a toilet roll just in case. Avoid unpurified water (bottled mineral water is widely available), stay away from uncooked food, such as salads, and be sure to peel or wash fruit and veg. Diarrhoea and stomach complaints are common in Morocco and children are even more susceptible than adults; pack some rehydration sachets.

ACCOMMODATION

If you decide to come to Marrakech with your children, the first thing you need to decide is where you want to stay. Although riads are the height of fashion, they are not all well suited to children. They tend to be peaceful, intimate spaces, with rooms arranged off a central courtyard with no activities or places to play –

fine if you have a quiet, well-behaved child, but a potential nightmare otherwise. In this respect it's worth noting that **Riad Ifoulki** (*see p51*) is arranged so that certain parts can be separated off by doors, behind which families can have their own courtyard and rooms. **Villa Vanille** (*see p61*) in the Palmeraie is also reasonably priced and great for kids; owners Pierre and Pia's two children always play with young guests.

The alternative is to go for one of the larger five star-style hotels (*see p39* **The chain gang**) in the Hivernage district. Otherwise, the **Coralia Club Palmariva** is one of the few hotels in the city that claims specifically to cater for children. The hotel complex is huge, so much so that rollerblades are handed out to help get around. Facilities include the Baboo Kids Village, a playgroup and activity centre for four- to 12-year-olds that is open seven days a week. Activities range from golf and archery to canoeing, and most are included in the price. There's also the nearby **Palmeraie Golf Palace**, another large resort complex with heaps of activities, including a kiddies' adventure playground, horse and pony stables and camel rides. Both the Palmariva and Golf Palace are out in the Palmeraie, some distance north of the Medina, and involve lots of taxiing around, which could be an issue.

The majority of hotels will not charge for children under the age of two. Between two and 12 years, so long as the room is being shared with parents, children are commonly charged around 50 per cent of adult rates.

Note that budget hotels are unlikely to have adequate bathroom facilities for small children – they are often communal.

Coralia Club Palmariva

Route de Fes, km6 (024 32 90 36). **Rates** 720dh per person per day (half board); 50% discount under-12s. **Credit** AmEx, MC, V.

Palmeraie Golf Palace

Palmeraie Golf Palace Hotel & Resort, Palmeraie (024 30 10 10/fax 024 30 63 66/www.pgp.co.ma). **Rates** from 3,900dh double; free under-4s. **Credit** AmEx, MC, V.

TRANSPORT

If you decide to rent a car for a day trip or plan to do some exploring by taxi, do not expect child seats, although international rental companies are most likely to have them; phone to check (*see p225*). The spectacular panoramas out of the car window – especially in the south – should be enough to keep the little ones interested, but it's worth bringing something to keep them entertained on long journeys. Make sure you have enough water and food, as shops may be few and far between on the open road.

BABYSITTING

Most riads and hotels can provide babysitters upon request. Most won't speak English, but the language of play is universal.

Activities

There's not a great deal specifically for children to do in Marrakech itself, although the surrounding area has a fair number of pools and sports facilities. Most kids will be just as taken by the unfamiliar sights, sounds and smells of Marrakech as their parents – it's not as if the city has any shortage of visual stimulation. For a wonderful take on Marrakech from a child's perspective, read Esther Freud's autobiographical novel *Hideous Kinky*.

Carriage rides

Place de Foucault, Medina. **Map** p69.
A ride in a brightly painted horse-drawn carriage (*calèche*) is great fun. They seat around four and can be hired for a circuit of the walls, which is a pretty ride, or taken even further afield up and through the Palmeraie. The wall circuit will probably take an hour or more; the Palmeraie run two or three hours. The rate is officially 80dh an hour, but be prepared to negotiate down from 100dh or so. Note that the rate is per carriage not per person. Pick them up on the north side of place de Foucault, midway between the Koutoubia Mosque and Jemaa El Fna.

Jemaa El Fna

Map p69.
Children love the Jemaa El Fna. During the day there are dancing monkeys and snake charmers, while the water carriers with their bright red outfits can easily be mistaken for clowns. At night food stalls are set up, displaying all kinds of strange things to eat, and there are acrobats, fire-eaters and magicians. *See also pp68-71.* **Photo** *p144*.

Kawkab Jeu

1 rue Imam Chafii, Kawkab Centre, Hivernage (024 43 89 29). **Open** 8.30am-10pm daily. **No credit cards. Map** p254 B3.
Next door to the Royal Tennis Club, Kawkab Jeu is a coffee shop (big on crêpes and fancy ice-creams) with both an indoor play area for the really little 'uns, plus an outdoor playground with swings, slides, climbing frames and so on. For young teens there's table football, table tennis and video games.

Tansift Garden

Circuit de la Palmeraie (024 30 87 86). **Open** 10am-3pm, 5.30-10pm daily. **Credit** MC, V.
Just off the main road that winds through the Palmerie, the Tansift Garden is a combination of playground and coffee shop. Plastic tables are set up among the palm trees, where children can run and play and scream their lungs out without bothering anyone. There are also slides, swings, monkey bars and camel rides in the parking lot.

Arts & Entertainment

Parks & outdoor spaces

The city's parks and gardens (*see pp91-94*) are generally of limited interest to most children. The exception is the **Menara Gardens**, which has a big water-filled basin at its centre, home to huge and greedy fish. Children can buy bags of bread from a kiosk and feed them. In Guéliz, **Jnane El-Harti** (*see p89*) has a play area with sandpits, climbing frames and a big dinosaur.

Menara Gardens
Avenue de la Menara, Hivernage (no phone). **Open** 5am-6.30pm daily. **Admission** free. **Map** p251 A5.

Sports & leisure

The range of distractions increases with the age of your children. If they're able to swing a club or stay astride, then the **Royal Golf Club** has a kids' club every Wednesday and Saturday and the **Palmeraie Golf Palace** has a weekly pony club. The Golf Palace also has a **bowling alley**, which is open 4.30pm-1am daily and is accessible to non-residents (unlike the pool).

For a day rate of 100dh-250dh per person, including lunch, **Club Med** will bus you from its Medina premises to its site in the Palmeraie for pool access and a full range of sporting activities. Some half hour's drive south of the city, **Le Relais du Lac**, a lakeside site with mountain views, offers something similar. A driver will pick you up in Marrakech and drive you down there for a day of darts, canoeing, pedal boats, donkey rides, biking, volleyball and badminton, with lunch included. The price is 450dh per person (under-12s half-price).

La Plage Rouge is another pool worth investigating. It's on the route de l'Ourika, about 15km (9.5 miles) south of the Medina. The pool is large, and the tropical setting is alluring. There's a free bus service from Marrakech every hour, plus a hammam and restaurant. **Oasiria** is another another wet and wild hotspot, with water slides, a wave pool, a wading pool and a pirate boat.

Club Med
Place de Foucault, Medina (024 44 40 16). **Pool admission** 250dh; 150dh 12-17s; 100dh 4-11s. **Credit** MC, V. **Map** p250/p252 B5.

Oasira
Route D'Amezmiz, km4 (024 38 04 38/www.oasiria.com). **Open** 10am-6pm daily. Closed Sept-Mar. **Admission** 170dh full day; 130dh half day. **No credit cards.**

Palmeraie Golf Palace
Palmeraie Golf Palace Hotel & Resort, Palmeraie (024 30 10 10/fax 044 30 63 66/www.pgp.co.ma). **Credit** AmEx, MC, V.

The charms of **Jemaa El Fna**. *See p144.*

La Plage Rouge
Route de l'Ourika, km10 (024 37 80 86/024 37 80 87). **Admission** 150dh (incl transport & sunlounger). **No credit cards.**

Le Relais du Lac
Barrage de Lalla Takerkoust (mobile 061 24 24 54/ 061 18 74 72). **No credit cards.**

Royal Golf Club
Ancienne route de Ouarzazate, km2 (024 40 98 28). **Open** *Summer* sunrise-sunset daily. *Winter* 9am-2.30pm daily. **Credit** MC, V.

Restaurants

Shame on us for promoting it, but the kids do love **McDonald's**. Marrakech has three: one up by the Marjane hypermarket, a few minutes' drive north of town on the Casablanca road, one at Marjane itself, and the other in central Guéliz on place du 16 Novembre. **Catanzaro** (*see p106*) is the sole restaurant, so far as we know, that has a children's menu.

Shopping

For nappies and baby food you'll have to make the trek to **Marjane** (*see p123*), as most small grocery stores don't stock them. UHT and powdered milk, however, are easily available. For clothing try **Jacardi** on avenue Mohammed V in Guéliz (no phone). For toyshops, again, hit Marjane or there's **La Drogerie** (163 avenue Mohammed V, 044 43 07 27) in Guéliz. Just round the corner, **Articles pour le Bébé** (68 rue de la Liberté, 024 43 12 00) specialises in – you guessed it – baby needs.

Film

Hollywood's favourite film location is also home to an indigenous industry.

Alejandro González Iñárritu's 2006 movie *Babel*, in which Brad Pitt and Cate Blanchett's ill-fated Saharan holiday forms the centrepiece of a sprawling, transcontinental story, was that very rare thing indeed – an international film in which Morocco appears as itself.

Generally, it's playing somewhere else. In recent years Morocco has become an all-purpose backdrop for an assortment of foreign filmmakers. It stood in for Tibet in Martin Scorsese's *Kundun*, Somalia in Ridley Scott's *Black Hawk Down* and Ethiopia in Renny Harlin's *Exorcist: The Beginning* in 2004. It was a generic North Africa for Matthew McConaughey and Penélope Cruz in *Sahara*, for Jean-Claude Van Damme in *Legionnaire* and for Ridley Scott's *Gladiator*. It's also a popular substitute for the Holy Land: Ben Kingsley was a cable TV Moses here, Willem Dafoe was Jesus in Scorsese's *The Last Temptation of Christ*, and there always seems to be some TV Bible epic or another in production at one of the two studios in Ouarzazate, the pre-desert town that's home to Morocco's biggest film facilities.

The aftermath of 11 September 2001 has only accelerated the phenomenon of Morocco as adaptable bit-player. More and more stories have scenes in the Middle East and elsewhere in the Islamic world, just as insurers and production companies baulk at the increased danger of filming in such places. Casablanca stood in for Beirut in Paul Gaghan's *Syriana*, and Paul Greengrass used the Atlas as Afghanistan for scenes he shot, but later discarded, for *United 93*. Morocco appears as Afghanistan again in Mike Nicholls' *Charlie Wilson's War* (in post-production at the time of writing).

And Morocco as Morocco? Well, Bertolucci's adaptation of Paul Bowles' *The Sheltering Sky* was shot in Tangier as well as the Sahara, and is probably the most evocative take on the landscape's mysterious charms. And Gillies Mackinnon brought Esther Freud's *Hideous Kinky* to the screen, a sparky Western take on Marrakech and the Moroccans. After that we have to go back to 1956 and Hitchcock's *The Man Who Knew Too Much*. Morocco's signature image on screen is, of course, *Casablanca*. But Rick's Café never existed, and Bogart and Bergman never left the Warner Bros backlot.

SWORDS, SANDALS AND SAVINGS

The $457-million, multiple-Oscar-winning success of *Gladiator* inspired a brief flurry of sword-and-sandal epics. Wolfgang Petersen's *Troy* might have relocated to Mexico after jitters about the Iraq war, but Ridley Scott flew back in for *Kingdom of Heaven*, and Oliver Stone turned up to shoot *Alexander*.

Appearing as a guest of honour at the 2004 Marrakech Film Festival, Stone grandly declared: 'Without Morocco there would be no

Homegrown talents take on Hollywood hotshots in the local cinemas.

film. It is the place where East meets West.' He went on to elaborate the more prosaic reason that makes Morocco attractive: cost. 'We tried to make the film in Hollywood. But when we factored in all the unit costs in California we were way over budget. In Morocco we could run 500 to 2,000 extras a day. It's not possible to do this kind of movie in America.' In America, an extra earns $100 a day. In Morocco it's $15.

But it's not just a question of financial savings. Ever since David Lean filmed much of *Lawrence of Arabia* around Ouarzazate, plenty of directors have capitalised on Morocco's versatile landscapes and deserts. For *Alexander*, Oliver Stone used Essaouira for Greece, the Atlas Mountains as the Hindu Kush and a plain outside Marrakech for his battle scenes. All this and 300 sunny days a year.

MOROCCO'S GAINS AND LOSSES

What's good for Hollywood is also good for Morocco. A major production like *Alexander* brings an investment of around $60 million, and up to around 10,000 people get work as extras and crew. Not to mention the £30,000 leading man Colin Farrell supposedly clocked up at the bar of Marrakech's Le Meridien.

Enlightened government policies regarding foreign filmmaking in Morocco have also boosted the indigenous film sector. To receive a production licence, at least one producer must be Morocco-based. In addition, ten per cent of all domestic box office revenue goes towards funding Moroccan movies, of which there are usually between ten and 12 a year. But while foreign productions provide locals with an opportunity to learn or hone cinematic skills, they also lure technical expertise away from Moroccan films and encourage indigenous professionals to charge American rates.

The local industry faces other difficulties. In a country of about 150 cinemas, Moroccan films can rarely pay for themselves. Nor does it help that the local Arabic is not widely understood beyond Morocco and Algeria. In any case, many Moroccan films are French co-productions and are often in French. Not surprisingly, emigration to Europe is a common theme (in 2001's *Au-delà de Gibraltar*, for example), as are the difficulties of love in an Islamic society and of life in general in a desperately poor one. They are popular with local audiences (Moroccan films represented just two per cent of those shown in 2002, but bagged eight per cent of the year's attendance), but few have excited much international attention outside of the festival circuit. Nabil Ayouch's realist fable *Ali Zaoua: Prince de la Rue* and Laila Marrakchi's glossy teen movie *Marock* (see *p147*) both got limited European distribution, but these are exceptions.

Cinemas

Marrakech has just a handful of city-centre cinemas, plus one new multiplex. Programming is a mix of Hollywood blockbusters, Bollywood films, martial arts pictures and mainstream French releases. This is a francophone country; films are usually dubbed in French with Arabic subtitling, so unless you can speak one or read the other, your cinema-going experience is likely to be a disappointing one. Especially as Marrakchis are notorious for making a lot of noise during the film.

In addition to the cinemas listed below (the pick of a poor crop), films are shown roughly twice a week at the **Institut Français** (Route de Targa, Jebel Guéliz, 024 44 69 30, 20dh), which has a more eclectic programming remit.

Cinéma le Colisée

Boulevard Mohammed Zerktouni, Guéliz (024 44 88 93). **Tickets** 15dh-25dh Mon; 25dh-35dh Tue-Sun. **No credit cards**. **Map** p254 A2.
This place trumpets itself as 'the best cinema in Morocco' and it's certainly the best in Marrakech – a comfortable, modern venue with excellent sightlines.

Cinéma Rif

Daoudiate (024 30 31 46). **Tickets** 15dh. **No credit cards**. **Map** p249 D1.
A barn-like Moorish movie palace with a balcony, red carpets on the steps and (sometimes) tea served in the forecourt.

Megarama

Jardins de l'Aguedal (090 10 20 20/www. megarama.info/marrakech). **Tickets** 29dh-45dh. **No credit cards**.
Marrakech enters the multiplex era with this ten-screen complex, just behind Pasha. The building, a concrete hulk topped with Berber-style crenellations, is like a pre-Saharan version of Californian mall architecture; inside, you could be just about anywhere.

Saada

Quartier Hay Hassani, Douar Laasker (024 34 70 28). **Tickets** 15dh. **No credit cards**.
An auditorium in 1950s style, again with carpets and tea, in a dusty neighbourhood square off the Essaouira road, past the railway station.

International Film Festival

The Marrakech International Film Festival (www.festival-marrakech.com), held in December for the past few years, is an ambitious, multifaceted event with a determinedly global remit. Under the patronage of His Majesty King Mohammed VI (a film buff, apparently), with his younger brother Prince Moulay Rachid as president and powerful UniFrance chief Daniel Toscan du Plantier as director, the festival has managed to attract a good deal of star-power and media attention. Francis Ford Coppola, Martin Scorsese, Oliver Stone, Alan Parker, Sean Connery and Catherine Deneuve have all made the trip. Some insiders believe the festival could attract even more luminaries if it ironed out a tendency to make protocol mistakes and offered filmmakers a better forum to present their work.

But the main raison d'être of the event, reaching its seventh year in 2007, is to encourage international filmmakers to shoot in Morocco – and this it does very well. Hence screenings and competition take second place to the lavish

parties thrown every night by sponsors, aiming to match the King's dinner that opens the event. From a total of around 100 films from 22 countries, there were 15 in competition in 2006; Dominique Graf's *Der Rote Kakadu*, a romance set in communist East Germany, won the awards for Best Film and Best Actor (Max Riemelt).

But much of the excitement comes from the festival's screening venues, which include the Jemaa El Fna and the Badii Palace. Tickets are available for almost all films on a first-come-first-served basis from the cinema box offices; the parties, however, are invite-only.

Reel Morocco

They're unlikely to be playing in a cinema near you any time soon – but just in case, here are a selection of Moroccan movies that made their mark.

Al Hall
(Ahmed El Maanouni, 1981)
Released abroad as *Trances*, this documentary tracks the history of Nass El-Ghiwane, the pioneering group who merged traditional influences with protest lyrics.

À la Recherche du Mari de ma Femme
(Mohammed Abderrahman Tazi, 1995)
A comedy about a man who repudiates his third wife and then tries to get her back, *Looking for My Wife's Husband* was the biggest-grossing Moroccan film ever.

Ali Zaoua, Prince de la Rue
(Nabil Ayouch, 2001)
A compelling mix of compassion, realism and sentiment earned this tale of young Casablanca street kids (played by homeless children) 44 film festival prizes and an international release.

Un Amour à Casablanca
(Abdelkader Lagtaâ, 1991)
This gritty, daring love story depicted a Casablanca of sex, prostitution, drugs and alcohol, that no one had seen on screen before. It won two prizes at the 1991 Meknès film festival, and opened up a new way of seeing and filming Morocco.

Bab Al-Sama Maftuh
(Farida Ben Lyziad, 1989)
A Door in the Sky recounts the story of a young emigré who returns to Fès to visit her dying father and befriends the woman reciting the Qur'ran at his funeral. Together they decide to transform her father's house into a women's refuge.

Badis
(Mohammed Abderraham Tazi, 1988)
Two women oppressed by village life rebel and are punished by a fatal stoning. Tazi shot the film in the actual village of the same name, using locals as extras.

Hallak Hai El Foukara
(Mohammed Reggab, 1982)
Hatred and passion drive a tense narrative in *The Hairdresser of the Poor Quarter*, in which a rich man who controls a district extorts from a poor hairdresser whose salon he wants to replace with a school of Qur'anic learning.

Keïd Ensa
(Farida Ben Lyziad, 1999)
Women's Wiles is a traditional tale adapted for the cinema, in which a young woman marries a sultan and, after an argument, finds herself a prisoner in the harem.

Marock
(Laila Marrakchi, 2005)
Deft coming-of-age love story in which an Arab girl and Jewish boy fall for each other in the milieu of the wealthy, French-speaking Casablancan middle-class.

Mektoub
(Nabil Ayouch, 1997)
Thriller in which a doctor's wife is kidnapped and raped in Tangier. Her husband gets involved in a revenge killing, and the couple rebuild their relationship on a trip to the south.

What a Wonderful World
(Faouzi Bensaïdi, 2007)
Writer/director Bensaïdi plays a hitman who has a phone affair with a traffic cop in a Casablanca of disillusion and vast contrasts. Inventive visuals compensate for an occasionally stuttering narrative.

Arts & Entertainment

Galleries

Art's getting serious.

'Art follows money, and Marrakech is beckoning.' That was our conclusion when we surveyed the art scene in the last edition of *Time Out Marrakech*. And indeed, two years on, the accelerating flow of Western cash has been accompanied by a number of new gallery openings. Les Atlassides has closed, but **Galerie Rê** has replaced it to represent both young and established Moroccan artists. The new **Galerie 127** became the first photographic gallery in North Africa. The **Light Gallery** opened up in the Kasbah with an ambitious programme of international contemporary work. And **Lawrence-Arnott** opened a gallery in Marrakech to match its long-established business in Tangier. Suddenly everything looks a lot more serious.

THE ORIENTALISM EXPRESS

Islam's aversion to representational forms has historically channelled artistic impulses into decorative work rather than fine art. This is as true in Morocco as it is everywhere in the Muslim world. And what goes for Morocco goes double for artisanal Marrakech, where the primacy of crafts over arts has only been encouraged by the city's dialogue with Western style and decor.

It wasn't until European painters began coming to North Africa in the 19th century that Morocco was first captured on canvas. Adventuring artists were captivated by the clear light and rich colours. It also helped that pictures of fearsome desert warriors and dusky harem girls sold well back home. The 80 or so canvases produced by **Eugène Delacroix** on a visit to Morocco and Algeria in 1823 diverted French painters from the traditional pilgrimage to Italy and set them scurrying all over North Africa instead.

Delacroix defined the style that became known as Orientalism. Today it's widely derided for treating its subjects as colourful curiosities, but it motivated **Henri Matisse** to settle in Tangier for a productive stint, now regarded as the culmination of his Fauve period. Matisse protégé **Raoul Dufy** travelled to Marrakech and painted the typically cartoony *Couscous Served at the Residence of the Pasha*, but few other painters made it this far south.

Galerie 127. *See p149.*

The notable exception was **Jacques Majorelle**, a tuberculosis sufferer who came on the advice of his doctor. He settled here in 1923, building a villa and later adding the gardens that perpetuate his name (*see p92*). Majorelle's work still falls under the heading 'Orientalist' but is redeemed by his apparent empathy with his subjects; that and a superbly graphic sense of line and colour. Some of Majorelle's most striking works were posters to promote exotic Maroc. He's also noted for his attachment to a particularly intense shade of cobalt that now goes by the name 'Majorelle Blue'.

MODERNISM AND BEYOND

It was only after independence in 1956 that Moroccan artists began to emerge with their own styles, mostly abstract, naive or calligraphic, and mostly in the north and on the coast. Many were trained at the fine arts school in Tetouan, founded in 1945 and one of only two in Morocco (the other, founded in 1950, is in Casablanca). Tangier used to have cash and international connections, and still has Morocco's only contemporary art museum. Nearby Asilah hosts an annual art festival, hitting its 29th edition in August 2007 with three weeks of exhibitions and workshops. But there's never been a Marrakech school or style, and there's little sense of a coherent scene.

One of the key figures of Moroccan modernism, **Farid Belkahia**, is a Marrakchi. Born in 1934, he works with Berber symbols (spirals, hands) and traditional materials (sheepskin, pigments) and still lives in Marrakech. If Belkahia is the city's fine-art founding father, **Mohammed Melehi** is its current power, less important as a painter of gaudy abstracts than as president of Morocco's oldest artists' association and co-founder of the Asilah festival. Although Asilah-born, he too now lives in Marrakech. There's also writer »and painter **Mahi Binebine**, back in his home town after decades abroad. The sadness of his pieces – constricted, tormented faces and figures – is said to be inspired by the 20-year imprisonment of his brother for his part in a 1970s attempted coup. Other Marrakech artists to look out for include Pop painter **Hassan Hajjaj**, photographer **Hicham Benouhoud** and calligraphy painter **Nouredine Chater**.

Apart from galleries, there are other moves to anchor art in the area. Bearded abstractionist **Mohammed Morabiti** has opened a place called **El-Maquam** (024 48 40 02, 061 19 58 59) in Tahanaout, 28 kilometres (17 miles) south of Marrakech on the Asni road. There are rooms and ateliers for artists to stay and work, a small gallery, a bookshop, and a 'literary café' that hosts occasional readings. **Miloud Labied**, a

local painter of the Belkahia generation whose canvases remind the viewer of Paul Klee, has long supposed to be setting up something similar in the village of Mejjat, near Amizmiz, but seems to be moving rather slowly.

Galleries

Apart from places listed below, the boutique **Lun'art Gallery** (*see p133*) has a small selection of modern Moroccan art for sale. **Noir sur Blanc** (48 rue Yugoslavie) also shows contemporary art; it recently featured Mahi Binebine. The **Musée de Marrakech** (*see p77*) hosts regularly changing temporary exhibitions and there's a permanent display of work by Jacques Majorelle at **the Museum of Islamic Art** (*see p92*) in the Majorelle Gardens.

Dar Cherifa

8 Derb Charfa Lakbir, Mouassine, Medina (024 42 64 63/www.marrakech-riads.net). Open 9am-7pm daily. No credit cards. Map p250 C4.
This gorgeous townhouse is the Medina's premier exhibition space. Parts of the building date back to the 16th century and it has been lovingly restored by owner Abdelatif Ben Abdellah, who's taken great pains to expose the carved beams and stucco work while leaving walls and floors bare and free of distraction. Regular exhibitions lean towards resident foreign artists, but there have also been shows by Moroccan artists Hassan Hajjaj and Milaudi Nouiga. The space also includes a small library, tea and coffee are served, and there's a light lunch menu too.

Galerie 127

127 avenue Mohammed V, Guéliz (024 43 26 67/ galerie127mohammedV@arnott-lawrence.com). Open 11am-7pm Tue-Sat. No credit cards. Map p254 B2.
When Nathalie Locatelli opened Galerie 127 in February 2006 it became the very first photo gallery in the Maghreb and only the third in all Africa (the others are in Dakar and Bamako). It's an appealingly simple space – a converted apartment with tall windows and walls left unsurfaced – and got off to a good start with an opening show by Tony Catany. The king bought 30 of the photographs. Locatelli has continued with work by other big names in contemporary photography, mostly French or France-based, such as portraits by Carole Bellaiche and Gérard Rondeau, Alejandra Figueroa's images of ancient statues, and Bernard Faucon's 'staged photography'.

Galerie d'Art Lawrence-Arnott

Immeuble El-Khalil, Avenue Hassan II, Guéliz (024 43 04 99/gallery@arnott-lawrence.com). Open 9.30am-12.30pm, 3.30-6.30pm Mon, or by appointment Credit MC, V. Map p254 B3.
Just as art follows money, so do estate agents. Both arrived together in June 2005 when Philip Arnott and John Lawrence set up their second gallery in Morocco – along with an adjacent branch of Moroccan Properties, their real estate company. It's

Galerie Rê.

hard to escape the feeling that the artists they exhibit, mostly native or expatriate painters of 'Moroccan' subjects – neo-Orientalist noble savages, villages set in hazy landscapes, scurrying figures in jellebas – are simply chosen to adorn the walls of the half-million-euro second homes they're also trying to flog next door. The Moroccan Properties website even suggests as much. In Tangier, where there's been a Lawrence-Arnott gallery since 1991, there is some connection with the local art scene. In Marrakech, they're outsiders. And it shows.

Galerie Bleue

119 avenue Mohammed V, Guéliz (066 19 21 29). **Open** 10am-1pm, 4-8pm Tue-Sun. **Credit** MC, V. **Map** p254 A2.
A handsome but low-key space devoted to solo shows by contemporary French and Moroccan artists. There never seemed to be much going on here, and there's perhaps even less of a vibe now that Lawrence-Arnott has turned up to tap the same market for inoffensive figurative painting.

Galerie Rê

Résidence Al-Andalus III, angle rue de la Mosquée and Ibn Touert No.3, Guéliz (024 43 22 58). **Open** 930am-1pm, 3-8pm Tue-Sat; 3-8pm Sun. **Credit** MC, V. **Map** p254 B2.
With a background of collecting Berber textiles and running a New York gallery specialising in Egyptian art, Lucien Viola opened this serious and lavishly designed contemporary gallery in late 2006. His intention was to pick up where the now closed Les Atlassides left off – with the involvement of that gallery's Christine and Alain Gorius. A splendid staircase rises through the centre of the space to a small mezzanine. Downstairs is for changing exhibitions by mostly 'Moroccan and Mediterranean' artists. An opening show by French painter Sébastien Pignon was followed by recent work from M'Barek Bouchichi, who lives near Zagora, and sculptures by the Marrakech-based American, Lori Park. Upstairs is work from established Moroccan artists such as Abdelkarim Ouazzani, Tibari Kantour and Mohammed Lagzouli. Viola's next project is to open a museum of ancient textiles in the souks.

Light Gallery

2 derb Chtouka, Kasbah (072 61 42 10/light. marrakech@gmail.com). **Open** 11am-7pm Tue-Sun. **No credit cards. Map** 252 C9.
The newest arrival on the Marrakech scene is an internationally oriented contemporary art gallery in the Kasbah, just down the derb from Les Jardins de la Medina. Founded by Marcelle Danan, Julie Caignault and Nicolas Carré, it kicked off at the beginning of 2007 with photographs of neon and fluorescent lights by Gilles Coulon, then moved on to drawings by Swiss painter Mathias Schauwecker. It's a big, bright, modern space where they also sell a few clothes, intend to start selling books, and have a few small photos for sale from the likes of Robert Mapplethorpe, Helmut Newton and Martin Parr.

Matisse Art Gallery

61 rue Yougoslavie, No.43 passage Ghandouri, Guéliz (024 44 83 26/www.matisse-art-gallery.com). **Open** 9am-1pm, 3.30-8pm Mon-Sat. **Credit** MC, V. **Map** p254 A2.
A decent space devoted to solo shows by young Moroccan artists such as calligraphy painters Nouredine Chater and Nouredine Daifellah, and figurative painter Driss Jebrane. More established names are also exhibited, such as Farid Belkahia and Hassan El-Glaoui (the late son of the former 'Lord of the Atlas' was devoted to painting horses). Upstairs are some vintage Orientalist canvases.

Ministerio del Gusto

22 Derb Azouz El-Mouassine, off rue Sidi El-Yamami, Mouassine, Medina (024 42 64 55). **Open** 9am-noon, 4-7pm Mon-Sat. **Credit** MC, V. **Map** p250 B5.
Showroom for the design talents and eclectic tastes of owners Alessandra Lippini and Fabrizio Bizzarri, this eccentric space also hosts occasional exhibitions; when these are over Alessandra and Fabrizio continue stocking work by the artists they like. These include Essaouira-based English artist Micol, the American photographer Martin H M Schreiber, Italian multimediaist Maurizio Vetrugno, Indonesian painter Ribka and Marrakchi Pop artist Hassan Hajjaj.

Arts & Entertainment

Gay

Where the boys are.

When it comes to homosexuality, Morocco is a paradoxical place. Gay sex is forbidden by law – punishable by six months to three years' imprisonment. A 'gay identity' exists only among a small, socially elite group of Moroccans. Yet sex among men is, and always has been, common.

The lack of rigid categories of gay and straight and the fluidity of sexual boundaries have a lot to do with the strong cultural idea that only the passive partner in intercourse is 'gay' (in other words, unmacho).

With attitudes like these, it's not surprising that there is a lot of gay sex about, or that Morocco has become a gay travel destination. Despite the legal situation, gay sex is generally tolerated if it's discreet, although police have been known to arrest Moroccans walking with Europeans late at night on charges of prostitution (leaving their Western companion alone). And unusually, in 2004 a 66-year-old British man was jailed for a year for having sex with a man and corrupting a minor (two young people were involved, one aged 16, the other 18). One could speculate that the case was a response to recent pressure in the Moroccan media for the authorities to crack down on gay sex tourism.

THE SWINGING '60S

Back in the 1960s, the British playwright Joe Orton famously shagged his way around Tangier, which he dubbed the 'Costa del Sodomy' (his holiday debauchery is documented in the *Joe Orton Diaries*). But Morocco's queer credentials started even earlier: back in 1931, bisexual American author Paul Bowles visited Tangier with gay composer Aaron Copeland (on the advice of Gertrude Stein, no less). He fell in love with the place and immortalised it in his 1949 novel *The Sheltering Sky*.

During the 1950s and 1960s, bohemians and artists arrived in droves, including a sizeable queer contigent, lured by the promise of drugs and handsome young men. In addition to Orton, famous gay visitors included Tennessee Williams, William Burroughs, Allen Ginsberg, Kenneth Williams, Jack Kerouac, Kenneth Halliwell and Truman Capote.

Since inheriting international favoured status, Marrakech has taken up the reins from Tangier as Morocco's most gay-friendly

city. Young colts are attracted from all over the country, eager for the freedom of playing away from home. There also remains the traditional heavy presence of old queens from Europe and America on tour in passionate pursuit of young delicacies, plus a newer, younger crowd of sophisticated weekend-away gays attracted by the glamour of Marrakech, staple of the fashion mags.

CRUISE CONTROL

None of this amounts to any kind of gay community, but there is a lot of action going on – so much so that a single man walking alone might be approached at any time of day, and more especially at night. Male prostitutes are a slick and practised crowd (we wouldn't be surprised if they carry credit-card swipers), used to being spoiled by wealthy Europeans eager to spend on sex. Prime hangouts include the **Café les Négociants** in Guéliz (*see p116*), the **Café Atlas** opposite, and several of the seedier nightclubs round place de la Liberté, notably **Diamant Noir** (*see p156*). Not everyone giving you a come-hither glance will be a rent boy, but put it like this: being poor here won't make you many new friends.

Avenue Mohammed V, between place de la Liberté and the Koutoubia Mosque, doubles as a cruising area after midnight, but again, it's a search for money rather than love that propels. Romantic souls head for avenue El-Yarmouk and a bench beneath the Old City walls, haunt of men looking for a bit of companionship. The biggest gay pick-up joint of all, though, is Jemaa El Fna. Straight tourists pass through oblivious, but among the circled audiences crowding the entertainers there are plenty of locking eyes. Likely prospects are approached from behind and a hardened 'expression of interest' none too discreetly pushed against them.

Pick-up by internet is increasingly popular and facilitated by the proliferation of internet cafés. Local favourite is www.cybermen.com (Moroccan area code: mar). Cyber-contacts are quickly translated into mobile numbers and hence to meetings. Personal ads and responses also feature at www.kelma.org, which includes the online e-zine 'Kelmaghreb', focusing on gay issues in North Africa.

Music

Elusive and inspiring, the city's music scene is well worth seeking out.

Long before the words 'world' and 'music' got chummy with each other, Morocco was one of the few developing countries whose music had any kind of audience in Europe or America. Paul Bowles toured the country in the late 1950s with a tape recorder and a commission from the US Library of Congress, aiming to capture examples of endangered music from all regions. Another Tangier resident, Brion Gysin, established diplomatic relations with the Master Musicians of Joujouka, who went on to work with Brian Jones. Robert Plant and Jimmy Page recorded their *No Quarter* album in Marrakech with a gnawa master or two in 1994, and Blur spent a month here recording 2003's *Think Tank*.

But despite this ongoing Maroc 'n' roll dialogue, Moroccan music remains relatively unknown outside of the Francophone world, and relatively inaudible for visitors to Morocco. There might be Berber music and Arab music, Jewish music and the music of the descendants of slaves, music to accompany dance and music that goes with storytelling, music for harvest festivals and music for circumcision rituals, classical music rooted in medieval Andalucía and pop music that belongs to the urbanised Arab cultures of today. But there aren't many easy ways to hear it. There's no real performance tradition in the western sense, and precious few concert venues. Most musicians confine their appearances mostly to private ceremonies and religious events, and there's no real Moroccan music industry to make anything happen.

ANCIENT GRIKA

With its own instruments and tunings, rhythms and sounds, Berber music (called *grika* – 'improvisation') is entirely different from Arabic music. It's rootsy, rural stuff that's traditionally performed at community celebrations, especially harvest and religious festivals. The sound is heavily percussive, with harsh shrieks from the *ghaita* – an instrument related to the oboe. The music is composed of several fairly simple parts, intricately woven together and extended into performances that can last for days, with musicians taking breaks as others step in to replace them. The ritualised formula has changed little over the centuries.

Prime exponents of *grika* are the **Master Musicians of Joujouka**, described by William Burroughs as 'the world's oldest rock 'n' roll band'. According to their website, the musicians

– from the village of Joujouka in the foothills of the Rif – have been passing their tunes and traditions from father to son for 4,000 years. Prior to French rule, they were court musicians to seven sultans. In the rock era, since they were recorded by Brian Jones, they've played with Ornette Coleman, Bill Laswell and Talvin Singh, and the Stones, minus Jones, used them on 1989's *Steel Wheels* album.

VIVE LE TRANCE

If Berber music comes across as elemental, bordering on mystical, it's got nothing on gnawa (also spelled gnaoua).

The name refers both to the music and its practitioners. The gnawa trace their ancestry back to the Sudan and sub-Saharan Africa – 'gnawa' may derive from the same root as Ghana or Guinea – whence they were dragged to Morocco as slaves. To reflect their difficult history, the gnawa claim spiritual descent from Bilal, the Ethiopian slave who suffered much before becoming the Prophet's first *muezzin*.

Gnawa communities are concentrated mostly in the southern, less Europeanised parts of the country – notably Marrakech and Essaouira – though there are gnawa communities all over the country. A strong oral tradition has kept alive the culture of their ancestors, and gnawa is the best-preserved manifestation of the black African aesthetic within Morocco.

At its simplest, gnawa is just drum and bass. The *gimbri*, a long-necked lute, is the main component, combining a fat acoustic bass sound with a metallic rattle. Accompaniment comes from the insistent clatter of chunky iron castanets, *karakeb*. Bigger ensembles add drums, call-and-response vocals, and lots of dancing. It's repetitive, hypnotic stuff, built around looping riffs. You might not get it at first, but after a while your body can't help but respond.

At their most authentic, gnawa performances are part of all-night healing rituals involving trance and possession. Different powers in the gnawa spirit world are denoted by different colours (seven in all), and the different colours by different music. At a *lila* (from the Arabic word for 'night') ritual, one of the musicians will play until whatever colour is dominating proceedings reveals itself.

Back in the mundane world, gnawa lyrics are riddled with references to the pain of slavery and exile, and the turmoil of dislocation. In this

The new sound of Marrakech

Collecting the source sounds of Marrakech and inventing the new sound of the city were Philippe Lauro Baranès' aims when he set up KamarStudios, back in 1999. A corner of the studio, which occupies a modest riad in the Medina, is equipped with DJ decks and recording equipment, but there's perhaps more here than meets the eye. The gnawa consider it a house inhabited by *mlouks* – spirits.

The music of the gnawa was the 'source sound' Baranès (pictured, right), an urbane Parisian who's had one foot in Marrakech for about 25 years, had in mind. But why? 'Because it's the oldest trance music in Africa,' he replies, speaking of the music's origins in the south Nile area, from where the ancestors of the gnawa were centuries ago brought to Morocco as slaves. Indeed, the gnawa ritual music that Baranès set about collecting is so old that it contains words in dead languages that even the gnawa no longer understand.

Seven painstaking years on, KamarStudios (www.kamarstudios.com) has finally released a four-CD package, *The Black Album* by Marrakech Undermoon – a project name for Baranès, the gnawa musicians involved, and the young Marrakchi DJs with whom he collaborates. It took a while to get the gnawa's confidence, but soon the Kamar courtyard became the scene of several *lilas*, the trance rituals that are gnawa music in its most authentic form. Two of the CDs contain an impressive complete recording of the 'black' part of their seven-colour cycle, made in 2003.

But that's only half of the story. Baranès wanted to prove that, given the chance, young Moroccans could cut it at an international level that transcended mere 'local' interest. So, from the beginning, the project also involved two young Marrakchi DJs: DJ Zitroz (Khalid Icame, pictured left) and DJ Folani (Abderrazak Akhoullii). Initially Baranès brought a hip hop DJ over from New York to help them learn composition and recording techniques. Soon they were proficient on their own.

While recording the gnawa, they also sampled sounds that they integrated into new tracks. To their surprise, the results sounded very much like Berlin minimal techno. *The Black Album*'s third CD contains the results of these experiments. They resist the hackneyed fusion approach that characterises most western musicians' work with the gnawa,

instead using their music as inspiration in seeking the 'new sound of Marrakech'.

'The Sound of Marrakech' is how Baranès bills Kamar's electro-house and minimal club nights with DJ Zitroz and others, currently held one Saturday a month at Théâtro (*see p156*). Kamar also stages performances of gnawa dance and music, and undertakes 'sound design' projects. He also intends to record the other six sections of a complete gnawa *lila*.

The club music and activities and gnawa shows and recordings – the two kinds of trance music – meet but never quite touch. You could listen to the 'minimal trance' CD and, despite the occasional vocals from gnawa singer Said Damir (pictured, front), hardly guess at its cultural starting point. Baranès argues that a set by DJ Zitroz is more like the 'spiral' of a gnawa ritual than the linear motion of a set by a European DJ, but it's a difficult point to demonstrate. 'How we play house is completely inspired by the way a trance night happens' says Baranès, but then laughs. 'You know how it is, the metaphysical in the left hand, clubbing in the right hand...' There's room for heaven and earth in the KamarStudios philosophy.

The Black Album is available at Kifkif in Marrakech (*see p133*) and Essaouira (*see p176*). It currently has no UK distribution.

sense gnawa is similar to both blues and reggae, speaking the universal language of suffering. But it also has much in common with European trance or techno, in which music ceases to have a beginning, middle or end, and instead becomes one enveloping continuum of sound and rhythm.

GLOBAL GNAWA

Although marginal in Moroccan society, gnawa has made an impact on both the local and global music scenes – particularly since the Festival d'Essaouira (see p153 **Gnawa grooves**) gave it an annual focus and international respect. A music of loops, spaces and extended durations, gnawa lends itself easily to fusion experiments and collaborations. Perhaps too easily. Most gnawa encounters with the wider world of music are little more than boring old jazzers soloing over the rhythms.

Attempts to merge gnawa with other musics have been going on since the 1970s. The torch was lit by long-haired Casablancan five-piece **Nass El Ghiwane**, who played traditional instruments and fused gnawa with elements of popular Egyptian and Lebanese song. That, and a political edge, gave them Bob Marley-like status across North Africa. The band leader died in a plane crash in the 1980s, but two of the group play on under the original name.

Gnawan fusionist **Hassan Hakmoun** cut his teeth playing around Jemaa El Fna, before moving to New York in the mid 1980s, where he made the impressive *Gift of the Gnawa* (1991), featuring legendary trumpeter Don Cherry and Richard Horowitz, an avant-garde musician and composer (contributor to the soundtrack of Bertolucci's *The Sheltering Sky*), and sometime resident of Marrakech.

Gnawa fusion also made radical moves forward with Arabic techno pioneers **Aisha Kandisha's Jarring Effects** – although their momentum has slowed since founding member Habib El Malak left the band to become a politician in Marrakech. Paris-based **Gnawa Diffusion** blend gnawa with ragga and reggae. In the UK, three-piece **Momo** peddle their version of gnawan 'dar' (house) to a clubbing crowd, while DJ **U-Cef** mixes samples of Moroccan music with just about anything.

Back in Morocco, there is little market for anything too edgy. Most home-grown innovations are social rather than musical, and recent years have seen the emergence of women's gnawa. The most high-profile group is **B'net Marrakech** (Women of Marrakech), five taboo-breaking women (gnawa has always been a male preserve) who do weddings, births – and international world music festivals. Their debut CD *Chamaa* included songs about love, demonic possession and the national football team.

And with the innovative Sound of Marrakech club evenings and Marrakech Undermoon project (see p153 **Sounds of Marrakech**), the trance music of the gnawa has finally encountered the trance music of Europe.

MASTERS AT WORK

Where to see music in Marrakech? The short answer is, 'nowhere'. Or almost nowhere: there's a near-total absence of concert halls and live music clubs. **The Musica Bar** (see p120), **VIPRoom** (see p156), **Afric'n Chic** (see p117), **Le Senz** (see p156) and **Montecristo** (see p120) all feature live bands of one sort or another. In the first two that means the Arab equivalent of cheesy cabaret, and in the others an assortment of derivative second-rate local acts or French fusioneers who can't get a gig back home. Still, the number of venues offering live music seems to be on the increase, and perhaps Marrakech will in time develop a live scene worthy of more serious attention. Otherwise, there's the Jemaa El Fna. It's filled with musicians, solo and in groups, but these are nothing more than street buskers. The costumed gnawa playing in restaurants tend to be a cut above, but it's still not the real deal.

According to **Brahim El Belkani**, respectable gnawa musicians just don't do that sort of stuff. El Belkani is a *maalim*, or master, one of only eight such gnawa dignitaries in Marrakech. He's scornful of playing for 'tips', and makes his living as a butcher. But he's not above turning out for international festivals or visiting stars. On his music room wall there are photos of Brahim with Dizzy Gillespie, Page and Plant and Carlos Santana. But chances of witnessing such masters at work occur only at major cultural jamborees.

FESTIVALS

There are no music festivals in Marrakech, but over on the coast there's the **Festival d'Essaouira** (see p177 **Gnawa grooves**), a joyous, four-day jam session. There's more jazz than trance, but it's the only event at which all the masters come out to play.

Essaouira also hosts autumn's **Festival des Andalousies Atlantiques**, which focuses on arabo-andalucian music and flamenco (www.festivaldesandalousies.com), and the **Printemps des Alizés** classical music festival each spring.

The most important music festival in Morocco is the **Festival de Fès des Musiques Sacrées du Monde** (www.fesfestival.com), held each June. In late May, there's also the annual **Festival des Musiques de Desert** (www.festivaldudesert.ma), which takes place in various locations around the Tafilelt oasis.

Nightlife

Talented new local DJs are the brightest hope for the city's club scene.

Clubbing heaven? The dancefloor at **Paradise Club**. *See p156.*

The 2005 opening of the enormous **Pacha** complex has, to some extent, put Marrakech on the international clubbing map. At the very least, it draws habitués of Pacha outposts in Spain, the UK and elsewhere for occasional party weekends. But to read it as evidence that Marrakech now has some kind of world-class nightlife scene would be to make a grave mistake.

Clubs here, mostly located in international chain hotels or out in the Palmeraie, remain almost entirely the preserve of foreigners and the wealthy Moroccan middle-class. There is no clubbing tradition here at all, and even if they suddenly acquired an interest in drinking alcohol and dancing to house music all night, most Marrakchis would have to hoard their dirhams for weeks to afford the 100dh-150dh entrance fee and a cocktail or two. Even then, the doormen probably wouldn't let them in.

Inside, the gaudy ambience of most places reflects their role as the stomping ground of the nouveax riches. Decent soundsystems and creative music policies often take second place to cigar bars and fancy restaurants, while most of the guests seem to have copied their look from the cheesiest styles on Fashion TV. As for the music, expect a mix of last year's house, a bit of jazzy Latino, Arab pop and Euro cheese.

Far from vibing the place up, Pacha's arrival seems to have had the opposite effect, with many deciding they simply can't compete. Nikki Beach is no longer a club, and the White Room, newly-opened when we compiled the last edition of *Time Out Marrakech*, has already thrown in the towel and become an 'oriental cabaret' instead.

That said, a handful of Moroccan DJs are developing their own sensual take on the turntables. Look out for DJ Zitroz, DJ-Unes, Leo Veil, Miko or Mednas, though all of these are more likely to be found playing in Rabat, home of Platinium Skhirat, probably Morocco's best club. Of those names, DJ Zitroz (aka Khalid Icame), is the only Marrakchi. At his best when working with minimal techno, Zitroz is part of the Sound of Marrakech crew (*see p153*), who at the time of writing had a once-a-month Saturday night residency at **Théatro**.

What clubbing information there is can be found (in French only) on two local what's-on portals, www.madein-marrakech.com and www.maroceve.com. The former has paid-for listings only; the latter is more impartial, but you have to sift out Marrakech nightlife information from listings for the whole of Morocco. Check your options before heading out, as the scene looks set for further changes.

Don't turn up anywhere before midnight, or you'll find staff outnumbering customers – and most of the latter will also be 'working', if you catch our drift. Pacha and Théatro are the only places that really fill up on week nights.

Actor'S
Hotel Medina Spa, Avenue Mohammed VI, Guéliz (reservation 067 52 63 92/ 061 06 41 16). **Open** 11pm-4am daily. **Admission** 150dh Mon-Thur, Sun; 200dh Fri, Sat. **No credit cards. Map** p254 B4.
Opened in December 2006, this place was still struggling to find its feet in early 2007. Music is a mix of '80s hits, rock, Spanish stuff and the odd trance or techno number, which suits a club that isn't yet sure who its audience ought to be. The circular bars are a nice touch; you can look across and meet the glance of whoever's waiting to be served on the other side, making it a good place to meet people. But only time will tell what kind of people those are likely to be.

Diamant Noir
Hotel Marrakech, place de la Liberté, avenue Mohammed V, Guéliz (024 43 43 51). **Open** 10pm-4am daily. **Admission** 80dh Mon-Thur, Sun; 100dh Fri, Sat. **No credit cards. Map** p254 C3.
Spurned by the smart set, Diamant Noir nevertheless remains popular with party boys and girls and a smattering of expats, including the Euro queens. It's a non-judgemental crowd, making it something of a refuge for Moroccan gays. Scout out the talent going in from the vantage of the neighbouring house pizzeria before descending to the sub-basement dancefloor (passing a couple of bar levels and pool area en route). Music is a better-than-average mix of Arabesque and electrobeats, spun by competent DJs.

Pacha
Boulevard Mohammed VI, Zone hôtelière de l'Aguedal (061 10 28 87/www.pachamarrakech.com). **Open** 11.30pm-6.30am daily. **Admission** 100dh Thur; 150dh Fri, Sat. **Credit** MC, V.
Pacha is an enormous complex which, apart from the club itself, also includes two restaurants – Jana and Crystal (*see p112*) – as well as a chill-out lounge and swimming pool. The dancefloor and bars can accommodate up to 3,000 smiley souls, and guest DJs are flown in most weekends. The names include many of those you'll find elsewhere on the international Pacha circuit. The club is some 7km (four miles) south of town, so getting there and back can be pricey.

Paradise Club
Kempinski Mansour Eddahbi, avenue de France, Hivernage (024 33 91 00). **Open** 10.30pm-4am daily. **Admission** 150dh (incl 1 drink). **Credit** MC, V. **Map** p254 A4.

Before Pacha, Paradise was the largest club in town. It always attracted an unexciting, moneyed crowd, which was predominantly Moroccan. Some of them are still around, but these days it's even less happening than ever. A grand flight of luminous steps leads down to the main arena, where spacious enclaves of seating encircle a relatively small dancefloor. A vast upper level offers the added distractions of pool and table football, as well as prime viewing of the occasionally impressive light show. **Photo** *p155*.

Le Senz
Palmeraie Golf Palace, Palmeraie (024 30 10 10). **Open** 11pm-3.30am daily. **Admission** 100dh Mon-Thur, Sun; 150dh Fri, Sat (incl 1 drink). **Credit** MC, V.
Formerly New Feeling, and a hangout of the current king back in his princely days, Le Senz has had a makeover along with a name change. It now usually features some kind of live band at the beginning of the evening. A raised glass dance podium allows for maximum exhibitionism; on the dancefloor below, DJs play an unimaginative selection of dance hits. Weekends can get so busy that it is virtually impossible to get a drink at the bar. Sit-outs are best spent on the smaller upper gallery, which is usually pleasantly empty. Be warned: taxis charge a minimum of 100dh each way to get out here from the Medina.

Théâtro
Hotel Es Saadi, avenue El-Qadissia, Hivernage (024 44 88 11/www.essaadi.com). **Admission** 150dh. **Open** 11.30pm-5am daily. **Credit** MC, V. **Map** p254 C5.
Theatro opened in 2004 and quickly established itself as the club least dependent on out-of-towners. This is where you'll find the hippest, best-informed locals. The venue was once a theatre; now, the stalls are filled with sofas, while the balcony is tiered with throw cushions. A series of semi-private, gauze-veiled crash crèches fill the stage, while the former orchestra pit houses a long curved bar, well stocked with chilled champagne and Red Bull. The sound system is thunderous, and psychedelic cinema projections entertain the eye – it's just a pity no one thought to leave space for a dancefloor. Look out for nights by Sound of Marrakech (*see p153*), as well as occasional international names such as Andy Morris.

VIP Room
Place de la Liberté, avenue Mohammed V, Guéliz (024 43 45 69). **Open** 9pm-4am daily. **Admission** 150dh (incl 1 drink). **Credit** MC, V. **Map** p254 C3.
Hailed as the Studio 54 of Marrakech when it opened several years ago, VIP Room falls an abyss short of those ambitions – but it's still worth a visit. Flounce down the neon-striped tunnel to the upper-basement level, where a jobbing Arabic orchestra saws away at Middle Eastern classics while couples canoodle in the semi-gloom. Down in the nightclub proper is a circular dancefloor, overhung by a sci-fi spider-like light rig. Equally alarming are the leather-clad local ladies who, between sultry demands of random men to 'light their cigarettes', shoot a mean game of pool.

Sport & Fitness

The great outdoors on your doorstep.

Palmeraie Golf Palace. *See p158.*

Marrakech and sport may not seem a natural partnership, but bear in mind that the city is surrounded by mountains and desert, natural habitats for adventure sports. In addition, the powers that be, in their wisdom, are promoting Marrakech as a golfing destination, and thirsty oases of lush green grass are appearing around the city's dry environs. Of course golf, quad-biking and the like are strictly for the moneyed-up tourist; there is very little municipal sports provision for the city's people.

Like most of the rest of the world, Moroccans are obsessed with football. The national team have made it to three World Cup finals (most recently in 1998 in France). Marrakchis are also great fans of their local team (*see p162* **Lions of the Atlas**). But it's on the track or the marathon course that Moroccans really excel. The country has produced several champion middle- and long-distance runners, including Hicham El-Guerrouj, five times world 1,500 metres champion; Said Aouita, the former 1,500, 2,000, 3,000 and 5,000 metres world record holder, and London Marathon winner Abdelkader El-Moaziz.

Spectator sports

Gates for league football games at El-Harti Stadium are counted in the hundreds rather than thousands. The top local soccer team is **Kawkab** ('KAC'; *see p162* **Lions of** the Atlas). Next best are **Najm Sport Marrakech**, a second division semi-pro side in perpetual money trouble, whose players are forced to earn their keep elsewhere.

Daoudiate Stadium

Route les Philistines, off avenue Palestine, Hay Mohammadi, Daoudiate.
An indoor stadium that's the venue of choice for all non-footballing sports events of any significance.

El-Harti Stadium

Jnane El-Harti, Guéliz (024 42 06 66). **Map** p254 B3.
Home to the Kawkab and Najm football teams. It seats just 15,000 and facilities are sparse. Tickets are usually purchased on the day, but sometimes in advance for big games.

Active sports

Climbing

The Todra Gorge on the southern side of the Atlas Mountains is the best known and most widely climbed bit of Morocco, but there are also plenty of places to climb in the Marrakech region. Most of these sites are unknown and largely undeveloped.

High Country

31 Bab Amadel, Amizmiz (024 33 21 82/www.highcountry.co.uk). **Open** 8.30am-5pm Mon-Fri.
High Country is a reputable, locally based outfit offering rock climbing. It's a British- and American-run operation that arranges climbs for groups of four or more using sites deep in the Atlas Mountains.

Cycling

The roads of the Ourika and Drâa valleys, and the weaving passes of the Atlas mountains, are challenging and exhilarating terrain for cyclists.

You can rent quality bicycles from **Action Sports Loisirs** (1 boulevard Yacoub El-Mansour, apartment 4, Guéliz, 024 43 09 31, mobile 061 24 01 45). **D and O Adventures** (www.dandoadventures.com), based in Morocco and Canada, has more than 15 years experience of organising tailor-made trips for individuals and groups. It offers cycling, mountain biking and combined hiking and cycling in the High Atlas, including several day trips.

Golf

For good or ill, Marrakech is being touted as the next big destination for golfers. Around a dozen new courses and complexes are currently under construction outside the city, but this being Morocco, it's not happening overnight. The three courses that already exist are excellent, and do not require handicap

certificates. Most golfers find the summer months too hot to play – most visit between October and May. The international Open du Maroc is held every April.

With average temperatures for most of the year a grass-withering 25˚C-38˚C (77˚F-100˚F), and minimal precipitation, the popularity of golf in Morocco may seem a little incongruous. Perhaps it's more than mere coincidence that Morocco's previous monarch, King Hassan II, was a golfing fanatic. He played as often as the royal schedule allowed and employed a squadron of caddies, one of whom was responsible for gripping the royal cigarette with a pair of silver tongs while the king swung his club. Thereafter building golf courses became an important part of the royal vision for the modernisation of the country.

Golf d'Amelkis

Route de Ouarzazate, km 12 (024 40 44 14). **Open** 7am-6.30pm daily. **Rates** *18 holes* 500 dh; *daily green fees* 700dh; *caddies* 100dh; *hire clubs* 300 dh. **Course length** 5,774m. **Credit** MC, V.
The newest course in Marrakech, the Amelkis ('flower of the oasis' in Berber) is a rolling landscape of baize-like greenery – and real desert sandtraps – fringed by sumptuous Moorish fantasy villas. The ultra-modern championship course has hosted the Moroccan Open. Caddies are obligatory if you are not using a golf buggy. The pro-shop is well stocked, although the hire clubs looked as if they belonged to the pre-independence era; staff say they are getting new ones soon. The Berber-style clubhouse may look a bit gimmicky but it is lovely inside and the facilities and restaurant are top-notch. Only about 15 minutes drive south-east of the Medina.

Palmeraie Golf Palace

Palmeraie Golf Palace Hotel and Resort, Palmeraie (golf club 024 36 87 66/www.pgpmarrakech.com). **Open** 7am-7pm daily. **Rates** *18 holes* 500 dh; *daily green fees* 500dh; *caddies* 80dh; *hire clubs* 260 dh. **Course length** 6,200m. **Credit** AmEx, MC, V.
This somewhat kitsch and extremely expensive resort has everything: horse riding, tennis, swimming pools with waterslides and probably the best golf course in the region. Designed by America's most famous course architect, Robert Trent Jones, it recently hosted the French PGA championship. No expense is spared on the upkeep of the 18 holes, which are in great condition. It is the longest of Marrakech's courses, and a further nine holes are due to open in November 2007. Facilities include a golf academy with three professionals. There are discounts on green fees if you are staying at the Palmeraie Golf Palace Hotel. **Photo** *p157.*

Royal Golf Club

Ancienne Route de Ouarzazate km 2 (024 40 47 05). **Open** 7am-6pm daily. **Rates** *daily green fees* 500dh; *caddies for 18 holes* 80dh; . **Course length** 5,268m. **Credit** MC, V.

This colonial-style golf course is the oldest in Morocco. It was built in the 1920s by the despotic Thami El-Glaoui, to impress his British guests. To irrigate the course, water was diverted from farmland – a fact that was of no concern to the pasha. These days the course is a little rough around the edges, but it oozes history and has stunning views of the Atlas mountains. In an attempt to upgrade the set-up, the management have set up a David Leadbetter teaching academy, and a new restaurant and club house have recently been added, although both are slightly spartan. The hire clubs, like much of the course, have seen better days.

Horse-riding

Marrakech has its horsey set, comprised of expats and moneyed locals. For the latter group, it's very much a status thing; the current king's aunt, Amina El-Alawi, is the president of the Royal Association Equestre, and the sport enjoys powerful royal patronage.

Les Cavaliers d'Atlas

Ait Ourir (village 35mins outside Marrakech) (072 84 55 79/064 90 34 49/www.lescavaliersdatlas.com). **Open** 8am-6pm daily. **Rates** 900dh per day; 580dh per half day. **No credit cards**.

Surf Morocco

It might be better known for its souks, but Morocco also boasts 3,500 kilometres of coastline and an abundance of stunning surf spots – from shallow beach breaks to bone-crunching barrels. As such, it's justifiably popular with starry-eyed surfers craving exotic adventures but unable to afford the pipe dreams of Hawaii or Fiji.

Most tend to descend on the bustling fishing town of **Taghazout**, 100 kilometres (62 miles) south of Essaouira (and just 18 kilometres, 11 miles, north of Agadir). Its surroundings are the stuff of postcards – the bottle-green Atlantic, the beaches fringed with wooden fishing boats and peppered with seafarers repairing their nets – but it's the waves themselves that draw surfers from across the world, consistently clean and catering to everyone from swell-shy howies to hardened water walkers.

Banana Beach, for example, gives beginners a leg-up with its lightweight and leisurely break, seldom topping four feet in summer. At the other end of the scale are legendary spots like **Anchor Point**, a kilometre north of the town centre, which underpins one of the longest right-hand breaks on earth with a mean current, occasionally merciless crowds and a rather alarmingly placed pier; or **Killer Point**, three kilometres (two miles) out of Taghazout, with barrelling waves that regularly rear up to 12 feet in peak season.

The area's popularity means that first-timers are well served by a wealth of hire shops, surf schools and affordable beachside accommodation. Anyone worried about their ability to string the various elements of a trip together can instead leave the legwork to reputable UK-based tour company **Surf Maroc** (01794 322709/www.surfmaroc.co.uk),

which offers a range of accommodation options from basic room and board to luxuriously furnished apartments, literally overlooking the beaches, and with various optional extras like coaching and hire of cars or equipment.

Alternatively, those seeking a surf safari further off the beaten track might prefer to ride the scenic coast road south of Agadir to lesser-known **Sidi Ifni**, once a Spanish colony, now a colourful town teeming with life, but with decidedly fewer peroxided locks or 'hang-ten' hand signals per square metre than its more northerly neighbours. Recent years have seen a number of surf-style cafés and bars open along the beachfront, but there's still little in the way of equipment hire (although you can usually persuade locals to lend you a board in an emergency). The fact that the main wave is a reef break (significantly less pleasant to get hurled on to than a sandbar) means that only intermediate or experienced surfers need apply. For accommodation, head straight to the family-run and famously friendly **Suerta Loca** (which means 'crazy luck'; 7 Plaza Mulay Yousef, 48 87 53 50, 190dh per night) – part hotel, part heaving community centre – or the **Bellevue** (11 Place Hassan, 48 87 50 72, 200dh per night).

Lastly, the beaches of **Essaouira** are largely uncrowded and well suited to beginners in the summer months. Sandy **Sidi Kaouki**, 30 kilometres (15 miles) outside the town, has just been linked to it by a major road development, leading many to predict a forthcoming boom in surf-related tourism. Powerful north-easterly trade winds on this stretch of coast means that it's more usually frequented by windsurfers (*see p179* **Wind City Afrika**).

Arts & Entertainment

Taking a corner at **Atlas Karting**.

The stable can accommodate beginners as well as accomplished riders. The price includes pick-up from your hotel.

Club Equestre de la Palmeraie

Palmeraie Golf Palace Hotel & Resort, Palmeraie (024 36 87 93/www.pgp.co.ma). **Open** *Winter* 8am-noon, 3-6pm daily. *Summer* 8-11am, 3-8pm daily (Wed & Sat pm reserved for club members). **Rates** *Horses* 150dh per hr; 800dh per day. *Ponies* 50dh per 15mins; 90dh per hr. **No credit cards**.

Part of the Palmeraie Golf Palace resort (*see p158*), the Club Equestre has extensive stables with an adjacent training area for beginners. Experienced riders are led out into the groves of the Palmeraie for a canter.

Jebel Atlas

Golf Palmier Club, Club Boulahrir, route de Fes, km 8 (024 32 94 51). **Open** 9am-6pm Tue-Sun. **Rates** 170dh per hr. **Credit** MC, V.

This beautifully constructed, Swiss-run site has a great atmosphere, and caters to riders of all levels. After a session in the saddle, head to the relaxing and well-appointed clubhouse. Accommodation is also available at the club, as well as swimming, mini-golf and tennis facilities.

Royal Club Equestre de Marrakech

Route d'Amizmiz, km 4 (024 38 18 49). **Open** 8am-noon, 2-6pm Tue-Sun. **Rates** *Horses* 150dh per hr. *Ponies* 15dh per 15mins. **No credit cards**.

The trainers are often ex-national equestrian competitors at this state-owned establishment. It is very well-run and has a wonderfully relaxed atmosphere. Longer group trips don't have fixed prices or times, so it's best to call beforehand.

Karting & quad biking

Why Marrakech is such a magnet for karting and quad operators is a mystery, but their numbers continue to grow steadily. Quad novices receive a short training session before being allowed to roam wild.

Atlas Karting

Route de Safi (061 23 76 87). **Open** 8am-7pm daily. **Rates** *Karts* 100dh 10mins; 250dh 30mins; 300dh 40mins; 450dh 1hr. *Quads* 500dh for 90mins pilot; 340dh passenger. **No credit cards**.

Owned and run by a French karting pro, this is a fully competitive course, challenging and fun to drive. It's the venue for an annual 24-hour marathon and is on the European karting competitive circuit. The company also has quad bikes and offers a full-day adventure package comprising half a day on the karts and half on the quads, hotel pick-up included. We should think so. **Photo** *p160*.

Nakhil Quad

Route de Palmeraie (061 15 99 10). **Open** 9am-noon, 2-5pm daily. **Rates** 500dh for 2hrs pilot; 340dh passenger. **No credit cards**.

Tucked away behind the Coralia Club hotel, Nakhil was the first place with quads in Marrakech. However, the machines are a little old and not as well maintained as they could be. The location is great, allowing for fantastic rides through the Palmeraie and its villages.

Microlights & hot-air balloons

Ciel d'Afrique (024 43 28 43, www.ceil dafrique.info) also organises hot-air ballooning over the city and desert.

ULM

Km 22, route de Tahanahout (071 66 13 50/ www.ulm-maroc.com). **Open** by appointment only. **Rates** 750dh for 15mins, 2,520dh per hr. **No credit cards**.

Two French pilots have wangled the necessary flight authorisation and since January 2005 have been taking passengers up and over the Pink City. They have also teamed up with fellow air enthusiasts to offer all-day packages that include microlight flights, hang gliding and hot-air ballooning; rates start at 2,000dh per person.

Running

The international success of Morocco's long- and middle-distance runners (*see p157*) has proved a national inspiration. Sweat-stained runners are a common sight on the wide road that rings the age-old walls of Marrakech Medina. There are plenty of running clubs in town, whose members compete in local, regional and national competitions at all levels. The main spectator event is the annual **Marrakech International Marathon**, which takes place at the end of January (usually the coolest time of the year). It attracts more than 6,000 professional and amateur athletes and has been increasing in stature since its inception nearly 20 years ago. The marathon starts and finishes in the Jemaa El Fna and the circuit goes around the city walls and through the Palmeraie. There is also a half-marathon and a race for children. For further details see www.marathon-marrakech.com.

If the Marrakech marathon isn't tough enough for you, then try the **Marathon des Sables** – a six day, 240-kilometre (150-mile) endurance run across a section of the Sahara near Ouarzazate. The MDS, as it's known, takes place at the end of March and beginning of April, just when it's getting seriously hot (49°C/120F), and is equivalent to five and half standard marathons. Runners must carry a lightweight backpack with all the clothing, food and supplies they need for the week, and are supplied with a measly nine-litre ration of water for each day. At night, participants sleep on the ground in Berber tents. Surprisingly around 700 people pay just short of $5,000 each for the privilege of competing, with Brits making up the largest proportion (more than 200 competed last year). Only one person has died while competing; in fact, the MDS is littered with legendary stories of survival. In 1994 Mauro Prosperi, a police officer from Rome, got lost in a sandstorm and wandered several hundred miles off course. He somehow survived the next nine days on boiled urine and dead bats.

Skiing

Oukaimeden (*see p201*), 70 kilometres (43 miles) south of Marrakech, has a number of chair lifts and ski runs, and at 2,650 metres, it's as high as many Alpine resorts. However snow falls are unpredictable, so there is no guarantee that you will actually get to ski, even in the peak season, which runs from December to March. Artificial snow is nowhere to be seen, although that could be set to change as investors from the UAE are planning to transform what has until now been a rather paltry collection of sheds and ski lifts into state of the art facilities. One of their first priorities should be to update the equipment – the current range of '80s boots and skis look more like something from *Star Wars* than contemporary mountain wear.

At the moment Oukaimeden has just seven lifts and eight pistes, including an impressive black run that would be no disgrace in a top European or American ski resort. Après ski is limited, unless huddling around a solitary roadside tagine stand is your idea of a night out. If you're travelling to Oukaimeden by taxi you will need to hire a driver for the day, as it is almost impossible to find a free taxi in the resort itself.

If you really want to get back to basics, you could consider ski touring with a mule from the village of Imlil below Jbel Toubkal. You can use the refuge that sits at 3,500 metres as your base camp (it will feel like Everest in temperature if nothing else) and from here you can trek up half a dozen different peaks and have couloirs and untrammelled powder all to yourself.

Lions of the Atlas

Marrakech isn't a big football town. The local team, Kawkab (KAC Marrakech), last won the national championship (GNFE League) and cup (Coupe du Trône) in the early 1990s. But loyal fans still turn up in their – well – hundreds at the sparse **El-Harti stadium** (pictured below, *see p158*) in Guéliz.

Elsewhere in Morocco – particularly Casablanca – football is a lifelong passion. Moroccans took to the game in the early 1900s. The Spanish introduced it to Ceuta and Ifni; the French to Fes, Tangier and Casablanca. A local league was set up in 1916, won by CA Casablanca, and the city soon became the powerbase for the Moroccan game. Fierce competition bred world-class players, who exported their talents to the professional game in France. The prime example was Casablanca-born Larbi Ben Barek, who became a hero at Olympique Marseille and went on to play many times for the French national team. Ben Barek was a figurehead in the pre-Independence game.

Morocco was the first African nation to compete at a modern World Cup finals – in Mexico in 1970. Having beaten major European teams in friendlies during the 1960s, the Lions of the Atlas gave eventual semi-finalists West Germany a huge fright, falling to a late goal to lose 2-1. Star of the side was Mohammedia striker Ahmed Faras, who would lead his country to their only African Cup of Nations victory in 1976.

Morocco's darkest footballing hour was a 5-1 defeat at the hands of rivals Algeria in 1979. After this débacle, King Hassan II, who understood football's power as a unifier, ploughed resources into the game, allowing more players to turn professional. The fruits of that investment were realised when the Lions reached the World Cup finals in Mexico in 1986 and finished top of their group ahead of England – only to be knocked out again by those pesky West Germans. They made it again in 1994 and 1998, and were narrowly pipped at the post for qualification in 2006 by neighbouring Tunisia.

Arts & Entertainment

There is more information about skiing in Morocco on the Sport Travel website (www.sporttravel-maroc.com).

Swimming

Fewer hotels than might be expected have pools, thanks to the space restrictions of the Medina. Those places that do usually zealously enforce a guests-only policy. Exceptions are few: the the **Sofitel** (*see p39* **The chain gang**; pool open 8.30am-6.30pm daily) charges 300dh, which includes lunch. **Hotel El Andalous** (avenue du Président Kennedy, 024 44 82 26, pool open 8.30am-6.30pm daily) charges 150dh including lunch, which is served from noon to 2pm, and the **Jardins de la Koutoubia** (*see p41*) charges 150dh by reservation only, but if the hotel is busy the pool is closed to non-guests.

A new alternative to the hotels are the club/restaurants with pools out of town. You get relative peace, greenery, good food and a swim; the only drawback is that you need your own transport.

Forget municipal pools in the Medina; there are only three, and they are usually reserved for local swimming clubs. At other times they're filled with horny little boys who'd be highly amused at a foreigner in their midst and would wet themselves at the sight of a woman in a swimsuit.

Beldi Country Club
Km 6, route de Barrage (024 44 42 21). **Open** 10am-6pm daily. **Pool** 200dh per person, 320dh per couple. **No credit cards.**
Rambling gardens and lots of private spaces, with a wonderful large pool. Lunch is served for an additional 220dh.

L'Oliveraie de Marigha
Route d'Amizmiz (024 48 42 81). **Open** 10am-6pm daily. **Pool** 160dh per person. **Credit** MC, V.
A 300sq m pool one hour's drive from Marrakech in the heart of an old olive grove. The cover charge includes lunch, but not drinks.

Tennis

Most of the large hotels have tennis courts but, as with their swimming pools, use of them tends to be restricted to guests. One exception is the **Palmeraie Golf Palace** (*see p158*), where both squash and tennis courts are available for hire to the general public at 100dh per hour.

Royal Tennis Club de Marrakech
Rue Oued El-Makhazine, Jnane El Harti, Guéliz (024 43 19 02). **Open** 7am-8pm daily. **Rates** 100dh per hr. **No credit cards. Map** p250 B3.

As much a social club as a sports centre, this is where Marrakech's well-heeled families come to play. There are only six courts and the place is very popular, so reservations are essential.

Health & fitness

Gyms/fitness centres

Weightlifting and bodybuilding are beloved of Moroccan men across all social classes. There are probably over 100 small- to medium-sized gyms in Marrakech. Every area of the city has one. They all have equipment for weight training and possibly some of the following: boxing, judo, karate and taekwondo. Day rates are uncommon, but offering to pay an upfront nominal fee is likely to gain you access. Cheaper gyms and fitness centres tend to be dominated by men, and women will certainly not feel comfortable. Most of the larger hotels (*see p39* **The chain gang**) offer gym access to non-guests for around 180dh-200dh per hour.

Kawkab Sportif du Marrakech
Battement Lahbess, Bab Doukkala, Medina (024 43 31 33). **Open** 6am-10pm daily. **Rates** 270dh-300dh per mth. **No credit cards. Map** p250 A3.

Nakhil Gym
75 rue Ibn Aicha, Guéliz (024 43 92 90). **Open** 8am-10pm daily. **Rates** 270dh-300dh per mth. **No credit cards. Map** p254 A2.
This place also offers aerobics classes for women three days a week.

Hammams

Anyone who's visited the bathhouses of Turkey or Syria is in for a big disappointment. The public hammams of Marrakech are a pedestrian lot. But if they're lacking in architectural finery, they are rich in social significance – and they do a good job of getting a body clean.

The advent of internal plumbing for all has meant that hammam-going is no longer a necessary ritual, but many who live in the Medina will still go at least once a week to meet friends and gossip. For the uninitiated, entering a hammam can be a baffling experience. After paying (prices are set by the state at 7dh for men and 7.50dh for women), leave your clothes (and a little *baksheesh*) with the attendant. Men keep their shorts on, women go naked (all hammams are single sex). There are three rooms: one cool, one hot, one very hot. The idea is to spend as long as you can in the hottest room then retreat to the less-hot place and douse yourself with water. In public hammams there's usually a 'trainer' who, for an additional fee, will deliver a massage. You should bring your own towels.

Arts & Entertainment

It's increasingly common these days for hotels to include a hammam. Use tends to be restricted to guests only, but there are exceptions: these include **Maison Arabe**, **Bains de Marrakech** and **Palais Rhoul**.

Hammam El Bacha

20 rue Fatima Zohra, Medina (no phone). **Open** *Men* 7am-1pm daily. *Women* 1-9pm daily. **Rates** 7dh men; 7.50dh women; massage 50dh. **No credit cards**. **Map** p250 B4.

Probably the best-known hammam in town, thanks to its past role as local soak for the servants and staff of the Dar El-Bacha opposite. It boasts impressive dimensions and a 6m (20ft) high cupola, but it's very badly maintained – don't count on coming out any cleaner than you went in.

Hammam El Grmai

Bab Aylen, Medina (no phone). **Open** *Men* 7am-1pm daily. *Women* 1-9pm daily. **Rates** 7dh men; 7.50dh women; massage 50dh. **No credit cards**. **Map** p251 F5.

This place has the old-fashioned basin from which you collect water to wash in a bowl (modern hammams have taps). In the changing areas the floor is covered with *hsira* mats made of grass or palm leaves; interiors throughout are done out in *tadelakt*. Unlike modern hammams at which you pay on entry, here you pay as you leave.

Hammam Menara

Quartier Essaada (no phone). **Open** *Men* 10am-9pm Tue, Thur, Sat. *Women* 10am-9pm Mon, Wed, Fri, Sun. **Rates** 60dh; massage 60dh. **No credit cards**.

The Menara is the first of a new breed of high-end 'luxury' hammams aimed at the local market. It's beautifully done with individual *vasques* with marble stools (so you don't have to sit on the floor), and the scrubdown with the *kissa* (loofah mitten) takes place on a slab. There's a pleasant salon in which to relax afterwards. It's located out beyond the Menara Gardens but most taxi drivers know how to find it.

Maison Arabe

1 Derb Assehbe, Bab Doukkala (024 38 70 10/ www.lamaisonarabe.com). **Open** by appointment only. **Credit** MC, V. **Map** p250 A4.

The ultimate in self-indulgence – a hammam with rubdown (*gommage*) administered by a vicious pro, followed by an all-over body treatment. Another package includes the most thorough of massages.

Palais Rhoul

Route de Fès, Palmeraie (024 32 94 94/www.palais rhoul.com). **Open** by appointment only. **Rates** 400dh. **Credit** MC, V.

The Palais Rhoul is a ridiculously opulent and exclusive Palmeraie villa, which lies beyond the means of most ordinary human beings. It is possible to breathe in its rarefied air, though, by booking a visit to the hammam. It's the most beautiful setting in which most of us are ever likely to voluntarily sweat buckets. Best of all is the massage, with manipulation of

Sultana. *See p165.*

joints so vigorous that victims are reduced to jelly. Slither into the cool basin afterwards to be revived with fresh mint tea. It's the best pampering money can buy – but don't forget to factor in the cost of getting out to the Palmeraie and back.

Massage

Almost all riads offer massage, though it's not always much good: it can just seem like an experiment to see how much oil your skin can absorb. As with most things in Marrakech, quality comes at a price. We are particularly keen on the **Palais Rhoul** (*see above*).

Ahmed Bissi

067 75 91 76/ahmed@gmail.com. **Open** By appointment only. **Rates** 600dh per hour. **No credit cards**.

A fixture of the Marrakech spa scene for over 10 years, Ahmed has worked with the best and has finally decided to work by appointment. He uses a mixture of techniques, depending on what your body needs, and is deservedly popular.

Pia Westh

Villa Vanille dour Bellaguid, Sidi Brahim, route de Palmeraie (063 72 79 77/scoubia@menara.ma). **Open** By appointment only. **Rates** 450dh-550dh per session. **Credit** V.

Westh has been trained by Axelsons in Stockholm and specialises in *tui na*, which is a medicinal massage with a 2,000-year history in China of efficacy against a range of ailments from chronic pain to allergies. *Tui na* works by addressing the *qi*, or internal energy, of the patient to balance their overall state of health. Westh has also recently completed a diploma in Swedish massage.

Spas

Not too long ago rituals of relaxation and well-being in Marrakech started and ended with readings from the Qur'an or visits to a shrine. That's history. Spas and associated treatments are becoming big news. However, it's still early days and the scene remains undeveloped. As yet there seems to be nobody with any kind of interesting signature treatment. Proper training is also lacking. An alternative option is Richard Branson's **Kasbah Tamadot** (*see p196*), which has been investing heavily in staff.

Bains de Marrakech

Riad Mehdi, 2 Derb Sedra, Bab Agnaou, Medina (024 38 14 28/www.lesbainsdemarrakech.com). **Open** 9am-1pm, 3-8pm daily. **Rates** treatments from 200dh-400dh; day packages up to 1600dh. **Credit** MC, V. **Map** p250 B8.

Attached to the Riad Mehdi, just inside the Bab Agnaou, is this extensive spa complex occupying several rooms and a courtyard of an old Medina house. An array of treatments include all manner of baths and body wraps – with essential oils, algae, refreshing mint and orange blossom milk – as well as various massages. It's one of the only places in town that does a shiatsu massage.

Hotel Hivernage & Spa

Angle avenue Echouhada & rue des Temples, Hivernage (024 42 41 00/www.hivernage-hotel.com). **Open** 9am-10pm daily. **Rates** treatments from 150dh-750dh; day packages 1,500dh. **Credit** AmEx, MC, V. **Map** p254 C4.

The Hotel Hivernage is a smart, mid-range new build just a few minutes walk from the Bab Jedid and Mamounia. It has a dedicated spa with a separate section for men and women, both kitted out with state-of-the-art equipment. Staff are notably smiley and welcoming and most of them speak English. It's a great place to come as a couple.

L'Oriental Spa

Hotel Es Saadi, avenue El-Qadissia, Hivernage (024 44 88 11/www.essaadi.com). **Open** 9.30am-12.30pm, 2.30-7.30pm daily. **Rates** treatments from 250dh; day packages from 1,300dh. **Credit** AmEx, MC, V. **Map** p254 C5.

The Hotel Es Saadi (*see p59*) is a long-standing Marrakech fixture, now with a stunning-looking spa. Day packages are available.

Secrets de Marrakech

62 rue de la Liberte, Guéliz (024 43 48 48). **Open** 10am-8.30pm Mon-Sat. **Rates** treatments from 400dh; day packages from 650dh. **No credit cards.** **Map** p254 B2.

A small establishment and more personal than other spas, it's something of a rarity in that it is not attached to a hotel; it offers correspondingly fewer treatments. A menu of light snacks and fruit salads is served on the terrace.

Sofitel Marrakech

Rue Harroun Errachid, Hivernage (024 42 56 00, www.sofitel.com). **Open** 9am-9.30pm daily. **Rates** treatments 500dh-1,000dh; day packages from 2,000dh. **Credit** AmEx, MC, V. **Map** p254 C5.

The Sofitel group has the most experience of any of the spa operators in town, so it's no surprise that this is the number one spa in Marrakech. Staff are well trained (diploma-holders, the lot) and thoroughly professional, and the world-class facilities cleverly grouped into a series of appealing packages. It's essential to book well in advance; weekends are reserved exclusively for hotel guests.

Sultana

Rue de la Kasbah, Kasbah (024 38 80 08/www.la sultana marrakech.com). **Open** 10am-8pm daily. **Rates** treatments from 275dh; day packages from 1,100dh. **Credit** AmEx, MC, V. **Map** p252 B8.

The Sultana (*see p47*) is a five-star hotel located in the Medina; its spa opened in December 2004. It's a lovely little complex with an intimate, grotto-like feel. We are very fond of the free Jacuzzi that comes with all treatments. Hammam treatments come with a special aromatic body massage; body wraps with argan oil also feature.

Yoga

Olivier Lefèbvre

063 54 40 59/olivieryoga@gmail.com. **Open** By appointment only. **Rates** 450dh-550dh per session. Olivier has been teaching yoga for 10 years. He offers individual sessions in his studio for 450dh per lesson (these usually last from one and a half to two hours) or will visit your hotel for 550dh bringing mats with him. Book well in advance. At the time of writing, he is in the process of building a brand new yoga studio that should be open in autumn 2007. He will have guest teachers from overseas and organise intensive yoga weekends throughout Morocco all year round.

TRANSPORT & TRAVEL

Essaouira

Features

Maps

Essaouira

Atlantic winds, big seas and gnawa.

Southern Morocco's most interesting coastal town – and the one most easily reached from Marrakech – offers both a contrast and an escape. There's a point on the road, about two-thirds of the way there, where the villages stop being pink and green and start being blue and white – the colours of earth and vegetation replaced by the colours of sea and sky. This elemental reorientation is matched by a change in climate. Where Marrakech is hot and arid, Essaouira is subject to winds that keep at bay the searing temperatures of the interior.

It's around three hours away by bus, quicker by car or taxi, and, while just about doable as a day trip, travellers tend to linger here. Out on a limb from the rail network and until recently with no airport (it now has a small one with flights to Paris and Casablanca), Essaouira long managed to retain a laid-back timelessness all of its own. That's now changing, a victim of the town's accelerating popularity amid the same mix of foreign investment and state-encouraged development of tourist infra-structure that is pumping up Marrakech.

That said, it's still a relatively relaxing place, and a charming one too. Sandy-coloured ramparts shelter a clean and bright Medina built around French piazzas, carved archways and whitewashed lanes and alleys. The fishing port provides a constant fresh catch for local restaurants, while the wide, sandy beaches to the south, combined with high winds of up to 40 knots, have put Essaouira on the international windsurfing map.

It's also probably the best place to be in Morocco during Ramadan. Many cafés and restaurants remain open through the day, unlike in most Moroccan towns, and the atmosphere in the evening is crowded but fairly calm when locals come out to socialise in the streets and cafés. Essaouira can also claim to be one of the cleanest and freshest Moroccan towns, with no vehicles in the Medina, regular street sweeping, and the Alizés winds keeping the temperature to an equable average of 22°C (72°F).

THE PERNICIOUS WEED

In 1878 British consul Charles Payton observed of the locals that 'they are a tough and hardy race these Moorish fishermen, bronzed and leathery of skin, sinewy of limb and yet not too fond of hard work… They would rather smoke the pernicious hasheesh in a foul and frowsy den of the back slums of the Moorish quarter than live out on the rippling sea.'

The westerners arriving in ever-increasing numbers today may still note the locals' talent to be comfortable doing nothing, even when they're not smoking the pernicious weed. This relaxed attitude is just as well, although it's being challenged by the pace of change. Despite the town's increasing popularity, all the renovations going on, and its designation as a UNESCO World Heritage Site, there is high unemployment and considerable poverty. Factories lie empty in the industrial quarter north of the Medina and the port no longer provides a living. Meanwhile, over ten per cent of the Medina's 16,000 houses – some 1,700 properties – are now owned by Europeans. The accompanying upswing in property prices is pushing the poorest Souiris out to the city limits. But locals know that the town is now largely dependent on tourism and this reinforces their instinctive tolerance – only occasionally tested by behaviour considered inappropriate in a Muslim country.

History

Essaouira has attracted travellers since the seventh century BC, when the Phoenicians established their furthest outpost in Africa on one of its islands. During the first century BC, King Juba II extracted purple dye from Essaouira's murex shells for the Romans. The dyeworks were also on what are still known as the Iles Purpuraires. In the 15th century, the Portuguese occupied Mogador, as it was then called, and built fortifications around the harbour. The town was one of their major bases until they abandoned it in 1541. Sir Francis Drake ate his Christmas lunch on the Ile de Mogador in 1577.

In 1765 the local ruler, Sultan Sidi Mohammed Ben Abdellah, captured a French vessel and hired one of its passengers – French architect Théodore Cornut – to redesign the place. The sultan wanted a fortified southern base to counter trouble from the port of Agadir to the south, threatening revolt at the time; but he also wanted an open city for foreign traders. A grid street layout was drawn up and the sultan shipped in black slaves from the Sudanese empire to begin building what was to become the most important port on the North African coast. The gnawa brotherhood of mystic musicians first set foot on Moroccan soil as part of this shackled workforce. With the work completed, Mogador became Essaouira. (It was to revert to Mogador again when the French arrived in 1912,

and then become Essaouira again at independence in 1956.)

A sizeable Jewish community was welcomed, numbering around 9,000 at its peak, and British and European merchants were drawn by protected trade status and a harbour free from customs duties. For a long time, Essaouira was the only Moroccan port on the Atlantic coast that was open to European trade, and it prospered greatly until the French arrived in 1912. It is said that Marshall Lyautey visited Essaouira on a Saturday when the Jewish community was at prayer, took one look at the deserted streets, and decided to make Casablanca the principal port. Trade began slipping away. The town slid into further decline with the departure of all but a handful of the Jewish community following independence in 1956.

CLAIMS TO FAME

Orson Welles stayed here on and off in 1949-50, shooting much of his wonderful *Othello*. There are many scenes on the ramparts, and the murder of Rodrigo was staged in a local hammam. Locals pitched in as extras, earning two dirhams a day, plus bread and a tin of sardines. In 1992, after a special screening of the restored version attended by King Mohammed VI (then Crown Prince), a small park outside the Medina's south-west corner was officially named place Orson Welles. The Prince also unveiled a memorial sculpture by local craftsman Samu Mustapha that is curiously unrecognisable as either Welles or Othello. More recently, Essaouira was used as a location for both Ridley Scott's *Kingdom of Heaven* and Oliver Stone's *Alexander*.

In the late 1960s, Essaouira and the neighbouring village of **Diabat** were inked on the hippy map. Celebrity visitors included Tennessee Williams, Margaret Trudeau and Cat Stevens, who, now Yusuf Islam, still returns each summer. Most celebrated of the lot, though, was **Jimi Hendrix**, whose brief visit in 1969 has generated a wealth of myth (*see p186* **Castles made of sand**). Otherwise, the influence of the hippies lingers on in the school of naïve painters and in the annual music festival in June, which sees 200,000 revellers decend upon the town (*see p177* **Gnawa grooves**).

Sightseeing

As in Marrakech, Essaouira has next to nothing in the way of formal sights such as monuments and museums. The Medina itself is one big sight, with highlights including the ramparts,

Skala de la Ville.

PLACE MOULAY HASSAN AND THE PORT

Connecting the Medina to the port, place Moulay Hassan is Essaouira's social centre. You can sit at any of the cafés and watch the theatre of the town unfolding. Early in the morning, fishermen pass by on their way to work, and the first wave of itinerant musicians and shoe-shine boys appears. By 10am or 11am the café tables have begun their secondary function – as al fresco offices from which most Souiris conduct business at some time or another. Purveyors of sunglasses, watches and carpets sweep from table to table, only occasionally selling something. By now tourists have started to appear, buying the previous day's international newspapers from **Jack's Kiosk** (*see p187*).

Apart from the cafés at street level, place Moulay Hassan is also overlooked by the balconies of **Beau Rivage** (*see p174*), one of the better budget hotels, and the terrace of **Taros** (*see p184*), a multi-purpose venue in prime position above the corner with rue de la Skala. It's entrance is just a few yards off the square down rue de la Skala; it stands among a clutch of interesting shops. **Galerie Aida** (*see p185*) stocks second-hand *objets d'art* and books; **Bazaar Mehdi** (*see p185*) is the place for rugs and carpets. Carry on down here and you end up at the Skala de la Ville.

The port, although pleasant at any time of day, is most interesting in the late afternoon when the fishing fleet rolls back into the harbour. Essaouira is Morocco's third-largest fishing port after Agadir and Safi. The catch is auctioned between 3pm and 5pm at the market hall just outside the port gates, and fresh fish are grilled and served up at **stalls** (*see p183*) on the port side of place Moulay Hassan.

If you want to go fishing yourself, you can hire a boat from the kiosk of the **Societé Navette des Iles** (064 32 64 93/www. mogador-iles.com) on the quayside near Chez Sam (*see p183*) for 200dh per person for three hours. The Societé also offers a '*promenade en mer*' – an hour-long drift around the bay on a 70-seater tourist boat – for 80dh a head; fizzy drinks and junk food extra.

SKALA DE LA VILLE

The narrow rue de la Skala leads from place Moulay Hassan along the inside of the sea wall. It's also possible to get here by ducking through the spooky tunnel-like alley that leads off place Moulay Hassan by the Café de France. The entrance to **Dar Loulema** (*see p176*) can be found in this gloomy area, the dark heart of the Kasbah.

the **souks** and the **Mellah**. You can march from one end to the other in ten minutes; a more leisurely exploration, however, can take days. The **port** is a separate entity, worthy of at least a stroll. Connecting the two is the **place Moulay Hassan**, the town's social nexus, which you'll pass through at least a dozen times a day.

Arriving by car from Marrakech, you'll most likely enter the Medina through the arch of **Bab Sbaâ**, one of five gates. (By bus, you'll enter thriough **Bab Marrakech**.) Beyond Bab Sbaâ, avenue du Caire has the town's useless tourist information office on the left, and the police further down on the opposite side. The few cross streets around here also contain several hotels, galleries and restaurants and a rowdy Moroccan bar, but it's a strangely detached corner of town, separate from both the Kasbah area and the rest of the Medina.

The narrow, shady avenue du Caire intersects the broad, open avenue Oqba Ibn Nafia, spine of the Medina. Left, this leads out to the port. Right, it dips under an arch, changes its name to avenue de l'Istiqlal, and becomes Essaouira's main commercial thoroughfare. Opposite avenue du Caire, the arch in the wall leads into the Kasbah district and, bearing left, to the place Moulay Hassan.

Rue de la Skala leads to the **Skala de la Ville**, where you can walk on top of the ramparts. There is one ramp up to the top near the junction with rue Ibn Rochd at the southern end, and another near the junction with rue Derb Laâlouj at the northern end. Locals gather here to watch the sunset and lovers cuddle in the crenellations, where ancient cannon offer places to perch. At the far end is the tower of the **North Bastion**, the top of which offers good views across the Mellah and Kasbah.

Painters lay out their work for sale on and around the ramparts. Artisans sculpting *thuja* – a local coniferous hardwood with a smell like peppery cedar – have their workshops in the arches below and here you can find all manner of carvings and marquetry.

From near the North Bastion, rue Derb Laâlouj leads back into the heart of the Medina, past a variety of handicraft and antique shops, a handful of restaurants including the excellent **Silvestro** (*see p184*), and Essaouira's lone museum, the **Musée Sidi Mohamed Ben Abdellah** (*see p171*).

At one time Essaouira was known as the Sanhedrin (Jewish cultural centre) of North Africa. As recently as the 1950s the city still claimed 32 official **synagogues**. One of those that still functions remains at 2 derb Ziry Ben Atiyah, which is the last lane on the right off rue Derb Laâlouj before it intersects with avenue Sidi Mohammed Ben Abdellah. The synagogue was founded by British merchants from Manchester; at the height of Essaouira's importance this section of the Kasbah was the location of various consulates and administrative buildings.

Musée Sidi Mohammed Ben Abdellah

7 Derb Laâlouj (024 47 23 00). **Open** 8.30am-6pm Mon, Wed-Sun. **Admission** 10dh.
This renovated 19th-century mansion was used as the town hall during the Protectorate and hosts a fairly boring collection of weapons, woodwork and carpetry. There are also gnawa costumes and musical instruments and a few pictures of old Essaouira.

THE MELLAH

British merchants outnumbered other nationalities during the 19th century to the extent that 80 per cent of the town's trade was with Britain and sterling was the favoured currency. Muslims were not permitted to

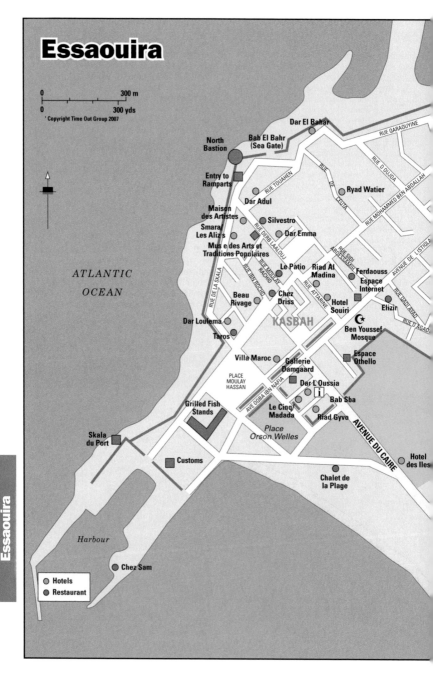

Essaouira

0   300 m
0   300 yds
' Copyright Time Out Group 2007

ATLANTIC
OCEAN

Dar El Bahar
RUE QARAOUYINE

Bab El Bahr
(Sea Gate)

North
Bastion

RUE D'OUJDA

Entry to
Ramparts

RUE TOUAHEN

Ryad Watier

RUE MOHAMMED BEN ABDALLAH

Dar Adul

Maison
des Artistes

RUE DERB LAALOUJ

Silvestro

Smara
Les Alizés

Dar Emma

RUE SIDI ABDESSMAIH

Musée des Arts et
Traditions Populaires

AVENUE DE L'ISTIQLA

RUE DE CEUTA

Le Patio

Riad Al
Madina

Ferdaouss

RUE DE LA SKALA

RUE BOULAF
RACHID

RUE ATTARINE

Espace
Internet

RUE DADI AYAD

Beau
Rivage

Chez
Driss

Hotel
Souiri

Elizir

RUE IBN ROCHD

RUE D'AGAO

Dar Loulema

KASBAH

Ben Youssef
Mosque

Taros

Espace
Othello

Villa Maroc

Gallerie
Damgaard

PLACE
MOULAY
HASSAN

AVE OQBA IBN NAFIA

Dar L'Oussia

i

Bab Sba

Grilled Fish
Stands

Le Cinq/
Madada

Riad Gyvo

AVENUE DU CAIRE

Place
Orson Welles

Skala
du Port

Hotel
des Iles

Customs

Chalet de
la Plage

Harbour

Chez Sam

○ Hotels
● Restaurant

Essaouira

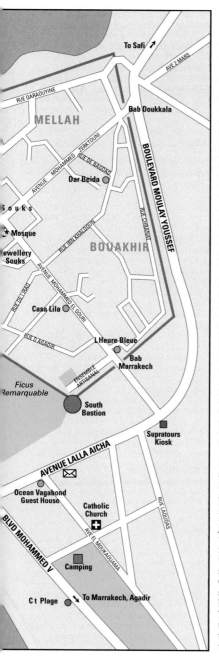

conduct financial transactions, so the sultan brought in Jews from all over the kingdom; by 1900 they outnumbered the locals. All but the wealthiest lived in the Mellah district between the North Bastion and Bab Doukkala, an area that has been neglected since most of the Jews emigrated to Israel in the 1950s and 1960s.

The **Mellah** can be found by following the alleys just inside the ramparts beyond the Skala de la Ville – turn down rue Touahen off rue Derb Laâlouj – or by following avenue Sidi Mohammed Ben Abdellah. When the shops and businesses start to peter out, the Mellah begins. These days its alleys are grubby and dilapidated; some houses look ready to fall down. It was always a gloomy quarter; until the end of the 19th century it was even locked up at night. The family of Leslie Hore-Belisha, British Minister of War in 1939 and inventor of the belisha beacon, lived at 56 rue de Mellah. These days there are perhaps two dozen Jews left in Essaouira, some still distilling fiery *eau de vie de figues*, but they don't necessarily live around here.

At the northern end of the Mellah is **Bab Doukkala**. Just outside of the gate is the **Consul's cemetery**, another reminder of the town's cosmopolitan past. It's crammed with the graves of British officials from the days when Mogador had as many links with Manchester as with Rabat. Over the road, tombstones are packed tightly together in the old Jewish cemetery, where graves are reputed to be five layers deep.

THE SOUKS

Leading south-west from Bab Doukkala, avenue Zerktouni is a busy commercial street of butchers and vegetable stalls. The narrow lanes of the **Chabanat** district on the eastern side are full of tiny workshops.

In the centre of the Medina, the **souks** (*photo p175*) are in cloistered arcades around the intersection of avenue Mohammed Zerktouni and avenue Mohammed El-Qouri, another busy street leading at right-angles towards Bab Marrakech and the hotels **Casa Lila** (*see p176*) and **L'Heure Bleue** (*see p178*). First on the left as you come under the arch from avenue Zerktouni is the **grain market**. Slaves were auctioned here until the early 20th century. Now there are small shops, including **Kifkif** (*see p187*) and **Chez Aicha** (*see p184*). The next cloistered square along, the **Joutiya**, comes to life between 4pm and 5pm for a daily auction. The auctioneers walk in a circle holding up old alarm clocks, fishing reels, slippers, transistor radios – like a demented Moroccan version of *The Generation Game*.

On the other side of the avenue, the **fish and spice souk** is lively and interesting, but beware of unscrupulous stallholders, expert at the hard sell. It is here that Souiri women come to buy chameleons, hedgehogs and various weird and wonderful plants for use in sorcery and magic.

Beyond this point, avenue Zerktouni turns into avenue de l'Istiqlal. The **jewellery souk** is on the left, curling around the outside of the mosque. It's a surprisingly quiet corner where it's possible to browse in peace. Avenue de l'Istiqlal offers Essaouira's most upmarket stretch of shopping. **Trésor** (*see p188*) and **Mogador Music** (*see p187*) are along here, as is cybercafé **Éspace Internet** (*see p188*). Turn down rue Malek Ben Morhal to find the traditional pharmacy, **Azurette**, and left into rue d'Agadir to find the **Elizir** restaurant (*see p183*).

After the arched Kasbah gate, avenue de l'Istiqlal changes names again, becoming avenue Oqba Ibn Nafia. We are now back in the neighbourhood around Bab Sbaâ. **Galerie Damgaard** (*see p188*), a commercial gallery that has nurtured Essaouira's naïve school of painters, can be found on this stretch.

THE BEACHES AND DIABET

Essaouira has wonderful beaches, but the north-westerly winds, known as the Alizés, make it cold and choppy for bathing. It's ideal for windsurfing, though (*see p179* **Wind City Afrika**). To the north of town, the **Plage de Safi** can be dangerous when it's blowy, but is nice when it's warm and usually less crowded than the main beach.

The main beach stretches for miles to the south, backed by dunes once the town peters out. Closer to the Medina it serves as a venue for football. There's always a game going on and at weekends there are several played simultaneously, their kick-offs timed by the tides. You'll also find guys with camels, or they will find you, insistently offering rides. It can be fun to trek around the bay to the ruined old fort of **Borj El Berod**, but wait until you find a camel guy you feel comfortable with, and agree a firm price before setting off.

The village of **Diabat** is a few miles further south and a little inland, on a ridge overlooking the scrubby dunes. In the late 1960s it hosted a hippy community, and legends of a visit made by Jimi Hendrix abound (*see p186* **Castles made of sand**). Any lingering flavour of those times is, however, rapidly being obliterated by the enormous golf resort under construction between the village and the ocean. Diabat's main street now overlooks one of the fairways.

There is further large-scale development occurring along the coast. A whole new town, **Essaouria Al Jadida** (meaning 'New Essaouria'), is going up near the airport. The airport in turn is being expanded, and budget airlines will surely ferry increasing numbers of tourists. And the small surfer haven of **Sidi Kaouki** (*see p179* **Wind City Afrika**), 25 kilometres (15.5 miles) south of Essaouira, which at the time of writing still didn't even have running water, will shortly be overwhelmed by a 220-room resort hotel with pools, luxury bungalows and gardens.

Where to stay

There's no shortage of accommodation in Essaouira, but it's still wise to book in advance if you've got your heart set on a particular guesthouse, and essential if you want to secure anything at all over Christmas or Easter and during the gnawa festival in late June (*see p177* **Gnawa grooves**). Happily, there are rooms to suit all budgets and there's no such thing as a bad location – most places are a few minutes' walk from the central place Moulay Hassan and the fishing port.

As in the Marrakech Medina, small *maisons d'hôtes* have proliferated in the last few years. Old Essaouira houses are set around open courtyards and tend to be smaller and less fussy than their Marrakchi equivalents. Most rooms in such places overlook the inner patio, but Essaouira also boasts rooms with ocean glimpses and roof terraces affording cinematic vistas of sea and sky. On the other hand, terrace breakfasts can be prey to high winds, and some houses on the ocean side fight a running battle with damp. This is a town where you will be glad of a log fire or central heating in winter.

Self-contained accommodation is also available (*see p180*).

Beau Rivage

14 place Moulay Hassan (024 47 59 25/www. essaouiranet.com/beaurivage). **Rates** 350dh double; 500dh suite. **Credit** MC, V.
The pick of the inexpensive options, Beau Rivage has been operating above the Café Opera on the Medina's main square since 1939 – and was renovated in 2002. There are 15 bedrooms and six suites. All are clean, colourful and bright and have toilets and showers en suite. Rooms on the second floor also have balconies overlooking the square. The location can be noisy but is as central as it gets; though still offering big views from the roof terrace, it is cosier and more sheltered than those places overlooking the ramparts. Breakfast is extra, but it's just as easy to nip downstairs for croissants from Chez Driss and a coffee at one of the tables on the square. *Restaurant.*

Eggs, tagines, spices and much more in the **souks**. *See p173.*

Casa Lila

94 rue Med El-Qorry (024 47 55 45/www.riad-casalila.com). **Rates** 825dh-1,600dh. **Credit** MC, V.
Half-way between the souks and Bab Marrakech, this tasteful, unfussy *maison d'hote* has eight rooms and suites plus one two-bedroom apartment ranged around the usual central courtyard. Most of the rooms come equipped with baths (three just have showers) and all except the apartment boast open fires. Common areas include a salon off the courtyard and a rambling roof terrace. It's all nicely decorated in bold pinks and purples with lots of grey *tadelakt* in the bathrooms, complemented by a few well-chosen knicknacks.
Heating.

Dar Adul

63 rue Touahen (tel/fax 024 47 3910/mobile 071 52 02 21/www.dar-adul.com). **Rates** 500dh single; 600dh-880dh double; 990dh quadruple.
No credit cards.
Houses on the ocean side of the Medina need a lot of maintenance if they're not to fall into decline and the five bedrooms of this unpretentious French-owned former notary's house were recently renovated to good effect. The owners also added – the first in Essaouira – a skylight to close off the atrium in inclement conditions. The shared sitting room with open fire is comfortable and there are excellent views from the roof terrace, where breakfast is served when it's not too windy.
Heating.

Dar Al Bahar

1 rue Touahen (024 47 68 31/www.daralbahar.com).
Rates 385dh-770dh double; 660dh-770dh triple; 1,000dh apartment (sleeps two). **No credit cards**.
The 'House by the Sea' is right on the northern ramparts, with waves crashing on the rocks below – there's no place in town quite as close to the ocean. The French-Dutch couple who own the place have decorated their nine rooms in clean, bold colours, bright fabrics and local naïve art. Not all of them have sea views and they're not the biggest lodgings in town, but even the non-view ones are nice enough and more economically priced. The big roof terrace affords breakfast with a tang of sea spray.
Heating (100dh supplement).

Dar Loulema

2 rue Souss (024 47 53 46/mobile 061 24 76 61/ www.riadloulema.com). **Rates** 869dh-1,430dh double; 2,090dh suite (sleeps 4). **Credit** MC, V.
A well-run and straight-faced sort of place at the Kasbah end of the Medina, just behind the Taros café, which the terrace overlooks. It's a nice old house, more generously proportioned than many of its competitors. There are eight rooms, mostly named, and vaguely themed, after Moroccan cities, so 'Essaouira' is blue and white and 'Marrakech' is pink. Breakfast can be served in your room, on the terrace, in the patio, by the central fountain, in one of the living rooms with open fires – just about anywhere, really. Staff will also make dinner (180dh).
Cook. Heating.

Essaouira

Gnawa grooves

It's been described as the world's best jam session. Every June, around 200,000 people arrive for the **Festival d'Essaouira**, four days and nights of gnawa, world music and jazz. Among them are musicians from other parts of Africa, Europe, the USA and members of the gnawa brotherhood from all over Morocco.

The whole town turns into one big heaving party, like a Moroccan Notting Hill Carnival, or a mini Woodstock. There are several stages, the biggest in the square outside Bab Marrakech and on Place Moulay Hassan, with smaller events dotted about the Medina. Most of the concerts are free, in recent years with sponsorship from Pepsi and Moroccan mobile phone company Meditel. In 2006 Pat Metheny and Rachid Taha were on a bill dominated by gnawa masters, but also featuring acts from as far away as Brazil and Pakistan.

The gnawa (or gnaoua) are descendants of slaves from sub-Saharan Africa, now constituted as a itinerant brotherhood of healers and mystics. Their music is rooted in trance and possession rituals, where spirits are represented by colours and colours are represented by music. It's compellingly rhythmic stuff. Played on bass drums, clattering iron castanets and a sort of bass lute called a *guimbri*. However, the

gnawa aren't really professional performing musicians in the western sense and the Festival d'Essaouira is the one place where they all come out to play in public.

That public numbered around 20,000 for the first festival in 1998. These days there are ten times as many, mostly young Moroccan men, but also several thousand foreign visitors. Past guest performers have included Archie Shepp, Joe Zawinul, Ali Farka Toure, Oumou Sangaré and the Wailers. But the real stars of the show are gnawa masters such as Mohammed Ginia, H'Mida Boussou and Hamid El-Kasri, and in recent years a new generation of younger masters including Hicham Merchane and Boussou's son Hassan.

If there's a downside, it's that organisers invite too many bland Francophone artists and boring old jazzers. Still, the event has had a positive effect for both Essaouira and the gnawa. Once looked down upon and regarded with suspicion, they are now a cultural treasure and given the nod from on high – the king's closest advisor, André Azoulay, is a regular festival attendee.

For more on the music of the gnawa (*see p152-154*). For the latest festival news and a more detailed schedule, visit www.festival-gnaoua.co.ma.

Dar L'Oussia

4 rue Mohammed ben Messaoud (024 78 37 56/ fax 024 47 27 77/www.darloussia.com). **Rates** 825dh-1,450dh double. **Credit** MC, V.

More of a hotel than a *maison d'hote*, this place near the Bab Sbaâ still consists of a house with rooms ranged around a central courtyard. It's just a very big house with a very grand courtyard, and 24 rooms in its upper reaches. Well fitted and colourfully decorated, these come in three categories. Standard rooms are a decent 25 square metres with king-size beds and big bathrooms. 'Deluxe' rooms are 35 square metres with bigger beds and bigger bathrooms. And 'junior suites' are a whopping 50 square metres with enormous beds and big bathrooms. To top it all there's a vast roof terrace, but the architectural highlight is the spectacular carved archway in the courtyard by the entrance. Beyond it there's a vaulted dining-room where the menu is prepared by a former chef from Taros (*see p184*). *Bar. Internet (wireless, on ground floor only). Restaurant.*

Dar Mimosas

Km1 Route d'Agadir (024 47 59 34/fax 44 78 52 74/www.darmimosas.com). **Rates** 3,800dh-5,900dh suite. **Credit** MC, V.

On the right-hand side of the Agadir road about a kilometre after it forks away from the route back to Marrakech, this is a walled compound of peace and luxury around the bay from Essaouira proper. Four suites and four villas are scattered in beautiful Italianate gardens. Two of the suites have their own gardens; the other two have terraces with views of the sea – 15 minutes' walk away across scrubby dunes. The villas have one or two bedrooms, sitting-rooms, well-equipped kitchens, two bathrooms each and walled gardens with fountains. All of the lodgings have log fires. You need never see another guest if you don't feel sociable, but it would be a shame to miss out on the gorgeous swimming pool, tiled in blue and white. The main house, coloured a brilliant terracotta, has dining rooms, TV room, a terrace, a well-stocked bar and the apartment of Morocco-born French owner Philippe Cachet. Service is nicely pitched between attentive and discreet and the food is excellent – they bake their own bread for breakfast and serve honey from their own hives. Ridley Scott, Orlando Bloom, the Pet Shop Boys and King Mohammed VI have been among the guests since it opened in September 2000. *Air-conditioning. Bar. Heating. Internet. Pool (outdoor). Restaurant. TV (satellite).*

L'Heure Bleue

2 rue Ibn Batouta, Bab Marrakech (024 78 34 34/ www.heure-bleue.com). **Rates** 3,080dh double; 3,300dh-3,900dh suite. **Credit** AmEx, MC, V.

This upmarket renovation of what was once a private mansion has 16 rooms and 19 suites around a spacious, leafy courtyard. It also has the Medina's only lift ascending to the Medina's only rooftop pool. The standard rooms (on the first floor) are spacious

Holding court at **Dar L'Oussia**.

African-themed – black marble, dark wood, zebra-patterned upholstery. Suites on the second floor, which get more light and seem better value, also come in Portuguese (blue and white), British colonial (19th-century engravings) and 'Eastern' (gold and burgundy) flavours. The British colonial theme – the 'clubroom' bar has big armchairs and mounted animal heads – seems pretentious and daft. There's also a DVD screening room, a beautiful hammam in black tadelakt, and a decent restaurant. *Air-conditioning. Bar. Hammam. Heating. Internet. Phone. Pool (outdoor). Restaurant. Solarium. TV/DVD.*

Hotel Smara

26 bis, rue de la Skala (024 47 56 55). **Rates** 76dh single; 104dh-196dh double; 174dh triple; 256dh quadruple. **No credit cards.**

Upstairs from Les Alizés Mogador (*see p183*) are simple rooms with bed, sink and table, overlooking the ramparts and ocean or (at the cheaper rate) nothing. Bathrooms and toilets are shared. Breakfast is an extra 14dh, or 18dh with juice. It's all basic and the staff are a bit brusque, but you can't argue with the prices. They also have apartments in the Medina.

Hotel Souiri

37 rue Lattarine (024 47 53 39/email souiri @menara.ma). **Rates** 100dh-220dh single; 150dh-310dh double; 225dh-375dh triple; 375dh-450dh quadruple; 600dh apartment. **Credit** MC, V.

Essaouira

The budget option when the Beau Rivage (*see p174*) or Hotel Smara (*see p178*) are full has a central location but no sea views. There are 39 cool and colourful rooms, of which 24 have bathrooms en suite. The apartment sounds like good value but we didn't get to see it. Nice stained glass throughout.
Satellite TV (in some rooms and in reception).

La Maison des Artistes

19 rue Derb Laâlouj (024 57 57 99/mobile 062 60 54 38/www.lamaisondesartistes.com). **Rates** 650dh-970dh double; 1,200dh-1,450dh suite. **Credit** MC, V.
A characterful French-run guesthouse making the most of its oceanfront location and the slightly eccentric taste of its original owners. It has six comfortable rooms, three overlooking the sea, three facing on to the patio, all furnished differently and some boasting intriguingly odd pieces. The suite is splendid, with the ocean on three sides and lording over it, the roof terrace like the bridge of a ship. It's pretty exposed, however, and can get a bit rattly in high winds. La Maison seems to be a home from home for an assortment of young and vaguely arty French folks, and whether you'll like it here depends greatly on whether you get on with the crowd. Manager Cyril is also proud of his 'Judeo-Berber' kitchen and lunch or dinner (150dh per person, non-residents 200dh, booking necessary) can be served on the terrace with the ocean view.
Cook. Heating. Internet (wireless in all rooms). TV(satellite).

Madada

5 rue Youssef El Fassi (024 47 55 12/www.madada.com). **Rates** 1,150dh double; 1,650dh suite. **Credit** MC, V.
At the south-west corner of the Medina, this is a smart and stylish six-room affair that, refreshingly, doesn't work too hard at looking 'Moroccan'. Upstairs from, and owned by the same people as Le Cinq restaurant (*see p183*), the accents are mostly Parisian rather than Souiri. The four rooms on the first floor have their own crenellated terraces overlooking the town and the port, but these are separated from each other only by wrought-iron fences and lack a feeling of privacy. Two of the rooms are on the roof, where breakfast is also served, and there's a panoramic view of the whole bay from a small upper level.
Airconditioning. Heating. Internet (wireless, in some areas).

Ocean Vagabond Guest House

4 Boulevard Lalla Aicha (024 47 92 22/fax 024 47 42 85/www.oceanvagabond.com). **Rates** 1,300dh-1,680dh double. **Credit** MC, V.
In a modern villa on the seafront, just a short walk outside the old city walls, Ocean Vagabond boasts a few features alien to converted medina houses, such as a garden and a pool. Opened by the crew from the Ocean Vagabond café and surf station, it's a breath of fresh air in all senses. Common areas are cool, bright, stylish and simple. The 14 rooms are

Wind City Afrika

With frequent high winds between March and September, Essaouira is Morocco's capital of windsurfing and has begun to market itself as such under the rubric 'Wind City Afrika'. Known as the Alizés, the north-westerly winds really are strong; wetsuits and sturdy sails are necessary. In winter, surfers can also be found on the town's broad and sandy beaches.

A 20-minute walk along the sea front (or short cab ride from Bab Smaâ), **Ocean Vagabond** is the best place to hire equipment and receive instruction for surfing, windsurfing and kite-surfing. It's also a good beach café for breakfasts, salads and pizzas with the sun on your face and your toes in the sand.

There is more hardcore windsurfing at **Sidi Kaouki**, 25 kilometres (15.5 miles) to the south of Essaouira, where a broad beach stretches for miles. The small village here is also popular with non-surfers in search of peace and quiet. All this may change with the completion of a 220-room resort hotel, under way in 2007. For now, there are several small hotels, including the **Auberge de la Plage** (024 47 66 00, www.kaouki.com) which also has horses and can arrange trekking. The No.5 bus runs regularly to Sidi Kaouki from outside Bab Doukkala. It's also possible to get there via grand taxi.

Ocean Vagabond

Boulevard Mohammed V (www.ocean vagabond.com). **Open** 8am-6pm daily. **No credit cards.**
Friendly French and Moroccan team offers instruction and provides equipment for surfing, windsurfing and kite-surfing. Windsurfing tuition starts at €120 for a six-hour starter course, including equipment. It's also a good beach café.

No Work Team

7 rue Houman El-Fatouaki (024 47 52 72). **Open** 9am-8.30pm daily. **No credit cards.**
Only distantly related to shops of the same name in Puerto Ventura and Tarifa, No Work Team caters for the windsurfing community with brand-name gear for all eventualities. Business is so good there are two locations.
Other location 2 rue Sqala (024 47 43 26).

themed ('Bali' is vaguely Indonesian, 'Geisha' vaguely Japanese, and so on). Try to get one of the four ('Dogon', 'Felluca', 'Pondichéry' and 'Inca') that have balconies with an ocean view (two others have balconies with a view of the Medina – and the post office). A garden bungalow is the place for pampering: it houses a hammam and rooms for massage, beauty treatments and a hairdresser.
Hammam. Heating. Internet (wireless). Pool (outdoor). Room service. TV (Satellite).

Riad Al Madina
9 rue Attarine (024 47 59 07/www.riadalmadina. com). **Rates** 814dh double; 1,064dh-2,364dh suite; 192dh extra bed. **Credit** MC, V.
Once the location of the Hippy Café, this is now a rather lackadaisical mid-price hotel that trades on the myth that Jimi Hendrix once stayed here. The beautiful courtyard is one of the nicest breakfast spots in town, but the rooms that overlook it, though decorated with colourful materials, tend to be poky, dark and full of tour groups. The owners recently bought the house next door and added a hammam (70dh) and 30 new rooms to make a total of 54.
Hammam. Heating. Restaurant. TV room.

Riad Gyvo
3 rue Mohammed Ben Messaoud (024 47 51 02/ www.riadgyvo.com). **Rates** 900dh-1,000dh double; 1,250dh apartment. **Credit** MC, V.
This big 200-year-old house in the corner of town by Bab Sbaâ is handy for arrivals or departures, but it's the space rather than the location that is the real draw. Many Essaouira guesthouses can feel a bit poky, but the three studios, two apartments and one terrace room arranged around the big central courtyard are all truly spacious, and all but one have their own kitchenettes. The apartments are particularly grand, and can sleep up to four, with a 200dh supplement per person beyond double occupancy (80dh for under-10s). The ground-floor rooms are a bit dark but there are sunbeds and genuinely panoramic views up on the roof terrace, where breakfast (60dh) can be served.
Heating. Parking. Room service. TV.

Ryad Watier
16 rue Ceuta (024 47 62 04/www.ryad-watier-maroc.com). **Rates** 935dh-1,650dh double. **Credit** (for stays of 4 nights or more) MC, V.
Open as a hotel since April 2005, the building was formerly a school, which means a more rambling, less predictable arrangement than in the usual converted Medina house. There are seven double rooms and three suites with two bedrooms, all with small writing desks (a rarity in Essaouira) and all en suite, but none with baths, only showers. There's also a big dining-room, a terrace on what used to be the playground, a hammam and a massage room, a pair of roof terraces, and a pretty decent library by Moroccan riad standards. Rooms and common areas are decorated with paintings and old film posters from the idiosyncratic collection of French owner

Jean Gabriel, for whom the whole thing is obviously a labour of love. Every picture tells a story which he'll cheerfully relate.
Hammam. Heating. Library.

Villa Maroc
10 rue Abdellah Ben Yassine (024 47 61 47/www. villa-maroc.com). **Rates** 1,050dh double; 1,350dh-1,700dh suite. **Credit** MC, V.
The first boutique hotel in Morocco when it opened in 1990, Villa Maroc is now a mature, well-known establishment. It's nicely located just inside the walls of the Kasbah quarter, its roof terraces overlooking the square and the fishing port. Twenty rooms and suites are nicely furnished and arranged around an intriguing warren of open terraces, narrow staircases and small, secluded spaces – the result of knocking together four old merchants' houses. No two rooms are alike; some are a bit cramped and gloomy, and the suites are built around a central patio, so you can hear what's happening on the next floor. The 'oriental spa' has a beautiful small ham-

Dar Beida. *See p181.*

mam for individuals or pairs, and offers a variety of massage and beauty treatments – also open to non-residents. Dinner is 200dh and the food, served in one of several small salons, uses ingredients from the owners' own farm. Non-residents are welcome, but must book by 5pm.

Bar. Hammam. Heating. Internet. Restaurant. Shop.

Houses & apartments

Apartments of one sort or another can be found via **Hotel Smara** (*see p178*), **Jack's Kiosk** (*see p187*), **Dar El Bahar** (*see 176*) and **Riad Gyvo** (*see p180*).

Dar Beida/Dar Emma

067 96 53 86 in Morocco/07768 352 190 in UK/ www.castlesinthesand.com.

For something a bit special, consider 'the White House'. Deep in a corner of the Medina, a twist or two off the tourist trail, this is a wonderful 200-year-old house owned by English partners Emma Wilson and Graham Carter. They've renovated and furnished with playful good taste, mixing Moroccan materials and flea-market finds with imported antiques and a retro vibe. The result manages to be both idiosyncratically stylish and unpretentiously comfortable. It can sleep up to four couples, has two bathrooms, two roof terraces, lounge, a small library, open fires and a well-equipped kitchen and comes with two amiable cats for £300 per person per week, with a minimum booking of three persons.

In addition, Emma Wilson also runs the less luxurious and slightly smaller **Dar Emma**. This compact 19th-century house in an alley off rue Derb Laâlouj has a kitchen, two double bedrooms and a roof terrace. The whole place can be rented at £600 a week for a couple, £700 a week for more.

Restaurants

Undoubtedly the best budget lunch in Essaouira is fresh fish, charcoal-grilled and eaten outside on the quayside. Well, it used

Fish stalls. *See p183.*

Essaouira

to be on the quayside. Some tidying-up initiative has moved the dozen or so stalls (**photo** *p182*) to a uniform blue and white, L-shaped cluster on the port side of place Moulay Hassan. There is now a list of fixed prices posted on a signboard (it's at the end furthest away from the water and includes a number for complaints, 024 78 40 33), so you don't have to haggle when ordering. Some of the stallholders can get a little too insistent when trying to usher you into their joint, but this shouldn't deter you from comparing the fresh catch on display before settling for a spot to snack. Your choice will be sprinkled with salt, grilled on the spot and served on a plastic plate with a slice of lemon and half a baguette. We favour Ali's stall at No.33, Les Bretons du Sud (067 19 42 34), but it's all much of a muchness. Prices range from 10dh for a plate of sardines to 400dh per kilo of lobster, with squid, sole, shrimp, bass, red mullet, urchin and crab costing anything in between. A 60dh set meal includes a selection, plus salad, but no alcohol is served. Stalls are open from 11am until 4pm every day.

Beyond the delights of fresh fish, Essaouira is no citadel of gastronomy. Still, good dinners can be tracked down in all price ranges, though you'll probably have to book or queue for a table in the best of the cheaper places.

In addition to restaurants listed here, dinner is also served to non-residents in most hotels and many guesthouses.

Les Alizés Mogador
26 rue Skala (024 47 68 19). **Open** *lunch* noon-3pm, *dinner* 1st service 7pm, 2nd service 9pm, daily. **Set meals** 95dh. **No credit cards**.
Opposite the wood workshops under the ramparts, and thus sheltered from the winds that lend the restaurant its name, this is one popular restaurant. It is known for its stone-arched interior, friendly, candlelit atmosphere, and above all for hearty portions of good and reasonably priced Moroccan home-cooking from a set menu. You can't make reservations, so expect to wait for a table sometimes – especially when it's feeding time for backpackers from the Hotel Smara upstairs.

Chalet de la Plage
1 boulevard Mohammed V (024 47 59 72/www.lechaletdelaplage). **Open** 6.30-10pm Mon, noon-2.30pm, 6.30-10pm Tue-Sat, noon-2.30pm Sun. **Main courses** 70dh-180dh. **Credit** AmEx, MC, V.
Built in 1893 entirely out of wood, this Essaouira beachside institution – just outside the Medina, opposite place Orson Welles – has been a restaurant forever. Good fish dishes are the highlight of a solid, unfussy menu, there's beer and a small wine list, and the overall vibe is friendly and efficient. It's at its best for lunch, when the terrace affords a tremendous panorama of the bay, from the guys touting

camel rides and the kids playing football in the foreground to the ruins of the Borj El-Berod on the headland. The owners have also opened a terrace café on the harbour side of the building, where coffee, tea and soft drinks can be enjoyed with an ocean view.

Chez Sam
Port de Pêche (024 47 62 38). **Open** noon-3pm, 7-10.30pm daily. **Main courses** 100dh-450dh. **Credit** Amex, MC, V.
Right by the harbour, the building is a waterside wooden shack, designed like a ship, cramped and full of clutter. Continuing in the nautical vein, you can even peer out of the portholes to see fishing boats bringing in the catch. It's a no-nonsense kind of place where you'll always get something edible even if you rarely get anything exceptional, but the staff seem to know what they're doing. The new balcony out the back, overlooking the entrance to the harbour, is a nice spot for lunch.

Le Cinq
7 rue Youssef El Fassi (024 78 47 26). **Open** 6.30-11.30pm Mon, Wed-Fri; noon-midnight Sat, Sun. **Main courses** 80dh-150dh. **No credit cards**.
Opened in June 2004, this warm, roomy place under the Madada Hotel (and kitted out by the same designers) has established itself as arguably the best restaurant in town. The dining-room is decorated in earthy tones with purple accents, outsize lampshades and lots of candles, providing a comfortable backdrop for Anne-Marie Teilloh's 'Atlantic' kitchen – essentially French with Spanish and Moroccan influences. On our last visit, only the vegetarian options were less than excellent, evidencing a lack of imagination familar in Morocco but alien to the rest of the otherwise laudibly creative menu here. Leave some room for the wonderful desserts.

Côté Plage
Boulevard Mohammed V (024 47 90 00). **Open** noon-3pm, 7-10.30pm daily. **Main courses** 70dh-170dh. **Credit** AmEx, MC, V.
On the promenade opposite the Sofitel, by which it is owned and operated, this is a good spot for mildly upmarket beachside lunches and interminable menu descriptions, both epitomised by the likes of Duo de Melon du Pays au Jambon Cru de Parme et Pain Tomate or Escabêche d'Ombrine et Saumon Frais aux Épices de la Médina et Herbes Fraîches de l'Atlas, Toast Chaud. It's about a ten-minute stroll from the Medina. Barbecue on Sundays.

Elizir
1 rue de Agadir (024 47 21 03). **Main courses** 90dh-120dh. **Open** noon-3pm, 7.30pm-1am daily. **No credit cards**.
Elizir opened back in June 2006 with a Moroccan-Mediterranean menu and an atmosphere of idiosyncratic cool; it has already become one of the restaurants in town. Young owner Rharbaoui Abdellatif, who lived in Italy for a few years, still tinkers keenly with the stylish interior, where a few traditional elements set off an impressive

retro-futurist collection of 1960s plastic furniture and fittings in orange and white – all of them sourced in Moroccan flea markets. Meanwhile, he's serving a menu that veers from a camel tagine to home-made pasta via organic chicken and the catch of the day. In winter, ask for a table in the room with the open fire; in warmer months, go for the sheltered roof terrace. The louche, jazzy playlist sounds good wherever you're sitting. **Photo** *p185*.

Ferdaouss
27 rue Abdessalam Lebadi (024 47 36 55). **Open** 12.30-2.30pm, 6.30-10.30pm Tue-Sun. **Set meal** 95dh. **No credit cards.**
Ferdaouss is a cute and cosy place where the kitchen is bossed by a former chef from the Villa Maroc (*see p180*) and traditional Moroccan food is served with an imaginative twist at prices so reasonable that you usually need to book a couple of days in advance. It's quite a way down an alley off rue Sidi Mohammed Ben Abdellah in the central Medina, from which it is signposted. At the time of writing it was undergoing renovations.

Le Patio
28 rue Moulay Rachid (024 47 41 66). **Open** *tapas* 5.30-11pm, *dinner* 6.30-11pm Tue-Sun. **Main courses** 110dh-150dh. **Credit** MC, V.
Fish dishes are the highlight of a French-Moroccan menu, presented on a blackboard that can be hard to read in the dingy, candle-lit interior. The venue is an old house with a roofed-over courtyard, dark red palette, and fabrics hanging to create a tented effect. Tables are cramped though the room is spacious, and music is so insipid you almost don't notice it adds little to a rather bland atmosphere. That said, it's a good place to sample a selection from the day's catch, and there's a beautiful bar where you can order from a small but respectable tapas selection (around 35dh per item).

Silvestro
70 rue Derb Laâlouj (024 47 35 35). **Open** 11am-3pm, 7.30-11pm daily. **Main courses** 60dh-150dh. **No credit cards.**
This is a cool and unpretentious first-floor Italian restaurant. Run by Italians, it feels authentic, with an open kitchen, an espresso machine and a basic but sensible menu of antipasta, pasta and pizza. The food's all very well prepared and served with a smile. Accompany it with something from the short but reassuring list of Italian wines.

Taros
Place Moulay Hassan (024 47 64 07/www.taroscafe. com). **Open** 11am-4pm, 6pm-midnight Mon-Sat. **Main courses** 70dh-160dh. **Credit** MC, V.
Perched above the town's main square on a corner overlooking the sea, Taros is a multi-purpose venue with a prime location. It has a first-floor salon and library, where you can drink tea and read quietly in the afternoons or have a beer and listen to live music in the evenings (from Thursday to Saturday nights). Then there's a cocktail bar on the fine roof terrace

(serving Mojitos, Margaritas, Caipirinhas and the like) with tables and bar stools. Food is served in either area, and the menu offers a modest vegetarian selection, complemented by the best steaks in town. An art gallery and small shop round off this much-loved institution.

Cafes & bars

The cafés of place Moulay Hassan are all pretty similar, serving the same coffee, tea and soft drinks at outdoor tables, though **Café de France** has an interestingly dated interior. **Taros** (*see p184*) is as much a café as anything else and just about the only place where you can get a drink without a meal, apart from at the Moroccan bars, **Le Trou** and **Bar** (*see below*).

Chez Driss
10 rue El-Hajali (024 47 57 93). **Open** 7am-10pm daily. **No credit cards.**
The pâtisserie at the end of place Moulay Hassan, founded in 1925, serves a mouth-watering selection of croissants, tarts and cakes at prices everyone can afford. You can eat them with coffee here in the small, sheltered courtyard, or take them to one of the cafés with tables on the square (waiters are quite happy for you to consume food from off premises).

Bar
Boulevard Mohammed V (no phone). **Open** 9am-8pm daily. **No credit cards.**
Attached to the beachfront restaurant Chalet de la Plage (*see p183*) on the side furthest from the port, and accessed by a discreet entrance signed only with the single word 'Bar', this is a simple drinking den where Moroccans gather over cold bottles of Flag Spéciale either on a small terrace overlooking the sands or indoors in the cosy saloon. It's a friendly place, but it's their place.

Gelateria Dolce Freddo
25 place Moulay Hassan (063 57 19 28). **Open** 7.30am-10pm daily. **No credit cards.**
A prime location around the corner and facing across the open part of the town's main square is one reason why this is the most fashionable of the central cafés; good Italian coffee is another. A selection of garish ice-cream adds colour to the proceedings and helps keep outdoor tables full.

Le Trou
rue Mohammed El Ayachi (no phone). **Open** 11am-11.30pm daily. **No credit cards.**
At the cul-de-sac opposite and beyond the restaurant El-Yacoute, the entrance to 'the hole' is obvious at night, with a small barrow selling cigarettes and snacks outside, and a beery glow from within. It's a disreputable sort of place, full of fishermen in jellabas drinking bottles of Stork beer, with a drunken hubbub and the occasional row. Tourists are tolerated rather than welcomed.

Essaouira

Shopping

Essaouira is a good place for shopping. It lacks the quantity of Marrakech, but has pretty much all the variety, plus its own local specialities, such as argan oil (a cosmetic and medicinal oil from the nuts or argan trees, exclusive to Morocco) and products sculpted from *thuja* wood. The spice souk is hassly but elsewhere you're mostly left to browse in peace and there are some interesting individual shops.

Afalkay Art

9 place Moulay Hassan (024 47 60 89). **Open** 9am-8pm daily. **Credit** AmEx, MC, V.

The one-stop shop for all your Essaouiran woodcraft needs. Searching the wood workshops under the ramparts might turn up the odd different item, but pretty much anything they can make out of fragrant *thuja* wood – from tiny inlaid boxes to great big treasure chests, toy camels to bathroom cabinets – can be found somewhere in this big barn of a place opposite the cafés of place Moulay Hassan. Staff speak English and are used to shipping larger items.

Azurrette

12 rue Malek Ben Morhal (024 47 41 53). **Open** 9.30am-8pm daily. **No credit cards**.

At some remove from the hassle and hustle of the spice souk, this traditional Moroccan pharmacy has the largest herb and spice selection in the Medina

and also offers perfumes, pigments, remedies, incense and essential oils. The big, cool space is lined with shelves of common condiments, exotic ingredients, mysterious herbs and colourful powders, all in glass jars or baskets. English is spoken by amiable young owner Ahmed, who's happy to explain what's what.

Bazaar Mehdi

5 rue de la Skala (024 47 59 81). **Open** 9am-8pm daily. **Credit** AmEx, MC, V.

As good a place as any to buy a Moroccan carpet. It's no match for the big dealers of Marrakech, but there are literally heaps of rugs, with floorspace to lay them out and nimble helpers to unfurl them. Owner Mustapha is a good sort, speaks excellent English, and will provide detailed biographies of each carpet. Don't expect any bargains, though. If nothing here takes your fancy, there are other carpet shops further up rue de la Skala.

Chez Aicha

116 place aux Grains (024 47 43 35). **Open** 9am-8pm daily. **Credit** MC, V.

Moroccan ceramics can be a pretty standard affair – and much Essaouiran pottery is poorly glazed and chips easily. Aicha Hemmou's stock is a cut above. It's mostly Berber pottery, made near Marrakech. Some of the designs are a bit fussy, but others are clean-lined in warm, solid colours. There's also a bit of glassware and argan oil in gift bottles.

Elizir: idiosyncratic cool and eclectic food. *See p185*.

Chez Boujmaa

1 avenue Allal Ben Abdellah (024 47 56 58).
Open 8am-midnight daily. **No credit cards**.
Expats call this small, central grocery shop 'Fortnum & Mason's'. That's a bit of a stretch, but Chez Boujmaa is the place to find English teas and biscuits, plus a range of Italian pasta and parma ham, French cheeses and tinned haricots. And at the basic deli counter they'll make up a sandwich to your specifications.

Galerie Aida

2 rue de la Skala (024 47 62 90). **Open** 10am-1pm, 3-8pm daily. **Credit** AmEx, MC, V.

A big place filled to bursting with an intriguing selection of old jewellery, paintings, glassware, crockery and other Moroccan antiques, plus a small but good (and pricey) selection of secondhand books.

Galerie Jama

22 rue Ibn Rochd (024 78 58 97). **Open** 9am-noon, 1-9pm daily. **Credit** AmEx, MC, V.
The brother of Mustapha from Bazaar Mehdi offers an interesting and nicely displayed selection of antiques and old pieces – silver jewellery, select ceramics, ancient wooden doors, vintage kaftans, treasure chests and old portraits of King Mohammed V.

Castles made of sand

1967. And Jimi didn't visit Morocco until July 1969.

Just ten days long, it was the only vacation Hendrix ever took. Stressed out after the break-up of the Jimi Hendrix Experience, moving from London to New York, getting busted by the Mounties in Toronto, and rehearsing a new band, Jimi accepted his friend Deering Howe's suggestion that they go to Morocco, and ran off in defiance of his management. The pair flew to Casablanca in late July, where they met up with two Moroccans they knew from New York, Stella Douglas and Colette Mimram.

They stayed at the Casablanca Meridien, the Mamounia in Marrakech and the Hotel des Iles in Essaouira, travelling by limo and doing tourist things – eating out, smoking kif, shopping for clothes. Far from jamming with local musicians, Hendrix enjoyed his anonymity and kept a low profile. He had a spooky fortune-teller experience, conducted a romance with Colette Mimram, and spent an evening in Essaouira with a couple of actors from the Living Theater. But he didn't meet Timothy Leary, bought no islands, probably didn't visit Diabat, certainly didn't stay at the Riad Al Madina, and likely never even saw the Borj El-Berod.

It's a lot of myth from a short visit, but that's what you get from a good rock legend. By 6 August Hendrix was on his way back to New York, stopping off in Paris to shag Brigitte Bardot. Twelve days later, he was playing Woodstock.

'Welcome to the village of Jimi Hendrix!' So runs the patter of shoeshine boys and dope dealers. 'Hendrix stayed here!' is the proud claim of at least two hotels. In nearby Diabat, where Jimi supposedly spent time with the hippy community, there is a Café Hendrix and a Hotel Hendrix, both overlooking the decidedly unrocking new golf resort.

Orson Welles may have a square named after him, but Hendrix is Essaouira's claim to street cred. The stories pour forth. Jimi jammed with the gnawa! He tried to buy one of the islands! He met with Timothy Leary! The most enduring tale is that he was inspired to write 'Castles Made of Sand' (which melt into the sea, eventually) by the ruins of the Borj El-Berod.

It seems almost plausible. The Borj El-Berod is a small, ruined fort at the ocean's edge, quite clearly melting into the sea. But the story has one small snag. 'Castles Made of Sand' appeared on the *Axis: Bold as Love* album, released on 1 December

The Gallery

19 Rue Moulay Ismael (067 96 53 86). **Open**
by appointment only. **No credit cards**.
In a small apartment space (with lots of stairs)
Emma Wilson of Dar Beida (*see p181*) offers an
intriguing selection of clothes, accessories and art-
works from a variety of sources. There are bags by
Lalla from London and clothes in reworked vintage
fabrics by Lola from Morocco, also some furniture,
'wonky donkeys' made of wood, and box-framed
'assemblages' by French artist Anne Marie Duprés.

Hassan Fakir

181 Souk Laghzel (070 23 00 17). **Open** 9am-8pm
daily. **No credit cards**.
Second on the right among the row of babouche
stalls as you turn into the fish and spice souk from
rue El-Fachtaly, Hassan sells the usual Moroccan
slippers and sandals and speaks decent English.

Jack's Kiosk

1 place Moulay Hassan (024 47 55 38). **Open**
9.30am-10.30pm daily. **No credit cards**.
In a key location on the square, Jack's is the place to
find the previous day's international newspapers
and other foreign periodicals, complemented by a
small selection of new and second-hand English,
French, German and Spanish books – mostly guides
and bestsellers. Jack also rents sea-view apartments
by the ramparts.

Kifkif

*204 Place du Marché aux Grains (061 08 20 41/
www.kifkifbystef.com)*. **Open** 10am-noon, 4-8pm
Mon-Sat. **No credit cards**.
This smaller sister shop to the Kifkif in Marrakech
(*see p133*) sells the same eclectic assortment of
colourful bags and purses, nice notebooks, electric
lamps, jewellery and lots of things for children.

Mogador Music

52 avenue de l'Istiqlal (070 72 57 79). **Open** 10am-
10pm daily. **No credit cards**.
Gnawa, arabo-andalusian, *grika*, bellydance, rai,
desert blues – Mogador Music is well stocked with
all varieties of North African and West Saharan
music on CD and cassette. If you can't find it here
you probably won't find it anywhere: owners
Youssef and Azza know their stuff and distribute to
all the other music shops.
Other locations 1 place Chefchaouen (061 72 83 62).

Ouchen Mohamed

4 rue El Attarine (024 47 68 61). **Open** 9am-9pm
daily. **No credit cards**.
On a corner by the Riad Al Madina (*see p180*),
Ouchen Mohamed is our favourite of the various
leatherwork shops. It's good for pouffes, bags and
belts, but there's also a big slipper selection and a
few non-leather items, such as boxes, mirrors and
old musical instruments.

Riri d'Arabie

66 rue Boutouil (024 47 45 15). **Open** 10am-7pm daily. **No credit cards.**

French exile Richard Brecquehais accumulates intriguing bric-a-brac, some of which he sells on as *objets trouvés*, some of which he arranges in his own eccentric way, matching pictures to frames or ornaments to shelving units. The result is a small curiosity shop of old postcards, framed mirrors, ancient signs, out-of-date toys and a scatter-brained sense of comedy. If you feel like sitting down, he also sells juices (10dh) and a few hot snacks (35dh).

Trésor

57 avenue de l'Istiqlal (064 84 17 73). **Open** 9am-8.30pm daily. **Credit** AmEx, MC, V.

On the Medina's main avenue, jeweller Khalid Hasnaoui speaks good English and offers a more discerning selection than that found in the nearby jewellers' souk. It's a mixture of Berber, Arab, Tuareg and other pieces – some old, some new, and some new but using old designs. Look out for work in the local filigree style, made by Essaouiran Jews.

Galleries

The naïve school of painting for which Essaouira has become famous began in the 1950s with the mystical painting and sculpture of local artist **Boujemaâ Lakhdar** (1941-89). During the 1960s, visiting hippies painted psychedelic murals (none have survived) and this undoubtedly encouraged the Souiris to pick up their brushes and experiment with colour. **Galerie Damgaard** is the place to see the most serious results, but you'll find paintings and sculpture on sale all over town – sometimes alongside handicrafts, sometimes in tiny artists' studios-cum-shops.

In addition to the galleries, the **Gallery** (*see p187*) shop stocks art by French artist Anne Marie Duprés – fascinating boxed scenarios made out of old postcards, product packaging, plastic toys, and other found objects.

On place Moulay Hassan, look out for young local artist Mustapha Elharchi (066 92 68 88). Confined to a wheelchair, he holds the paintbrush in his mouth to produce small abstract watercolours. You can buy his unframed naïve miniatures, fresh from the easel, for just 20dh each.

Espace Othello

9 rue Mohammed Layachi (024 47 50 95). **Open** 9am-8pm daily. **Credit** AmEx, MC, V.

The extremely mixed bag of work by artists from Essaouira and beyond includes some small pieces as well as large paintings and sculptures. There's some interesting stuff here, but you have to poke around a bit to find it. The gallery's architecture is a worth a look in its own right. It's behind the Hotel Sahara.

Galerie Damgaard

Avenue Oqba Ibn Nafiaa (024 78 44 46). **Open** 9am-1pm, 3-7pm daily. **Credit** AmEx, MC, V.

Danish expat Frédéric Damgaard opened Essaouira's only serious commercial gallery in 1988 and helped to develop the work of around 20 local artists – known as the 'Essaouira school'. It's bright and colourful, almost hallucinogenic work, heavy with folk symbolism and pointillist techniques. Gnawa artist Mohammed Tabal is the star: his 'paintings of ideas' are inspired by the gnawa trance universe of colour-coded spirits. We also like the paint-splattered wooden furniture sculptures of Saïd Ouarzaz and the dreamlike canvases of Abdelkader Bentajar. After Damgaard's recent retirement, we're worried that things might stagnate under new ownership.

Getting there

By bus

Supratours (024 43 55 25) runs a bus service from its depot next door to Marrakech railway station; departures for Essaouira are at 8.30am, 11am, 3.30pm and 7pm daily. Buy tickets (one-way 65dh) the day before as the bus fills up for the three-and-a-half-hour journey. In Essaouira buses arrive at and leave from the south side of the big square outside Bab Marrakech, where tickets are sold at a kiosk (024 47 53 17) next to the Telecom building. Departure times are 6.10am, noon, 4pm ,6.45pm daily.

By taxi

Shared grand taxis from Marrakech (80dh per person) leave from Bab Doukkala. Coming back, they leave from outside Essaouira's *gare routière*. You can also hire your own taxi for around 700dh. From Essaouira, we'd recommend Taxi Mustapha (061 20 71 68).

By air

At the time of writing, Royal Air Maroc (www. royalairmaroc.com) was running three daily flights from Paris and thrice-weekly flights from Casablanca to the tiny Aéroport de Mogador. But the terminal is being expanded; Atlas Blue (www.atlas-blue.com) will likely lead the pack of budget airlines.

Resources

Internet

Espace Internet Café *5 avenue de l'Istiqlal (024 47 50 65).* **Open** 24 hours daily. **No credit cards.**

Police

Avenue du Caire (emergencies 19).

Post Office

Avenue El-Moqaoumah. **Open** 8am-6pm Mon-Fri; 8am-noon Sat.

Tourist Information

10 rue du Caire, BP 261 (024 78 35 32/www. tourisme.gov.ma). **Open** 9am-noon, 2-4.30pm Mon-Fri.

The High Atlas
& Sahara

Features

Maps

Getting Started

The beautiful south – just hours from Marrakech.

The south was always the unruly part of Morocco. Few Europeans dared venture into the High Atlas or journey through the expanse of the Moroccan Sahara before the French Foreign Legion built roads and garrisons in the 1920s and '30s. To ascend into the dramatic mountain valleys and pass through the lush oases of the South is still somehow to venture into another world. Even if you're never off the mobile phone network and stay only in tasteful riads, the desert can still be a raw and salutary experience, and the Atlas sometimes might as well be Tibet. Coming back, tired and dusty, from the point where civilisation peters out in the desert sands, makes Marrakech feel like New York City.

The landscape might seem inhospitable but in most places people are unbelievably friendly. They're also unbelievably poor, and often the former is a result of the latter – they're happy to make contact with you in case it leads to a money-making transaction. But then, if it doesn't, they're happy to talk to you anyway. Most Moroccans love to laugh and many are incorrigibly curious about the world you come from and the life you lead – as alien to them as theirs is to you. It's depressing to see children begging, though, and everywhere you'll run into kids trying to scam a dirham or two, sometimes very ingeniously. If you want to give them something useful rather than money or 'bonbons', take a few ballpoint pens. Kids are always asking for 'un stylo'.

Where to go

South of Marrakech, there are two main passes over the High Atlas. The **Tizi-n-Test** (*see p199*), to the south-west, runs up past the 12th-century mosque of Tin Mal, snakes over

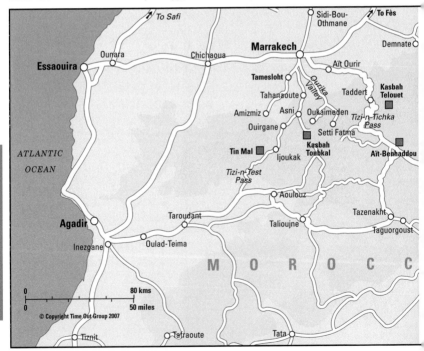

the spectacular pass, and hairpins down to the Sous Valley and the pre-Saharan town of Taroundant. The **Tizi-n-Tichka** (*see p203*) to the south-east runs over the mountains near the kasbah of Telouet, and then down to Ouarzazate and the edge of the Sahara. In between the two, another road follows the **Ourika Valley** (*see p201*) into the High Atlas as far as the village of Setti Fatma and its waterfalls. This is the easiest trip from Marrakech and it's a popular day-excursion for both Marrakchis and tourists.

Ouarzazate is basically the gateway to the desert, and here it's possible either to head further south down the palmeraie of the **Drâa Valley** (*see p218*) until both road and river sink into the sand at M'Hamid, or bear east along the rugged **Dadès Valley** (*see p208*), taking in the Dadès and Todra gorges. Further east lies the great **Tafilelt Oasis** and the dunes of **Merzouga** (*see p216*), which can be reached from either the Drâa or Dadès valleys.

Whichever route takes your fancy, there are basically two kinds of country south of Marrakech: the colourful mountains of the High Atlas, and the stony plains and lush oases of the Moroccan Sahara.

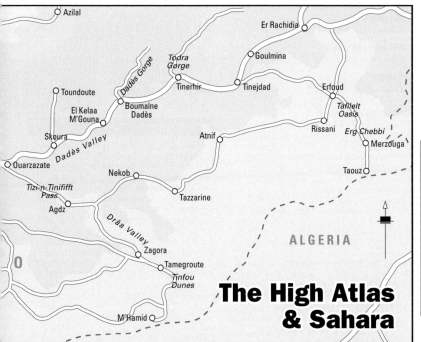

The High Atlas & Sahara

The south

Film location
Aït Benhaddou. *See p205.*

Waterfalls
Cascades d'Ouzoud. *See p194.*

Trekking base
Imlil. *See p196.*

Local museum
Ksar El-Khorbat. *See p212.*

Sand dunes
Merzouga. *See p216.*

Camel trekking
M'Hamid. *See p222.*

Skiing
Oukaimeden. *See p202.*

Palmeraie
Skoura. *See p208.*

City walls
Taroudant. *See p200.*

Kasbah
Telouet. *See p204.*

Mountain pass
Tizi-n-Test. *See p199.*

Gorge
Todra. *See p211.*

THE HIGH ATLAS

There are some serious peaks in the Atlas. At 4,167 metres (13,667 feet), Jebel Toubkal is the highest mountain in North Africa. But you don't need to be a climber to enjoy the spectacular landscape and various valley roads take you into – over – some of the most interesting areas.

Rugged and remote, throughout history the Atlas has been home to an assortment of Berber tribes, and every now and then one of them has come galloping down to conquer the rest of the country and establish a new dynasty. These tribes were never really conquered by anyone, and their traditions are very different from those of urban Moroccans. The women, for example, wear headscarves but are never veiled and have skirts in bright, clashing patterns. They also seem to do all the work: you see them carrying huge bales of brushwood on their backs while the men sit around smoking and talking.

They live in villages up on the valley sides looking on clear streams, rugged skyscrapes, wriggling roads and verdant valley floors. In spring, like the clothes of the women, it's all one big patchwork of colour.

THE SAHARA

Strictly speaking, the area south of the Atlas is the pre-Sahara, rather than the full-blown desert itself, but the aridity is palpable the minute you cross the watershed, and the pattern of lush oases separated by barren stretches begins just beyond the town of Ouarzazate.

An oasis – called a palmeraie in Morocco – is an area of densely cultivated land, anchored by palm trees, with other crops grown beneath. In the palmeraies you'll also find *ksour* (fortified tribal villages) and kasbahs (fortified family mansions) made out of *pisé* mud and straw. Most of these aren't anywhere near as old as they look (feudal days ended less than a century ago) and they decay fairly quickly once abandoned, melting back into the landscape. The great oases, however, have been inhabited for centuries, if not millennia. *See also pp32-4.*

There are both Berber and Arab settlements in the Sahara, and at the far end of the road also Tuaregs and Sahrawis, though not everyone wearing a blue robe and turban is a genuine 'blue man' of the desert. Many dress that way just to help sell their souvenirs or camel treks. *See p221* **Who are the Tuaregs?**

While the areas covered in the following chapters are mostly a kind of Sahara Touristique, the desert can still be dangerous and should be treated with respect. Don't venture off the road unless you know where you're going.

When to go

The best time to visit any of these places is in the spring (mid March to May), when all is lush and the almond trees are in bloom. October and November are fine temperature-wise too, though you don't get the greenery. But forget the Sahara between June and September: it's unbearably hot and there are sandstorms. In winter the nights can be cold but the days are clear and bright and not too hot. The Atlas is wonderful in the summer, however: Marrakchis scoot up there just to escape from the heat of the city, and you may well want to follow their example. There is sometimes snow in winter, and even skiing between February and April at Oukaimeden (*see p202*). Snow will also occasionally close both the Tizi-n-Tichka and the Tizi-n-Test, and in winter it's best to check the situation before setting out.

Market day

Most of the towns and villages on the Haouz plain and in the Atlas have some kind of weekly market. People ride in from outlying settlements on bikes and donkeys, as much for the buzz and gossip as for the buying and selling. The typical market spreads over a couple of roadside fields, or occupies some dusty, dedicated area on the edge of a settlement. And one of the first things you'll notice is the donkey park, where the beasts are tethered in rows.

Here you can also buy a donkey, or trade an old one in part exchange. (Those too old to work may be sold to the zoo in Rabat, where they're rewarded for a patient lifetime of toil by being fed to the lions and tigers.)

At the market's heart will be stalls and groundsheet pitches of agricultural produce. But all the best fruit and veg goes straight to the cities and what's left at these markets is bruised, bargain-basement stuff. There will also be sellers of groceries and cigarettes, cheap clothing, cassettes (music and Islamic sermons) and farming implements, plus a few people touting souvenirs and trinkets – and looking to latch on to someone like you.

Sheep and cattle will be auctioned off to one side. Tagines will be simmering somewhere. There's typically also a row of busy Berber barbers, each cropping hair in their own makeshift cubicle.

Interesting though these markets are, the people attending are dirt poor, and if you visit one we recommend leaving the shiny camera and designer shades back at the riad. Not that they're liable to get stolen, but you might feel a little self-conscious about such ostentatious displays of wealth.

Markets within day-tripping distance of Marrakech are held on the following days:
● Monday: **Dar Caid Ourika** near Aghmat (*see p201*) in the Ourika Valley.
● Tuesday: **Amizmiz** (*see p194*) and **Tahanaoute** (*see p196*).
● Thursday: **Ouirgane** (*see p197*); **Setti Fatma** (*see p202*) and **Touama** (32km/ 20 miles east on the Tizi-n-Tichka road).
● Friday: **Aghmat** (*see p201*) and **Tamesloht** (*see p194*).
● Saturday: **Asni** (*see p196*).
● Sunday: **Chichaoua** (52km/32 miles east of Marrakech on the Essaouira road).

Away days

There are plenty of destinations within day-tripping distance of Marrakech. Along the routes covered in detail in other chapters, **Imlil** and **Tin Mal** on the Tizi-n-Test road (*see p196*), Telouet on the Tizi-n-Tichka road (*see p203*) and the whole of the **Ourika Valley** (*see p201*) can be done as day trips. Otherwise, there are decent excursions in two other directions – to the south-west, and to the east.

Route d'Amizmiz

Leave Marrakech as if heading for the Tizi-n-Test, and then fork right soon after the Royal Club Equestre. After a further 15 minutes' drive is the turning for **Tamesloht**, home of a potters' co-operative. The village also boasts ancient olive oil presses with gigantic grindstones until recently driven by mules – decommissioned when the villagers were given modern machinery. They are located '*derrière la commune*'. There's also a rambling kasbah still partially occupied by descendants of the village founders, and next to it a Shrine of Moulay Abdellah with a minaret that appears to be toppling under the weight of an enormous storks' nest. Visitors can drop by the offices of the Association Tamesloht (place Sour Souika) for additional information and directions.

South of Tamesloht, the fertile landscape becomes a brilliant patchwork of greenery. Visible to the left is **Kasbah Oumnast**, a location for Martin Scorsese's *The Last Temptation of Christ* and Gillies MacKinnon's *Hideous Kinky*. A little *baksheesh* will likely persuade the guardian to show you around.

Eight kilometres (five miles) further south, the road swings on to a perilously narrow looking bridge over the Oued N'fis before looping around to hug the shore of the **Barrage Lalla Takerkost**, a sizeable reservoir with the mountains as backdrop. There are several restaurants and campsites in the area, the best of which is the **Relais du Lac** (061 24 24 54/061 18 74 72). It has a grassy garden beside the water's edge, where tagines and couscous are served al fresco.

The road ends at **Amizmiz** (pronounced 'Amsmiz'), 55 kilometres (34 miles) south-west of Marrakech. The town has a rather dilapidated kasbah and a former mellah (Jewish quarter), as well as a Thursday market that's one of the biggest in the region (*see p193* **Market day**). There are regular buses and *grand taxis* between Marrakech (from Bab Er Rob) and Amizmiz. The journey takes just over an hour.

Cascades d'Ouzoud

The route de Fes runs east out of Marrakech. After ten kilometres (six miles) there's a right-hand turn on to the road for Demnate and Azilal. After 40 kilometres (24 miles) skirting the foothills of the Atlas, look for a right turn down to the village of Timinoutine, which is on the edge of the Lac des Aït Aadel. Also known as the **Barrage Moulay Youssef**, this is another large reservoir with a High Atlas backdrop. The scenery is gorgeous and it's a popular picnic spot for Marrakchis.

At Demnate, a side road runs south to **Imi-n-Ifri**, which scores with a natural rock bridge, a slippery grotto and fossilised dinosaur footprints. East from Demnate on the way to Azilal is a signposted turn-off north for the **Cascades d'Ouzoud**: the biggest waterfall in Morocco, it plunges 110 metres in three tiers down to a picturesque pool overlooked by cafés, where people will want to 'guide' you down, though help isn't really necessary. By car it should take about two-and-a-half hours from Marrakech. For anyone who doesn't fancy going straight back, the **Riad Cascades d'Ouzoud** (023 45 96 58, www.ouzoud.com, 750dh double) is rustically tasteful. Two buses a day run from Marrakech to Azilal, and from here you can hire a grand taxi for the 20-minute backtrack to the falls. Make that trip on a Thursday to coincide with Azilal's weekly market (*see p193* **Market day**).

Where to stay

Most hotels in the region are pretty basic, but there are exceptions, and riad culture is seeping south from Marrakech. Most places will try to sell you half-board – room plus dinner – and more often than not this is a good idea. Apart from in Ouarzazate (and that's not exactly a gourmet paradise either), there are almost no decent restaurants anywhere outside of the hotels. Even most hotels will only serve the same old couscous and tagines, which seem to be the only things anyone knows how to cook. There are some upmarket exceptions, but expect to return thoroughly sick of Moroccan food.

The High Atlas.

Getting around

It's possible to reach most places mentioned
in these chapters by bus, but we'd recommend
travelling that way only if you've got one
destination in mind and intend to go there,
hang around for a while, and then return.

The *grand taxi* network is a little more
flexible, and the shared ones aren't much more
expensive than buses, but they're often just as
cramped. You can get to everywhere on the
main roads this way, and also to a lot of places
off them by hiring your own taxi. Make sure
the price is clearly agreed beforehand.

But the best way to explore is by renting
both car and driver. Car hire isn't exactly
cheap: 350dh-500dh per day for a Fiat Uno,
depending on the season; about 600dh per
day for something with air-conditioning; and
1,200dh per day upwards for a 4x4. Drivers are
more affordable, adding about 300dh per day to
the deal. Most car-hire companies can sort out a
driver who knows the routes, so why not enjoy
the scenery while someone else deals with the
hairpin bends and donkey carts?

A 4x4 is great for exploring remote mountain
valleys and the more deserted bits of desert, but
unless otherwise stated, everywhere we write
about can be reached by Fiat Uno. Filling
stations are infrequent so top up whenever
possible. Pack a torch and some toilet paper.
For more details on car rental, including
contacts, see *p225*.

Specialist tours

Independent travel in southern Morocco is
manageable and inexpensive, but if time is
short, or if you're interested in trekking, safari,
cycling or cooking, it can be worth enlisting the
help of the experts.

For more options on places to stay take a
look at **www.travelintelligence.com** or
www.iescape.com, which provides honest
reviews of dozens of select hotels scattered
throughout the Atlas and pre-Sahara, and
also offers a booking service.

Best of Morocco
*Seend Park, Seend, Wiltshire SN12 6NZ (01380 828
533/www.morocco-travel.com).*
A leading tour operator with over 30 years as a
Morocco specialist, with all the in-depth knowledge
that suggests. Tours are tailor-made to suit individual needs, including flights, transfers, hotels and
travel, but must be a minimum of four nights.
Activities on offer include cooking, trekking, skiing
and camel trekking. Recommended.

Destination Evasion
*Villa El-Borj, rue Khalid Ben Oualid, Guéliz (024 44
73 75/www.destination-evasion.com).*
Based in Marrakech but with years of experience in
southern Morocco, Pierre Yves Marais and Beatrix
Maximo specialise in organising trips in the Atlas.
They can provide whatever clients want, from yoga
sessions in secluded valleys to ballooning over the
dunes. They cater for groups from two to 200.

Tizi-n-Test to Taroudant

Drive every mountain.

The road to Taroudant heads directly south out of Marrakech, winds over the Tizi-n-Test pass, and snakes down to the Sous Valley. It then cruises west through argan country (*see p200* **Argan: elixir of everything**) into Taroudant – a distance of 223 kilometres (138 miles).

That's about a five-hour drive. If getting to Taroudant is what it's all about then it's easier to take what looks on the map like a longer route – the highway west from Marrakech to Chichaoua and then south over the Tizi Maachou with all the Agadir traffic. But to go that way would be to miss out on one of the most spectacular drives in North Africa.

About 100 kilometres (62 miles) or two hours' drive from Marrakech, Tin Mal is also doable as a day trip. On the way, Moulay Brahim (*see p196*) sports a shrine to Moulay Brahim (who else?), Asni (*see p196*) hosts a Saturday morning souk, and Ouirgane (*see p197*) offers a couple of good hotels and some fine dining. An alternative trip is to bear left at Asni up to Imlil and maybe have an overnight stay at the Kasbah du Toubkal (*see p198*).

Heading towards the Tizi-n-Test, after Tin Mal there's not much but the road itself – but hey, what a road it is.

It's a tricky one, though, for drivers without much experience of mountains. Originally built by the French in 1928, it's well surfaced and contoured, but loops and twists like a sack of serpents and in places is treacherously narrow. The stretch after the pass hairpins around blind corners all the way down on to the plain, and it's only half as wide again as your car. The Gorges of Moulay Brahim below Asni are another stretch that demands a little respect. You wouldn't want to come off this road, for precisely the same topographical reasons that make it so worth driving in the first place.

All this makes it sound more dangerous than it is. There isn't too much traffic and frankly, stuck among all the trucks, we find the Agadir road much more scary as well as much less interesting.

Snow sometimes closes the Tizi-n-Test in winter. There's a sign on the way out of Marrakech that warns if the pass isn't open, and another one just after Tahanaoute.

Buses that run all the way to Taroudant via the Tizi-n-Test tend to leave Marrakech very early in the morning (5am or 6am) and take

seven to eight hours. If you're heading for one of the classier hotels in these parts, such as the Kasbah du Toubkal or the Gazelle d'Or (*see p200*), they can arrange a car to collect you from Marrakech.

Moulay Brahim & Asni

It's a boring administrative sort of town but **Tahanaoute** is the only feature of note on the plain between Marrakech and the mountains. After it, though, the road gets picturesque, winding uphill through the Gorges of Moulay Brahim. Drive carefully.

Moulay Brahim also has a village named after him, which is off up to the right just before Asni, and in the middle of the village he has a green-roofed shrine – entry forbidden to non-Muslims. Nearby stalls sell charms, incense, nougat, chameleons and other esoteric supplies. Moulay Brahim is said to sort out female fertility problems, if asked nicely. This is a popular summer day-trip destination for Marrakchi families and it can get quite bustly in a bank holiday sort of way.

Asni is a few kilometres beyond the gorges. Its approach is lined with poplar and willow trees. The lively Saturday souk draws people from all over the area and it's worth a look if you're here on the day, but expect hassle from trinket-sellers. The village is bigger than it first appears, with clumps of houses dotted about the valley. But there's nothing else to see here.

Beyond Asni the road continues up towards Ouirgane and Tin Mal; *see p197 and 199*. The road for Imlil forks off to the left.

Imlil

The road to Imlil hugs the side of a broad valley, its bottom a wide bed of shale. Not far out of Asni, surrounded by high walls and cypresses, is the restored **Kasbah Tamadot** (*see p197*), part of Richard Branson's portfolio of Virgin hotels. Further up the valley, across on the far side and perched above green pastoral enclosures and walnut groves, is the hilltop hamlet of **Aksar Soual**. Everyone will tell you the story of how, in 1999, Aksar Soual was unexpectedly descended upon by a fleet of big black SUVs with accompanying helicopter support. It was

Mosque at **Tin Mal**. *See p199*.

Hillary Clinton, visiting her niece who lives up here and is married to a local Berber guide.

The surfaced road comes to a halt at **Imlil**, beyond which the valley forks. This small village serves as the centre for trekking in the region, lying, as it does, at the foot of **Jebel Toubkal** – at 4,167 metres, North Africa's highest peak. Guides can be hired at the Bureau des Guides in the centre of the village. There are also several small café/restaurants and a sprinkling of souvenir shops.

Where to stay

The best place to stay – indeed, one of the main reasons to head in this direction – is the **Kasbah Du Toubkal** (*see p198*), but there is also some basic budget accommodation in Imlil and, on our last visit, some other small hotels under construction.

Further up the valley, accessible by mule or 4x4, the **Douar Samra** (024 37 86 05, www.douar-samra.com, half board 444dh per person) offers modest accommodation in the hamlet of Tamatert. There are seven sweet rooms, a small hammam and dining room in the main house, plus two bungalows. Owner Jacqueline Brandt describes it as a 'hobbit house', built around living rock and with lots of slightly rickety wooden stairs – perilous when her family of shitsu dogs get underfoot.

Back down towards Asni, Richard Branson's **Kasbah Tamadot** (024 36 82 00/fax 024 36 82 11/www.virgin.com/kasbah, 3,405dh-7,816dh double) feels like it's on another planet. Built in the 1920s as the residence of the caid of the valley, and acquired by Branson from the Italian-American antique dealer Luciano Tempo, it's kitted out with every luxury amid four hectares of landscaped gardens. Yes, there are pools and tennis courts and talented international chefs, and, like Kasbah du Toubkal, it too has provided money for community projects. But it's totally detached from local life and ultimately rather soulless.

Ouirgane

Ouirgane ('weer-gan') at first seems like the tiniest place, consisting of little more than its two well-known hotels – La Roseraie and the Au Sanglier Qui Fume – on either side of the Oued Nifis. But after a while you realise that the houses are hidden in forest and scattered up the valley sides, safe from occasional flash flooding. It's a pretty location, in a basin surrounded by wooded mountains, with glimpses of Toubkal towering highest of all. There's a Jewish hamlet (deserted) nearby to the south-east, and a primitive salt factory (operational) back down the main road and off to the west. You'll need a guide to find either. It's also the most comfortable base from which to do Tin Mal, though if you don't have your own transport this will involve commandeering a taxi. But Ouirgane is a place for chilling rather than sightseeing, with a little light walking on the side. It's also a good lunch stop, as both the hotels have decent restaurants.

La Roseraie (044 43 91 28, www.la roseraie.ma, from 1,800dh double) is a peaceful place set among rose gardens and groves of lime and lemon. It has two restaurants, indoor and outdoor pools, a hammam, a tennis court,

The High Atlas & Sahara

Kasbah du Toubkal

A wonderful restoration of an abandoned kasbah perched on an outcrop above Imlil, Kasbah du Toubkal is both one of the most atmospheric places to stay in southern Morocco, and an admirable exercise in the delicate balancing act that is 'sustainable tourism'.

From the start, it was conceived as a partnership with the local community. The idea of transforming the derelict kasbah came to adventure tour operator Mike McHugo and his financial consultant brother Chris in 1989 when they were staying in Imlil with mountain guide and community leader, Hajj Maurice. The three set about acquiring the crumbling ruin.

To plans from British architect John Bothamley, it was restored by village craftsmen in vernacular style. The result is lodgings that are comfortable rather than glossy magazine fodder, but who needs radical lampshades when from every window and terrace there are breathtaking mountain views? The McHugos describe the result, opened in 1995, as a 'Berber hospitality centre' rather than a hotel, staffed by locals rather than outside professionals. Other community employment comes as work for the muleteers who transport guests (and everything else) up from the village on their beasts of burden, and a commitment to local sourcing wherever possible.

McHugo's company Discover Ltd also helped set up and continues to support a village association, through which Imlil has acquired an ambulance, a communal hammam and a rubbish collection system. They are now looking at ways to add value to local agriculture, and a five per cent levy on all bills provides funds for further projects. In sustainable tourism terms, Kasbah du Toubkal ticks all the boxes – respect for local traditions, low carbon footprint, benefits for the community, tourism as a dialogue between cultures. It also makes pragmatic sense. As long as locals are happy about the place, they won't be throwing rocks at trekkers.

Arriving on muleback, guests enter the compound by a tower constructed for Martin Scorsese's *Kundun* – the kasbah was used as a location. Accommodation ranges from simple dorm rooms to a huge, split-level apartment suite with a 12-metre glass wall

opening from the lounge on to one of its two terraces. Food is hearty rather than haute cuisine, vegetarians are well catered for, and though the Kasbah has no alcohol licence, guests are welcome to bring (and uncork) their own.

Staff can arrange every kind of trek from short rambles to ascents of Toubkal and the Kasbah has recently opened a comfortable trekking lodge with three en-suite bedrooms in a nearby valley, about four hours walk away. A visit here is also doable as a daytrip from Marrakech (€85 per person): at 9am a car picks you up in the city, ferries you up here for a lunch, a spot of walking, and a visit to a Berber house, then returns you by 6pm.

Kasbah du Toubkal

BP31, Imlil, Asni (024 48 56 11/fax 024 48 56 36/www.kasbahdutoubkal.com). **Rates** dorm 300dh (up to three); double 1,500dh-2,000dh; suite 2,500dh-4,300dh. **Credit** MC, V.
Bicycles. Car hire (4x4). Cook. Garden. Hammam. Library. Mountain guides. Mules. Trekking.

and facilities for hunting, shooting and riding. More basic and perhaps better value, the **Au Sanglier Qui Fume** (044 48 57 07, fax 044 48 57 09, www.ausanglierquifume.com, 605dh-8150dh half-board for two) is a friendly French-run inn, opened in 1945, that has 22 cabin-style rooms and suites with log fires, an outdoor pool, a convivial bar and a restaurant serving good French country cooking. Mountain bikes can also be rented.

Tin Mal

Beyond Ouirgane, it all begins to feel rockier and more remote. The twisting road climbs high up the valley sides, with riverside cultivation glowing green far below while flat-roofed Berber villages blend into the stony background above the fertile stretches.

The village of **Ijoujak** has several basic cafés, some of which also offer rooms. Just after it, on the right, is the kasbah of **Talaat -n-Yacoub**. This, and the other kasbahs that crown strategic heights in the area, were all fortresses of the Goundafi tribe, who ran the Tizi-n-Test until 'pacified' by the French. Though they look ancient, the kasbahs mostly date from the late 19th and early 20th centuries – a reminder that the feudal era is still a living memory around here.

About three kilometres past the kasbah, a track to the right leads down and across the river to **Tin Mal**. The ancient mosque, built in 1153, stands above the undistinguished modern village. Soon after you arrive, someone will appear with a key to let you in.

How much more remote must this valley have been in the early 12th century? Yet back then it became the spiritual heart of the Almohad Empire. Around 1120 one Ibn Toumart arrived after much wandering to make a pest of himself in Marrakech with criticism of the ruling Almoravids. He was banished and retreated up here to seek the support of local tribes for his militant version of Islam. In 1125 he established his capital at Tin Mal, creating a sort of Moroccan Lhasa – a fortified religious community run with a pitiless, puritanical discipline. He and his supporters called themselves El-Muwahhidun ('the monotheists') – and hence their European name, the Almohads.

Ibn Toumart died in 1130 but his right-hand man, Abdel-Moumen, kept up his work. Tin Mal proved a good base, as the Almoravids' strength was in cavalry, and horses couldn't get up here. In 1144 Abdel-Moumen laid siege to Marrakech and went on to conquer the rest of Morocco, most of North Africa and much of Spain. Back here, in 1153, they used some of the loot to build the mosque that stands today. It was modelled after that of Tata, near Fes, and in turn provided the prototype for the Koutoubia in Marrakech, almost certainly built by the same craftsmen.

Tin Mal was a monument to Ibn Toumart and his doctrines. It also accommodated his tomb and that of other Almohad leaders. When the dynasty fell around the mid 13th century, Tin Mal was their last line of defence. It was taken by the Merenids in 1276, but even after that remained a place of pilgrimage. When the French turned up centuries later, the crumbling remnants of the mosque were home to a strange cult that worshipped the Stone of Sidi Wegweg.

Restoration had to wait until the 1990s, and has proceeded with funds raised in Morocco. There is no roof but the framework of sandy-coloured transverse arches is complete, offering receding perspectives of light and shade. For the non-Muslim visitor it's a rare chance to see inside a Moroccan mosque, but note that in mosque architecture the minaret is almost never above the mihrab, as it is here. Normally it's on the north wall, rather than the one facing east towards Mecca; no one knows why it's different at Tin Mal.

The precise future of the site is uncertain. Maybe it will become a museum, maybe a mosque, maybe some combination of the two and maybe it will stay exactly as it is. The roofless structure is currently used for prayers on Friday, which is the one day you can't visit. Tip the attendant with the key as you leave; he might point out the owl's nest, high overhead among the stalactite vaulting. But there isn't so much as a postcard on sale, and absolutely no information about anything.

The Tizi-n-Test

This pass (2,092 metres) is about 40 kilometres (25 miles) beyond Ijoujak. The final stretch is beautiful as the road curls up to the heights, and then suddenly reveals the most amazing view south across the plain of the Sous valley. There's a small café on the pass where you can stop and enjoy the panorama, as well as the view back towards Toubkal.

On the other side, the road loses height recklessly, descending 1,600 metres in little over 30 kilometres (18 miles). The twists and loops aren't too dangerous, but this is not a stretch to hurry. Take your time and enjoy the views that continue to present themselves until shortly before the road joins the P32, the main east–west route across southern Morocco, for the final run across prosperous farmland to Taroudant.

The High Atlas & Sahara

Taroudant

Enclosed by reddish ramparts, with a back-drop of the High Atlas, commanding the trade routes across a plain, kitted out with souks – Taroudant is often considered to be a junior Marrakech. It has its pretensions. In the early 16th century it was the Saadian capital. They, and the gold they hauled up from the Sahara, built the well-preserved *pisé* walls that remain the town's most prominent feature. Later the Roudanis, as the inhabitants are called, joined a rebellion against Moulay Ismail. In 1787 Ismail took the town, destroyed the Saadian palaces, slaughtered the locals, and brought in a whole new Berber population from the Rif.

He left behind his own fortress – what is now the Kasbah, one of the town's poorest and most crowded quarters – and the walls. A ride around their crenellated five-kilometre (three-mile) circumference – either in a horse-drawn calèche (from outside the Hotel Palais Salam, about 50dh per hour) or by bicycle (a place on avenue Mohammed V, just east of place Assareg, rents them for 10dh per hour) – Taroudant's only standard tourist activity. On the way, check out the foul-smelling tanneries, on the western side, outside Bab Targhount.

There are two souks: the **Marché Berbère**, where the locals buy groceries; and the **Arab Souk**, more focused on traditional crafts. Local guides may show you an ancient *foundouk* (merchants' hostel) 'used in the French film *Ali Baba*' (we've never heard of it either) or lead you to one of the local sculptors who work with limestone. It's also a good place to buy Berber jewellery.

The Arab Souk is west of **place Assareg**, the town's main square. Settling at a café and watching the laid-back daily life of this modest pre-Saharan market town, you realise that really it's nothing much like Marrakech at all.

Where to stay

The **Hotel Palais Salam** (028 85 25 01, fax 048 85 25 54, pasalam@agadirnet.net.ma, from 935dh double) is housed in a 19th-century palace – built into the ramparts of the Kasbah quarter – which was formerly the governor's residence. The best hotel in town, it has three restaurants and is the only place to get a beer, but it's a little cheesy – there's piped music by a pool shaped like a Moroccan horseshoe arch.

A few kilometres out of town is the **Gazelle d'Or** (028 85 20 39, fax 048 85 26 54, www.gazelledor.com, from 2,250dh per person half board). It was built in 1961 as a Belgian baron's hunting lodge and has been a hotel since 1972. There are 30 grand bungalows set in enormous grounds, with tennis, croquet and an organic farm. The lunch buffet, served by the pool, is splendid, and exorbitant rates include dinner at what is considered one of Morocco's finest restaurants (jacket required). Regular guests include Jacques Chirac and Bryan Ferry.

Taroudant's best budget beds are at the **Hotel Taroudant** (place Assareg, 028 85 24 16, 500dh double), a fading institution with a flavour of French colonial times.

Argan: elixir of everything

Goats clambering about in argan trees is part of tourist mythology in south-west Morocco. And you may actually see them doing it. Round here grow the world's only argan trees. A botanical relic from a remote era, the fussy argan only flourishes inland between Essaouira and Sidi Ifni, in an area that has been declared a UNESCO Biosphere Reserve.

Spiny and knotted, argan trees look similar to olive trees and they too bear a fruit from which oil can be extracted. This is where the goats come in. Some graze in the trees, others are fed the fruits after harvesting in `spring. The goat's digestive system is the means by which the tough fruit is stripped from the recalcitrant nut. Yes, the nuts are collected from goat droppings. They are then split, toasted, pulped, pressed – it takes 30 kilogrammes of nuts to make one litre of oil.

After all that, you'd better believe the product is highly prized. Berbers have long used the oil to help heal scars and ease rheumatic pain. Rich in vitamin E, it's good for the skin and has become a staple of Moroccan massage and beauty treatments. Modern research has pronounced argan oil efficacious in reducing cholesterol and countering arteriosclerosis. Taken internally it also proves to be very tasty – sweet and rich, great for drizzling or bread-dunking. Useful as conversation piece as well as exotic ingredient, it's a good (if pricey) gift for a foodie friend: it costs around 150dh per litre.

Resourceful locals have found one other use for the argan. In tourist areas, kids hover near grazing goats. When the cameras come out, the kids demand dirhams – or they'll frighten the goats from the branches.

The Ourika Valley

A big gulp of mountain air.

Ourika is a spectacular valley cut deep into the High Atlas and an easy way to get a taste of mountain air. It's not a pass – the road stops at Setti Fatma, 63 kilometres (39 miles) from Marrakech – and unless you're interested in skiing or trekking it's more of a day trip than a fully fledged excursion. Marrakchis nip up here for a break from the summer heat. But there are places to stay if you want to experience the peace of the valley after the daytime traffic has all gone home.

This is also the way to get to Oukaimeden, home to Morocco's best skiing. At the time of writing, work was just beginning on a billion-euro 'golf and skiing' development near the existing resort, the anticipated scale of which is likely to affect the whole area. Expect new roads (one may link Oukaimeden with Asni

Setti Fatma. See p202.

via Imlil; *see p196*), substantial improvements to the existing ones, and, of course, a whole lot more traffic.

Buses and *grand taxis* leave from outside Marrakech's Bab Er Rob. Make sure you're getting one that goes all the way to Setti Fatma, as most local traffic heads only as far as Arhbalou, 24 kilometres (15 miles) short. The journey takes about two hours. Buses head to Oukaimeden in winter. If you want to go there at another time of year and don't have your own transport, you'll have to hire a taxi for the day from Marrakech, although it might also be possible to find one in Arhbalou.

To Arhbalou

The route d'Ourika begins at the fountain roundabout of Bab Jedid, by the Mamounia Hotel. The road follows that stretch of the walls which encloses the Agdal Gardens before crossing 34 kilometres (21 miles) of agricultural flatland.

There are two possible side excursions. **Aghmat** was the first Almoravid capital of the region. It is now a small village, and has a 1960s mausoleum dedicated to Youssef Ibn Tachfine, founder of Marrakech. **Tnine de l'Ourika** has a Monday souk and is home to **Nectarome** (*see p124*), an organic garden of aromatic plants and a shop selling wellness products made with their essential oils. Beyond here, Berber villages cling to steep valley sides, camouflaged against a red-earth backdrop that forms a brilliant contrast with the deep, luminous greens of the valley floor and cultivated terraces. Terracotta pottery, made from this local earth, is on sale at stalls all along the road, sometimes shaped as a wild boar, a local speciality.

There's nothing much at Arhbalou, except for the turn-off to Oukaimeden (*see p202*). On the stretch beyond it, there are a few decent hotels which also double as lunch spots, notably the French-owned **Auberge le Maquis** (024 48 45 31, www.le-maquis.com, 800dh double incl dinner), just before the roadside settlement of Oulmès (no relation to the fizzy water), and **Ramuntcho** (024 48 45 21, www.ramuntcho.ma, 600dh double), which has a wonderful terrace for lunch and a *salon de thé* that's perfect for a nap afterwards.

Walk of the Seven Waterfalls.

Setti Fatma

After a final gorge-like stretch, with cafés and houses along the opposite bank reached by perilous-looking rope bridges, the road peters out at Setti Fatma. The village is nothing special – lots of cafés and souvenir shops, with satellite dishes on breeze-block houses – but the setting is wonderful, ringed by mountains with lots of streams and grassy terraces. If you arrive in mid August there's a big four-day *moussem*, an event that's both a religious celebration and sociable fair. The village also has a *bureau de guides* (near the Hotel Asgaour) where you can arrange an assortment of treks and hikes; Noureddine (070 78 10 96) is the English-speaking one.

The shortest and simplest hike is the **Walk of the Seven Waterfalls**. On the other side of the river from the main body of the village – reached by footbridges made of bundled branches (tourists pick their way across these with trepidation; locals spring over them like mountain goats) – are a number of small tagine and brochette joints. Concealed behind these cafés is a steep-sided valley, and a climb up it will bring you to the first of the seven cascades. It's quite a strenuous scramble, over big river boulders and up a cliff or two. Anyone will point (or lead) the way, and there's a basic café at the foot of the first waterfall where you can rest with a cool drink. The other six are a more serious climb.

There is some rudimentary accommodation. **La Perle d'Ourika** (061 56 73 29, 140dh double), south of the main village, is friendly and about as stylish as it gets up here. The **Hotel Asgaour** (066 41 64 19, 70dh-150dh double) in the village proper has 26 basic rooms, some with shower, overlooking the river.

Oukaimeden

The road up here hairpins all the way from the valley, though in a fairly gentle fashion, rising eventually to 2,650 metres. This is Morocco's best ski resort, though facilities are old-fashioned and conditions unreliable. The season runs from December to May but snow is most likely to be found between February and April. Casablancans scurry down here at the first hint of it. These are no slopes for beginners but anyone can go up the ski lift, once the highest in the world and still, at 3,273 metres, the highest in Africa. It's not always in operation, though.

All this will soon pale in comparison to 'the first ski and golfing resort in the Middle East and North Africa' – a gigantic development by the UAE's Emaar Properties, which promises 2,000 hotel rooms, 300 retail units, 25,000 square metres of business and conference facilities, and lots of Dubai bling. Work was just beginning in early 2007. *See also p161.*

The area's other attraction is the prehistoric rock carvings – of animals, weapons, battle scenes, and symbols with forgotten meanings – that can be found nearby with the help of a guide. Look for the book *Gravures Rupestres du Haut Atlas* by Susan Searight and Danièle Hourbette, which might be on sale at the CAF Réfuge (*see below*) or in Marrakech.

The **CAF Réfuge** (024 31 90 36, www.cafmaroc.co.ma, 220dh double) has both dorm beds and private rooms, and is a good place to find guides and check out trekking possibilities. The **Chez Juju** (024 31 90 05, www.hotelchezjuju.com, 790dh half-board) has a decent bar and restaurant, clean rooms and hot showers.

In summer, the area below Oukaimeden becomes what is known as an alpine prairie. The pastures are opened on 10 August, and after that become crowded with Berber tents and livestock. Compared to the ski resort, it's a scene not just from another season, but from another age. And once the new development is completed, it'll seem like another planet.

Tizi-n-Tichka to Ouarzazate

A spectacular mountain pass descends to the desert's edge.

The fortified village and kasbah at **Ait Benhaddou**. *See p205.*

Running south-east out of Marrakech, the P31 courses across the plain, then cuts into the High Atlas to snake spectacularly over the range's loftiest pass – the Tizi-n-Tichka. It then descends into the arid pre-Sahara and down to Ouarzazate, rightly considered the gateway to the desert, as well as being the centre of Morocco's film industry. Along the way, there are interesting side trips to the kasbahs of Telouet and Aït Benhaddou.

It's only 196 kilometres (122 miles) to Ouarzazate, and it's a pretty decent road, originally built by the French Foreign Legion in 1931 and recently improved. But the mountains demand respect so leave a good four hours for the journey – longer if you decide to stop at Telouet or Aït Benhaddou. And if you're not in a hurry, there are places to stay on the way.

There are several Ouarzazate buses daily from Marrakech's *gare routière*. Journey time is about four hours. One bus a day leaves Bab Ghemat (map p253 F6) in Marrakech for Telouet in the early afternoon; the return journey is at 7am, but to reach Aït Benhaddou by public transport it's necessary to go to Ouarzazate and then backtrack.

The Tizi-n-Tichka

About 50 kilometres (31 miles) south-east of Marrakech, the road begins to climb into the mountains. It's a spine-tingling journey, each bend revealing a new panorama. On the way up, the fertile slopes are shrouded in forest or terraced for cultivation, and Berber villages can be seen clinging to vertiginous gradients. The mountains here are full of semi-precious stones

Snowcapped peaks in the High Atlas.

change to a more arid landscape, leaving little doubt that the desert is where you're headed. The turn-off to Telouet is just a few kilometres further on the left.

Telouet

The village and kasbah of Telouet is a 21-kilometre (13-mile) detour deep into the remote heart of the mountains. Scattered settlements hang between barren peaks and luminous green valleys. In spring there is almond blossom everywhere. Kestrels and vultures weave in the blue skies above. The village of Telouet is tiny, dominated, as is the whole valley, by the slowly crumbling kasbah of the Glaoui clan.

For centuries, before the French built the Tichka road, this was the southern side of the main pass over the High Atlas. In the late 19th century, control of that pass was in the hands of the Glaoui clan – one of three tribes that dominated the ungovernable south of Morocco. After coming to national prominence following their assistance to Sultan Moulay Hassan in 1893, the Glaoua greatly expanded this kasbah, which remained their stronghold and last line of defence. However, while Thami El-Glaoui (see p17 **Lord of the Atlas**), as pasha of Marrakech, ran the South on behalf of the Protectorate, the kasbah passed into control of his obstinately anti-French in-law Hammou. This was enough to stall French 'pacification' of the South until the 1930s, and they built the Tichka road, following a much trickier route, simply to avoid the fortress. It was abandoned upon Thami El-Glaoui's death in 1956. There have been several failed attempts to rescue the kasbah – all foiled by complicated inheritance laws, which mean the site is jointly owned by all the descendants of the Glaoui, whose myriad permissions would be needed for any transfer of ownership.

The **kasbah** is reached by following the road around the edge of the village. Entry is by donation (maybe 20dh) and someone will appear with a bunch of keys to let you in and show you around. After lying empty for half a century, much of the fortress is in advanced disrepair and out of bounds for safety reasons. The main thing to see is the reception hall, built in 1942 and, alongside the ornately traditional decoration in cedarwood, stucco and mosaic, equipped with sockets for electric appliances – odd, among such apparently medieval surrounds. At the end of the hall is a delicate iron window grille that frames a commanding view of the valley below. You can also climb up steep, dark stairs to a terrace that offers a sense of the whole picturesquely decaying structure, its towers inhabited only by storks.

and roadside sellers angle melon-sized geodes, broken in half, to show you the glittering light reflected by the red or green crystals within. A closer look reveals that some have been painted to appear more vivid for the passing motorist.

There are various places to take a breather. About 15 kilometres (nine miles) before the pass, the village of **Taddert** is the busiest halt. It's divided into two parts; the higher of the two has a better choice of cafés, some of which overlook the valley below. A barrier is lowered here when the pass is closed, and this is where the snow plough is garaged.

Beyond Taddert it's all much more barren and the road gets quite hairy in places – looping and twisting and running along the knife's edge of exposed ridges. Small shops selling minerals and fossils are perched in some seemingly impossible places. There's a point where you can stop and look back down over the hairpins you have just ascended.

The pass, at 2,260 metres (7,415 feet), is reached with little fanfare. There are a couple of masts and a few more stalls selling rocks. Beyond it there's an immediate and dramatic

Where to stay & eat

Right by the kasbah, the pocket-sized **Lion d'Or** (no phone, 150dh double) has a handful of basic rooms. The **Auberge Restaurant Telouet** (024 89 07 17, www.telouet.com, 200dh-260dh double), which overlooks the kasbah from further back down the road, is marginally more sophisticated, and has a Berber-tented dining area across the road (menus 60dh-80dh). Additional rooms in adjacent buildings are also available.

But if you want to overnight or linger in these parts, by far the nicest place is **Irocha** (067 73 70 02, www.irocha.com, 800dh double incl dinner). This small *maison d'hôte* is in a quiet spot, perched above the P31 (from which it's well signposted) at Tisselday, half way between the Telouet turn-off and Aït Benhaddou. The simple rooms, all but two of which surround a quiet courtyard, have a number of tasteful touches, nice rugs and en suite showers. There's also a terrace overlooking the verdant valley floor and a dining room with generous windows, some interesting old books, and a few decent CDs. They've recently added a traditional wooden hammam and a swimming pool, and the food is among the best in southern Morocco. Cooking lessons are offered for 450dh per person.

Aït Benhaddou

If you have a 4x4 and about seven hours to spare, it's possible to go from Telouet to Aït Benhaddou via Anmiter (last stop for buses) and 36 kilometres (22 miles) of rough piste down what used to be the main route through this area. Sticking with the main P31, the turn-off for Aït Benhaddou is 11 kilometres (seven miles) south of the hamlet of Amerzgane (itself 50 kilometres south of the turn-off for Telouet). If you're already exhausted from your trip over the pass, it may make more sense to do Aït Benhaddou as a backtracking day trip from Ouarzazate (24 kilometres, or 14 miles, south), or as a last sight on the way back to Marrakech.

Whichever, it shouldn't be missed. The fortified village (*ksar*) and complex of kasbahs is one of the most striking and best preserved in southern Morocco, appearing to tumble down a slope above the Oued Mellah. It's also probably the most famous, used as a location in David Lean's *Lawrence of Arabia*, Robert Aldrich's *Sodom and Gomorrah*, Franco Zeffirelli's *Jesus of Nazareth* and Ridley Scott's *Gladiator*. But the film and tourist industries have only slowed Aït Benhaddou's decline from the importance it formerly had for its position on the old Saharan caravan route. The

population is dwindling fast and the village is now under the protection of UNESCO.

The road brings you to the far side of the river, where there is a cluster of hotels, cafés and souvenir shops. In spring it can be necessary to paddle (or occasionally wade) through water across the ford. Locals will inevitably appear to guide you over the stepping stones or through the passages and stairways of the village. The owner of the principal kasbah, which is said to be 400 years old though no one really knows how long Aït Benhaddou has been here, charges 5dh to let you see the view from his terrace. The ancient fortified granary (*agadir*) at the top of the complex is also worth the uphill clamber.

There's another kasbah, this one dating from the 17th century, ten kilometres (six miles) up the road at **Tamdaght**, also often used as a film location. You can look around but it's not in very good condition and there's little to see inside. Beyond there you need a 4x4 to follow the piste up to Telouet.

Where to stay & eat

The cluster of businesses on the other side of the river testify to the importance of Aït Benhaddou on the tourist route, if no longer on the trade route. There isn't much reason to hang about but if you do want to stay then the **Hotel la Kasbah** (024 89 03 02, 360dh-500dh double incl breakfast) has a pool, a hammam (50dh) and, in some of the more expensive rooms, air-conditioning. Across the road, the **Auberge El-Ouidane** is now an annexe of la Kasbah, where you can lunch on a roof terrace with a view across the river. Even if you don't have time to visit Aït Benhaddou proper, it's worthwhile pausing up here. Try the spicy Berber omelette.

Ouarzazate

Pronounced 'wa-zah-zat', this doggedly unpicturesque town sits in prime position where the Dades and Drâa valleys fork off from the High Atlas route, and where the route de Taroudant winds in from the west.

It was founded by the French in 1928 as a regional capital and Foreign Legion outpost and still retains both a garrison and a drably functional air, with concrete buildings all along avenue Mohammed V, its one main street. Film industry folk use its five-star facilities and backpackers are increasingly drawn by the range of exotic tourism on offer, but few others will find much cause to linger. On the other hand, its size and strategic position as gateway to the Sahara means that if travelling

Who are the Berbers?

The original inhabitants of North Africa, the Berbers were resident from Egypt to the Atlantic for millennia before the Arabs began heading west from the Arabian peninsula in the seventh century. They were probably around as long ago as the Upper Paleolithic era; they were first mentioned in writing around 3000 BC, by the ancient Egyptians.

Invaders and traders came and went – Phoenicians, Romans, Vandals, Byzantines, Alans – some leaving their mark on the Berbers, but none managing to eradicate their languages and traditions altogether. The name 'Berber' was probably given to them by the Romans – it's the same word as 'Barbarian', originally a Greek term. The Berbers call themselves the Imazigen ('free men'; singular Amazigh).

Before the Arabs arrived, most Berbers were Christian. St Augustine was a Berber, as were several Roman emperors. The Arab newcomers weren't able to conquer the Berbers (they settled for living beside them), but they were able to convert them. By the eighth century most had become Muslim, though communities of Berber Jews survived in North Africa right up until the 1950s and 1960s, when most of them moved to Israel.

The Moors who conquered Iberia in 711 were mostly Berbers, as was their leader, Tariq ibn Ziyad, who gave his name to Gibraltar ('Jebel Tariq' – the mountain of Tariq). The dynasties who presided over Morocco's golden age were all Berber: the Almoravids, who founded Marrakech, and the Almohads and Merenids who succeeded them. It wasn't until the 16th century and the coming of the Saadians that Morocco was first ruled by Arabs.

Today there remain significant Berber populations in Algeria, Libya, Tunisia, Mauritania and Egypt, as well as emigrant communities in Belgium, France, the Netherlands and Israel. But the biggest Berber population of all is in Morocco, where they comprise anything between 30 and 40 per cent of the population.

Of course, in reality, it's all got mixed up. Arab intermarriage with Berbers down the centuries means that most Moroccans have at least some Berber ancestry. Berbers have survived more as a culture than a race, and their traditions are most strongly rooted in the regions too remote for anyone to conquer.

Though many have moved to the cities, the three main Berber groups in Morocco are based in the Rif mountains, the Middle Atlas, and the High Atlas and Sahara. And there's no one physical type. Riffian Berbers from the north are often pale-skinned with fair or reddish hair, high cheekbones and green eyes. Southern Berbers are usually dark-haired and brown-eyed, with skin shading from olive to black.

During the Protectorate, the French favoured the Berbers – the Glaoui, for example, who ran southern Morocco as colonial proxies, are a Berber tribe. But after independence, Berber traditions were ignored or suppressed in the interests of forging a Moroccan national identity. However, in recent decades Berber culture has been experiencing a revival. King Mohammed VI, whose mother is a Berber, appointed the Berber Driss Jettou as prime minister and founded a Royal Institute for Amazigh Culture. A written form of the Berber language, Tamazight, has been standardised using the ancient Tifinagh alphabet, and Berber activists agitate for Tamazight to join Arabic as an official language. There are Amazigh associations, films, books, festivals, newspapers and websites. The Berbers are very much back.

in the South you're almost bound to end up spending a night here sooner or later.

The mid 18th-century **Taouirt Kasbah** (8am-6pm daily, admission 10dh), at the eastern end of town, is Ouarzazate's one historical sight and the only thing remaining from before the Protectorate. During the 1930s, when the Glaoua were at their prime, this was one of the largest kasbahs in the area, housing lots of the clan's lesser-known members, plus hundreds of servants and slaves. These days much of it is ruined, although some is being restored under UNESCO auspices. A big section is still inhabited. The part that faces the main road has been maintained, and this is what gets shown to visitors – the principal courtyard, the former harem, and a few other rooms around a central airwell.

Next door is **La Musée Regional de la Résistance et de l'Armée de Libération de Ouarzazate** (8.30am-4.30pm, closed Sat, Sun, admission free), which contains a fascinatingly boring display of photos, most of them too high on the wall to look at, and a few old objects kept in dusty cabinets.

Some of the town's poorest inhabitants live in the ramshackle old quarter behind the kasbah – all there was of the town before the French built the rest – and here you can wander freely if you don't mind acquiring a small entourage of kids hassling for dirhams and would-be guides. Opposite the kasbah entrance is the **Ensemble Artisanal** (open 9am-noon, 2.30-6pm daily), a cluster of stalls and shops selling fixed-price arts and crafts.

Tiffoultoute (open 8am-7pm) is another Glaoui kasbah, just outside town on the bypass (head back towards Marrakech, then turn left at the roundabout). Well preserved and dramatically located between the river and a palmeraie, these days it offers a restaurant and accommodation for tour groups.

The other face of Ouarzazate is its connection to the film industry, which dates back to David Lean shooting some of *Lawrence of Arabia* around here. Bertolucci's *The Sheltering Sky*, Martin Scorsese's *Kundun* and Ridley Scott's *Gladiator* and *Kingdom of Heaven* have been among the many other films to make use of the area's good light, cheap labour and variety of mountain and desert locations.

The **Atlas Corporation Studios** (024 88 21 66, www.atlasstudios.com, open 8am-6pm daily, admission 30dh), seven kilometres (four miles) west of town, were built in the early 1980s and can be toured when there's no filming. You can look at the Tibetan monastery built for *Kundun*, a fighter plane made for *Jewel of the Nile*, a fake medina alley and Egyptian temple sets from the *Asterix* movie. It all has a run-down air. A little further out of town, the **CLA Studios** (www.cla-studios.com), owned by Dino de Laurentis and Cinecittà, were built in 2004. A sign encourages you to stop and visit (and the Jerusalem set for *Kingdom of Heaven* might be worth a look) but they've not been letting anyone in every time we've passed by.

Where to stay

Ouarzazate has hotels for all budgets but a preponderance of four- and five-star places geared to the package tourist. **Dar Daif** (three kilometres off the Zagora road, 024 85 42 32, fax 024 85 40 75, www.dardaif.ma, 1100dh double incl dinner) is one of the few *maisons d'hôtes*. It's in a converted kasbah on the tatty outskirts and has 12 rooms with a 'typical Sahara' theme. There's a hammam and a pool too. No alcohol, though.

The 234-room **Berbère Palace** (Quartier Mansour Eddahbi, 024 88 31 05, fax 024 88 30 71, mberpala@iam.net, 2,000dh-3,600dh double, breakfast 130dh) is our pick of the three big five-stars, with air-conditioned bungalows, a big pool, hammam, jacuzzi, tennis courts and even a small football pitch. The **Riad Salam** (avenue Mohammed V, 024 88 33 35, fax 024 88 27 66, www.salamhotelmaroc.com, 700dh double, breakfast 70dh) is comfortable. The same chain also has a branch at the Atlas studios (Oscar Salam, 024 88 22 12, fax 024, 88 21 80, 450dh double, breakfast 70dh). The **Hotel Bab Sahara** (place El-Mouahidine, 024 88 47 22, 130dh double) offers basic budget beds on a recently pedestrianised central square; it's also local HQ for the US Peace Corps.

Where to eat & drink

Ouarzazate's relatively cosmopolitan dining doesn't seem much on the way out from Marrakech, but feels like heaven on the way back from the Sahara. **Chez Dimitri** (22 avenue Mohammed V, 024 88 73 46, average 150dh) is a Ouarzazate institution, founded in 1928 and serving moussaka alongside French and Moroccan dishes. The new **Relais Saint Exupéry** (13 boulevard Moulay Abdellah, 024 88 77 79, www.relaissaintexupery.com, average 250dh) offers upmarket French dining in aviation-themed surrounds. **Pizzeria Venezia** (avenue Moulay Rachid, 024 88 24 58, average 70dh-100dh) has decent pizzas and the next-door **Obélix** (024 88 71 17, average 120dh) serves Moroccan and international dishes in an atmosphere of high kitsch, with props from *The Mummy* and *Gladiator*. The nearby **Datte d'Or** (024 88 71 17, menus 110dh-160dh) is cosy and has reasonable set menus.

The Dadès Valley & the Gorges

Walk the kasbahs – then spend midnight in an oasis.

Stretching east from Ouarzazate, the Dadès Valley runs between the High Atlas to the north and the bare, jagged formations of the Jebel Sarho to the south. It's sometimes referred to as the Valley of the Kasbahs, which is appropriate – there are dozens of them. And almost every valley here is dubbed the Valley of Something Or Other.

The Dadès is also the most barren of the southern valleys, but the juxtaposition with such rugged surrounds just makes the oases seem all the more beautiful. North of the main road, from Boumalne du Dadès and Tinerhir respectively, are the gorges of Dadès and Todra (**photo p212**), dramatic cuts into the Atlas that are well worth detouring for.

Skoura, at the westernmost end of the Dadès Valley, can be done in a day trip from Ouarzazate. The Dadès Gorge too. But trying to pack in the Todra Gorge as well is pushing it. There's decent accommodation along the route, and all this can be done with overnight stops on the way to the Tafilelt (*see pp213-16*).

Infrequent buses run along the main road and grand taxis shuttle between the bigger towns. If you don't have your own transport and want to visit the gorges, you can commandeer taxis at Boumalne or Tinerhir, and hotels can also arrange transport. But this is an area where it really does make sense to have a 4x4 to explore a little of the Atlas beyond the various valleys or gorges, or to detour into the strange, sculpted landscapes of the Jebel Sarho.

Skoura

About 40 kilometres (25 miles) east of Ouarzazate, Skoura is a big oasis but a small settlement. The main road bypasses what there is of the town centre – just one street with a few basic shops, a couple of down-at-heel cafés and signs still pointing to a long-closed women's goat's cheese cooperative. Most of the population is scattered about the extensive palmeraie, which is beautiful, and sprinkled with kasbahs. If you want to explore some of these, it's worth considering a guide for the day, most easily arranged through your hotel.

One of the kasbahs, on the far side of the *oued* (wadi, or dry river bed) from the road, to the west of the centre behind **Kasbah Ben Moro** (*see below*), is the famous **Amridil** (open dawn-sunset daily, admission 10dh), which features on both the 50-dirham note and on the packaging of Marrakesh Orange Juice (an example sits proudly on display). Built by a Middle Atlas tribe in the 17th century, it's now being restored with local labour and foreign donations. Resident guide Aziz Sadikln brings everything to life with humour as he shows you around. Aziz can also do a tour of the oasis; call him on 064 91 45 53.

Another dramatic old kasbah, **Dar Aït Sidi El-Mati**, is ten minutes' walk to the south-west of Amridil. And if you're still not kasbahed out after that there are plenty of others, including ones you can stay in.

The road that heads north out of Skoura up to the village of **Toundoute** is a beautiful drive through what's known locally as the Vallée des Amandes (Valley of the Almonds).

Where to stay & eat

Kasbah Ben Moro (024 85 21 16, www.kasbahbenmoro.com, 650dh double) is on the Ouarzazate road, two kilometres (1.2 miles) short of Skoura proper. It was founded by a Spanish exile in the 18th century and in 2000 turned into a modern 16-room hotel by a Spanish expat from Cadiz. The rooms are cosy but dark – but that's a kasbah for you. Breakfast is an extra 40dh and there's a 150dh lunch or dinner menu.

Deep in the palmeraie, the artfully luxurious **Dar Ahlam** (024 85 22 39, www.darahlam.com, 7,900dh double) is the kasbah as designer labyrinth – the ground floor is a maze of corridors and salons – artfully exploited each evening. The gag is that you find your way from one of nine austere but tasteful suites or three sumptuous garden villas to the enormous lounge, then they escort you to where you'll eat dinner – somewhere different from the evening before, with different place settings and different food. You'd have to stay

The filmic scenery around the **Dadès Valley** is a showstopper.

here for about ten days before you dined in the same place twice. The kitchen is excellent, as it should be at these prices. Also thrown in is a gorgeous hammam, professional masseur, swimming pool set in lush gardens, three small libraries, and the use of a 4x4 and experienced guide (the price drops a little if you forgo the car and guide). The hotel makes its own luxurious soaps and shampoos and you can enjoy them in big bathtubs, or buy some to take home at the small but interesting shop.

Out on the far edge of the oasis, **Sawadi** (024 85 23 41, www.sawadi.ma, 1,280-2,560dh double) offers more modest accomodation and is a great option for travellers with children. As

well as houses and bungalows scattered among big grounds and equipped to accommodate groups of all sizes, there's a pool and a small farm with a flock of sheep and donkeys to ride. It also supplies meat and veg for the kitchen. The place had just changed hands when we looked around and new owner Philippe Ferrer Mora was busy with construction. It should reopen in summer 2007, with a playground, mini-golf, boules and a conference centre.

The friendly, family-run **Gîte Tiriguioute** (024 85 20 68, bouarif_elhachmi@hotmail.com, 500dh double incl dinner), three kilometres (two miles) out of town, is the nearest thing to a budget option.

Skoura. *See p208.*

There isn't really anywhere to eat outside of the hotels, but if pushed then **Café Atlas** is probably the best place on the lone main street.

El-Kelaa M'Gouna

Fifty barren kilometres (30 miles) east of Skoura, the oasis resumes at El-Kelaa, which ribbons along the road. It's famous for its rose products. All over the country, women rub rosewater into their face and hands, and most of it comes from here. It seems the most Moroccan of things, yet it was French perfumiers who, in the early 20th century, realised that this area offered ideal growing conditions for the leafy rosa centifolia. You'd barely notice them among the palms when they're not blooming, but there are hundreds of thousands of rose bushes around here. The harvest is in May, celebrated by a rose festival with dances, processions and lots of petal-throwing.

Essences are distilled at two factories and every other shop sells rose soap, rose skin cream, rose shampoo, rose shower gel and, of course, rosewater. It's not otherwise a very interesting place, though there's also a dagger-making cooperative.

With a 4x4 you can drive north towards **Tourbist** through what's known, naturally, as the Vallée des Roses. From here you can follow the piste around to the top of the Dadès Gorge.

There's not much reason to linger around El-Kelaa, but the old-school **Hotel les Roses** (024 83 63 36, fax 024 83 60 07, 320dh double), up by an old kasbah, is a three-star with 102 rooms, good views, a pool, the town's only bar and a bit of faded grandeur.

Dadès Gorge

Leaving El-Kelaa and continuing east, ribbon development continues for another 20 kilometres (12 miles) or so, with kasbahs left to crumble among new buildings made from concrete rather than *pisé*. There's not much of interest at the next major settlement, **Boumalne Dadès**, but it does mark the mouth of the Dadès Gorge.

The road into the gorge swoops and twists, climbing high up the steep valley sides through curvaceous formations of red rock and old kasbahs on rugged outcrops. The valley is at its most dramatic and gorge-like after the village of **Aït Oudinar**, about 27 kilometres (17 miles) along, where it turns into a deep, reddish canyon – though only for a couple of hundred metres.

It's a good road up to this point, but from here it gets more difficult. You'll need a 4x4 to proceed beyond Msemrir, but could then take the spectacular piste that runs east over the mountains to **Aït Hani**, whence you can come back down through **Todra**. This is also excellent hiking territory, and any hotel can arrange guides and excursions.

Back on the main Dadès Valley road, just east of Boumalne Dadès, is the turning for the **Vallée des Oiseaux** (Valley of the Birds), signposted to **Ikniouin**. Here amateur ornithologists can spot Houbara bustards, Egyptian vultures, eagle owls and bar-tailed desert larks.

Where to stay & eat

Clambering up the steep valley side shortly before the canyon, **Chez Pierre** (024 83 02 67, chezpierre@menara.ma, 570dh double, closed Aug & 2wks mid Feb) is the most sophisticated option for either sleeping or eating. It's Belgian-run and has eight simple, spacious rooms, a small pool and a restaurant serving excellent food that includes vegetarian options. A little further up but still south of the canyon, **La Kasbah de la Vallée** (tel/fax 024 83 17 17, kasbah_de_lavallee@yahoo.fr, 400dh double) is big and friendly, with rooms in varying configurations, as well as a much-appreciated alcohol licence.

Just on the other (north) side of the canyon is the **Berbére de la Montagne** (024 83 02 28,

280dh-560dh double incl dinner), which has six rooms with showers and four without. All are well furnished.

Back down towards Boumalne, **the Kasbah Aït Arbi** (024 83 17 23, fax 024 83 01 31, 70dh-140dh double) in the hamlet of the same name is the star budget option. The cheaper rooms are on the roof with wonderful views, but the showers are two floors below (the other rooms have their own).

Off to the left as the road east leaves Boumalne, **Le Soleil Bleu** (024 83 01 63, fax 024 83 03 94, le_soleilbleu@yahoo.fr, 320dh-550dh double) is a good, basic hotel overlooking the town. It's popular with birdwatchers, and the visitors' books record what they've spotted.

Tinerhir

There's another desolate stretch beyond Boumalne, but after about 50 kilometres (30 miles) the road arrives in Tinerhir, the most interesting town on this road. The new part of it ribbons east and west along the road; the old part stretches out in huge kasbah-dotted palmeraies to the north and south. There's a pocket-sized medina where you can find rug-weavers from the Aït Atta tribe at work on their looms. The carpets these women make are brilliantly coloured and of high quality, but you'll need an interpreter to negotiate as few speak anything but Berber. The main street is called the rue des Femmes because it mostly sells kaftans and suchlike. There are also lots of spice merchants. The small mellah (Jewish quarter) on the far side of the medina, closed off

behind a big wooden door, is these days occupied by about 20 Berber families.

The modern part of town has all mod cons – post office, banks, cybercafés, and a small supermarket that's the last stop for alcohol. It's on the south side of the main road, between Kasbah Lamrani and the old centre. Opposite Kasbah Lamrani is where you'll find Tinerhir's Monday souk.

Where to stay & eat

Kasbah Lamrani (024 83 50 17, fax 024 83 50 27, www.kasbahlamrani.com, 560dh double) has 22 rooms kitted with air-conditioning, heating, telephones, fridges, TVs and nice bathrooms. There's also a pool and three restaurants. It's all slightly Disneyfied, but that's common in mid-range places in these parts, and this hotel is very well-run. The **Hotel Todra** (avenue Hassan II, 024 83 42 49, fax 024 83 45 65, 160dh-320dh double) is well-placed for exploring the Medina, and is atmospherically old-school with lots of dark wooden panelling and heavy furniture. Go for the more expensive rooms as some of the cheaper ones don't have windows.

Todra Gorge

The road up to Todra winds north around the edge of **Tinerhir**'s lush palmeraie. There are a couple of spots here with good views back over the town.

Once in the valley, the road runs along the bottom, never climbing the sides as the road does in Dadès. After about ten kilometres (six

Tell it to the tourists

In any tourist economy, locals have their little jokes for the visitor. They're the common currency of cross-cultural exchange, designed to throw light upon their traditions, foster international understanding, affirm shared humanity through the precious gift of laughter – and sell you some useless damn thing you don't need. The gag in southern Morocco is to translate the function of everyday items into terms the foreigner will understand. Once you've wandered around a few souks and kasbahs, you'll have heard these many times, but no harm in being ahead of the game.

Berber massage Sex.
Berber Mercedes A donkey. *See also* Berber taxi.

Berber pharmacy A herbalist's shop; the place to buy Berber viagra.
Berber taxi A donkey. See also Berber Mercedes.
Berber telephone The narrow airwell that's an architectural feature in Berber kasbahs. Apart from admitting light and air to lower levels, these allow communication between different floors. 'Fatima! Where's the couscous?'
Berber viagra Ginseng. *See also* Berber pharmacy.
Berber whisky Mint tea. Sometimes used with scarcely a hint of irony, as Moroccans credit their national hot beverage with powers that, to the foreigner, it simply does not seem to possess. 'I've drunk too much Berber whisky,' you may hear someone moan.

The High Atlas & Sahara

miles) of palmeraie and campsites, the road fords the river and beyond this someone will usually be waiting to charge you 10dh to proceed. It's worth getting out and walking to enjoy the last, canyon-like stretch – it's not as narrow as at Dadès but it's much grander and more spectacular. Here the cliffs rise to about 300 metres, and provide a habitat for assorted birdlife, including a pair of Bonelli's eagles. There are two hotels here on the other side of a cold, clear stream, which is crossed by stepping stones, carefully placed just far enough apart that you might want to pay the boys who hang around to offer a helping hand in return for dirhams.

With a 4x4 it's possible to head on up beyond the gorge and follow the mountainous piste from Aït Hani to Msemrir, and then enter the Dadès Gorge from the north.

Going back down the road towards Tinerhir, notice the **Source des Poissons Sacrés**, a spring-fed pool full of 'sacred' fish, these days on the grounds of a rather tawdry campsite. We wouldn't recommend staying here, but you can go and have a look at the fish. According to local folklore, bathing in here on three successive Friday afternoons will help women conceive.

Where to stay

This enclosed section of the gorge is an atmospheric place to stay the night, and feels remote despite being just 15 kilometres (nine miles) north of busy Tinerhir. At the bottom of the cliffs, next to each other on the side of the river, are two hotels: **Les Roches** (024 89 51 34, h-les-roches@hotmail.com, 400dh double) and **Yasmina** (024 89 51 18, fax 024 89 50 75, www.todragorge.com, 360dh double incl dinner). Yasmina has the better restaurant, plus it has a tented 'Berber' dining area by the river, but there's not a lot to choose between these places. Both are unremarkable buildings.

Tinejdad

Beyond Tinerhir the road continues in the direction of Er Rachidia. After about 50 kilometres (30 miles), just short of Tinejdad, there's an eccentric roadside attraction on the left-hand side. The **Sources de Lalla Mimouna** (8am-sunset daily, admission 50dh) is a walled garden housing an assortment of small 'museums' (of agriculture, manuscripts, horses), each built around a gurgling spring. It's the pet project of multilingual Zaïd Abboa, who also owns the Galerie d'Art (really more of a museum and antique shop) in downtown Tinejdad. It's on the main road, which is

otherwise full of shops selling chickens. There are also some antiques and paintings on sale at the Sources. The springs themselves are disappointingly devoid of special significance.

On the outskirts of Tinejdad, a left turn at the sign for the **Musée des Oasis** leads, after a few twists and turns, to the beautiful 18th-century **Ksar El-Khorbat**. Part of this fortified village has been transformed into a fascinating museum of oasis life (admission 20dh). It's the best exhibit this side of the Atlas: well organised with informative captions in five languages, supplied by Spanish writer Roger Mimó.

Just after Tinejdad there's a turn-off to Erfoud and the Tafilelt (*see pp213-16*), which takes you through towns inhabited by members of the once widely feared Aït Atta tribe.

Where to stay & eat

To go with the museum, Mimó and his Moroccan partners have also opened a restaurant and converted some village houses into a six-room hotel (**El Khorbat**, 035 88 03 55, fax 035 88 03 57, www.elkhorbat.com, 600dh-800dh double incl dinner). The rooms, all with en suite bathrooms but few other luxuries, are big and dark and cool – great when it's hot, but not so welcoming in winter. The restaurant (menus 70dh-150dh) serves both Spanish and Moroccan dishes. Icy gazpacho is a welcome treat during a hot Sahara lunchtime, and if you're ever going to try camel tagine, this is probably the place to do it.

Todra Gorge.
See p211.

The Tafilelt & Merzouga

The desert trade routes may have gone, but the camels are still here.

Art imitating life in **Rissani**. *See p214.*

Historically, the Tafilelt Oasis was the most important area south of the Atlas. Taroudant, Telouet and the Drâa Valley might all have had their moments, but the Tafilelt was where the medieval city of Sijilmassa once stood, nexus of desert trade routes, raking in gold from across the Sahara. It was the Talifelt that in 1893 sent Moulay Hassan and his tax-collecting expedition scurrying back over the Atlas with its tail between its legs, thus inadvertently hastening the end of independent Morocco and giving the Glaoui a leg-up to power. And it was from here that the Alaouites, three centuries ago, sallied forth to become the dynasty that still rules Morocco today.

You wouldn't guess any of this from a quick look at the area's two major settlements today, bureaucratic Erfoud and impoverished Rissani. The area long ago stopped being on the way to somewhere and started being the end of the line. (The Algerian border isn't far away to

either south or east.) But the Tafilelt does retain a kind of brooding quality, thanks to its decaying kasbahs, ancient palm groves and vague royal connections. This last has meant that traditionally it was a place to dispatch the more troublesome members of the ruling family to, out of sight and far from the centre of power.

Most travellers who get this far carry straight on through to Merzouga and the dunes of Erg Chebbi, which are one of the great sights of Morocco. This should be your plan too. But Rissani is worth spending some time in, either coming or going, and there is life to the south of Merzouga too.

You can get here by road from the Dadès Valley via the turn-off at Tinejdad (*see p212*). Buses run from Tinehrir to Tinejdad, and from Tinejdad to Erfoud, but you will not be able to do much around here without your own transport. Driving to or from the Drâa Valley there's a road that runs east–west through the empty quarter south of the Jebel Sarho, connecting with the Drâa Valley between Agdz and Zagora.

Erfoud

Erfoud is a mostly French-built administrative town that, on account of having the most mod cons within striking distance of the photogenic Merzouga dunes, also has connections with the film business. It's a desultory sort of place – a frontier town with a gridlike street pattern and ideas above its station. But it's where you'll find essential facilities such as banks and a pharmacy, and there's a Sunday souk and an October date festival.

The one unique local item is a kind of fossil-rich black marble. This is polished up and used for tabletops and bar counters. By another process, the stone is sculpted to bring the fossils into relief on everything from ashtrays to washbasins. The results are mostly quite kitsch, as can be seen at **Manar Marbre** (035 57 81 25, www.manarmarbre.com, open 8am-noon, 2-6pm daily) a few hundred metres up the Tinehrir road. At the showroom here you can see or buy every imaginable kind of black marble item and look round the not very interesting factory.

Erfoud has a clutch of old-school four- and five-star hotels, suitable for housing film crews and correspondingly overpriced. The best is probably the **Hotel Salam** (035 57 66 65, fax 035 57 81 92, double 560dh), which has a pool, gardens, bar and sauna and is just about the first thing you'll see arriving from the Dadès – it's at the junction of Erfoud's main street and the road from Tinerhir. Six kilometres to the north of Erfoud is the Spanish-owned **Kasbah Xaluca** (035 57 84 50, fax 055 57 84 49, www.xaluca.com, 625dh double), a walled enclosure around a central pool with a pizza restaurant. The rooms have air-conditioning and bathrooms with sculpted fossil fittings. DJs play nightly in the Tent Royale, and there's every kind of excursion, trek, rental, hike, adventure and experience on offer. It's the Tafilelt's stag-party destination.

Rissani

Around 20 kilometres (12 miles) south of Erfoud, Rissani (**photo** *p213*) is an untidy village with a small modern central core, and *ksour* and kasbahs scattered throughout its extensive palmeraie. This is the home town of the Alaouite dynasty, which started feeling expansive in the early 17th century and had taken power by 1664.

Before that it was the site of Sijilmassa, founded in the mid eighth century by Berber heretics. At the heart of such a fertile oasis, and at the nexus of trade routes connecting West Africa to Morocco and Europe – and Morocco to the rest of North Africa and the Middle East – Sijilmassa quickly became a great trading centre and dominated the South for five centuries. Huge caravans would set out from here heading first for the Saharan salt mines in what today is Mali, then to the Niger region, where salt was traded for gold, then back across the Sahara laden with gold, ebony, ostrich feathers and slaves. Meanwhile, coins from Sijilmassa have been found as far away as Akabar in Jordan.

The place was never the same after the Portuguese opened up maritime routes to sub-Saharan Africa, and Sijilmassa long ago sank back into the sands. Such ruins as there are can be found on the north side of Rissani, near the outlying hamlet of **El-Mansouria**, where a gate known locally as the Bab Errih probably dates from the Merenid period. (You can ask for directions at the nearby Hotel Kasbah Asmaa, three kilometres – two miles – towards Erfoud.) The other faint traces of Sijilmassa are really only of academic interest. A few archaeological finds are on display at the small and not very interesting museum of the **Centre d'Étude et de Recherches Alaouite** (open 8.30am-6.30pm Mon-Fri) on the north side of Rissani's main square – basically a handful of dusty pots. It also hosts temporary exhibitions.

The ancestors of the current ruling Alaouite dynasty in Morocco settled in the region in the 13th century. Off the road running towards Merzouga, just after the village peters out into the desert, there are signposts directing you to the **Mausoleum of Moulay Ali Cherif**, founder of the dynasty, who was buried here in 1640. It's a modern building, an older one having been destroyed by flash flooding in the mid 1950s, and entrance is forbidden to non-Muslims.

Beyond the mausoleum is a signposted turn on to the **Circuit Touristique**, a 21-kilometre (13 mile) loop around the *ksour* and kasbahs of the palmeraie. The first point of interest is the 19th-century **Ksar Akbar**, once used to house disgraced members of the Alaouite family. About two kilometres (one mile) further on is the grand **Ksar Ouled Abdelhalim**, built for Moulay Hassan's brother around the turn of the 20th century and touted as the 'Alhambra of the Tafilelt'. Its remains include imposing towers, cloistered courtyards and ornate gateways that do give a flavour of former grandeur. The whole circuit takes in a number of other kasbahs and *ksours* – some in an advanced state of erosion, others still housing a substantial part of Rissani's population.

Hump-backed holidays

Here's a challenge. In the region of Erg Chebbi, or on the lower reaches of the Drâa Valley road, see if you can find anyone at all who *can't* help arrange you a camel trek. It sometimes seems as if every last hotelier, guide, waiter, shopkeeper or random pedestrian is touting some kind of hump-backed experience. Since the 1990s, the camel-trek business has been booming to the point that extra camels were brought in from Mali.

Camels aren't native to the region; they were introduced from Asia around 2,000 years ago. The 'ship of the desert' is a remarkable beast. Camels can last up to seven days with little or no food or water and, when they do drink, slurp up 20 gallons (91 litres) in ten minutes. They can carry huge loads, their hide is used to make tents, and their dung can be used as fuel for fires even without being dried.

It was these special talents that made trans-Saharan trade routes possible. That trade is now long gone. You do sometimes see small camel trains moving stuff around within the bigger oases, and there are still some genuine nomads knocking about between the smaller ones, but the only volume item camels carry into the desert these days is tourists.

And why not? You didn't come this far just to sit in a hotel. And while oases are cool, a taste of the desert's shattering stillness is what's needed to complete the experience. The camel is the only authentic way to get it.

They're easy enough to ride. It's a small surprise when you first clamber aboard and the beast stands up, rocking you forward and back as it hoists you disconcertingly high. But after that it's steady going, if a little jolting on a downhill stretch.

Camel treks can involve anything from a sandy sleepover to a fearsome 14-day lurch between Merzouga and M'hamid. Most hotels have their own permanent encampments out in the dunes, and a night in one of these offers the quickest desert fix. You'll typically find a horseshoe arrangement of semi-permanent structures – often wood draped with sackcloth to look like a tent – with carpets spread out to cover the sand. While you watch a desert sunset, your guides will be preparing tagines. After eating, get them to turn off the generator so you can hear the silence, and gaze into the clearest night sky you've ever seen.

Camel treks cost around 300dh per person per day, with trimmings negotiable. Forget it between April and September, when the heat is just too intense. The trek organisers below have good reputations and speak English. They also do 4x4 excursions at around 1,200dh per day.

Adventures With Ali

Nomad Palace, Merzouga (061 56 36 11/fax 055 57 79 50/www.adventureswithali.com).
No credit cards.
Ali Mouni can sort everything from a three-hour ride and a night at an oasis in the dunes, to tailor-made treks accommodating specialist interests. His brother Hassan has a camel called Jimi Hendrix, and was Hillary Clinton's camel-handler when she came this way.

Sahara Services

Next to Restaurant Dune d'Or, M'Hamid (061 77 67 66/ www.saharaservices.info).
No credit cards.
Abdelkhalek Benalila organises a variety of treks into the dunes around M'Hamid and can offer all-in deals that include transport to and from Marrakech, a night at the Dar Azawad and camels out to Erg Chigaga and what they call the 'Sacred Oasis'.

The High Atlas & Sahara

If you carry along the Merzouga road past the Mausoleum turn-off and take the next left, the first big, intact structure on the right is the 19th-century **Ksar El-Fida**. Formerly an Alouite residence, in May 2005 it was opened as a museum by Prince Moulay Rachid (www.museeksarelfida.org). There's a reasonably interesting collection of rugs, chests, swords and costumes from the region, and in late May it's one of several venues for the annual **Festival des Musiques de Desert** (www.festivaldudesert.ma).

Back downtown, Rissani has a lively souk on Sunday, Tuesday and Thursday, drawing people from all over the area to buy and sell everything from dates to doorknobs. There's also an animal market behind it, with donkeys, sheep and camels on sale. Souk days are good for people-watching, and there are some strategically placed cafés with terraces, but after that, once you've done the crap museum there's not much else to see.

We wouldn't recommend staying in Rissani, but if you do, the **Hotel Kasbah Asmaa** (035 77 40 83, fax 055 57 54 94, 400dh double) is certainly the best place, just north of the village, with comfortable but unremarkable rooms, and a pool set among gardens. There aren't many eating options, though on market days you'll find a tagine or two on sale around the colonnaded souk.

Merzouga

Until recently the road ran out at Rissani and proceeding to Merzouga and the dunes of Erg Chebbi involved setting off across 30 kilometres (20 miles) of piste. Now there's good paved road to Merzouga village and beyond to Taouz near the Algerian border.

There's nothing much at Merzouga itself but squat, flat-roofed houses, a few general stores, some extremely basic café-hotels, and a couple of carpet dealers. The real attraction here are the dunes looming over to the east of the road and to the north of the village. About 27 kilometres (17 miles) from north to south and eight kilometres (five miles) from east to west, **Erg Chebbi** is a huge, shifting expanse of pink sand that looks exactly how the desert always looks in the movies – probably because many of them were shot right here. But the celluloid image doesn't quite prepare you for the precise beauty of the sand, its contours and peaks picked out by shadow, its colours shifting from pink to gold against a backdrop of clear blue sky and particularly vivid at either dawn or sunset.

But it's not the world's quietest piece of desert. This area has long been a big tourist attraction. Around two dozen hotels nudge up to the western edge of the sands, and in the late afternoon there are both tourists and locals running around on quads and motorbikes, as well as camel-trekking trains setting off to overnight at the small oasis that lies out of sight among the dunes. *See p215* **Humpbacked holidays**.

Camels aren't the only wildlife here. Birders should look out for Egyptian nightjars, fulvous chatterers and blue-cheeked bee-eaters. Best of all, however, is when there's been enough rainfall for a shallow seasonal lake to appear to the north-west of the village, usually in late spring, which sometimes attracts large flocks of pink flamingos – a particularly exotic sight out here in the arid wilderness.

Where to stay & eat

There are hotels dotted all along the western fringes of the dunes, and getting to the more northerly of these involves a rattle across bumpy piste from the road between Rissani and Merzouga. Individual establishments are well signposted. The only electricity comes from generators, so expect no power late at night or in the middle of the day.

All the hotels sell half-board, which makes sense around here as there aren't any cafés or restaurants. The **Auberge Kasbah**

Derkaoua (025 57 71 40, www.auberge
derkaoua.com, 1,100dh double incl dinner,
closed Jan, June-Aug), the northernmost hotel
along the fringes of the sand, was the first
around here, established in the late 1980s,
and it remains probably the best place to stay.
Set in its own small oasis, it has an assortment
of rooms and bungalows, a bar and restaurant
serving good French Moroccan food, a
swimming pool, tennis court, and its own
desert encampment not far away. You'll
sometimes hear it referred to as Chez Michel,
after the now deceased original owner.

If you're looking for something cheaper,
then the **Auberge du Sud** (061 21 61 66,
fax 035 57 86 31, www.aubergedusud.com,
300dh-440dh double incl dinner) is probably
a good bet. The cheap rooms are comfortable,
though without frills; while it's clear that some
thought has been put into the more expensive
ones. All rooms have showers, and some
were recently rebuilt after flash floods in
May 2006 washed a corner of the place clean
away. It fared better than the unfortunate
Riad Maria nearby, however, which was so
badly damaged by flood water that it is no
longer in business.

Erg Chebbi. *See p216.*

South of Merzouga

The road from Rissani continues all the way
to Taouz. About eight kilometres (five miles)
south of Merzouga is a gnawa village called
Khamlia, populated by the Berber-speaking
descendants of black African slaves. The sun-
blasted scattering of poor, flat-roofed *pisé*
houses feels like it could have been lifted
whole from the other side of the Sahara. As
with gnawa everywhere, music is one of the
locals' main pursuits and there are several
family bands here. You can sometimes find
them playing at the village's small cultural
centre, or you can locate the house of the family
Zaid on Khamlia's south-east side. Go in, say
hello, and settle on cushions in the room to the
left. Someone will bring you mint tea, and then
musicians in white robes will appear to play
and dance – drummers, castanet players and
a guy on a *gimbri*. It's excellent entertainment.
Tip them 50dh or buy their CD.

Sixteen kilometres (ten miles) further on, past
salt flats and dry lake beds, is the village of
Taouz. It's little more than a military outpost
by the Algerian border, but if you like being
stared at then this is the place.

The Drâa Valley

Barren beauty and garden groves.

The River Drâa begins where the Oued Dadès, Oued Mellah and other streams come together at Ouarzazate, and theoretically it runs all the way to the Atlantic Ocean, some 750 kilometres (465 miles) distant. But the last time it actually managed that feat was in 1989. More usually, it vanishes into the sand near M'Hamid, the town that marks the end of the Drâa Valley route, some ten kilometres (six miles) short of the Algerian border.

Beyond M'Hamid, all travel is by camel, and you start measuring journeys in days, not hours. But before that, the Drâa Valley between Agdz and Zagora is a heartbreakingly beautiful drive past palm groves, kasbahs and geology in the raw.

Buses run south from Ouarzazate with reasonable frequency as far as Zagora, but from there onwards services are spotty. *Grand taxis* run between the bigger villages and are the best way of getting around, but any kind of traffic gets sparse towards M'Hamid.

Drâa Valley

The arid, stony plains south of Ouarzazate are breathtakingly bleak – flatlands of brown rubble as far as the eye can see. The road does get quite dramatic, though, as it winds up through the layered rock formations of the **Jebel Sarho** to the 1,600 metre (5,250 foot) **Tizi-n-Tinififft pass**.

On the other side of the pass, **Agdz** (**photo** *p222*) is a small market town with a few carpet shops and a Thursday souk. The **Hotel Kissane** (024 84 30 44, fax 024 84 32 59, 300dh double) has a decent restaurant and a pool. If you're not depending on public transport, there are a couple of nearby kasbahs worth looking at: the turn-off for **Tamnougalk** is on the left roughly six kilometres (four miles) past Agdz and the kasbah is down a further three kilometres of piste; the more palatial Glaoui kasbah of **Timiderte** is eight kilometres (five miles) further south.

Agdz is overlooked by the 1,500-metre (4,921-foot) **Jebel Kissane** (**photo** *p220*), which looks like a single mountain until you draw abreast and realise it's actually one end of a long, brooding range. This is also where the Drâa Valley oasis begins. The next 100 kilometres (62 miles) is a long, verdant strip

cut into the desert. Every last scrap of fertile land is planted to grow olives, lemons, oranges, almonds, cereals and, most of all, dates, which are the valley's principal crop. Dates like lots of water and are sweetest and plumpest where it is hottest. A Moroccan saying has it that date palms have 'their heads in fire and their feet in water'. Dense with such trees, the Drâa Valley produces some of the finest dates in North Africa. Local kids stand by the road trying to sell boxes of them to passing motorists.

The road runs along the edge of the fertile area. On the other side, where nothing will grow, there are dozens of red-ochre *ksour* – fortified Berber villages. The last stretch runs through the Jebel Azlag gorge before emerging on to the palm-filled plain that is the Zagora oasis.

Zagora

Like Ouarzazate, present-day Zagora is a colonial creation, built by the French as a garrison and administrative centre. But the oasis has been inhabited for millennia. There's an 11th-century Almoravid fortress, built to guard the Sahara trade route, on top of Jebel Zagora at the end of town. And the Saadians would set out from around here at the beginning of the 16th century to conquer first Taroudant, then the rest of Morocco.

This trading history is acknowledged in the town's famous sign that shows a camel train and the legend 'Timbuktu, 52 days'. It used to stand outside the Préfecture, facing traffic as it left Zagora heading south. But a few years ago the original was replaced by a more modern, less characterful version, and moved over the road to an obscure position. Mad, given that the sign is this inauspicious town's only landmark. Local souvenir merchants sell versions of the old sign as paintings, plates and postcards.

The Préfecture is at one end of the long, dull main street – boulevard Mohammed V – and pretty much anything you might want to find is along here: post office, banks, cafés, army barracks. There's a large souk on Wednesdays and Sundays, at which the biggest section is given over to dates, compressed and packed into plastic sacks. Common types include the small, black

The stark and stony **Tizi-n-Tinififft pass**. *See p218.*

bousthami and the light, olive-coloured *bouzeki*. But the sweet *boufeggou* date, whose sugar content delays decomposition, is the most important – highly nutritious and edible for up to four years if dried properly.

There's not much else going on in Zagora proper and it isn't the friendliest of towns. Expect a fair bit of hassle from locals in search of a buck. Over the river, the adjacent hamlet of **Amazrou** is more interesting. The palmeraie is wonderfully dense and lush, and crossed by paths that afford a good stroll. The nearby **Kasbah des Juifs** was, as its name suggests, built and formerly inhabited by Jews. They all left in the 1960s and local Berbers now make silver jewellery by old Jewish methods, using clay moulds. You can visit them at work making fibulas, brooches worn by Berber women (one below the right shoulder if not married, one below each shoulder if married or divorced). Any local will guide you round the kasbah, which has underground passageways that are still partially inhabited.

Where to stay & eat

La Fibule du Drâa (024 84 73 18, fax 024 84 72 71, fibule@menara.ma, 450dh double) is a small and friendly complex built around a pool on the edge of the Amazrou palmeraie. It has a basic but decent restaurant and a bar. Nearby, among the palms (take the path along the irrigation canal), is the **Riad Lamane** (024 84 83 88, fax 024 84 83 89, www.riad lamane.com, 1200dh double including dinner). As its name suggests, this is a *maison d'hôte* with 14 rooms, each with a private bathroom. Decor verges on the kitsch but proportions are gratifyingly grand. There's an indoor restaurant or you can eat in the pretty garden by the small swimming pool. The **Riad Salam** (boulevard Mohammed V, 024 84 74 00 fax 024 84 75 51, www.salamhotelmaroc.com, 545dh double) is on the way into town and has big air-conditioned rooms, some with TV, as well as a pool and two restaurants. It's an efficient sort of place, but a bit lacking in character. The hotels have the best restaurants.

Tamegroute & Tinfou

Around 18 kilometres (11 miles) south of Zagora, the town of **Tamegroute** has long been an important religious centre. Its green-roofed *zaouia* (shrine) was founded in the 17th century and is headquarters of the Naciri Islamic brotherhood whose leaders, known as 'peacemakers of the desert' have traditionally been called upon to settle disputes between tribes or rival traders.

There's a *medersa* (Qur'anic school) along with the tomb of the Brotherhood's founder, a place of pilgrimage, but these are off-limits to non-Muslims. The main thing to see is the wonderful **library** (8am-3pm, 20dh donation), up a side street on the left of the main road. It was once much larger but there are still 4,000 volumes, carefully stored in glass-fronted cases, including an 11th-century gazelle-skin Qur'an as well as old books from as far afield as Egypt and Mali. The wizened librarian will sternly point out highlights: 'This Arab dictionary – Dictionary! History la ville de Fes – History! This Egyptian – Cairo! Cairo!!'

Drâa Valley.

Back by the minaret, there's also a cloistered courtyard that acts as a sanctuary for the infirm or mentally ill. People huddle in blankets, waiting for miracles or donations, or just for the next square meal. Around the corner on the left as you head south is a clutch of pottery shops selling cups, plates and tagines in the distinctive green glaze native to Tamegroute.

The same glaze is used for the green roof tiles on the nearby *zaouia*, as well as on mosques and royal buildings throughout Morocco.

About five kilometres (three miles) south of Tamegroute, at a place called **Tinfou**, is an isolated patch of sand dunes. It's only the size of a few football pitches, and you'll be sharing this Saharan experience with any

Who are the Tuaregs?

Here and there in southern Morocco, especially in the desert towns, you'll see people in bright blue robes, often accompanied by an indigo turban. This is the traditional outfit of the Tuareg, a nomadic Berber people often referred to as the 'Blue Men of the Sahara'.

Descendants of Berbers who once lived in what is now Libya, the Tuareg long ago decided they didn't care much for the Roman Empire, and moved southwards about 1,000 miles, deep into the central Sahara. There they adopted both the practice of camel nomadism and certain traditions of social organisation from the bedouin Arabs, who became their great rivals. For 2,000 years they controlled the five main trade routes that connected the cities south of the Sahara with the Mediterranean coast.

Despite resisting colonialism, they were eventually pacified by the French, and their tribal confederations were disbanded. Then, in the post-colonial period, the area they inhabited was carved up between Algeria, Mali, Libya, Niger and Burkina Faso. Now a people without a nation, their nomadic ways were disrupted by the new borders; increasing desertification made their life even harder. Many have now taken up farming or moved to the cities seeking work.

It was the Arabs who named them Tuareg, meaning 'forsaken by god'. But somewhere along the way, they became Islamised. Unlike most Muslims, though, they are a matrilinear people – and it's the men, not the women, who wear veils. They also have distinctive traditions in both jewellery and music. Tinariwen, the bluesmen of the Sahara, currently a big draw on the world music circuit, are a Tuareg band from Mali.

Like other Berbers, the Tuareg call themselves Imazighen, the 'free people', and it was they who kept alive the Tifinagh alphabet, now used to write Berber languages. It's a direct descendant of the ancient writing system of Numidia,

the Berber republic that once existed in what is now eastern Algeria and western Tunisia.

Despite the Tifinagh connection, most of the blue-robed folk in Morocco – like the man pictured below – are not Tuareg at all. Many Sahrawi, the descendants of nomadic Bedouins who inhabit the Western Sahara, wear similar blue dress. And some are Berbers dressing up for the tourists. Tuareg robes are favoured by guys touting camel rides everywhere from the dunes of Tinfou to the beaches of Essaouira.

The Tuareg identity remains strong. Like that of the Sahrawi, still at loggerheads with the Moroccan government over the ownership of Western Sahara, it is expressed in nationalist struggle against the countries that now control what were for so long their own desert lands.

The High Atlas & Sahara

Agdz. See p218.

number of tour groups, camel touts and kids trying to sell you animals made out of clay or palm leaves, but if you're not going all the way down to M'Hamid (*see below*) or across to Merzouga (*see p216*), this will be your only glimpse of desert sands.

M'Hamid

Beyond Tamegroute the road narrows and runs through mostly arid landscape for the next 70 kilometres (42 miles), crossing the barren **Jbel Bani** before coming back into oasis country at **Tagounite**. Before M'Hamid it's worth stopping off to see the small, private **museum** (open 6am-10pm, admission 15dh) in **Ouled Driss**. Follow the 'Musée' sign from the main road and a guide will pick you up. It's a beautiful 17th-century Berber house, once owned by the village chief, containing an exhibit of costumes, jewellery and tools. Above all, it's a cool place to lay back with the mint tea you'll be offered. Be careful on the uneven stairs, though – this is ankle-twisting territory.

M'Hamid is a tiny town that really does feel like the end of the line, fighting a losing battle against the sand. The locals, many of whom are Sahrawi, will stare like they've never seen a tourist before – although the entire town seems to be involved in the camel-trekking business (*see p215* **Hump-backed holidays**). You'll be beating away touts from the various agencies and turning down special deals for bivouacs at the 'Sacred Oasis' as soon as you step out of the car.

If you're not getting on a camel and swaying off to the sands of **Chigaga**, there isn't much to do, though the town is worth a stroll and a drive into the palmeraie is interesting. The Algerian border isn't far away; in the 1970s some of the kasbahs were destroyed by Polisario guerillas. Half the locals wear robes of Tuareg blue (men) or desert black (women) and the futuristic new Maroc Telecom public phones look odd among the tatty houses, sandy streets and shops selling chickens.

Where to stay & eat

Accommodation and dining in the town are basic, at best. The **Dunes d'Or** restaurant does simple meals (including some vegetarian choices) for 60dh, and has a couple of not very appealing rooms (but with shower) in the back, charged at 70dh a double. The **Hotel Iriqui** (024 88 57 99, www.iriqui.com, 180dh double) is better, but not much.

The best place in the area is **Dar Azawad** (024 84 87 30, www.darazawad.com, 1,000dh-1800dh double incl dinner) a French-owned *maison d'hôte* among the palms about four kilometres (2.5 miles) back towards Ouled Driss. In walled grounds there are 15 cool and tasteful bungalow rooms furnished with Moroccan items and fabrics, as well as simpler, tented rooms at a cheaper rate. (The tented rooms have showers en suite.) There's also a pool with bar, a hammam, dining room and a good French-Moroccan kitchen. Owner Vincent Jacquet creates a good atmosphere. The only problem is, you have to like dogs.

Directory

Features

Directory

Getting Around

Arriving & leaving

By air

Marrakech's international airport (Aéroport Marrakech Menara) is located just six kilometres (four miles) west of the city. From the airport forecourt to the city centre is a ten-minute drive. The airport information desk (9am-9pm daily) is in the check-in area. There are banks offering currency exchange in the arrivals hall, open 8am-6pm daily, plus two ATMs. For flight information, call 024 44 78 65 or 024 44 79 10.

Taxis wait outside the arrivals building. In a *petit taxi* (*see p225* **Taxis**) the official fare to anywhere in the Medina or Guéliz is 60dh (to the Palmeraie 120dh) but drivers usually demand more. Most will accept payment in dollars, euros or pounds at the equivalent dirham rate.

AIRLINES

Most airlines have their offices in Casablanca. An increasing number of budget carriers now fly to Morocco from Europe.

British Airways

Avenue des FAR, Casablanca (022 47 30 23). **Open** 8.30am-12.30pm, 2.30-6.30pm Mon-Sat. **Credit** AmEx, DC, MC, V.
The main British Airways office in Morocco is in Casablanca; you must call it to confirm all flights. The British Airways office located in Terminal 2 at the Airport is a sales-only agent. They cannot be reached by phone and the office is only open during BA flight times.

Royal Air Maroc (RAM)

197 avenue Mohammed V, Guéliz (024 42 55 00). **Open** 8.30am-12.15pm, 2.30-7pm Mon-Fri. **Credit** AmEx, DC, MC, V. **Map** p254 B2.

There is a 24-hour call centre (090 00 08 00) for flight reconfirmation, flight information and reservations. RAM continually changes and cancels flights at short notice so reconfirming is a must.

Atlas-blue

www.atlas-blue.com

EasyJet

www.easyjet.com

Ryanair

www.ryanair.com

Thomsonfly

www.thomsonfly.com

By rail

Trains are operated by the national railway company **ONCF** (024 44 77 68, www.oncf.org.ma). The train station is on the western edge of Guéliz, on avenue Hassan II. Marrakech is the southernmost terminus of two lines, both of which pass through Casablanca and Rabat; some trains then continue north to Tangier, others north-east to Oujda on the Algerian border via Meknes and Fès. A swarm of taxis meets each incoming train; make sure to get a *petit taxi* and not a more expensive big Mercedes. The fare into central Guéliz is 5dh-6dh; to the Medina 10dh. Alternatively, you can wait for bus No.3 or 8, which pass by the station en route to the place de Foucault for Jemaa El Fna.

By bus

The *gare routière* is just beyond the Medina walls at Bab Doukkala. Most long-distance buses terminate here, including those operated by national carrier **CTM** (024 43 39 33). Both the central Medina and Guéliz are walkable from

the station; a petit taxi will cost 5dh-6dh, or catch a local bus for place de Foucault (Jemaa El Fna). There is also a CTM office (which sells tickets) in Guéliz on boulevard Mohammed Zerktouni, a few doors along from the Cinema la Colisée, where buses also stop.

The superior buses run by **Supratours** (024 43 55 25), to and from Essaouira, Agadir, Laayoune and Dakhla only. They pull up at the forecourt of the company's own ticket terminus, next to the railway station (see above). Essaouira is a popular destination and the Supratour buses fill up fast, so it's wise to purchase your tickets at least a day in advance (for further details, *see p188*).

Public transport

Marrakech has a limited city bus network radiating from the Medina out to the suburbs. Other than along avenue Mohammed V, no buses operate within the confines of the city walls, where streets are prohibitively narrow. Few local bus services are of much use to visitors. The possible exceptions are those services that run between the Medina and Guéliz, which is a fairly long walk, but it's much less hassle (and still relatively inexpensive) to take a taxi.

Buses

City buses (024 43 39 33) are regular coaches with no air-conditioning. They charge a flat fee of 3dh payable to the driver. Beware: the drivers never have any change. All the following buses leave from place de Foucault, opposite the Hotel de Foucault, 100m west of the Jemaa El Fna:

Local bus routes

No.1 to Guéliz along avenue Mohammed V.
No.2 to Bab Doukkala for the *gare routière*.
No.3 to Douar Laskar via avenue Mohammed V, avenue Hassan II and the train station.
No.4 to Daoudiate (a northern suburb) by avenue Mohammed V.
No.8 to Douar Laskar via avenue Mohammed V, avenue Moulay Hassan and the train station.
No.10 to boulevard de Safi via Bab Doukkala and the *gare routière*.
No.11 to the airport via avenue de la Menara and the Menara Gardens.
No.14 to the train station.

Taxis

Taxis are plentiful and easy to find, whatever the time of day or night. They are also cheap enough that it makes little sense bothering with buses. The standard ride is known as a **petit taxi** (lettered on the side of the car as such) and is usually a little khaki-coloured four-door Fiat, Simca or similar. By law, they can carry a maximum of three passengers. Drivers are reluctant to use the meter. Asking for them to switch it on sometimes works, otherwise it's just a question of knowing the right fare. From Jemaa El Fna to Guéliz costs around 6dh; from Jemaa El Fna to the Palmeraie around 40dh. Expect to pay about 50 per cent more after about 8pm (9pm in summer).

Grand taxis (again, lettered as such) are bigger cars that can squeeze in six people and are normally more expensive. They loiter outside hotels and the railway station. Avoid them, unless you are a group of four or more or are travelling long distance: some grand taxis operate like minibuses running fixed routes to outlying suburbs, villages and towns, and even as far as Essaouira and Agadir.

Note, it is mandatory for front-seat passengers to wear seat belts in a taxi.

Driving

A car can be useful for venturing out of the city, especially for trips to the south, but unless you are a resident (making shopping trips, running the kids to school) a car is of limited use within Marrakech itself. For short-term visitors, taxis are cheap and plentiful and easily hired by the day for around 250dh in and around the city; ask your hotel for help finding a reputable driver.

Vehicles drive on the right in Morocco. The French rule of giving priority to traffic from the right is observed at roundabouts and junctions: in other words cars coming on to a roundabout have priority over those already on it. Speed limits are 40km/h (25mph) in urban areas, 100km/h (62mph) on main roads, 120km/h (74mph) on autoroutes. There are on-the-spot fines for speeding and other traffic offences. It is compulsory to wear seatbelts.

Be very wary when driving at night as cyclists and moped riders often have no lights. Neither do sheep, goats and pedestrians, and street lighting can be poor. In the case of an accident, report to the nearest *gendarmerie* to obtain a written report, otherwise insurance will be invalid.

Car hire

To hire a car, you must be over 21, have a full current driving licence and carry a passport or national identity card. Rental isn't cheap; daily rates with a local agency start at about 400dh (around £25/$50 at the time of writing) for a Fiat Palio, Citroen Saxo or Peugeot 205 with unlimited mileage. A Toyota Corolla kicks in at

about 700dh (£44/$86) per day, a Toyota Avencis at 950dh (£60/£118). At the internationals like Avis, Budget or Hertz, expect to pay about 25 per cent more.

The drawback with many of the local hire firms is the back-up service – cars may be ancient and unreliable, breakdown support lacking and replacement vehicles may not always be forthcoming.

Be aware that payments made in Morocco by credit card often incur an additional five per cent fee. This is one of several reasons why it works out cheaper to arrange your car rental in advance through the travel agent booking your flight or via the internet.

The major companies allow you to rent a car in one city and return it in another. Rental cars in Morocco are delivered empty of petrol and returned empty. Almost all agencies will deliver cars to your hotel and arrange pick-up at no extra charge but this service must be booked in advance.

If you are heading south over the mountains, remember that you are responsible for any damage if you take a car off-road or along unsuitable tracks. Four-wheel drives, such as a Toyota Landcruisers, are available from most hire companies and start at around 1,200dh (£75/$147) per day.

Always Car *15 rue Imam Chafi, Kawkab Centre, Guéliz (061 19 31 29)*. **Open** 8am-noon, 2.30-7pm daily. **Credit** MC, V. **Map** p254 B3. Always Car can organise anything from a two-door Fiat to a 4x4 to a minibus. Also has offices in Casablanca and Agadir, so cars can be dropped off there. English-speaking drivers also available.

Avis *137 avenue Mohammed V, Guéliz (024 43 25 25/fax 024 43 12 65/www.avis.com/avisrak@iam. net)*. **Open** 8am-7pm Mon-Sat; 8am-noon Sun. **Credit** AmEx, DC, MC, V. **Map** p254 B2.
Other locations: Aéroport Marrakech Menara (024 43 12 65). **Open** 8am-noon, 2-11pm Mon-Sat; 8am-noon Sun.

Directory

Budget *68 boulevard Mohammed Zerktouni, Guéliz (024 43 11 80/ www.budget rentacar.com).* **Open** 8am-noon, 2.30-7pm Mon-Fri; 9am-noon, 3-6pm Sat; 9am-noon Sun. **Credit** AmEx, MC, V. **Map** p254 A6.
Other locations: Aéroport Marrakech Menara (024 43 88 75). **Open** 7am-10pm daily.

Concorde Cars *154 avenue Mohammed V, Guéliz (024 43 11 16/fax 024 44 61 29/concordecar @iam.ma).* **Open** 8.30am-7.30pm Mon-Sat. **Credit** AmEx, DC, MC, V. **Map** p254 B2.

Europcar *63 boulevard Mohammed Zerktouni, Guéliz (024 43 12 28/ fax 024 31 02 30/www.europ car.com).* **Open** 8.30am-noon, 2.30-7pm Mon-Sat. **Credit** AmEx, MC, V. **Map** p254 B2.
Other locations: Aéroport Marrakech Menara (024 43 77 18). Open to meet incoming flights.

Fathi Cars *183 avenue Mohammed V, Guéliz (024 43 17 63).* **Open** 8.30am-12.30pm, 2.30-7pm Mon-Sat. **Credit** AmEx, DC, MC, V. **Map** p254 B2.

Hertz *154 avenue Mohammed V, Guéliz (024 43 13 94/www.hertz. com).* **Open** 8.30am-12.30pm, 2-6.30pm Mon-Sat. **Credit** AmEx, DC, MC, V. **Map** p254 B2.
Other locations: Aéroport Marrakech Menara (024 44 72 30). **Open** 8.30am-12.30pm, 2-6.30pm daily. Club Med (061 36 75 37). **Open** 9-11.30am, 5-7.30pm Mon-Fri, Sun.

Majestic Locations *21 rue Tarek Ibn Ziad, Guéliz (024 43 65 00/ fax 024 43 43 92/majesticloc @yahoo.fr).* **Open** 8.30am-12.30pm, 2.30-7pm Mon-Sat. **Credit** MC, V. **Map** p254 B2.

Parking

Wherever there's space to park vehicles you'll find a *gardien de voitures*. They're licensed by the local authority to look after parked vehicles and should be tipped about 10dh (the local rate is 2dh during the day, 5dh at night, but as a visitor you're not going to get away with paying that). Street-side parking is easy enough in the New City (look for the orange-painted kerbs) but troublesome in the Medina: the main parking spots are opposite the Préfecture de la Medina or on rue Ibn Rachid. Take note: red and white kerb markings mean no parking.

Repairs & services

The agents below should be able to help get you back on the road.

Garage Ourika

66 avenue Mohammed V, Guéliz (024 44 82 66). **Open** 8.30am-noon, 2.30-6.30pm Mon-Sat. **No credit cards**. **Map** p254 A1.
BMW, Fiat, Honda and Toyota specialist.

Garage Renault

route de Casablanca, Semlalia (024 30 10 08). **Open** 8am-noon, 2-6.30pm Mon-Sat. **No credit cards**.
Renault specialist.

Cycling

It's not quite China but humble bicycles, mopeds and motorbikes are a hugely popular mode of local transport – despite the inconvenience of widespread potholes, choking bus fumes and the perils of having to share the road with the average lunatic Marrakchi motorist. If you fancy taking to the streets on two wheels, try one of the places listed below for bike rentals.

In addition, there are also a couple of hire outfits at the northern end of **rue Beni Marine**, the small street running parallel to and between rue Bab Agnaou and rue Moulay Ismail. Guys with bikes for hire can also be found on the central grassy verge outside **Hotel Imperial Borj** (5 avenue Echouhada) and across from the **Hotel El Andalous** on avenue de Paris, both in Hivernage, and at the **Hotel de Foucault** (off place de Foucault) in the Medina, though none are affiliated to the hotels mentioned. In Guéliz try the **Hotel Toulousain** on rue Tarek ibn Ziad behind the old Marché Central. Prices are roughly 20dh per hour with negotiable daily rates.

Note that most rental places do not offer helmets or any kind of lock so if you want to leave the bike or

scooter anywhere it'll have to be with a gardien de voitures (*see above* **Parking**). Before taking a bike, check the gears and brakes as servicing is not always up to much.

Action Sports Loisirs

1 boulevard Yacoub El Mansour, apartment No.4, Guéliz (tel/fax 024 43 09 31/mobile 061 240 145). **Open** 8am-7pm Tue-Sun. **Bicycle rental** 150dh for 2hrs; 400dh per half-day. **No credit cards**. **Map** p254 A2.
Action Sports Loisirs has the best bikes in town, both in terms of quality of machines and attention to maintenance. Owner Alain rents bikes for all kinds of terrain, and also organises excursions for 800dh (including lunch and transport).

Marrakech Motos

31 avenue Abdelkarim El Khattabi, Guéliz (024 44 83 59/mobile 061 31 64 13). **Open** 9am-10pm daily. **Scooter rental** 250dh-300dh per day, depending on model. **No credit cards**. **Map** p254 A2.
Also known as Chez Jamal Boucetta.

Salah Eddine

18 rue de la Recette, Medina (061 87 31 45). **Open** 9am-9pm daily. **Bicycle rental** 10dh per hr; 100dh per day. **No credit cards**. **Map** p252 C6.
Salah Eddine operates from a basement room just around the corner from the Hotel Galia, off rue Bab Agnaou.

Walking

Walking is absolutely the only way to get around the Medina, which is where most visitors spend the bulk of their time. It's a compact area, perfect for exploring on foot. Many of the streets and alleys are too narrow for anything bigger than a motorcycle or donkey cart anyway.

Be sure to pack a pair of comfortable, flat-soled shoes because the streets in the Medina are rarely paved and full of ruts and potholes. Visitors coming any time from November to April should bring cheap and/or waterproof footwear because the slightest bit of rain turns the whole of the Medina to a mudbath.

Resources

Addresses

In the newer quarters of the city, streets are well signposted in both French and Arabic. This is not the case in the Medina: major streets do have dual-script signs but the majority of smaller alleyways have signs in Arabic only, or simply no signs at all. Most of the time, when looking for a specific street or place, the only option is to ask the locals. If the person questioned doesn't know, they'll often try to find someone who does, and you'll probably end up with an escort.

When addressing an envelope, write the house number after the street name and place the postcode before the city, as in the following:

Monsieur Ledoux
avenue Mohammed V, 57
Marrakech-Medina
1050 Marrakech

Business

Casablanca is the country's economic centre, Rabat is the political capital and Marrakech is a modestly sized provincial city with a massive tourist trade. Big business is generally absent from the local scene, meaning that facilities for the powerbroker are few. If you are here doing business, don't expect deals to be closed in a single meeting, partly because of red tape, partly because haggling and hedging are standard practice, but also because getting to the point is often considered rude. Neither should you expect anyone to show up on time; why hurry when, as the local saying has it, 'A chance encounter is worth a thousand appointments'?

Business centres

Marrakech's few business centres are all in the large five-star hotels, including the Kempinski Mansour (024 33 91 00) and Le Meridien N'Fis (024 33 94 00). For others, *see p39* **The chain gang**. However, such services as there are tend to be reserved for guests. Faxes may be sent from some *téléboutiques* (*see p234* **Telephones**) and most cybercafés (*see p231*) will offer word-processing and printing.

Conferences

Marrakech has a fully equipped conference centre in the Palais de Congrès, which is managed by the **Hotel Kempinski Mansour** (024 33 91 00). Most other five stars also have more modest conference facilities.

Couriers

Within Marrakech, businesses use *petits taxis*. Note the number of the taxi (painted on the door) so if there's any problem later the police can track down the cabbie through the drivers' register – although this is rarely ever necessary. Pay as you would as a passenger. The following international couriers have offices in Marrakech:

DHL
133 avenue Abdelkarim El-Khattabi, Guéliz (024 43 76 47/www.dhl.com). **Open** 8am-12.30pm, 2.30-6.30pm Mon-Fri; 9am-1pm Sat. **Credit** MC, V. **Map** p254 A2.

FedEx
113 avenue Abdelkarim El-Khattabi, Guéliz (024 44 82 57). **Open** 8.15am-12.30pm, 2.15-6.30pm Mon-Fri; 8.30am-1pm Sat. **No credit cards. Map** p254 A2.

Consumer

There are no such things as consumer rights. You haggled for it and set your own price, in the course of which you examined the object in question. However, if you do have a genuine grievance, take it to the tourist police, who are usually good at settling matters promptly and usually in the favour of the visitor.

Customs

The following allowances apply to people bringing duty-free goods into Morocco: 400g

---

Travel advice

For up-to-date information on travel to a specific country – including the latest news on safety and security, health issues, local laws and customs – contact your home country government's department of foreign affairs. Most have websites with useful advice for travellers.

Australia
www.smartraveller.gov.au

New Zealand
www.safetravel.govt.nz

Canada
www.voyage.gc.ca

UK
www.fco.gov.uk/travel

Republic of Ireland
http://foreignaffairs.gov.ie

USA
http://travel.state.gov

Directory

of tobacco, 200 cigarettes or 50 cigars and 1 litre of spirits. The cap on foreign currency is set at €4,500 (£3,000), otherwise it must be declared upon entering the country.

Moroccan customs officials can be funny about electronic and photographic equipment. If it's just one or two items, obviously for your personal use, then you should be OK, but if they spot significant amounts of camera gear or a laptop, for example, you may have it written into your passport. Anything that can't be presented on leaving will be assumed to have been 'sold' and liable to a heavy duty tax. If the property has been stolen, you need police documentation to prove it.

Pets may be taken into Morocco as long as they have a medical certificate no more than ten days old and an anti-rabies certificate no more than six months old.

Disabled

Marrakech is tough on anyone with a mobility problem. Roads and pavements are uneven and pitted, and frequently rutted. Routes through the Medina are narrow and crowded and it's necessary to be nimble. Outside of the bigger hotels (the Mamounia, the Royal Mirage Marrakech and the Sofitel all lay claim to disabled facilities), few buildings make concessions to the disabled. In smaller hotels and riads, while facilities may be lacking, it's a given that people will try to make your stay as easy as possible but steps, if not stairs, are pretty much unavoidable. Problems may be compounded by the fact that banisters do not exist in traditional Moroccan homes, and you'll not find them in most riads and small hotels.

Drugs

Morocco is the world's largest cannabis producer and most of it is exported. Discreet use is tolerated and a significant minority still consume the stuff. It's smoked as *kif* (grass) in a long pipe called a *sebsi* or less traditionally as hash mixed with tobacco in European-style joints. It's also eaten in the notoriously hallucinogenic jam- or cake-like form of *majoun*.

However, Moroccan law maintains stiff penalties for sale or consumption so be careful. Some dealers double as police informers, angling for a share of the *baksheesh* you'll later pay to buy yourself out of trouble.

There are 60 or so Europeans in Moroccan jails and nearly all of them have been banged up for cannabis-related offences. To reduce the risk of joining them, follow these guidelines:

● Avoid street dealers. If you don't know any locals, the best bet is a younger souk stallholder who might have a bit under the counter. Don't ask. Wait for their approach.

● Never buy more than a small amount for personal use, and don't travel with any in your possession.

Electricity

Morocco operates on 220V AC. Plugs are of the European two-pin variety. If you forget to bring an adapter, they're available from electrical shops for around 25dh. Visitors from the USA will need to bring a transformer if they intend to use appliances from home.

Embassies & consulates

There's just the one diplomatic office in Marrakech, and that's the French one, of course. As a reminder of colonial days past, it occupies the most prominent site in the city, next to the Koutoubia Mosque. Its high blank wall fringes the place de Foucault. You'll find other embassies and consulates in Rabat and Casablanca.

British Consulate

17 boulevard de la Tour Hassan, Rabat (037 72 96 96/fax 037 70 45 31/www.britain.org.ma/ consular/services.html). **Open** 8.30am12.30pm, 1.30-4pm Mon-Thur; 8.30am-12.30pm Fri.
Also handles Irish and New Zealand consular affairs. In the event of an emergency in Marrakech, contact Residence Jaib (55 boulevard Mohammed Zerktouni, 024 43 60 78, mobile 061 14 84 44). Britain also has consulates in Casablanca and Tangier.

Canadian Consulate

13 rue Jaafar Es Sadiq, Agdal, Rabat (037 68 74 00/fax 037 67 21 87).
Also handles Australian consular affairs.

French Consulate

Rue Ibn Khaldun, Medina, Marrakech (024 38 82 00). **Open** 8.30-11.45am Mon-Fri. **Map** p252 B6.

US Consulate

2 avenue de Marrakech, Rabat (037 76 22 65/fax 037 76 56 61/ www.usembassy.ma). **Open** 8.30am-5.30pm Mon-Fri.
The US also has a consulate in Casablanca (8 Boulevard Moulay Youssef, 022 26 45 50).

Emergencies

Police 19
Fire service 15 or 024 43 04 15
Ambulance service 024 44 37 24

Health

Morocco has no reciprocal health care agreements with other countries, so taking out your own medical insurance is advisable. No vaccinations are required for Marrakech, although inoculation against hepatitis is a good idea. Travellers commonly complain of stomach upsets, but this is more often due to the change in diet than food poisoning. Bring along anti-diarrhoeal capsules, such as Imodium, and avoid tap water: bottled water is inexpensive and available at all restaurants and cafés.

Should you become ill, be warned: the Moroccan healthcare system is ropey. While good doctors can be found and pharmacies are surprisingly well stocked and knowledgeably staffed, for anyone afflicted with serious illness the best route to take is the one leading straight to the airport and home.

Contraception & abortion

You can purchase condoms as well as birth control pills over the counter at any pharmacy. If you aren't using birth control, bring an emergency morning-after pill kit with you if you think you might need one, as this is not available in Morocco.

Abortion is not openly discussed. It is unavailable to unmarried women; any doctor practising an abortion on an unmarried woman can be arrested and disbarred. However, married women who already have children seem to be able to have abortions discreetly without any problems. For non-Moroccans, contact an abortion clinic in Spain.

Dentists

Dental care in Marrakech is of a reasonable standard – discounting the wizened old guys on Jemaa El Fna with the trays of pliers and loose false teeth (although an otherwise perfectly sensible English friend of ours swears one of these guys cured her abscess). Offices and equipment may not be state of the art, but the practitioners are usually competent. However, getting appointments with the best guys isn't always easy.

Docteur Youssef Dassouli

Résidence Asmae, apartment No.6, 1st floor, above Pâtisserie Yum Yum, route de Targa (024 43 53 03, emergency contact 064 90 65 14). **Office hours** 9am-noon, 3.30-7pm Mon-Fri. **No credit cards.** English spoken.

Doctors

There's no shortage of doctors and specialists in Marrakech, but the trick is to find a good one. We can recommend the following:

Docteur Samir Bellmezouar

Polyclinique du Sud, rue Yougoslavie, Guéliz (061 24 32 27). **Office hours** *Emergency team* 24hrs daily. **No credit cards. Map** p250 A2. Doesn't speak English but does make house calls.

Doctor Béatrice Peiffer Lahrichi

Résidence Lafrasouk, 1st floor, 10 rue Oued El-Makhazine, Guéliz (024 43 53 29). **Office hours** 9am-12.30pm, 3.30-6.30pm Mon-Fri; 9am-12.30pm Sat. **No credit cards. Map** p254 B3. French doctor (speaks no English) working out of a very modern surgery with full lab facilities.

Doctor Frederic Reitzer

Above Café Zohra, Immeuble Moulay Youssef, 4th floor, rue de la Liberté, Guéliz (024 43 95 62/emergency contact 061 17 38 03). **Office hours** 9.30am-noon, 3.30-7pm Mon-Fri; 10am-noon Sat. **No credit cards. Map** p254 B2. Speaks English.

Docteur El-Oufir (gynaecologist)

125 avenue Mohammed V, Guéliz (024 43 18 28). **Office hours** 8.30am-1pm, 3.30-7pm Mon-Fri; 8.30am-1pm Sat. **No credit cards. Map** p254 B2. Speaks English.

Hospitals

The only place to go is the Polyclinique du Sud. This private clinic is frequented by the expat community and used by most insurance companies if their clients experience problems. Avoid public hospitals, where the severe lack of personnel, equipment and funding is shocking.

Polyclinique du Sud

rue Yougoslavie, Guéliz (024 44 79 99). **Open** 24hr emergency service. **Credit** MC, V. **Map** p254 A2.

Pharmacies

Pharmacies are clearly marked with a green cross and/or green crescent. There's at least one in every neighbourhood. The drugs may have strange names, but staff can usually translate. Most pharmacies are open 9am to 6-7pm Monday to Friday. Some may also open on Saturday mornings or afternoons. When closed, each pharmacy should display a list of alternative pharmacies open after hours. For addresses of some pharmacies, *see p139.*

Prescriptions

Next to anything can be bought over the counter without a prescription; about the only thing that raises eyebrows are condoms.

STDs, HIV & AIDS

Sexually transmitted diseases, including HIV and AIDS, are present here. However, due to the cultural context, these problems are not readily discussed. There has been talk of free AIDS tests but, as with all things sexual, the problem in Morocco is largely ignored.

The Association de Lutte Contre le Sida (ALCS, or in English, the Association for the Fight Against AIDS) was set up in 1988, the first of its kind in the Middle East. Its headquarters are in Casablanca but it is active in 11 Moroccan cities including Marrakech. The ALCS can provide advice, prevention information and screening, as well as organise care for people living with HIV.

Directory

ALCS
association de lutte contre le sida

"they support the ALCS"

Pierre Bergè, Sida Info Service Casablanca City, Mairie de Paris et Mairie de Marseille, Conseil Règional du Grand Casablanca et Conseil Règional de l'Ile de France, AIDES, Global fund to fight AIDS, Tubercolosis and Malaria, GlaxoSmithkline Fondation OMNIPAR, Maroc Telecom, ONA RAM, UN, MAE France, ESTHER, American Women's Club, Marrakech Film Festival...

We need your financial support to continue and develop our work in giving people living with HIV access to information and treatment, and to ensure that Morocco remains a country with low numbers of HIV/Aids sufferers.

To contribute, please make payments to:
Wafabank Place du marché
Agence PLM Place des Halles-Maârif IM°
Account No: 019 780 000 022 010 12186
Swift Code: WAFAMAMC

AGADIR - CASABLANCA - FES - GUELMIM - MARRAKECH MEKNES
OUJDA - RABAT - TANGER - TAROUDANT - TETOUAN
e-mail : alcs@menara.ma - site web : www.alcsmaroc.org

Sidaction

ALCS
*17 avenue Massira El-Khadra
Maarif, Casablanca (022 99 42 42/
www.alcsmaroc.org).*

ID

You are meant to carry ID at
all times. Moroccans have
identity cards but a passport
is fine for foreign visitors, or
better still, a photocopy, so
you can leave the original at
the hotel. Valid ID is essential
when checking into a hotel,
hiring a car, changing or
paying with travellers'
cheques (and sometimes just
changing foreign currency)
and collecting poste restante.

Insurance

All travellers should take
out personal travel insurance
to cover trip cancellation,
emergency medical costs
and loss or theft of baggage
or money. If you're going
horse-riding, skiing or
mountaineering, get extra
'dangerous sports' cover.

Keep a record of your policy
number and the emergency
telephone number with you.

Internet

Computers are expensive
in Morocco, so most people
resort to private internet
centres. In the Medina they're
concentrated along rue Bab
Agnaou, with at least half a
dozen; in Guéliz the best are
up around place Abdel-
Moumen. Prices are about
10dh an hour. The cheapest
internet access is offered at
the Arset Abdelsalam,
Marrakech's 'internet park',
opposite the Ensemble
Artisanal (map p252 A5),
which has several public-
access terminals in a glass
building at the park entrance
charged at 5dh per hour.

ISPs tend to be
oversubscribed and download
times can be painfully slow.

Though broadband is
gradually creeping in, you
might want to take along a
book wherever you go surfing
the internet. We're not kidding.

If you are lugging around
your own laptop, then you can
get connected in some of the
better hotels by using an RJ-11
standard telephone connector.
However, few of the major
ISPs have any sort of local
access number for Morocco
and you will have to call long
distance to log on. Between
high telephone tariffs and
lengthy download times this
can prove costly. That said,
as more places get hooked
up to broadband, things will
surely improve. More and more
hotels are offering a Wi-Fi
service, for instance; some may
even lend you a computer. And
Le Café du Livre (*see p116*),
and other cafés like it, offer
free Wi-Fi to their customers.

Internet service providers (ISPs)

Ménara (Maroc Télécom's ISP,
www.menara.ma) is available
to those with a landline. To
subscribe, visit the Maroc
Télécom office (*see p234*
Telephones). The other
option is Wanadoo (081 00
63 63, www.wanadoo.ma)
prepaid cards (10hrs for 50dh;
20hrs for 70dh). These cards
don't include the telephone
communications needed to
access the server. Wanadoo
cards can be purchased at
Marjane (route de Casablanca,
024 31 37 24), Magawork (1
Résidence Maniss La Youne,
boulevard Aila Fassi, 024 33
13 92) or Buraliste Bouargan
(168 avenue Mohammed V,
Guéliz, 024 43 02 57).

Internet access

Askmy
*6 boulevard Mohammed Zerktouni,
Guéliz (024 43 06 02).* **Open** 8am-
2am daily. **No credit cards**.
Map p254 A2.

The best internet centre in
Marrakech, with 14 state-of-the-
art computers and fast 128kbps
connections. Rates are higher
(12dh per hour), but it's worth it.

Cyber Club
*avenue Mohammed V (next to Café
Koutoubia), Medina (no phone).*
Open 9.30am-1pm, 3-10.30pm daily.
No credit cards. **Map** p250/252 B5.
Right across from the Koutoubia, a
small sign points down a flight of
steps to this basement room with 11
online terminals.

Mohammed Yasin Cyber Café
38 rue Bab Agnaou, Medina.
Open 7am-midnight daily.
Map p252 C6.
Close to the Pâtisserie des Princes,
this is the best of the street's internet
providers courtesy of its super-fast
connection speeds and 16 terminals.

Left luggage

There are no left luggage
facilities at Marrakech's
international airport. Bags can
be left at the railway station
for 10dh per day, and staff
insist that they are padlocked.

Legal help

Embassies and consulates (*see
p228*) can assist nationals in
emergencies and provide a list
of English-speaking lawyers.

Lost property

In general, if you've lost it,
forget it. If you've lost
something on public transport,
call the transport operator,
who should, in principle, hang
on to lost property – but don't
hold your breath.

Maps

There is no commercially
available map of Marrakech.

A small city plan is inset
on most of the Morocco maps
but while these are good for
overviews of the city they
lack the detail required for
navigating the Medina. At
present, the maps in this
book are as good as it gets.

The best overall map of the country is the Michelin sheet 959, on a scale of 1:1,000,000 with a 1:600,000 inset of the Marrakech area, useful for anyone heading over the Atlas. Decent alternatives include Hildebrand's (1:900,000) and GeoCenter (1:800,000).

Media

Foreign publications

English-language publications are easy to come by. Expect to find the major dailies (usually just 24 hours old) including the *Guardian, Telegraph, The Times, Daily Mail* and *Sun*, plus the Sundays and those weekly international digests put out by some of the broadsheets. There will also usually be the *International Herald Tribune, Time, Newsweek* and *The Economist* plus sundry fashion, style and interiors magazines. For details of newsagents that stock foreign papers, *see p138*.

Magazines

Most mags are in French, the best being *Medina* and *Maison du Maroc*: the former is a Morocco travel magazine with places that will interest tourists, the latter is the local equivalent of *Homes & Gardens*. There is also a new English magazine called *Last Exit Marrakech*: distributed widely on the streets, it offers a free introduction to the city.

Newspapers

There are both French and Arabic papers. Though there is increasing editorial freedom, national dailies tend to restrict their coverage to the goings-on of the royal family, sports and local events (sound familiar?). There's little in the way of foreign news. If you read French, the best paper is the daily *Le Figaro*, printed in Casablanca.

Television

Most hotels and riads that offer TV have satellite with BBC World, CNN, French TV5 and occasionally Sky channels.

Money

Local currency is the Moroccan dirham, abbreviated dh (in this book) and sometimes MDH, or MAD. There are 100 centimes to a dirham. Coins come in denominations of 5, 10, 20 and 50 centimes (all useless) and 1, 2, 5 and 10dh. There are two different types of 5dh coin in circulation: a large silver-coloured version and a smaller new bi-metal issue (which is similar to the 10dh coin but smaller). It's confusing. Small change is useful for things like tips and taxi fares and should be hoarded. Banknotes come in denominations of 20, 50, 100 and 200dh. (There is also a 10dh note but this is being phased out.)

Excess dirhams can be exchanged for euros or dollars (pounds sterling are often not available) at a bank. You may be asked to show the exchange receipts from when you converted your hard currency into dirhams – this is because banks will only allow you to change back up to half the amount of Moroccan currency originally purchased.

At the time of writing, conversion between currencies was 10dh = 60p or US$1.20.

ATMs

Cashpoints, or *guichets automatiques*, are common in most Moroccan towns and cities, and it's perfectly possible to travel on plastic – although it's always wise to carry at least a couple of days' 'survival money' in cash. Most ATMs are connected to the international banking systems and issue dirhams on most European and US debit and credit cards. If the ATM carries only a Visa symbol, don't go there; it will only process locally issued Visa cards and may well swallow the international variety (we've heard tales of this happening). Instead look for machines bearing the Cirrus, Link and Maestro symbols.

Most banks set a daily withdrawal limit of 2,000dh (currently around £120) per day on ATM withdrawals. If you need more, go to an exchange bureau with your card and passport and get a cash advance. Or try Wafa Bank (213 avenue Mohammed V, Guéliz), which allows withdrawals of up to 8,000dh (£490) if your home bank permits it.

ATMs are concentrated along rue Bab Agnaou in the Medina and around place Abdel-Moumen in Guéliz. Beware of Monday mornings; machines are often empty.

Banks

The main local banks are Banque Commerciale du Maroc (BCM), Banque Marocaine du Commerce Extérieur (BMCE), Banque Marocaine du Commerce et de l'Industrie (BMCI) and Crédit du Maroc. All have agreements with major international banks. The heaviest concentration of bank branches is around place Abdel-Moumen in Guéliz. For opening hours, *see below*. Note that the BMCI on boulevard Mohammed Zerktouni (round the corner from Café Atlas) is open at weekends and on public holidays.

Bureaux de change

Almost all banks have a bureaux de change counter, as do most major hotels of three stars and up. The exchange rate is set by the Bank of Morocco and is uniform. No commission is charged. When changing money you will usually be asked to show your passport. There's a convenient exchange window on rue Bab Agnaou, 100 metres along from Jemaa El Fna.

Credit cards

MasterCard and Visa are widely accepted at shops, restaurants and hotels; American Express less so. Places that accept AmEx often add five per cent to cover the cost of the transaction. It's wise to carry cash back-up because management will often claim that the machine is 'broken' or that your card won't go through – they aren't keen on the delay in payment that comes with credit cards. Most establishments can do a manual transaction ('*au sabot*') and phone for authorisation.

Credit-card fraud is also a problem in Morocco, so keep all receipts to check against your statement. Chip and PIN has yet to reach Morocco.

BMCE banks will give cash advances on MasterCard and Visa up to around 5,000dh.

American Express is represented in Marrakech by Voyages Schwartz (024 43 33 21), whose offices are in the Immeuble Moutaouskil, 1 rue Mauritanie, Guéliz (map p254 B3). It won't give cash advances but it will issue a letter of credit that you can then use to get cash at any Crédit du Maroc bank.

Lost/stolen credit cards

All lines of the companies listed below have English-speaking staff and are open 24hrs daily.
American Express 00 973 256 834
Barclaycard 00 44 1604 230 230
Diners Club 022 99 455/00 44 1252 513 500
MasterCard 00 1636 722 7111
Switch 00 870 000459

Travellers' cheques

Travellers' cheques are accepted by most banks. Stick to well-known brands like Thomas Cook and American Express. A commission is usually charged (around 20dh-25dh per transaction), no matter the number of cheques or amount cashed. The Banque El-Maghreb is an exception in charging nothing. Some hotels and shops will also accept travellers' cheques as payment.

Opening hours

Opening times listed in this book should be taken more as guidelines than gospel (many places close in the afternoon for a siesta, which is not always reflected in the times we have given). As a rule of thumb the working week is Monday to Friday, with a half-day on Saturday. Note that hours vary in summer (from around 15 June to the end of September) and during Ramadan (*see p234* **Islamic holidays**), when business open and close later.
Banks 8.30-11.30am, 2.30-3.30pm Mon-Fri.
Shops 9am-1pm, 3-7pm Mon-Sat.
Museums & tourist sights Usually closed Tue.

Police

Crime against visitors is rare and physical violence almost unheard of. You do need to watch your pockets and bags, though, particularly around Jemaa El Fna. If you are robbed or have a complaint against an unscrupulous taxi driver or souk merchant, go to the office of the Brigade Touristique (*see below*).

Note, if you are the victim of crime outside Marrakech, then you must make a report to the local police wherever the incident occurred – do not wait until your return to the city.

Police stations

The main police station (Hôtel de Police; map p250 B3) is on rue Oued El-Makhazine in Guéliz near the Jnane El-Harti park. There's also an office of the tourist police (Brigade Touristique; 024 38 46 01) on the north side of Jemaa El Fna.

Postal services

The main post office (PTT Centrale) is on place du 16 Novembre, Guéliz, halfway along avenue Mohammed V (across from the McDonald's). It's open 8am-2pm Mon-Sat. There is a second, smaller PTT in the Medina on rue Moulay Ismail, between Jemaa El Fna and the Koutoubia Mosque, open 8am-noon and 3-6pm Mon-Fri (winter) and 8am-3pm (summer). Stamps are sold at a dedicated *timbres* counter, but can also be bought at a *tabac* or at the reception desks of big hotels. Parcels should be taken unwrapped for examination.

Mail delivery is painfully slow. Post offices provide an express mail service (EMS), also known as *poste rapide*. For really urgent mail, it's safer to use an international courier company, *see p227*.

Poste restante

Poste restante is not always reliable, but if you want to give it a go, have the letters addressed to 'Poste Restante, PTT Centrale, Marrakech', and make sure that the surname is clear. A passport will be needed to pick up any mail.

Religion

Islam underpins society, places of worship are prominent and religious festivals are a highlight of the annual calendar. Sex

Islamic holidays

Of all the Islamic holidays, **Ramadan** is the most significant and the one that has the greatest impact on the visitor. This is the Muslim month of fasting. Many Moroccans abstain from food, drink and cigarettes between sunrise and sunset. Many cafés and restaurants will close during the day. It's also bad form to flaunt your non-participation by smoking or eating in the street. Ramadan nights are some of the busiest of the year as, come sundown, eateries are packed with large groups communally breaking their fast, a meal known as *iftar*. Jemaa El Fna gets particularly wild.

The end of Ramadan is marked by the two-day feast of **Eid al-Fitr** ('the small feast'). A few months later the feast of **Eid al-Adha** ('the festival of sacrifice') commemorates Abraham's sacrifice of a ram instead of his son. It's not a good time for sheep as every family that can afford to emulates the Patriarch's deed by slaughtering an animal.

Three weeks after Eid El-Kebir is **Moharram**, the Muslim New Year. The other big Muslim holiday is **Mouloud**, a celebration of the birthday of the Prophet Mohammed.

Islamic religious holidays are based on a lunar calendar, approximately 11 days shorter than the Gregorian (Western) calendar. This means that Islamic holidays shift forward by 11 days each year.

	2007	**2008**	**2009**
Ramadan	13 Sept	2 Sept	22 Aug
Eid al-Fitr	13 Oct	2 Oct	21 Sept
Eid al-Adha	20 Dec	9 Dec	28 Nov
Moharram	20 Jan	10 Jan	29 Dec
Mouloud	31 Mar	20 Mar	9 Mar

Note, these dates are approximate as the exact start of the celebrations depends on the sighting of the full moon.

before marriage is taboo. Islam may be tough on alcohol, but the Moroccans are more liberal when it comes to drugs (*see p228*). Although every district has its mosque, few Moroccans perform the required five daily cycles of prayer. Many only attend the mosque on noon Friday, the main weekly prayer session. But most Moroccans make an effort to observe Ramadan; *see above* **Islamic holidays**.

Christian

Church of St Anne
rue El-Imam Ali, Guéliz (024 43 05 85). Map p254 B3.

Catholic services are held in French, but there is an interdenominational service delivered in English at 10.30am Sunday (9.30am during July) with tea and coffee afterwards.

Smoking

Morocco is firmly in thrall to nicotine. Non-smokers are outcasts and few cafés and restaurants recognise the concept of a clean-air environment (Marrakech is a good place to start smoking). Foreign cigarette brands cost 32dh, or about £2, for 20, while the best of the domestic product goes for even less. Passive smoking or active, it's your choice.

The Institut Français de Marrakech offers a selection of reasonably priced classes in Arabic to foreigners and can recommend tutors for private study. An intensive 40-hour summer course is available for 700dh. Marrakech also has the Cadi Ayyad University but this is of little interest to the average foreign visitor.

Institut Français de Marrakech
route de Targa, Jebel Guéliz (024 44 69 30/fax 024 44 74 97).

Cadi Ayyad University
avenue Prince Moulay Abdellah, BP 511, Guéliz (024 43 48 13/fax 024 43 44 94/www.ucam.ac.ma).

Telephones

Telephoning abroad from Marrakech is no problem. Either use the cardphones that are dotted around town (cards are bought from post offices, *tabacs* or news vendors) or one of the numerous *téléboutiques*. The latter are identified by a blue and white sign depicting a telephone receiver. They are small premises with anything from two to a dozen coin-operated phones in booths. The overseer supplies change. International calls require a minimum of three 5dh coins.

In the Medina there's at least one *téléboutique* on every main street. Off-peak rates apply from midnight to 7am weekdays, from 12.30pm Saturday and all day Sunday.

Dialling & codes

To call abroad dial 00, then the country code followed by the telephone number. When calling within Morocco you need to dial the three-digit area code even if you are calling from the same area. For instance, if you are making a local call within Marrakech, you must still dial 024. Mobiles begin with the prefix 06 or 07 or 01.

Morocco country code 212

Area codes
Casablanca 022
Essaouira 024
Fes 035
Marrakech 024
Ouarzazte & the south 024
Rabat/Tangier 037

Faxes

Most, but not all, *téléboutiques* will send a fax for you. Faxes to international destinations will cost around 70dh.

Mobile phones

There are two main mobile service providers offering a pay-as-you-go option: the national operator Maroc-Télécom and Méditel. Most European networks have arrangements with one of the two so that visitors can use their mobiles in Morocco (note: it's expensive). Alternatively, mobile users can buy a pre-paid SIM card from either of the Moroccan network operators. For a charge of 200dh you are provided with a local number through which calls can be made at favourable rates.

Maroc-Télécom (Agence Guéliz Mobile)
avenue Mohammed V (opposite McDonald's), Guéliz (024 43 44 53/fax 024 43 10 23/www.iam.ma). **Open** 8.30am-noon, 2-7pm Mon-Fri; 8.30am-1pm Sat. **Credit** MC, V. **Map** p254 B2.

Méditel
279 avenue Mohammed V, Guéliz (024 42 74 44). **Open** 9am-noon, 3-9.30pm daily. **No credit cards.** **Map** p254 B2.

Aloha
15 avenue Mohammed V, Guéliz (024 42 00 34/fax 024 42 00 32). **Open** 9am-9pm Mon-Sat. **No credit cards.** **Map** p254 A1. Méditel franchise.

Ilaicom
117 avenue Houmann El-Fetouaki, Medina (024 38 59 63). **Open** 10am-1pm, 3.30-7.30pm Mon-Sat. **Credit** MC, V. **Map** p252 C7. Méditel franchise.

Kent 2
40 avenue Abdelkarim El-Khattabi, Guéliz (024 44 84 38/fax 024 42 00 32). **Open** 9.30am-9pm Mon-Sat. **No credit cards.** **Map** p250 A2. Méditel franchise.

Le Portable
8 rue Fatima Zohra, Medina (024 44 22 28). **Open** 9.30am-1pm, 3.30-8pm daily. **No credit cards.** **Map** p250 B4.

Operator services

The international operator can be accessed by dialling 120. To make a reverse charge call say *'Je voudrais téléphoner en PCV'* but you will wait. To get the domestic operator dial 10. For directory enquiries dial 16, but operators don't speak English.

Time

Morocco follows GMT all year round (it's on the same time as Britain and Ireland in winter but an hour behind during British Summer Time, from late March to late October).

Tipping

Tipping is expected in cafés and restaurants (round up the bill or add 10-15 per cent), by guides and porters, and by anyone else that renders you any sort of small service. Five or ten dirhams is sufficient.

It is not necessary to tip taxi drivers, who can just be content with overcharging.

Toilets

Public toilets are a rarity – use the facilities when in bars, hotels and restaurants. They're usually decent enough (and occasionally stunning, as at Comptoir, *see p111*). It's a good idea to carry tissues as toilet paper is not always

available; most people use the water hose to sluice themselves clean. The wastebasket beside the toilet is for used tissues. At cafés the toilet attendant expects a few dirhams as a tip; it's bad form not to oblige.

Tourist information

The ONMT (Office National Marocain du Tourisme) has a fairly useless presence in Marrakech. Basic tourist informatioin can also be found at its website, www.visitmorocco.com.

ONMT
ONMT, place Abdel-Moumen, Guéliz (024 43 61 31). **Open** 8.30am-noon, 2.30-6.30pm Mon-Fri; 9am-noon, 3-6pm Sat. **Map** p254 A1.

International offices

London *205 Regent Street, W1R 7DE (+44 20 7437 0073).*
New York *20 East 46th Street, suite 1201, 10017 (+1 212 55 72 520).*
Paris *161 rue Saint Honoré, 75001 (+1 42 60 63 50).*

Visas & immigration

All visitors to Morocco need a passport to enter (it should be valid for at least six months beyond the date of entry. No visas are required for nationals of Australia, Britain, Canada, Ireland, New Zealand, the US and most EU countries. If in doubt check with your local Moroccan embassy.

Travellers can stay in Morocco for three months from the time of entry. Extensions require applying for an official residence permit – a tedious procedure. First you must open a bank account in Morocco, which requires a minimum of 20,000dh (£1,250) in your account and an *attestation de résidence* from your hotel or landlord. Then you need to go to the Bureau

Directory

des Etrangers equipped with your passport, seven passport photos, two copies of the *attestation*, two copies of your bank statement, and a 60dh stamp (available from any *tabac*). Once the forms have been filled out twice you should receive a residence permit a few weeks later.

For a simpler option, leave the country for a few days and re-enter, gaining a new three-month stamp.

Bureau des Etrangers
Comissariat Central, Guéliz. **Open** 8am-noon, 2-6pm Mon-Thur; 8am-noon Fri.

When to go

Though Marrakech gets lots of sunshine, December and January can be overcast and rainy. Still, Marrakech makes for a good winter retreat with daily temperatures of around 15-20°C (59-68°F). Evenings can be chilly though (you need to stay in a hotel that has heating).

March to May is the perfect time to visit but beware of price hikes at Easter. Summers can be oppressive with temperatures averaging 30-35°C (86-95°F), peaking at 40°C (104°F). Things cool off in September. Hotel rates soar over Christmas.

Public holidays

Morocco's six secular holidays occupy a day each. Banks, offices and civil service institutions close, but many shops stay open and public transport runs as usual.

1 January New Year's Day
1 May Labour Day (Fête du Travail)
30 July Feast of the Throne (Fête du Trône), commemorating the present king's accession
14 August Allegiance Day
6 November Day of the Green March (Marche Vert), commemorating the retaking of Spanish-held Saharan territories
18 November Independence Day

Religious holidays (*see p234* **Islamic holidays**) occupy

two or three days and if these happen to fall midweek then the government commonly extends the holiday to cover the whole working week.

Festivals

Six years old in 2007, the **Marrakech International Film Festival** is the city's most prestigious cultural event. In past years the festival has been held in September and December but it's now in late November: *see p147*. The **Marrakech Popular Arts Festival**, a week-long festival in July, features storytellers, dancers and bands.

Outside of Marrakech, there's the annual **Festival d'Essaouira** (*see p177*), held each June in the pretty Atlantic port town.

Women

Though Marrakech is a Muslim country, the dress code for women is not strict – with a few provisos. Leave the minis and micros behind. Shorts are out too. Wear trousers or dresses and skirts that reach the knee or lower; baggy is the way to go. In conservative areas such as the northern Medina, it's a good idea to keep shoulders covered.

In touristy areas such as Jemaa El Fna and the souks, you may get hit on, so avoid direct eye contact and don't smile at men. Ignore come-ons or obnoxious comments. If a man is persistent, raise your voice so others can hear; someone may intervene on your behalf.

Work

Most foreign residents of Marrakech are retired or living on incomes derived in their home countries; but if you can prove that regular transfers of funds are being made into a Moroccan bank account, it shouldn't be a problem to obtain a *carte de séjour* (residence permit). Earning your keep as a foreigner in Marrakech is a harder task as international companies (hotels, for example) tend to do their hiring abroad.

Teachers with recognised qualifications (CELTS) could inquire at the American Language Center where English is taught to locals.

American Language Centre (ALC)
3 impasse des Moulins, boulevard Mohammed Zerktouni, Guéliz (024 44 72 59). **Open** 9am-noon, 3-7pm Mon-Fri; 9am-noon Sat.

Weather report

	Temperature (°C/°F) Average high	Rainfall (inches/mm)
Jan	21/70	1.1/28
Feb	22/72	1.2/30
Mar	23/73	1.2/30
Apr	26/79	1.1/28
May	29/84	0.7/18
June	30/86	0.3/7.6
July	33/91	0.1/2.5
Aug	36/97	0.1/2.5
Sept	31/88	0.3/7.6
Oct	28/82	1.0/25
Nov	24/75	1.3/33
Dec	21/70	1.3/33

Glossary

Architecture

bab gate
dar house
fundouk medieval merchants' inn arranged around a central courtyard with stabling on the gound floor, sleeping quarters above
hammam traditional bathhouse
kasbah traditional Berber fortress/palace
koubba domed tomb
mashrabiya fretworked wooden screens traditionally used for windows
Mauresque French colonial version of neo-Moorish architecture
méchouar parade ground
medersa Koranic school for the teaching of Islamic law and scriptures
mihrab prayer niche facing towards Mecca in a mosque
minbar pulpit in a mosque for the reading of the Koran, usually free-standing
muqarna Moorish ceiling ornamentation resembling stalactites
pisé mud reinforced with straw and lime, and the primary building material of Marrakech
riad house with a central courtyard garden
tadelakt moisture-resistant polished plaster wall surface
zaouia shrine of a holy man, usually also doubling as a theology school
zelije coloured tilework typical of Moorish decoration

Around town

agdal walled garden
arset quarter
calèche horse-drawn carriage
derb alley
hôtel de ville city hall
jnane market garden
maison d'hôte guest house
medina Arabic for 'city', often used to mean the 'old city'
marché market
mellah traditional Jewish quarter
place square
souk bazaar or market

Culture

babouche traditional leather slippers, typically yellow
baksheesh a tip or kickback
baraka blessings
ben son of (also spelled ibn)
Berber the indigenous tribes people of southern Morocco
bidonvilles unplanned slum dwellings on the outskirts of town
douar tribe
Fassi adjective for someone from Fès
gnawa semi-mystical brotherhood of muscians descended from black African slaves. Also the name of the music they play
haj pilgrimage to Mecca which observant Muslims are expected to perform at least once during their lifetime. Also the honorific title of someone who has made the pilgrimage
hijab headscarf warn by some Muslim women
jellaba traditional men's robe
jinn souls without bodies, usually malevolent (also spelled djinn)
kif the local marijuana, cultivated extensively in the Rif Mountains
leila all-night gnawa music performance (the word literally means 'night')
maalim master craftsman or master of any profession, including musician
majoun a cake or jam of marijuana
Marrakchi adjective for someone from Marrakech
muezzin the man who makes the call to prayer
oud musical instrument, like a lute
oued wadi or dried river bed
sidi saint
Souari adjective for someone from Essaouira
wali regional governor appointed by the king

Food

briouettes little envelopes of paper-thin *ouarka* (filo) pastry wrapped around ground meat, rice or cheese and deep fried, served as an hors d'oeuvre
chakchouka dessert of light pastry filled with fruit
couscous coarse-ground semolina flour. Also the name of the cooked dish
harira vegetable soup
pastilla *ouarka* (filo) pastry typically filled with a mixture of shredded pigeon, almonds and spices, served as an hors d'oeuvre
tajine slow-cooked stew of meat (usually lamb or chicken) and/or vegetables. Also the name of the conically lidded dish it's cooked in
trid shredded pigeon wrapped in a crêpe soaked in broth

History

Almohads Berber dynasty (1147-1269) that ruled out of Marrakech before relocating to Rabat
Almoravids Berber dynasty (1062-1147) that founded Marrakech
Green March Action by which Morocco seized the Spanish colony of Rio del Oro in the western Sahara in 1975
Merenids Berber dynasty (1248-1554) that ruled from northern Morocco
Saadians Arab dynasty (1549-1668) that oversaw a brief renaissance of imperial Marrakech
Treaty of Fès The act that formalised the imposition of French rule over Morocco in 1912

Vocabulary: French

In French, as in other Latin languages, the second person singular (you) has two forms. Phrases here are given in the more polite *vous* form. The *tu* form is used with family, friends, young children and pets; you should be careful not to use it with people you do not know sufficiently well, as it is considered rude. You will also find that courtesies such as *monsieur, madame* and *mademoiselle* are used much more than often their English equivalents.

General expressions

good morning/hello *bonjour*
good evening *bonsoir*
goodbye *au revoir*
hi (familiar) *salut*
OK *d'accord*; yes *oui*; no *non*
How are you? *Comment allez vous?/vous allez bien?*
How's it going? *Comment ça va?/ça va?* (familiar)
Sir/Mr *monsieur* (M)
Madam/Mrs *madame* (Mme)
Miss *mademoiselle* (Mlle)
please *s'il vous plaît*; thank you *merci*; thank you very much *merci beaucoup*
sorry *pardon*; excuse me *excusez-moi*
Do you speak English? *Parlez-vous anglais?*
I don't speak French *Je ne parle pas français*
I don't understand *Je ne comprends pas*
Speak more slowly, please *Parlez plus lentement, s'il vous plaît*
how much?/how many? *combien?*
Have you got change? *Avez-vous de la monnaie?*
I would like… *Je voudrais…*
it is *c'est*; it isn't *ce n'est pas*
good *bon* (m)/*bonne* (f); bad *mauvais* (m)/*mauvaise* (f)
small *petit* (m)/*petite* (f); big *grand* (m)/*grande* (f)
beautiful *beau* (m)/*belle* (f); well *bien*; badly *mal*
expensive *cher*; cheap *pas cher*

a bit *un peu*; a lot *beaucoup*; very *très*; with *avec*; without *sans*; and *et*; or *ou*; because *parce que*
who? *qui?*, when? *quand?*, which? *quel?*, where? *où?*, why? *pourquoi?*, how? *comment?*
at what time/when? *à quelle heure?*
forbidden *interdit/défendu*
out of order *hors service/en panne*
daily *tous les jours (tlj)*

Getting around

When is the next train for…? *C'est quand le prochain train pour…?*
ticket *un billet*; station *la gare*; platform *le quai*
bus/coach station *gare routière*
entrance *entrée*; exit *sortie*
left *gauche*; right *droite*;
interchange *correspondence*
straight on *tout droit*; far *loin*; near *pas loin/près d'ici*
street *la rue*; street map *le plan*; road map *la carte*
bank *la banque*; is there a bank near here? *est-ce qu'il y a une banque près d'ici?*
post office *La Poste*; a stamp *un timbre*

Sightseeing

museum *un musée*
church *une église*
exhibition *une exposition*; ticket (for museum) *un billet*; (for theatre,concert) *une place*
open *ouvert*; closed *fermé*
free *gratuit*; reduced price *un tarif réduit*

Accommodation

Do you have a room (for this evening/for two people)? *Avez-vous une chambre (pour ce soir/pour deux personnes)?*
full *complet*; room *une chambre*
bed *un lit*; double bed *un grand lit*; (a room with) twin beds *(une chambre) à deux lits*
with bath(room)/shower *avec (salle de) bain/douche*
breakfast *le petit déjeuner* included *compris*
lift *un ascenseur*
air-conditioned *climatisé*

At the café or restaurant

I'd like to book a table (for three/at 8pm) *Je voudrais réserver une table (pour trois personnes/à vingt heures)*
lunch *le déjeuner*; dinner *le dîner* coffee (espresso) *un café*; white coffee *un café au lait/café crème*; tea *le thé*
wine *le vin*; beer *la bière*
mineral water *eau minérale*; fizzy *gazeuse*; still *plate*
tap water *eau du robinet/une carafe d'eau*
the bill, please *l'addition, s'il vous plaît*

Behind the wheel

no parking *stationnement interdit/stationnement gênant*; speed limit 40 *rappel 40*
petrol *essence*; unleaded *sans plomb*

Numbers

0 *zéro*; 1 *un* (m), *une* (f); 2 *deux*; 3 *trois*; 4 *quatre*; 5 *cinq*; 6 *six*; 7 *sept*; 8 *huit*; 9 *neuf*; 10 *dix*; 11 *onze*; 12 *douze*; 13 *treize*; 14 *quatorze*; 15 *quinze*; 16 *seize*; 17 *dix-sept*; 18 *dix-huit*; 19 *dix-neuf*; 20 *vingt*; 21 *vingt-et-un*; 22 *vingt-deux*; 30 *trente*; 40 *quarante*; 50 *cinquante*; 60 *soixante*; 70 *soixante-dix*; 80 *quatre-vingts*; 90 *quatre-vingt-dix*; 100 *cent*; 1,000 *mille*; 1,000,000 *un million*.

Days, months & seasons

Monday *lundi*; Tuesday *mardi*; Wednesday *mercredi*; Thursday *jeudi*; Friday *vendredi*; Saturday *samedi*; Sunday *dimanche*.

January *janvier*, February *février*; March *mars*; April *avril*; May *mai*; June *juin*; July *juillet*; August *août*; September *septembre*; October *octobre*; November *novembre*; December *décembre*.

Spring *printemps*; summer *été*; autumn *automne*; winter *hiver*.

Vocabulary: Arabic

Within Marrakech (and other main towns and cities) you can get by in French, which is widely spoken by all educated Moroccans. However, a little effort with Arabic goes a long way, even if it is just a few stock phrases like 'hello' and 'goodbye'. Moroccan Arabic is a dialect of the standard Arabic language and is not the same as that spoken elsewhere in NorthAfrica and the Middle East, although there are some words and phrases in common. We should point out that transliteration from Arabic into English is a highly inexact science and a wide variety of spellings are possible for any given word (for example Koran vs Quran). In this guide we've tended to plump for whatever seemed the most straightforward. You are also likely to encounter Berber, which comes in three distinct dialects. Most Berber speakers will also be fluent in Arabic.

Arabic pronunciation

Arabic has numerous sounds that non-speakers have trouble in pronouncing but nobody is going to knock you for trying.

gh - like the French 'r', slightly rolled
kh - like the 'ch' in loch

Emergencies

leave me alone *esmahli la*
help! *tekni!*
help me, please *awenni afak*
call the police *ayyet el bolice*
thief *sheffar*
I'm lost *tweddert*

General expressions

good morning/hello *sabah el kheir/salaam aleikum*
good evening *masr el kheir*
goodbye *masalaama*

please *min fadlak* (to a male); *min fadlik* (to a female)
yes *aywa/anam*; no *la*
How are you? *labas/kifhalak (to a male)/kifhalik (to a female)*
thank you *shukran*
no thanks *la shukran*
sorry/excuse me *esmahli*
Do you speak English? *Itkelim Ingleezi?*
I don't speak Arabic *Metkelimsh Arabi*
I don't understand *Mafayimtish*
who? *shkun?*, why? *lash?*, which? *ashmen?*, where? *feyn?*
today *el youm*; tomorrow *ghedda*; yesterday *imbara*
God willing *inshalah*
never mind/so it goes *malish*
tips *baksheesh*
let's go *yalla*
passport *passeport*

Shopping

how much?/how many? *bekam?*
Do you have...? *Wahesh andakum...?*
Have you got change? *Maak sarf?*
credit card *kart kredi*
travellers' cheques *shek siyahi*
good *mleah*; bad *mish imleah*
small *seghir*; big *kebir*
beautiful *jameel*
that's expensive *ghali bezzaf*
enough *kafi*

Getting around

Where is...? *Feyn keyn...?*
Where is the hotel? *Feyn keyn el otel?*
airport *el mattar*
station *el mahatta*
bus/coach station *mahatta d'el ottobisat*
ticket office *maktab el werka*; ticket *werka*
train station *el gar*
bus stop *plasa d'el ottobisat*
museum *el mathaf*
embassy *el sifara*
pharmacy *farmasyan*
bank *el banka*
post office *el busta*; stamp *etnaber*
restaurant *el mattam*
mosque *jamaa*
left *yassar*; right *yemeen*
stop here *haten hinayer*
here *hina*; there *hinak*

Accommodation

Do you have a room? *Andak beit?*
key *srout*
room *beit*
sheet *eyzar*
shower *doush*
toilet *vaysay*
breakfast *iftar*

At the café or restaurant

table for... *tabla dyal...*
what's that? *shnu hada?*
I'm a vegetarian *makanakulsh elham*
I don't eat... *makanakulsh...*
meat *leham*
chicken *dzhazh*
fish *elhut*
bread *elkhobz*
coffee *qahwa*; tea *atay*
beer *birra*; wine *shshrab*
mineral water *sidi ali*
the bill, please *lahsab afak*

Numbers

0 *sifer*; 1 *wahid*; 2 *itnehn*; 3 *telata*; 4 *arbaa*; 5 *khamsa*; 6 *setta*; 7 *seba*; 8 *tamanya*; 9 *tesa*; 10 *ashra*; 11 *hadasha*; 12 *itnasha*; 13 *teltash*; 14 *arbatash*; 15 *khamstash*; 16 *settash*; 17 *sebatash*; 18 *tamantash*; 19 *tesatash*; 20 *eshreen*; 21 *wahid w'eshreen*; 22 *itnehn w'eshreen*; 30 *telateen*; 40 *arba'een*; 50 *khamseen*; 60 *setteen*; 70 *seba'een*; 80 *tamaneen*; 90 *tesa'een*; 100 *mea*; 1,000 *alef*.

Days, months & seasons

Monday *el itnehn*; Tuesday *el teleta*; Wednesday *el arbaar*; Thursday *el khemis*; Friday *el jomaa*; Saturday *el sebt*; Sunday *el ahad*.

January *yanayir*; February *fibraiyir*; March *maris*; April *abril*; May *mayu*; June *yunyu*; July *yulyu*; August *aghustus*; September *sibtimber*; October *oktobir*; November *nufimbir*; December *disimbir*.

Further Reference

Books

Fiction

Ben Jelloun, Tahar *This Blinding Absence of Light* (2004) Novel concerning the desert concentration camps in which King Hassan II held his political enemies, by Morocco's most acclaimed writer.

Binebine, Mahi *Welcome to Paradise* (2002) A ragtag group of the hopeful and the hopeless cower on a north Atlantic beach waiting for the boat that's to smuggle them into Europe. Highly moving.

Bowles, Paul *The Sheltering Sky* (1949) There's little in the writings of Morocco's most famous expat writer that relates to Marrakech, but his best-known novel hauntingly portrays the tribal life and deserts of North Africa.

Brady, James *Paris One* (1977) The thud of a body toppled off a roof into a dirt alley in Marrakech triggers bitching, sex and bloodletting in the Parisian fashion world.

Burroughs, William *The Naked Lunch* (1959) Compiled in Tangier from hoarded scraps of stories and typed up in a hotel room by Kerouac, who suggested the title.

Eggers, Dave *You Shall Know Our Velocity* (2003) Two whiney naïve American dopes set off round the world to give away $38,000, stopping in on Marrakech along the way.

Freud, Esther *Hideous Kinky* (1992) A child's view of hippy life in the Marrakech of the early 1970s; mum wants to be a Sufi, her two young girls just want to go home.

Goytisolo, Juan *Makbara* (1980) 'Spain's greatest living writer' is a long-standing resident of Marrakech. He also exhibits a cavalier way with grammar and punctuation.

Grenier, Richard *Marrakech One-Two* (1983) Slight comedy about an international crew in Morocco to film a life of the Prophet. Includes obligatory hostage taking and sex-crazed female Arab radicals.

Grimwood, Jon Courtenay *Stamping Butterflies* (2004) A would-be assassin holed up in a future version of Marrakech plots to kill the US president. Cutting edge Moroccan-tinged sci-fi from Britain's answer to William Gibson.

Hopkins, John *All I Wanted Was Company* (1999) This enjoyable short novel about love and solitude is mostly set in Tangier, but with sections of the story in Marrakech, the Atlas and the Sahara – all conveyed with a keen sense of place.

Taylor, Debbie *The Fourth Queen* (2003) Scots lass rises through the ranks of the harem in 18th-century Marrakech and has sex with a dwarf called Microphilius. Based on a true story, apparently.

Watkins, Paul *In the Blue Light of African Dreams* (1990) Lyrical tale of Foreign Legion flyers based in Mogador (Essaouira) who desert desert patrols to attempt the first aerial crossing of the Atlantic.

Non-fiction

Bowles, Paul *Their Heads Are Green* (1963) Short anthology of travel writings includes accounts of music-collecting in the Rif and a drive from Tangier to the Sahara via Marrakech.

Busi, Aldo *Sodomies in Eleven Point* (1988) Travels through Morocco and Tunisia in which museums and monuments take a back seat to gay sex.

Canetti, Elias *The Voices of Marrakech* (1967) A Nobel Prize winner's highly impressionistic tales and thumbnail sketches of the city. Yes, it's highly lyrical, but it's also a bit dull really.

Edwards, Brian T *Morocco Bound* (2005) Interesting deconstruction of America's cultural take on Morocco, from the movie Casablanca through Bowles and the Beats to the Marrakesh Express.

Harris, Walter *Morocco That Was* (1921) Correspondent of *The Times* who witnessed the downfall of the sultans and arrival of the French (1912) and documented all in a wickedly funny style.

Hopkins, John *The Tangier Diaries 1962-1979* (1997) 'Bill Willis calls my house "Scorpion Hall" there are so many. I keep viper serum and scorpion serum in the ice box in case someone gets bitten.' Magic stuff.

Howe, Marvine *Morocco: The Islamist Awakening and Other Challenges* (2005) Well-informed recent history of a Morocco torn between modernity and fundamentalism by veteran foreign correspondent returning to the country where she learned her trade.

Katz, Jonathan G *Murder in Marrakesh* (2006) Heavyweight history of how the 1907 lynching of Dr Émile Mauchamp in Marrakesh was exploited by the French in establishing the Protectorate.

Maxwell, Gavin *Lords of the Atlas* (1966) The single best book on Marrakech – an account of the rise and fall of the depotic Glaoui clan.

Mayne, Peter *A Year in Marrakesh* (1953) Account by a loafing Englishman of local alley life with drugs, casual sex and garden picnics. A bit of a wheeze.

Milton, Giles *White Gold* (2004) Action-packed popular history of white slaves in

18th-century Morocco, based on the memoirs of a Cornish cabin boy who became a personal slave of tyrannical sultan Moulay Ismail.
Rogerson, Barnaby *A Traveller's History of North Africa* (1998) Brief and readable overview covering Algeria, Tunisia and Libya as well as Morocco.
Rogerson, Barnaby *Marrakesh, Through Writers' Eyes* (2003) Terrific anthology of non-fiction writings on the city, from Ibn Battuta in 1325 to BBC radio reporters chasing down story tellers on the Jemaa El Fna in 2002.

Film

Babel
Alejandro González Iñárritu (2006)
Brad Pitt and Cate Blanchett star in the Moroccan section of a globalised narrative mosaic. Marrakech is only glimpsed; it's mostly set in the Saharan village of Tazarine.
Hideous Kinky
Gillies Mackinnon (1998)
Solid adaptation of the novel with Kate Winslet romanced by Moroccan-born Said Tagmaoui and loads of gorgeous local scenery.
The Man Who Knew Too Much
Alfred Hitchcock (1955)
Hitchcock's second take on the title begins with 30 minutes shot entirely on location in Marrakech. There's a murder at the Mouassine fountain and scenes featuring James Stewart and Doris Day at the Mamounia..
Moroccan Chronicles
Moumen Smihi (1999)
Haunting portmanteau of three fables: shot in Marrakech, Essaouira and Tangier.
Morocco
Josef von Sternberg (1930)
Marlene Dietrich vamps it up in Marrakech and elsewhere with legionnaire Gary Cooper. No plot to speak of.

Othello
Orson Welles (1951)
Shot in fits and starts over four years, on a dozen locations including Essaouira, where the film crew's prolonged stay was a huge boost to the local economy.
Our Man In Marrakesh
Don Sharp (1996)
Light hearted, stereotypical 1960s comedy spy romp concerning fixed UN votes and starring the excellent Terry-Thomas as a Moroccan caid. Almost entirely shot on location in Marrakech.
The Road to Morocco
David Butler (1942)
Like Webster's dictionary Bing (Crosby) and Bob (Hope) are Morocco bound, quipping and gagging as they vie for the hand of Dorothy Lamour.
The Sheltering Sky
Bernardo Bertolucci (1990)
Adaptation of the Bowles novel. American couple go down the drain in the desert.

Discography

For more general information *see pp152-4.*

Classical

Amina Alaoui *Alcaneara* (Auvidis Ethnic)
The great diva of Arab-Andalous music accompanied by three classical musicians. Ethereal and beautiful.
Moroccan Ensemble of Fès *Andalucían Music from Morocco* (Harmonia Mundi)
Good recordings of Moroccan classical music performed by one of Morocco's finest orchestras.

Berber & gnawa

B'net Marrakech *Chamaa* (Empreinte Digitale)
All-female ensemble from Marrakech who've been making a big impression on the European world music circuit.

Jil Jilala *Chamaa* (Blue Silver)
One of the most revered of all North African bands; this album shows why.
Lemchaheb *La Chanson Populaire Marocaine* (Club Du Disque Arabe)
A CD that captures the band raw before they went West.
Marrakech Undermoon *The Black Album* (KamarMusic) Excellent recordings of Gnawa ritual music mixed with trance and minimal techno tracks created from samples of Gnawa voices.
Najat Aatabou *The Voice Of The Atlas* (Globestyle)
Outspoken female Berber vocalist who sings in Berber, Arabic and French and has risen to major star status.
Nass El Ghiwane *Le Disque d'Or* (Blue Silver)
Classic album from the early 1970s features Nass at their finest.
Various *Gnawa Music of Marrakech: Night Spirit Masters* (Axiom US)
Great recording of gnawa musicians in the Medina, featuring Brahim El Belkani.
Various *Maroc: Musique Populaire* (Club du Disque Arabe)
CD of *grika* (improvised) folk music. Spookily intense.
Various *Morocco: Jilala Confraternity* (Ocora)
An important recording of a small Jilala ensemble who perform rituals in rural Morocco on request.

Western rock & pop

Blur *Think Tank* (Food)
Recorded in Marrakech and all the better for it as Britpop is superseded by 'soukpop'.
Crosby, Stills and Nash *Crosby, Stills and Nash* (Warner) CSN's 1969 debut album and the hippies are converging on Morocco.
Page and Plant *No Quarter* (Fontana) Jimmy and Robert reunite and go to Morocco.

Directory

Index

Note: page numbers in **bold** indicate section(s) giving key information on topic; *italics* indicate illustrations.

Place of interest and/or entertainment	�rectangle▪
Railway station	▪
Park	▢
City wall	▬
Area name	GUÉLIZ
Mosque	☪
Church	✚
Post office	✉

Maps

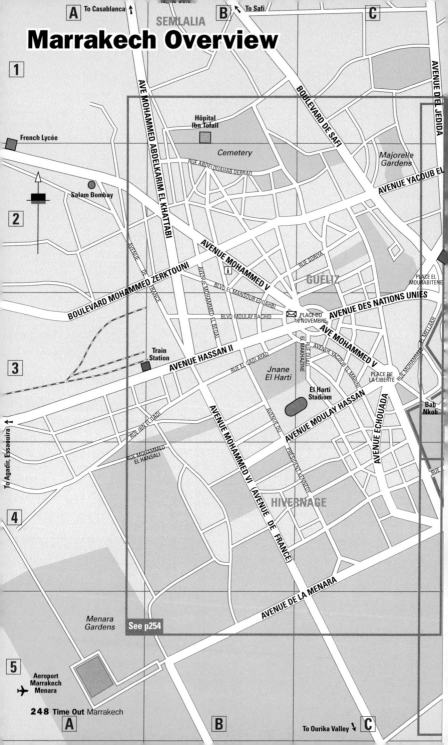

Marrakech Overview

SEMLALIA

B ↖ To Safi

C

French Lycée

Salam Bombay

Hôpital Ibn Tofail

Cemetery

RUE ABDELOUAHAB DERRAQ

Majorelle Gardens

AVENUE YACOUB EL

AVENUE DE EL JEDIDA

AVE MOHAMMED ABDELKARIM EL KHATTABI

BOULEVARD DE SAFI

AVENUE MOHAMMED V

BOULEVARD MOHAMMED ZERKTOUNI

AVENUE DE FRANCE

RUE SORIYA

GUELIZ

i

BLVD EL MANSOUR EDDAHBI

AVENUE MOHAMMED EL BEQAL

BLVD MOULAY RACHID

PLACE EL MOURABITENE

AVENUE DES NATIONS UNIES

PLACE DU 16 NOVEMBRE

AVE MOHAMMED V

RUE MOHAMMED

RUE EL MELLAKI

Train Station

AVENUE HASSAN II

RUE EL QADI AYAD

Jnane El Harti

RUE OUKA AYACOUB EL MARINI

AVENUE YACOUB EL MARINI

PLACE DE LA LIBERTE

RUE MOURABITINE

Bab Nkob

El Harti Stadium

RUE IBN EL QADI

AVENUE MOHAMMED VI (AVENUE DE FRANCE)

AVENUE MOULAY HASSAN

AVENUE ECHOUADA

RUE EL HANSALI

AVENUE DU PRESIDENT KENNEDY

HIVERNAGE

RUE

To Agadir, Essaouira ↑

Menara Gardens

See p254

AVENUE DE LA MENARA

Aeroport Marrakech Menara ✈

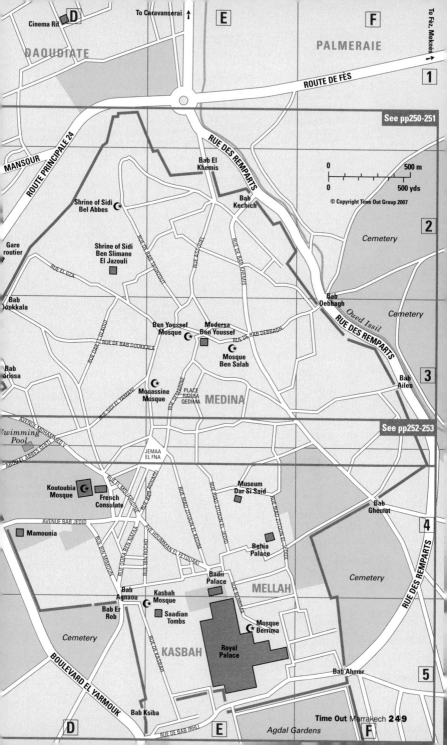

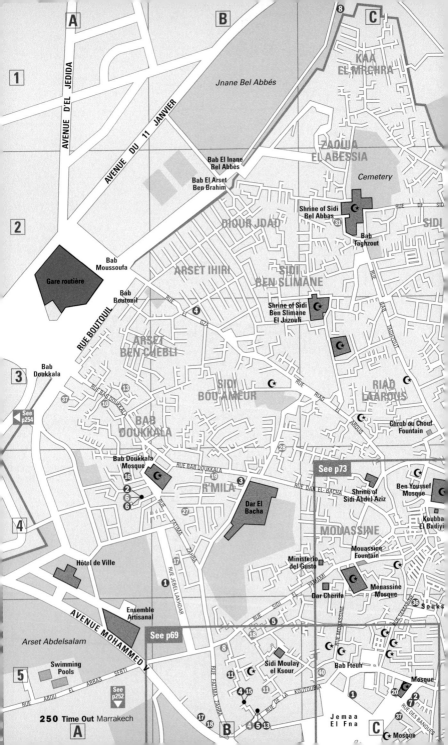

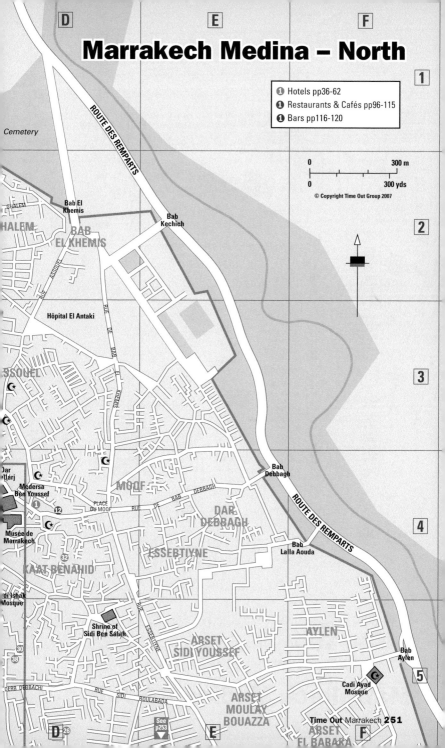

Marrakech Medina – North

1	Hotels pp36-62	
1	Restaurants & Cafés pp96-115	
1	Bars pp116-120	

0   300 m

0   300 yds

© Copyright Time Out Group 2007

Cemetery

Bab El Khemis

Bab Kechich

GHALEM

HALEM

BAB EL KHEMIS

RUE ASSOUEL

Hôpital El Antaki

RUE DE BAB EL KHEMIS

SSOUEL

Dar Harj

Medersa Ben Youssef

MOOF

RUE DE BAB DEBBAGH

Bab Debbagh

ROUTE DES REMPARTS

PLACE DU MOOF

DAR DEBBAGH

Musée de Marrakech

KAAT BENAHID

ESSEBTIYNE

Bab Lalla Aouda

di Ishak Mosque

Shrine of Sidi Ben Salah

RUE ESSEBTIYNE

ARSET SIDI YOUSSEF

AYLEN

DERB DEBBACHI

RUE SIDI BOULABADA

ARSET MOULAY BOUAZZA

Bab Aylen

Cadi Ayad Mosque

ROUTE DES REMPARTS

See p253 ▼

ARSET EL BARAKA

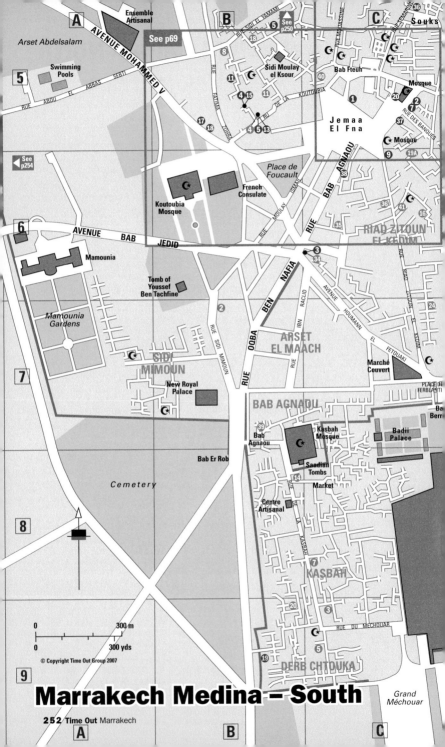

Marrakech Medina – South

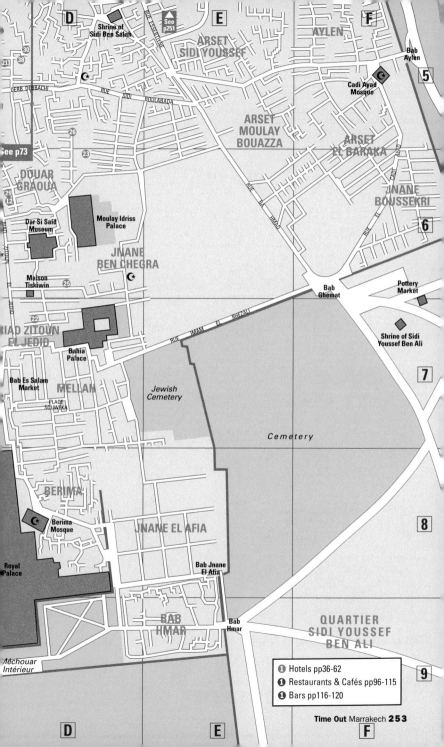

See p251

See p73

D

E

F

Shrine of
Sidi Ben Salah

ARSET
SIDI YOUSSEF

AYLEN

Bab
Aylen

5

OERB DEBBACHI

RUE SIDI BOULABADA

Cadi Ayad
Mosque

ARSET
MOULAY
BOUAZZA

ARSET
EL BARAKA

JNANE
BOUSSEKRI

DOUAR
GRAOUA

6

Dar Si Said
Museum

Moulay Idriss
Palace

RUE BAB HMAD

JNANE
BEN CHEGRA

Bab
Ghemat

Pottery
Market

Maison
Tiskiwin

RUE EL ARSA

RIAD ZITOUN
EL JEDID

RUE IMAM EL RHEZALI

Shrine of Sidi
Youssef Ben Ali

Bahia
Palace

7

Bab Es Salam
Market

MELLAH

Jewish
Cemetery

PLACE
SOUWEKA

Cemetery

BERIMA

8

Berima
Mosque

JNANE EL AFIA

Royal
Palace

Bab Jnane
El Afia

Bab
Hmar

QUARTIER
SIDI YOUSSEF
BEN ALI

BAB
HMAR

9

Méchouar
Intérieur

❶ Hotels pp36-62
❶ Restaurants & Cafés pp96-115
❶ Bars pp116-120

D

E

F

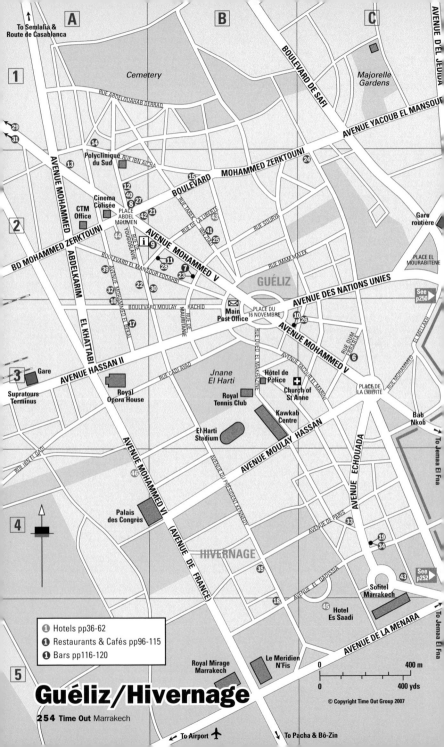

Guéliz/Hivernage

A

To Semlalia & Route de Casablanca

1

Cemetery

RUE ABDELOUAHAB DERRAQ

29
31

13
Polyclinique
du Sud

RUE IBN AICHA

14

12
40
Cinema
Colisée
CTM
Office
8
27
PLACE
ABDEL
MOUMEN
21
42
44

AVENUE MOHAMMED
BD MOHAMMED ZERKTOUNI
ABDELKARIM

2

RUE DE YOUGOSLAVIE
AVENUE MOHAMMED V
9
11
28
7
23

39
32
16
22
30

AVENUE MOHAMMED EL BEKAL
BOULEVARD MOULAY RACHID
17

B

BOULEVARD DE SAFI

BOULEVARD MOHAMMED ZERKTOUNI

15
RUE TAREK IBN ZIAD
RUE DE LA LIBERTÉ
43
41
25

RUE SOURYA

RUE IMAM MALEK

GUÉLIZ

Main
Post Office
PLACE DU
16 NOVEMBRE

AVENUE DES NATIONS UNIES
AVENUE MOHAMMED V
10
26

RUE OUM
ERRABIA
6

C

AVENUE D'EL JEDIDA

1

*Majorelle
Gardens*

AVENUE YACOUB EL MANSOUR

24

**Gare
routière**

PLACE EL
MOURABITENE

See
p250

PLACE DE
LA LIBERTÉ

**Bab
Nkob**

3

Gare
AVENUE HASSAN II

**Supratours
Terminus**
EL KHATTABI

RUE IBN EL GADI
RUE CADI AYAD
RUE DE LA MAURITANIE

*Jnane
El Harti*

Royal
Opera House

Royal
Tennis Club

El Harti
Stadium

AVENUE MOHAMMED VI (AVENUE DE FRANCE)

Hôtel de
Police
Church of
St Anne

Kawkab
Centre

AVENUE MOULAY HASSAN

AVENUE YACOUB EL MARINI
AVENUE DU PRÉSIDENT KENNEDY

PLACE DE
LA LIBERTÉ

To Jemaa El Fna

4

46

Palais
des Congrès

HIVERNAGE

35

AVENUE ECHOUADA

AVENUE DE PARIS

33

19
34

See
p252

43

**Sofitel
Marrakech**

To Jemaa El Fna

5

Royal Mirage
Marrakech

Le Meridien
N'Fis

18

AVENUE EL QADISSIA

45

**Hotel
Es Saadi**

AVENUE DE LA MENARA

❶ Hotels pp36-62
❶ Restaurants & Cafés pp96-115
❶ Bars pp116-120

0   400 m
0   400 yds

© Copyright Time Out Group 2007

254 Time Out Marrakech

To Airport ✈
To Pacha & Bô-Zin